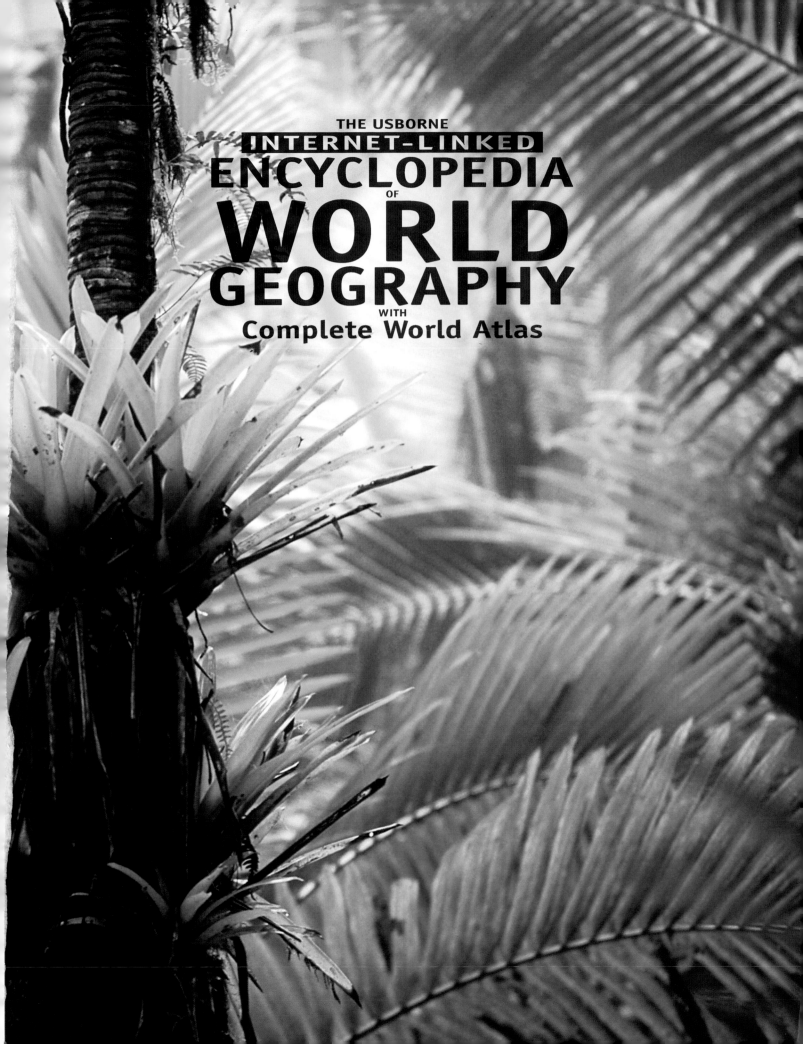

THE USBORNE
INTERNET-LINKED
ENCYCLOPEDIA
OF
WORLD
GEOGRAPHY
WITH
Complete World Atlas

THE USBORNE
INTERNET-LINKED
ENCYCLOPEDIA
OF
WORLD
GEOGRAPHY
WITH
Complete World Atlas

Gillian Doherty, Anna Claybourne and Susanna Davidson

Designers: Laura Fearn, Keith Newell, Stephen Moncrieff, Katrina Fearn, Melissa Alaverdy and Linda Penny

Project editor: Gillian Doherty

Additional contributors: Nathalie Abi-Ezzi,
Kamini Khanduri, Rebecca Treays and Stephanie Turnbull
Consultant cartographic editor: Craig Asquith
Cartography by European Map Graphics Ltd
Managing editor: Felicity Brooks
Managing designer: Stephen Wright
Cover design: Stephen Moncrieff and John Russell
Digital image processing: John Russell and Mike Olley
Picture research: Ruth King

Consultants:
Dr. Roger Trend, Senior Lecturer in Earth Science
and Geography Education, University of Exeter
Professor Michael Hitchcock, University of North London
Dr. William Chambers
Dr. Uwem Ite, Department of Geography, University of Lancaster
Susan Bermingham, Senior Lecturer, Institute of Education,
Manchester Metropolitan University
Dr. Stephanie Bunn, University of Manchester
Dr. Susan Pfisterer, Menzies Centre for Australian Studies,
King's College, University of London
Dr. Vivien Miller, Senior Lecturer in American Studies, Middlesex University
Dr. Francisco Dominguez, Head of Latin American Studies, Middlesex University
Dr. Elizabeth Bomberg, Department of Politics, University of Edinburgh
David Harrison, Professor of Tourism, Culture and Development,
University of North London

CONTENTS

INTERNET LINKS

This book contains descriptions of hundreds of recommended websites where you can find out more about people and places around the world. For links to these sites, go to the Usborne Quicklinks Website at **www.usborne-quicklinks.com** and enter the keyword "geography".

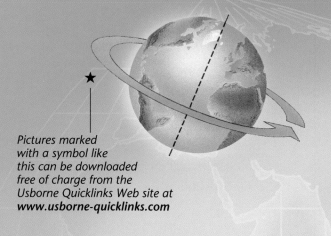

Pictures marked with a symbol like this can be downloaded free of charge from the Usborne Quicklinks Web site at **www.usborne-quicklinks.com**

Site availability

The links on the Usborne Quicklinks Website will be reviewed and updated regularly. If any of the sites becomes unavailable, we will, if possible, replace it with a suitable alternative. Occasionally, though, you may get a message saying that a website is unavailable. This may be temporary, so try again a few hours later, or even the next day.

Internet links

For links to all the websites described in this book, and for free downloadable pictures, go to **www.usborne-quicklinks.com** and enter the keyword "geography".

What you need

The websites described in this book can be accessed using a standard home computer and a web browser (the software that enables you to display information from the Internet.) It is best to make sure you have the most up-to-date version of your browser software. Recent versions have better security features and also enable you to view the latest developments in website design. You can find out how to check and update your browser in the Net Help area on the Usborne Quicklinks Website.

Downloadable pictures

Some of the pictures from this book can be downloaded from the Usborne Quicklinks Website and printed out for your own personal use. For example, you could use them to illustrate homework or a project. They must not be copied or distributed for any commercial purpose. Downloadable pictures have a ★ symbol beside them. To print out these pictures, follow the instructions on the Usborne Quicklinks Website at **www.usborne-quicklinks.com**

Things you can do

Here are some of the things you can do on the websites suggested in this book:

- Take a virtual tour of an oilrig, or climb to the summit of Everest

- Find facts and information about every country in the world

- View amazing NASA satellite images of the Earth

- Test your knowledge with online quizzes

Macintosh and QuickTime are trademarks of Apple computer, Inc., registered in the U.S.A. and other countries.
RealPlayer is a trademark of RealNetworks, Inc., registered in the U.S.A. and other countries.
Flash and Shockwave are trademarks of Macromedia, Inc., registered in the U.S.A. and other countries.

Help

For general help and advice on using the Internet, go to Usborne Quicklinks and click on Net Help.

To find out more about using your Web browser, click on your browser's Help menu and choose Contents and Index. You'll find a searchable dictionary containing tips on how to find your way around the Internet easily. For more up-to-the-minute technical support for your browser, click on Help and then Online Support. This will take you to the browser manufacturer's website.

Extras

Some websites need additional programs, called plug-ins, to play sounds, or to show videos, animations or 3-D images. If you go to a site and you do not have the necessary plug-in, a message should come up on the screen.

There is usually a button on the site that you can click on to download the plug-in. Alternatively, go to Usborne Quicklinks and click on Net Help. There you will find links to download plug-ins. Here is a list of plug-ins that you might need:

- **QuickTime** – lets you play video clips.

- **RealPlayer**® – lets you play video clips and sound files.

- **Flash**™ – lets you play animations.

- **Shockwave**® – lets you play animations and enjoy interactive sites.

Computer not essential
If you don't have use of the Internet, don't worry. This book is a complete, self-contained reference book on its own.

Computer viruses

A computer virus is a program that can damage your computer. A virus can get into your computer when you download programs from the Internet, or in an attachment (an extra file) that arrives with an email. We recommend that you use anti-virus software to protect your computer and that you update the software regularly.

Internet safety

When using the Internet, please make sure you follow these simple guidelines:

- Ask your parent's or guardian's permission before you connect to the Internet.

- If you write a message in a website guest book or on a message board, do not include your email address, real name, address or telephone number.

- If a website asks you to log in or register by typing your name or email address, ask the permission of an adult first.

- If you do receive email from someone you don't know, tell an adult and do not reply to the email.

- Never arrange to meet anyone you have talked to on the Internet.

We recommend that children using the Internet are supervised by a parent or teacher, that children do not use Internet Chat Rooms and that you use Internet filtering software to block unsuitable material. The websites described in this book have been selected by Usborne editors as suitable, in their opinion, for children, although no guarantees can be given and Usborne Publishing is not responsible for the accuracy or suitability of the information on any website other than its own.

The Earth and its moon

PLANET EARTH

OUR SOLAR SYSTEM

The Solar System is made up of the Sun and all the objects that travel around it, from planets and moons, to chunks of rock and ice and huge amounts of dust. At the moment, scientists know of nine planets that travel around the Sun.

This is a picture of the planet Saturn and some of its moons. Saturn is the one with the rings around it.

Planets

A planet is a large spherical object that travels around, or orbits, a particular star. As each planet moves, it also spins around on its axis (an imaginary line running through the planet).

The Sun

Stars

Stars are huge balls of hot gas which give off heat and light. The stars we see in the night sky only look tiny because they are far away. Our closest star is the Sun. It is about 146 million km (93 million miles) away. Light takes eight minutes to travel from the Sun to Earth.

Moons

Most of the planets in our Solar System have moons. A moon orbits a planet in the same way that a planet orbits a star. Earth has just one moon, but some planets have several. Saturn, for example, has at least 31 moons.

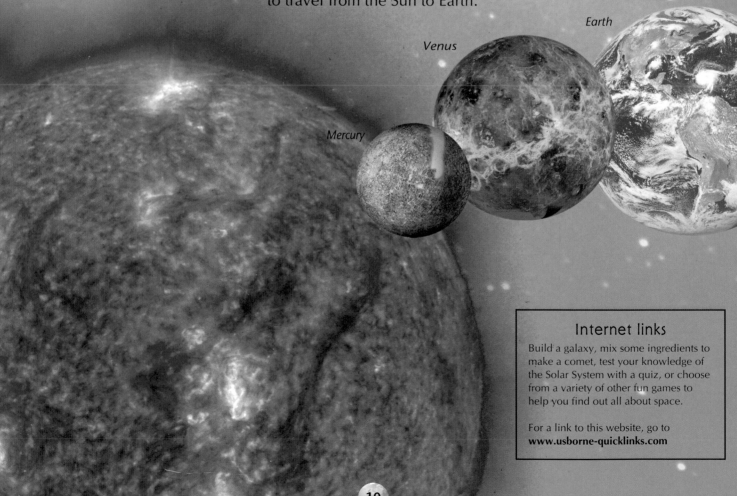

Mercury

Venus

Earth

Internet links

Build a galaxy, mix some ingredients to make a comet, test your knowledge of the Solar System with a quiz, or choose from a variety of other fun games to help you find out all about space.

For a link to this website, go to **www.usborne-quicklinks.com**

Uranus

Neptune

Pluto

Jupiter

Saturn

Mars

This picture shows the nine planets in our Solar System in the order they are from the Sun, though they are not to scale.

Space rocks

Asteroids and comets are pieces of rock, ice, dust and grit that whizz around our Solar System. Scientists believe that they are pieces left over from when the Solar System formed. The Solar System is also full of much smaller pieces of space debris called meteoroids. These may be grains of dust from comets, large chunks of rock or even shattered asteroids.

Galaxies

A galaxy is a group of many millions of stars. Galaxies are so big that it can take light thousands of years to travel across one. There are 6,000 million known galaxies in the universe, all of different shapes and sizes, but there could be many, many more. Galaxies are separated from each other by vast, empty spaces. Our Solar System is part of the Milky Way galaxy.

This picture shows stars in the southern part of the Milky Way galaxy.

THE EARTH

Factories like this one release harmful chemicals into the air, polluting the Earth's environment.

Earth is the third planet from the Sun. It is the only planet in our Solar System with the right conditions to support living things. The closest natural object to the Earth is the Moon, which is about 384,400km (240,250 miles) away.

Life on Earth

The Earth's distance from the Sun means that it has just the right amount of heat and light for life to flourish. Its combination of gases enables plants, animals and people to breathe, and it is warm enough for water to exist as a liquid. All of these things are essential for life on Earth.

This is a satellite photograph of the Earth taken from space. You can see the shapes of North America and the north of South America.

Earth in danger

As the number of people on Earth grows, we use more land, and our motor vehicles and industries release an increasing amount of waste, or pollution. This damages the environment: the land, oceans and the air we breathe. It is essential that we start taking more care of the Earth, before it is too late.

The Moon

Earth has only one moon. Most moons are very small compared with the planets they orbit, but our Moon is unusually large. It is about a quarter of the Earth's size.

The Moon does not make its own light, but it reflects the Sun's rays, so it can look very bright in the night sky.

Pulling power

Between objects in the Solar System there is an invisible force called gravity, which attracts, or pulls, things together. It is the Earth's gravity that holds the Moon in orbit around it.

The Moon's gravity affects the Earth too. It pulls on the water in Earth's oceans and seas, making the sea level rise and fall. These changing sea levels are called tides.

Satellites

Today, scientists are able to monitor vast areas of Earth from space. Devices called satellites orbit the Earth and send back information about our planet. The first satellite ever to go into space was launched by the U.S.S.R.* on October 4, 1957, to study the gases surrounding our planet. It was officially named

The Moon's surface is covered in craters. On a clear night, you can see the larger craters with your naked eye.

This is RADARSAT, Canada's first Earth observation satellite. It was launched in November 1995.

RADARSAT can produce high quality images of Earth's surface. It is used to monitor Earth's natural resources and the environment.

"Satellite 1957 Alpha 2", but became better known by its nickname "Sputnik", which is a Russian word meaning "little voyager".

Internet links

Website 1 Explore the Moon with the Apollo astronauts.

Website 2 Find out more about space and ongoing research projects.

For links to these websites, go to **www.usborne-quicklinks.com**

*U.S.S.R., 204

THE SEASONS

The Earth takes just over a year to orbit the Sun. As it makes its journey, different parts of the world receive different amounts of heat and light. This causes the seasons (spring, summer, autumn and winter).

Tilting Earth

The Earth is tilted at an angle as it travels around the Sun. This means that one half, or hemisphere, is usually closer to the Sun than the other. The hemisphere that is closer receives more heat and light energy than the one that is tilted away. So in this half it is summer, while in the other it is winter.

As the Earth orbits the Sun, the half that was closer to the Sun gradually moves farther away, so that eventually it becomes winter in this hemisphere and summer in the other. In June the Sun's rays are most concentrated at the Tropic of Cancer and in December they are most concentrated at the Tropic of Capricorn.

In June, it is summer in the Arctic. The warmer weather only lasts for six to eight weeks.

In autumn in Maine, northeast U.S.A., the leaves on the trees turn red and golden.

The diagram below shows how the seasons change as the Earth orbits the Sun.

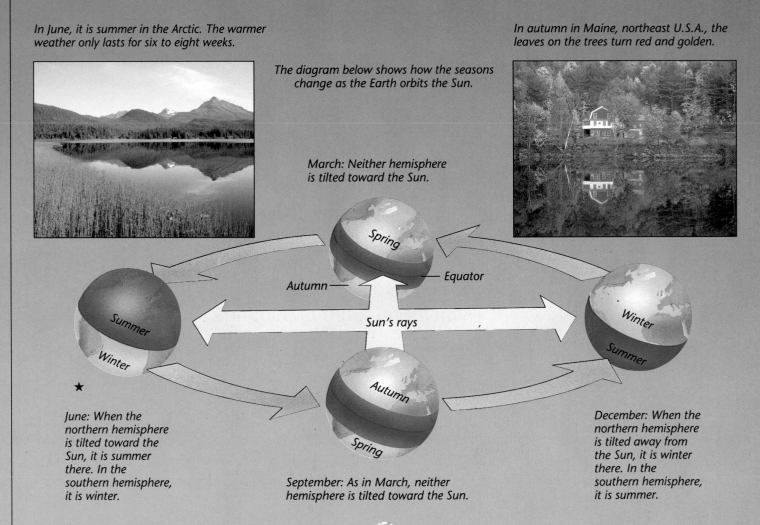

March: Neither hemisphere is tilted toward the Sun.

Spring

Autumn — — Equator

Summer

Winter

Sun's rays

Winter

Summer

Autumn

Spring

June: When the northern hemisphere is tilted toward the Sun, it is summer there. In the southern hemisphere, it is winter.

September: As in March, neither hemisphere is tilted toward the Sun.

December: When the northern hemisphere is tilted away from the Sun, it is winter there. In the southern hemisphere, it is summer.

The heat and light that the Sun gives out are essential for life on Earth.

Leap years

The time it takes for the Earth to orbit the Sun is called a solar year. A solar year is 365.26 days, but as it is more convenient to measure our calendar year in whole days, we round the number down to 365. In order to make up the difference, every four years we have to add an extra day to our calendar year, making it 366 days. These years are called leap years*. The additional day is February 29th. However, this does not make up the difference exactly, so very occasionally the extra day is not added.

Equatorial seasons

The Earth is hottest where the Sun's rays hit its surface full on. But because the Earth's surface is curved, in most places rays hit the ground at an angle. This causes them to spread out over a larger area, which makes their effect less intense.

Temperatures are also affected by the distance the Sun's rays have to travel through the Earth's atmosphere. Over greater distances, the Sun's rays lose more heat energy to the atmosphere, which makes temperatures cooler.

This picture shows how the Sun's rays spread out as they reach the Earth's surface.

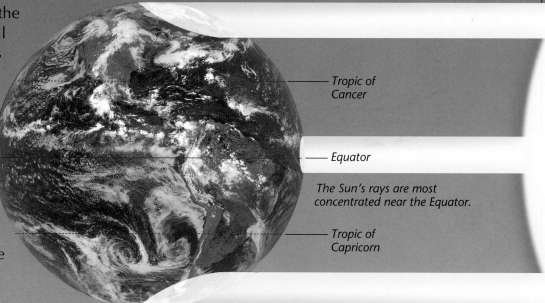

Tropic of Cancer

Equator

The Sun's rays are most concentrated near the Equator.

Tropic of Capricorn

The Sun's rays spread out at the poles and have farther to travel through the Earth's atmosphere.

Internet links

Website 1 Online activities about how the sun moves and what causes the seasons.

Website 2 See an animation showing how the seasons change as the Earth travels around the Sun.

For links to these websites, go to **www.usborne-quicklinks.com**

At the poles, the midday Sun is low on the horizon even in summer, making it cool.

At the Equator, the midday Sun is high in the sky all year round, so it is very hot.

*Leap years, 340

DAY AND NIGHT

When it's daytime in Australia, it's night-time in South America. This is because the Earth spins around on its axis as it orbits the Sun, so the part of the Earth that faces the Sun is constantly changing.

Rotating Earth

It takes 24 hours, or one day, for the Earth to spin around once on its axis. As it rotates, different parts of the world turn to face the Sun. The part of the Earth that is turned toward the Sun is in the light (daytime), but as it turns away from the Sun it becomes dark (night-time).

This diagram follows the change from day to night in one place (marked by the flag) as the Earth spins.

★

Path of orbit around the Sun

Sunrise and sunset

In the morning, you see the Sun "rise" in the sky. This is only an illusion. What is actually happening is that as your part of the Earth is turning to face the Sun, the movement of the Earth makes it seem as though the Sun is rising. When your part of the Earth turns away from the Sun at night, it looks as if the Sun is sinking in the sky until eventually it disappears over the horizon. This is called a sunset.

In the morning, the Sun looks as though it's rising, as your part of the Earth gradually turns to face it.

In the evening, the Sun seems to sink down in the sky, as your part of the Earth turns away from it.

Daylight hours

Everywhere in the world, apart from places that are on the Equator, days are longer in the summer than in the winter. This is because the hemisphere where it is summer receives more sunlight than the hemisphere where it is winter.

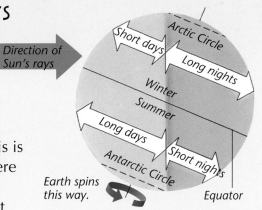

This diagram shows how the length of day and night varies depending on the time of year and where you are on the Earth.

Midnight Sun

In summer, when the northern hemisphere tilts toward the Sun, the regions north of the Arctic Circle don't turn away from the Sun, even at night. For this reason it is known as the Land of the Midnight Sun.

This shows the Sun in the Arctic Circle in the middle of the night.

Internet links

Website 1 Look at a map of the Earth to see the regions where it is day and where it is night at this moment.

Website 2 Play a game where you race against the clock to put the phases of the moon in order.

For links to these websites, go to
www.usborne-quicklinks.com

Moon shapes

The Moon doesn't give out any light of its own. It looks bright to us because we see the Sun's rays reflected off its surface. During the day, we can't usually see the Moon because the Sun is brighter.

As the Moon orbits the Sun and we see different amounts of its sunlit side, its shape seems to change as shown in these diagrams.

The pictures below show what the Moon looks like from Earth when it is in each of the positions numbered above.

1. New moon
2. Crescent
3. Half moon
4. Waxing
5. Full moon
6. Waning
7. Half moon
8. Crescent

INSIDE THE EARTH

The Earth is mainly solid. It has a rocky surface, but inside it has different layers, some of which are partly molten (melted). If you sliced through the Earth, you would see four main layers: the crust, the mantle, the outer core and the inner core.

This diagram shows the Earth's structure, though the layers are not drawn to scale.

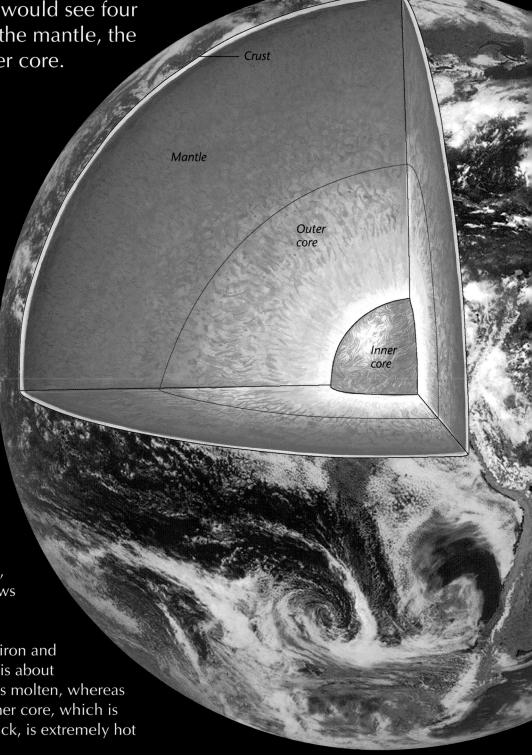

Crust

Mantle

Outer core

Inner core

Internet links

Find out how compasses work using the Earth's magnetism and learn how to make a compass of your own.

For a link to this website, go to **www.usborne-quicklinks.com**

Earth's layers

The crust is the thinnest layer. It is between 5km (3 miles) and 70km (43 miles) thick. Beneath the crust is the upper part of the mantle, and together these make up the lithosphere.

The mantle is made of silicon and magnesium. The region in the mantle at the bottom of the lithosphere, about 100km (62 miles) down, is partly molten. This layer flows very slowly.

The core is probably made of iron and nickel. The outer core, which is about 2,200km (1,400 miles) thick, is molten, whereas the inner core is solid. The inner core, which is about 1,300km (800 miles) thick, is extremely hot (about 6,000°C, or 10,800°F).

The Earth's crust

There are two different types of crust. Thick continental crust forms land, and much thinner oceanic crust makes up the ocean floors. Continental crust is made of granite and similar light rocks. Oceanic crust is made of a heavier rock called basalt.

★

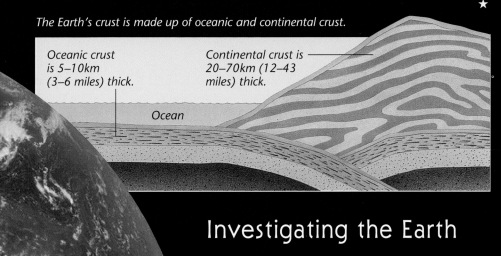

The Earth's crust is made up of oceanic and continental crust.

Oceanic crust is 5–10km (3–6 miles) thick.

Continental crust is 20–70km (12–43 miles) thick.

Ocean

Investigating the Earth

It's difficult to find out about the inside of the Earth. Geologists, who study rocks, find out about areas near the surface by drilling holes into the crust and collecting rock samples. But they can only drill a short distance below the surface.

Volcanic eruptions provide some information about material deep inside the Earth. But the main way that geologists find out about the Earth's structure is by studying earthquakes. During an earthquake, vibrations called seismic waves travel through the Earth. As they pass through different materials, they change speed and direction. By studying records of earthquakes, called seismograms, geologists try to determine what rocks are found at different depths.

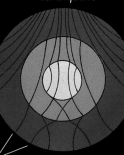

Earthquake

Paths of waves

This diagram shows how seismic waves change direction as they pass through the Earth.

Magnetic Earth

The Earth is magnetic, as if it had a huge magnetic bar inside. This may be caused by molten iron circulating in its core. The ends of this "magnet" are called the magnetic poles. These are not in exactly the same place as the geographic North and South Poles.

This diagram shows the Earth's magnetic field: the field of force surrounding it. The lines show the direction of the magnetic field.

Magnetic North Pole

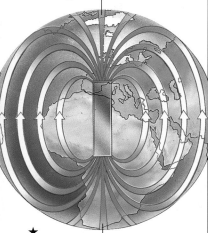

★
Magnetic South Pole

You can see the Earth's magnetism at work when you use a compass. The compass needle, which is magnetic, always points north. This is because it is pulled, or attracted, by the magnetic North Pole.

A compass's magnetic needle always points north.

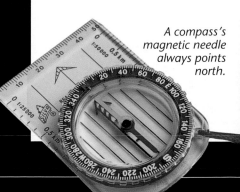

THE EARTH'S CRUST

The solid surface of the Earth is broken up into large pieces called lithospheric plates, which are made up of the Earth's crust and upper mantle. Many of the Earth's most spectacular features have been formed by the movement of these plates.

North American plate

Cocos plate

Caribbean plate

Plate boundaries

Nazca plate

Mantle

A moving surface

There are seven large plates and several smaller plates. The edges of the plates are called plate boundaries. The plates move on the partly molten layer of the mantle at a rate of about 5cm (2in) a year. As all the plates fit together, movement of one plate affects the others. The study of these plates and the way they move around is called plate tectonics.

Internet links

Read about plate structure and see an animated picture showing how the Earth's plates have changed position over time.

For a link to this website, go to
www.usborne-quicklinks.com

Ocean features

As plates on the ocean floor move apart, molten rock, or magma, from the mantle rises and fills the gap. Boundaries where this happens are called constructive boundaries. As the magma reaches the surface, it hardens to make new oceanic crust. The new crust sometimes forms islands or underwater mountain ranges, called ridges.

Oceanic crust   Ridge

Trench

Currents in the mantle

Plate boundaries   ★

When plates push together, underwater trenches form as one plate is forced below another. These boundaries are called destructive boundaries. The deepest trench, the Mariana Trench in the Pacific Ocean, is deeper than Mount Everest is tall.

This diagram shows how ridges and trenches form.

Shifting continents

As plates shift, the position of the oceans and continents on the Earth's surface changes. The maps on the right show how geologists think the continents may have shifted.

★

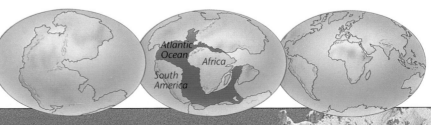

Geologists think that there was once a single supercontinent, which we call "Pangaea".

As new rock formed at plate boundaries, the floor of the Atlantic Ocean probably widened.

Today, South America and Africa are drifting apart at a rate of 3.5cm (1.5in) each year.

Atlantic Ocean

Africa

South America

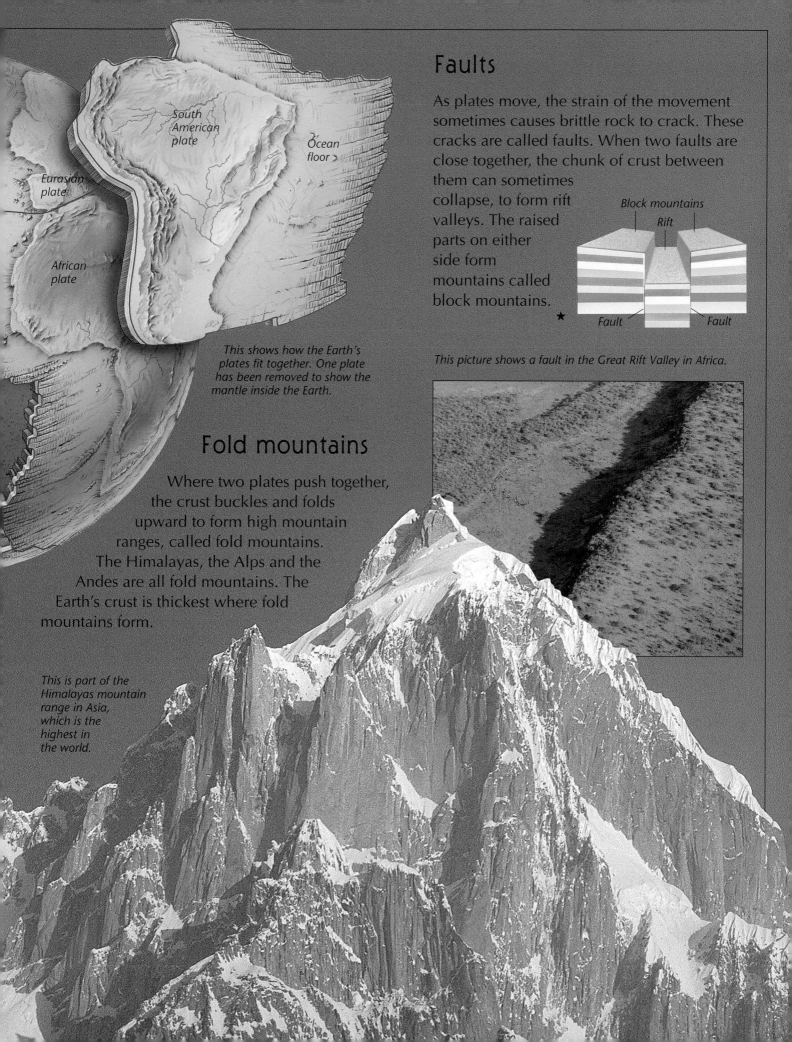

South American plate

Ocean floor

Eurasian plate

African plate

This shows how the Earth's plates fit together. One plate has been removed to show the mantle inside the Earth.

Faults

As plates move, the strain of the movement sometimes causes brittle rock to crack. These cracks are called faults. When two faults are close together, the chunk of crust between them can sometimes collapse, to form rift valleys. The raised parts on either side form mountains called block mountains.

Block mountains

Rift

Fault   Fault

★

This picture shows a fault in the Great Rift Valley in Africa.

Fold mountains

Where two plates push together, the crust buckles and folds upward to form high mountain ranges, called fold mountains. The Himalayas, the Alps and the Andes are all fold mountains. The Earth's crust is thickest where fold mountains form.

This is part of the Himalayas mountain range in Asia, which is the highest in the world.

ROCKS, MINERALS AND FOSSILS

The Earth's crust is made up of rock. There are three kinds of rocks: igneous, sedimentary and metamorphic. Over many years, rocks are sometimes transformed from one kind to another.

Igneous rock

Igneous rock gets its name from the Latin word for "fire", because it is formed from magma from inside the Earth. When the magma cools, it forms solid igneous rock. The way that the magma cools determines the kind of igneous rock that is formed.

Tuff is an igneous rock made from pieces of volcanic rock and crystals compressed together.

Obsidian is a shiny igneous rock formed when magma cools quickly.

Sedimentary rock

Sedimentary rock is made from tiny pieces of rocks and the decayed remains of plants and animals. These fragments, called sediment, are usually blown by winds, or carried by rivers, glaciers or landslides, to the sea, where they sink. The water and upper layers of sediment press down on the lower layers until, eventually, they form solid rock.

Chalk is a sedimentary rock made from tiny sea creatures.

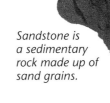

Sandstone is a sedimentary rock made up of sand grains.

The Grand Canyon, in the U.S.A., is a gorge formed by the Colorado River. You can see the layers of sandstone. Layers of rock like these are called strata.

Metamorphic rock

Metamorphic rock is rock that has been changed – for example, by heat from magma, or pressure caused by plate movements or very deep burial. It can be formed from igneous, sedimentary or other metamorphic rocks.

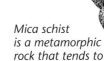

Marble is a metamorphic rock formed from limestone.

Mica schist is a metamorphic rock that tends to split into layers.

Minerals

Rocks are made from substances called minerals, which in turn are made up of simple chemical substances called elements. Some minerals are cut and polished to be used as gemstones.

These pictures show minerals in rocks and as gemstones.

Opal can be milky white, green, red, blue, black or brown.

Turquoise runs through rock in the form of veins.

Carnelian is a dark red stone.

Internet links

Discover more about different kinds of rocks and what they can tell us about the history of the Earth, then test your knowledge with an online quiz.

For a link to this website, go to **www.usborne-quicklinks.com**

Fossils

The shapes or remains of plants and animals that died long ago are sometimes preserved in rocks. They are called fossils. Fossils are formed when a dead plant or animal is buried by sediment which then turns to sedimentary rock.
Usually the remains decay, although hard parts such as teeth, shells and bones can sometimes survive. The space left by the plant or animal fills up with sediment or minerals which preserve its shape.

The fossil of an ammonite (an extinct sea creature)

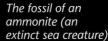

THE EARTH'S RESOURCES

T he Earth provides all sorts of useful rocks, minerals and other materials. We quarry stone and sand for building and glassmaking, extract over 60 types of metals, and mine hundreds of useful chemicals and compounds such as salt, talc and silicon.

Metals and minerals

Metals are among the most important materials we get from the Earth. They are strong, yet they can be beaten out into flat sheets or drawn out to make wire. They also conduct electricity and heat well. Some metals even have medical uses.

Most metals are found in ores, types of rocks that contain a metal in the form of a chemical compound. Metals are extracted from ores by mixing them with other chemicals to cause a reaction or by heating them strongly.

As well as metals and stone, the Earth also provides many other chemicals and elements. Their uses often depend on how hard they are.

Iron is extracted from its ore in a blast furnace.

Iron ore, coke (a type of coal) and limestone go in here.

The furnace is over 30m (100ft) tall.

Iron ore, coke and limestone react with each other in a blast furnace to make new chemicals, leaving the iron free.

Molten iron flows out here.

Hot air is blasted into the furnace.

Waste called slag comes out here.

★

People have used precious metals for centuries as settings for precious stones.

Internet links

Website 1 See beautiful microscopic photographs of rocks and minerals accompanied by helpful descriptions.

Website 2 Find out how to identify different minerals, grow crystals from salt and create your own mineral collection.

For links to these websites, go to **www.usborne-quicklinks.com**

The Mohs scale

The hardness or softness of minerals is measured on a scale of 1 to 10, called the Mohs scale. Soft minerals, such as talc, crumble easily into powder. At the other end of the scale are the hardest minerals, such as diamonds, which are used in cutting tools.

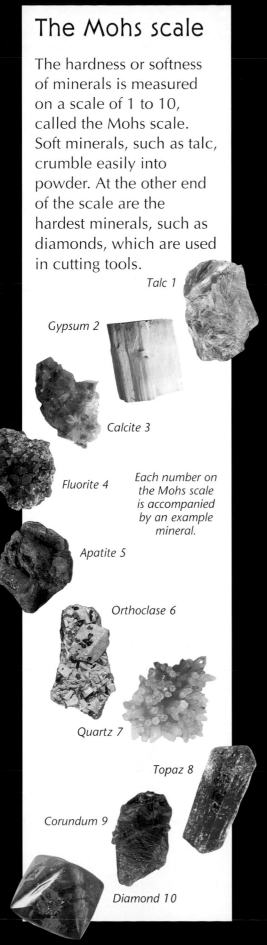

Talc 1

Gypsum 2

Calcite 3

Fluorite 4

Each number on the Mohs scale is accompanied by an example mineral.

Apatite 5

Orthoclase 6

Quartz 7

Topaz 8

Corundum 9

Diamond 10

Silicon chips

Silicon comes from a mineral called quartz. It has become very important in modern society, because it is used to make the electronic chips that run computers, digital watches, mobile phones and millions of other everyday appliances.

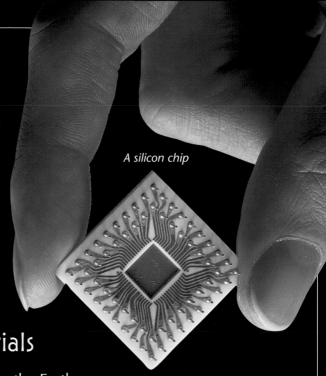

A silicon chip

Building materials

Rocks and minerals from the Earth are used to make bricks, cement, glass and other building materials. Stone for building is usually extracted from the ground in quarries. It's often so hard and heavy that explosives have to be used to blast it apart.

Sand is made of rocks, minerals and sometimes seashells, ground down to fragments by the action of water (which is why it is usually found near the sea). Concrete and glass are both made using sand.

The Taj Mahal is a huge Indian tomb. Its exterior is white marble.

ENERGY FROM THE EARTH

This huge structure is the top part of an oil platform, which sticks out above the sea's surface. It contains equipment for processing the oil, and living quarters for the workers.

The Earth's rocks, minerals and fossils contain energy which we can extract and use. Oil, gas and coal, which can be converted into heat and electricity, all come from the Earth. So do other forms of energy, such as nuclear energy.

Fossil fuels

Coal, oil and natural gas are fossil fuels. They are called this because, like fossils*, they form in the ground over a very long period of time from the bodies of dead plants and animals.

Coal is formed from trees and other plants. Layers of sand and clay gradually settled on top of them, and compressed them slowly into thick, underground layers, or seams, of coal.

Oil is formed from the bodies of tiny sea creatures. It is usually found in rocks under the seabed but may be found under land. Under certain conditions, natural gas is formed from dead plants and animals. Gas and oil are often found close together.

Extracting fuels

The coal we use comes from underground mines or opencast mines, which are huge, open holes dug in the ground. To extract oil and gas, a drill, supported by a structure called a rig, bores a hole into the ground or seabed. Sometimes the fuel flows out naturally, but usually water is pumped into the hole to force the oil or gas out.

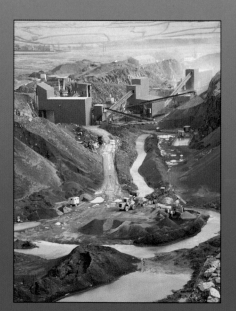

Coal being extracted from a mine at the surface of the ground, called an opencast mine.

NORTH CORMORANT

*Fossils, 23

Using fossil fuels

When a fossil fuel is burned, it releases energy, which is used to heat buildings and to run vehicle engines. In power stations, heat from fossil fuels is converted into electricity.

The world depends on fossil fuels. They provide more than three-quarters of the energy we use. But we use them up more quickly than they can form, so they are running out. In around two hundred years, humans will need to get most of their energy in other ways.

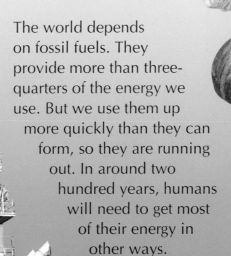

As well as providing energy, oil is used to make plastic, which is made into thousands of things, from bottles to polyester clothing.

Radiation

Some minerals found in the ground are radioactive. This means their atoms (the tiny particles they are made of) are unstable.

Instead of staying as they are, unstable minerals break up and send out particles or rays, known as radiation. As they break up, a type of energy called nuclear energy is released. Uranium, a metal, is the main radioactive mineral used to produce nuclear energy.

Internet links

Take a virtual tour of an oil platform or find out more about oil, oil products and how oil is processed.

For a link to this website, go to
www.usborne-quicklinks.com

This diagram shows how atoms of uranium produce nuclear energy.

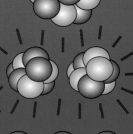

A tiny particle called a neutron is fired at the uranium nucleus.

This is the nucleus, or middle, of a uranium atom.

The nucleus splits, giving off heat.

More neutrons fly off the nucleus and split other uranium atoms.

SOIL

Soil covers over half of the Earth's land surface. It is vital to life on Earth, because it provides the food and conditions plants need to grow.

Internet links

Website 1 Explore the world of soil and find out what life would be like if you were half an inch tall.

Website 2 Find out how worms break down dead plants and animals.

For links to these websites, go to **www.usborne-quicklinks.com**

As they burrow through the soil, earthworms drag dead leaves and other organic matter down to the lower levels, and break them down into humus.

What's in the soil?

Soil is made up of particles of rocks and minerals, dead plant and animal matter, tiny living organisms, gases and water. The particles of rocks and minerals range from big chunks of stone to tiny mineral particles which get dissolved by the water in the soil. Some minerals are taken in by plants and used as food. These are called nutrients. The dead plant and animal matter is gradually broken down into a substance called humus, by all the tiny creatures, bacteria and fungi in the soil.

Humus is what makes soil fertile (easy for plants to grow in). Living things are a vital part of the soil. If they weren't there to break down dead plants and animals, the remains of things that have died would keep piling up on the Earth's surface.

The water in the soil comes from rain, and gases come from the air and from plants and animals. Plants absorb water and gases through their roots.

This earwig and her babies are among the thousands of insects and other small animals that live in soil.

Soil layers

If you looked at a slice of soil under the ground, you would see that it has several different layers, called horizons.

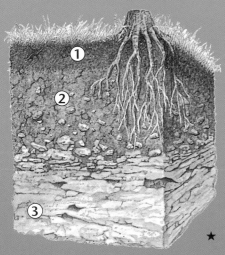

① *The topsoil contains a lot of humus and is full of tiny living creatures.*

② *Subsoil is made up of humus, rocks and minerals. Cracks and holes, or pores, in the subsoil help water to drain away, preventing the soil from getting too wet.*

③ *The rock that lies underneath the soil is called bedrock. Chunks of it sometimes break off into the soil.*

Types of soil

There are thousands and thousands of different types of soil. Some are more fertile than others, but different plants prefer different soils. Farmers can choose what to grow, depending on the type of soil they have on their land.

There are three main soil textures: sand, silt and clay. Sandy soil is rough and grainy. Silt has small particles, which are hard to see, while clay soil is made of fine particles, which bind together with water to form a thick, creamy mud. Clay is used to make pottery and china.

This picture shows parsnip roots reaching into the soil for water and minerals. Parsnips grow well in sandy and clay soils.

This hand contains sandy soil. Its grainy texture allows moisture to drain through it easily.

A handful of fertile soil contains up to six billion bacteria.

This hand contains loam soil. It is a very fertile soil containing a mixture of clay and sandy soils.

PROTECTING SOIL

Why do we need to take care of soil? The answer is that pollution, farming and cutting down trees can all damage soil and upset its natural balance. If we want to keep using the soil to grow food, we have to protect it, and replace all the chemicals that farming takes away.

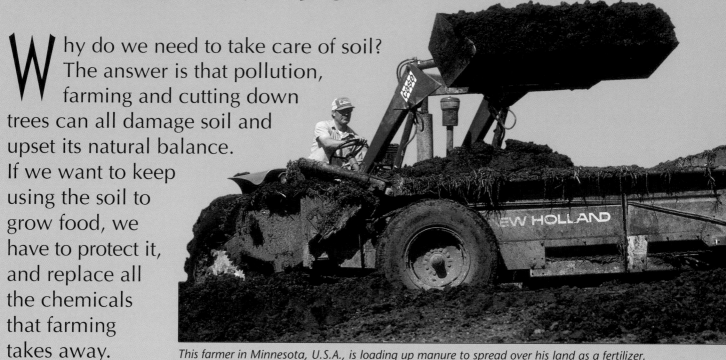

This farmer in Minnesota, U.S.A., is loading up manure to spread over his land as a fertilizer.

The soil cycle

Where there is no farming, soil is part of a continuous cycle. Minerals are gradually dissolved into the soil. Dead plants and animals fall onto the ground, begin to rot, and are broken down into humus*. The minerals and the humus provide nutrients (food) for new plants, and the cycle starts again. This means that the nutrients that are taken out of the soil eventually get put back in.

But, when soil is used for farming, the crops are taken away to be sold, instead of rotting back into the ground. This causes the soil to become gradually less fertile* as it loses its nutrients.

Fertilizing

The best way to replace the nutrients in soil is to add a fertilizer. Fertilizers contain chemicals, such as nitrates, which plants need in order to grow. Manure (animal dung) is a natural fertilizer, but many farmers use specially made chemical fertilizers. Sometimes, if farmers use too much fertilizer, the chemicals can leak out of the soil into rivers, causing pollution.

Crop rotation

Crop rotation means changing the crop grown on a piece of land each year. It helps to keep the soil fertile, especially if the land is sometimes left to "lie fallow". This means the farmer doesn't harvest the crop, but lets it rot back into the soil. Plants such as legumes (peas and beans) and clover make good fallow crops because they put nitrates into the soil instead of taking them out.

Bright yellow oilseed rape is used to make cooking oil and as food for animals. Oilseed rape crops are often rotated with other crops on farms in Europe.

*Fertile, 28; humus, 28

Soil erosion

In the natural environment, plants and trees hold soil together and stop it from being washed away by the rain or blown away by the wind. But when people chop down trees for firewood and farmers dig up the land to plant crops it leaves the bare soil exposed.

However, there are some ways to protect the soil. In some places, farmers can grow crops among the trees without cutting them down. If a main crop leaves bare patches of soil, a second crop called a cover crop can be planted in the gaps to stop it from eroding. In hilly areas, farmers build steps called terraces into the hillside to hold soil in place.

With the trees cut down, the soil on this hillside could soon be washed away.

This cover crop protects the soil between rows of rubber trees. It also lets farmers grow two crops on the same land.

Internet links

Take a closer look at soil and find out what it is made up of and why it's so important, before attempting some fun soil-related activities.

For a link to this website, go to
www.usborne-quicklinks.com

Lost forever

Ancient ruins show that there were once busy towns in places that are now desert, such as parts of Egypt and Saudi Arabia.

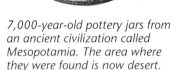

7,000-year-old pottery jars from an ancient civilization called Mesopotamia. The area where they were found is now desert.

The people who lived there may not have known how to look after soil and stop it from eroding. This may be why their civilizations died out.

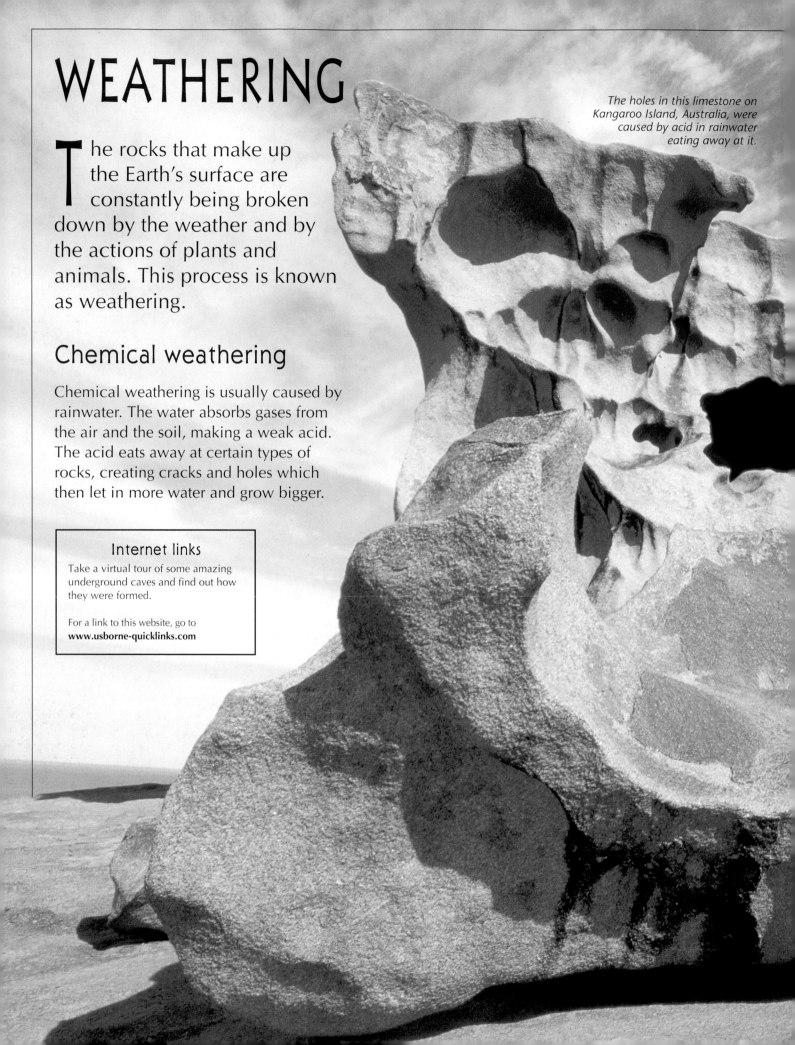

WEATHERING

The holes in this limestone on Kangaroo Island, Australia, were caused by acid in rainwater eating away at it.

The rocks that make up the Earth's surface are constantly being broken down by the weather and by the actions of plants and animals. This process is known as weathering.

Chemical weathering

Chemical weathering is usually caused by rainwater. The water absorbs gases from the air and the soil, making a weak acid. The acid eats away at certain types of rocks, creating cracks and holes which then let in more water and grow bigger.

Internet links

Take a virtual tour of some amazing underground caves and find out how they were formed.

For a link to this website, go to
www.usborne-quicklinks.com

Physical weathering

Heat makes most substances get bigger, or expand. When rocks are warmed by the Sun, they expand, and when they cool down at night they shrink, or contract. The outer layer of the rock expands more, because it is directly exposed to the Sun's heat. Eventually it separates from the rock and peels off. This is called exfoliation.

A type of weathering called freeze-thaw action occurs when water seeps into cracks in rock and then freezes and expands.

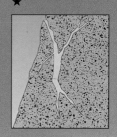
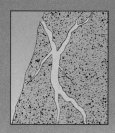

The process of freeze-thaw action begins when rain seeps into a small crack in rock.

The water freezes, expands and widens the crack. When the ice thaws, more water can seep in.

As the temperature rises and falls, the crack gradually grows until the rock breaks apart.

Biological weathering

Weathering caused by plants or animals is called biological weathering. For example, lichens, which are small organisms that grow on rocks, give out acidic chemicals which eat away at the rock surface. Animals burrowing and roots growing in the ground can also contribute to rocks breaking down.

As well as being dissolved by acidic rainwater, the Kangaroo Island rock on the left is being eaten away by lichens – the red areas on its surface.

Shaping the landscape

Because some rocks are harder and more resistant to weathering than others, they wear away at different rates. Harder rocks get left behind as outcrops, which stick up out of the surrounding land, or as long ridges. Over many years, weathering can produce amazing rock shapes, jutting mountain peaks and deep limestone caves*.

This cave is still being shaped by chemical weathering, as acidic water eats away at cracks in the rock.

EROSION

Erosion happens when wind, water, ice and gravity carry away particles of rock and soil that have been worn down by weathering*. Gradually, eroded material is carried downhill and into rivers, and most of it ends up being washed into the sea.

K2 in the Himalayas is 8,611m (28,250ft) high. It is relatively young and still has pointed peaks.

Mount Baker in Washington, U.S.A., is 3,285m (10,778ft) high. It has a flatter, worn shape, showing it was formed earlier in the Earth's history.

Wind and rain

Over hundreds of years, wind gradually blows away tiny particles from the surface of rocks. Many rocks contain different minerals, some harder than others. The wind wears them away at different rates, carving the rocks into wind sculptures.

Rain splashing onto rocks and soil washes away bigger particles and carries them into rivers. Farmers have to protect the soil* to prevent it all from eroding away in the rain.

These pinnacles in Arizona, U.S.A., are striated, which means the wind has carved their surfaces into narrow grooves.

Moving mountains

On mountains, particles of rocks and soil are pulled downhill by gravity. Chunks of rock that break off near the top of a mountain fall down the slopes, knocking off other chunks as they go. Often a covering of loose stones, called scree, collects at the bottom of a slope.

Humans can add to this kind of erosion. Rock climbers sometimes dislodge scree and set off rockfalls, and walkers can slowly wear mountain paths away.

Wearing flat

As erosion carries particles of rocks and soil away from mountains and high ground toward the sea, the Earth's land masses become lower and smoother. However, new islands and mountains are sometimes formed by volcanoes* erupting and by the plates* that make up the Earth's crust grinding together. So as old land is worn away, new land rises up to replace it.

34

This photo shows the bare hillside left behind after a landslide in North Carolina, U.S.A.

Internet links

Learn more about erosion and try an experiment to find out how rain shapes the Earth.

For a link to this website, go to
www.usborne-quicklinks.com

Landslides

A landslide is a mass of soil and rock suddenly slipping down a steep slope. Many landslides are caused by rainwater soaking into the soil and making it heavier. Landslides are particularly likely if water soaks into a layer of shale (a type of slippery rock made from compressed clay).

Preventing erosion

A certain amount of erosion is normal, and we could never stop it completely. In some places, though, we can try to slow it down.

On mountains that are popular with walkers, stone or wooden paths help to protect the land from being worn away by feet. In hilly areas, trees help to keep the soil in place and prevent landslides, so people have learned not to cut down hillside trees.

A worker planting vegetation to prevent erosion near a roadside

35

Plates, 20; soil erosion, 31; volcanoes, 38; weathering, 32

Lava flowing from the Kilauea volcano, Hawaii

EARTHQUAKES AND VOLCANOES

THE EXPLODING EARTH

An erupting volcano is one of the most dramatic sights in the natural world. Bubbling hot lava spews out of a hole in the Earth's crust and engulfs the land. Ash, dust and poisonous gases pour into the air and chunks of rock are hurled high into the sky.

Volcanoes

Volcanoes erupt when red-hot molten rock, called magma, from the Earth's mantle rises toward the surface. Eventually it builds up enough pressure to burst through the Earth's crust. Once magma has reached the surface of the Earth it is called lava.

A cross-section through a cone volcano

Dust, ash and gases —

Crater – the hole at the top of a volcano

Volcanic bomb

Vent – the main pipe up the middle of a volcano

Layers of volcanic ash – tiny particles of lava

Dyke – this leads from the vent to the surface

Magma chamber – place where magma collects below the Earth's crust

Growing

When a volcano erupts, the lava and ash it throws out eventually set as a solid layer of volcanic rock. As the layers build up, the volcano grows. Thick lava flows only a short way before setting, so it forms steep-sided cone volcanoes. Thinner lava flows farther before setting hard, so it forms shield volcanoes that have gently sloping sides.

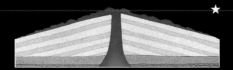

A cross-section through a shield volcano

Bombs and blocks

Volcanic bombs and blocks are thick lumps of molten lava which are blasted into the air as a volcano erupts. They start to cool and harden as they travel through the air. Blocks tend to be angular whereas bombs are more rounded.

Some blocks are the size of trucks.

As they twist through the air, some bombs form a "tail".

Tiny bombs shaped like drops form from very runny lava.

Dead or alive?

Volcanoes that erupt regularly are known as active volcanoes. Volcanoes that won't ever erupt again are called extinct volcanoes. Sometimes, people think a volcano is extinct when actually it is only dormant (sleeping). Volcanoes can lie dormant for thousands of years.

Internet links

Watch step-by-step animations of a volcano erupting and discover why volcanoes can be so deadly.

For a link to this Website, go to
www.usborne-quicklinks.com

Danger

Lava destroys everything it engulfs but, because it usually flows quite slowly, it rarely kills people. There is more danger from the hot gas, bombs and ash which can sweep down a volcano's slopes at speeds of 200kph (120mph). In AD79, when Mount Vesuvius in Italy erupted, the people of Pompeii were wiped out by poisonous gas and ash.

A plaster cast made from the hollow of a body left in the ash in Pompeii.

VOLCANIC VARIATIONS

Most volcanoes occur at weak spots on the Earth's crust where magma bursts through. Volcanoes erupt in different ways, depending on the thickness of the lava.

Hot spots

Some volcanoes form in the middle of plates. They may be caused by hot zones deep in the Earth's mantle. Scientists think that currents of warm rock called plumes rise slowly through the mantle and make magma which burns through the Earth's crust to make a hot spot volcano.

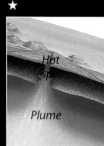
★

A diagram showing a hot spot volcano in the middle of a plate

Volcanoes with runny lava, like this, erupt gently.

Subduction zones

Volcanoes also occur at subduction zones. These are places where two plates collide head on and one plate is pushed down beneath the other. As the plate is forced deeper and deeper underground, it begins to melt, forming magma. This newly formed magma rises up through cracks in the surface and explodes in a volcano.

★

Spreading ridges

Whole mountain ranges of volcanoes can form at underwater boundaries where two plates* are moving apart. These are called spreading ridges. As the plates move apart, magma from the mantle rises to the surface. Most of it solidifies on the edge of the plates to make new crust, but some works its way up to the seabed, where it erupts as volcanoes.

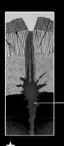

Spreading ridges form when plates move apart.

Rising magma

★

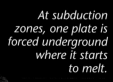

At subduction zones, one plate is forced underground where it starts to melt.

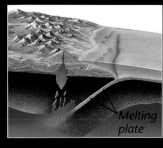

Melting plate

*Plates, 20

Lava

Not all volcanoes erupt in the same way. Some throw clouds of ash high into the air, while others have gentle lava fountains. The thicker and stickier the lava, the more gases are trapped within it. These gases create the pressure which makes a volcano erupt explosively. When lava is thin and runny, gases can escape more easily. They just bubble out of the top of the volcano.

Internet links

Build a volcano online and find out about different types of volcanoes around the world.

For a link to this website, go to
www.usborne-quicklinks.com

Hawaiian-type eruptions are usually gentle. They occur when lava is runny, so trapped gases bubble out easily.

Plinian-type eruptions are the most explosive. Trapped gases cause massive explosions as they escape, and huge amounts of volcanic ash are thrown high into the air.

NATURAL HOT WATER

In areas where volcanoes are found, there are often other dramatic natural features. Hot springs, jets of hot water and underwater chimneys that belch out black water can also be caused by volcanic activity.

Internet links

Take an online tour of the geysers in Yellowstone National Park, U.S.A.

For a link to this website, go to
www.usborne-quicklinks.com

Hot rock

In volcanic areas, when magma rises into the Earth's crust, it heats the rock around it. This rock might contain groundwater, which is rain or sea water that has seeped down into the Earth's crust through cracks in the surface. As the rock heats up, so does the groundwater around it, producing a natural supply of hot water.

Cold water

Rock heated by magma

Heated water

Hot rock heats up groundwater.

Hot springs

Groundwater heated by hot rock sometimes bubbles to the surface as a hot, or thermal, spring. The water usually contains minerals which have been dissolved from the rock below. Minerals from the water often build up around the edge of the spring.

This is the Morning Glory pool, one of many hot springs in Yellowstone National Park, U.S.A. The park has over 10,000 features, such as hot springs and geysers, that have been caused by hot, volcanic rock.

Black smokers

Around volcanic mountain ranges under the sea, hot springs sometimes emerge through holes in the seabed called hydrothermal vents.

Some vents, called black smokers, look like chimneys and puff out plumes of hot, cloudy black water. The water is cloudy because of the minerals it has dissolved from the hot rock. As minerals are deposited around the vent, the sides of the chimney build up. Some unusual creatures, such as tubeworms and blind spider crabs, live near black smokers. They feed on bacteria that live on the minerals given out by the vents.

Black smokers form on the seabed and puff out clouds of hot, black water. Some are as tall as 6m (20ft).

Geysers

A geyser is a jet of hot water and steam that shoots into the air from a hole in the ground. Geysers occur when heated groundwater gets trapped in a network of cracks under the Earth's surface. Because the water is trapped, it continues to heat up until it boils and forms steam. The pressure builds up until it forces the water to find a way out of the ground. This results in occasional bursts of hot water.

"Old Faithful" is a geyser in Yellowstone National Park, U.S.A. A fountain of hot water like this spurts out once every hour or so.

VOLCANIC ISLANDS

A volcanic island called White Island, off the coast of New Zealand

If a volcano on the seabed erupts enough times, it may become tall enough to reach the surface of the sea and begin to form an island. As ash and lava from repeated eruptions pile up around the vent, the island grows.

Hot spot islands

Hot spot volcanoes* under the sea sometimes grow into volcanic islands. Over thousands of years, a hot spot can produce a chain of volcanic islands. Scientists think that the rising plume remains in a fixed position inside the Earth's mantle, while the plate above moves. Over a long period of time, a volcanic island is carried away from the plume that caused it.

When an island moves away from a hot spot, the volcano becomes extinct as it loses its supply of magma. A new volcano then forms on the part of the plate lying above the plume. Eventually a chain of islands is formed.

Kauai
Oahu
Molokai
Maui
Hawaii
Plume

The Hawaiian island chain is made up of hot spot volcanic islands.

★

*Hot spots, 40

Internet links

Read more about volcanic islands and watch an animation of volcanic islands forming.

For a link to this website, go to **www.usborne-quicklinks.com**

An island is born

This picture shows steam and ash billowing from Surtsey, a volcanic island near Iceland.

In 1963, fishermen off the coast of Iceland saw smoke rising from the sea. They thought it must be a boat on fire. In fact, it wasn't smoke, but ash and steam from a volcano just below the water's surface.

During the next four years, the volcano erupted many times. As it emerged above the water, the eruptions became more explosive as the water pressure decreased. Lava and ash built up, until eventually they formed a volcanic island. The island was named Surtsey after Surt, the Nordic giant of fire.

Black beaches

Some volcanic islands have black sandy beaches. This is because they are formed from basalt lava which is black. When the lava runs down to meet the sea, it cools instantly. The change in temperature makes the lava shatter into tiny pieces which form the grains of sand.

A black sandy beach in Tahiti

LIVING WITH VOLCANOES

Despite the danger that active volcanoes present, many people choose to live on their slopes. Scientists are sometimes able to predict eruptions and warn those at risk.

Internet links

View amazing photographs of Mount St. Helens before, during and after its eruption in 1980.

For a link to this website, go to **www.usborne-quicklinks.com**

Monitoring volcanoes

Before a volcano erupts, the ground may change shape. This kind of change can be measured by instruments such as tiltmeters and geodimeters. The ground may also begin to tremble. This is known as volcanic tremor. It can be detected by seismometers.

Such instruments were used to monitor the Mount St. Helens volcano, Washington, U.S.A., in early 1980. They recorded a bulge swelling by 1.5m (5ft) per day. The area around the volcano was evacuated shortly before it erupted.

A group of experts monitoring the Mount St. Helens volcano were in a plane flying over it when the volcano began to shudder. This photograph of the eruption was taken as the pilot turned the plane to escape the blast.

The area around Mount St. Helens after the eruption. Despite the evacuation of the area, 61 people died.

A bulge on the side of Mount St. Helens swelled to 90m (295ft) before a massive eruption blasted away the side of the volcano.

Using volcanoes

Although volcanoes are usually a destructive force, they can also be put to productive uses. The ash from volcanoes contains minerals which make soil very fertile. As a result, the land around volcanoes is very good for farming. This is one of the reasons why people choose to live in such dangerous places.

EARTHQUAKE EFFECTS

An earthquake is a sudden release of energy that makes the ground tremble. The effects of a large earthquake can be devastating: the ground lurches violently and buildings sway from side to side, or may even collapse. However, earthquakes only occur in certain parts of the world and most earthquakes are not felt by people at all.

An apartment block in San Francisco, U.S.A., which has been damaged by an earthquake

Damaging effects

Earthquakes cause most damage when they occur in large towns and cities. During severe earthquakes, buildings and bridges collapse, and cracks called fissures may appear in the ground. There are also threats from hazards such as fire and flooding. These may be caused when underground gas pipes or water pipes crack during an earthquake.

The power of earthquakes

Over 800,000 earthquakes occur each year, but only around a hundred of these cause serious damage. Their power and effects are measured by seismologists, scientists who study earthquakes.

There are two scales for measuring earthquakes: the Richter scale and the Mercalli scale. The Richter scale measures the power of vibrations called seismic waves that travel through the ground when an earthquake happens. These tremors are registered using a device called a seismometer. Then a chart of the vibrations, known as a seismogram, is produced.

This is a device called a seismometer, which is used to measure ground vibrations.

This shows the devastation caused by an earthquake in Maharashtra, India, in 1993.

Internet links

Visit an online exhibition to find out more about how earthquakes are measured today and how they were measured in the past.

For a link to this website, go to **www.usborne-quicklinks.com**

Mercalli scale

The Mercalli scale rates earthquakes from I to XII according to the effects of the shaking, including the damage caused in different places. It is based on information from eyewitnesses.

These pictures show how earthquakes are rated using the Mercalli scale. Ratings below IV indicate very slight vibrations.

IV
People indoors may notice plates and windows start to rattle.

V
Small objects move and liquids in glasses and bowls splash around.

VI
Books and ornaments fall off shelves. Vibrations are felt indoors and outdoors.

VII
Walls crack and tiles and bricks fall from buildings.

VIII
Some weaker buildings collapse.

IX+
Many larger buildings collapse.

HOW EARTHQUAKES HAPPEN

Earthquakes are most common near plate boundaries*. The movement of the plates causes stress to build up in certain areas of rock. When this stress is suddenly released, the surrounding rock vibrates, causing an earthquake.

Fault lines

Earthquakes occur along cracks in the Earth's crust called faults. Faults can be tiny fractures or long cracks stretching over vast distances. They often occur when plates slide against each other, causing the rock to be twisted, stretched or squeezed until it splits. Boundaries where plates slide past each other in the same or in opposite directions are called conservative margins.

The North American plate moves 1cm (0.4in) a year.

San Francisco

San Andreas fault

The Pacific plate moves 6cm (2.4in) a year.

Los Angeles

San Diego

Earthquakes regularly occur along the San Andreas fault, on the west coast of North America. These plates slide in the same direction, but move at different speeds.

This diagram shows how some plates slide past each other in opposite directions.

An overhead view of the San Andreas fault

Releasing energy

If the jagged edges along a fault become jammed, energy builds up as the two edges strain against one another. Eventually, the stress becomes so great that one side is suddenly forced to give way, causing a jerking movement. The energy that has built up is released, making the surrounding rock vibrate in an earthquake.

A fault running through rock

Energy builds up at the point where the rocks become jammed.

*Plate boundaries, 20

The focus

The point where the rock gives way is called the focus. This is where the earthquake starts, usually about 5–15km (3–9 miles) underground. The point on the surface directly above the focus is called the epicentre*.

Internet links

Watch a movie of an earthquake, see animated diagrams that show how earthquakes happen and find out more about the ongoing attempts to predict earthquakes.

For a link to this website, go to
www.usborne-quicklinks.com

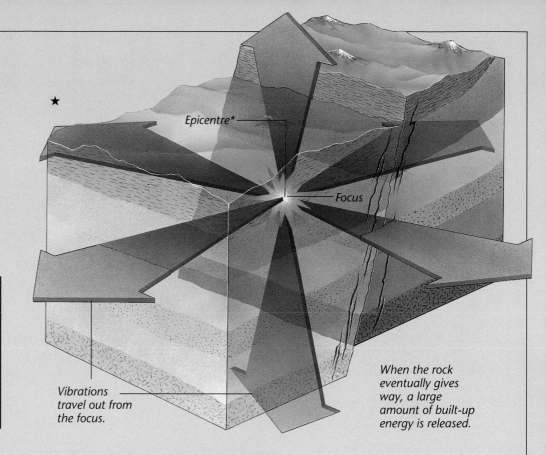

★

Epicentre*

Focus

Vibrations travel out from the focus.

When the rock eventually gives way, a large amount of built-up energy is released.

Seismic waves

Seismic waves are at their strongest nearest the focus and become weaker as they travel out. There are different types of seismic waves, each of which makes the rock it travels through vibrate in a different way.

Different types of seismic waves travel by distorting rock in different ways.

 Direction of waves

 Vibrations of the rock particles as the waves pass through

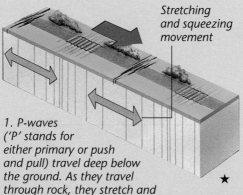

Stretching and squeezing movement

1. P-waves ('P' stands for either primary or push and pull) travel deep below the ground. As they travel through rock, they stretch and squeeze the rock particles.

★

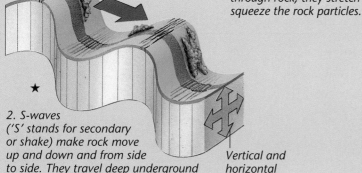

★

2. S-waves ('S' stands for secondary or shake) make rock move up and down and from side to side. They travel deep underground and can't move through liquid.

Vertical and horizontal movement

Circular movement

3. L-waves ('L' stands for long) only travel along the surface. Most earthquake damage is caused by this type of wave.

★

Aftershocks

Sometimes, not all of the energy that has built up is released during an earthquake. This may mean that after the main earthquake there are smaller tremors, known as aftershocks, as the remaining energy is released. Small amounts of energy may also be released before an earthquake occurs. This produces tremors known as foreshocks.

*Epicenter (U.S.A.)

EARTHQUAKE SAFETY

By monitoring faults, scientists can sometimes predict when and where earthquakes are likely to occur. This means that they can take steps to limit the damage caused by an earthquake or even prevent an earthquake from happening.

Seismic gaps

Stress that builds up at fault boundaries is often released gradually by slow movement known as fault creep. Earthquakes are less likely to happen in areas where fault creep occurs, because stress is being released. They are most likely to occur at sections of a fault where there has been no movement for many years. These sections are known as seismic gaps.

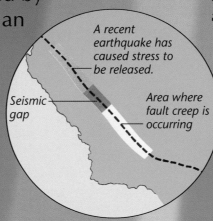

A recent earthquake has caused stress to be released.

Seismic gap

Area where fault creep is occurring

By identifying seismic gaps, scientists can carefully monitor areas where earthquakes are most likely to occur.

Monitoring faults

If the surface of the Earth suddenly starts to tilt, it may be a sign that an earthquake is about to happen. Devices called tiltmeters can measure tiny changes in the level of the ground. Horizontal movement along faults can be monitored using lasers. A laser beam from one side of the fault is bounced off a reflector on the other side, which reflects it back. A computer records the time it takes the beam to travel this distance. If the time changes, it shows that movement has taken place.

Scientists use lasers like these to detect ground movements. They can detect shifts as slight as 1mm (0.04in).

Preventing earthquakes

Earthquakes can be prevented by releasing jammed plates before too much stress builds up. This can be done by conducting a small explosion to shift the plates. Alternatively, drilling deep holes and injecting water into rocks reduces friction, enabling smoother movement along a fault.

Keeping safe

During an earthquake, if you are indoors, the safest place to be is under a solid table or desk. You should cover your eyes to protect them from flying glass and hold on tightly to the leg of the table. If you are outside, it's better to be in an open space, away from buildings, trees and power lines.

Internet links

You're the seismologist. Can you pinpoint where an earthquake began in an online game? Find out too, how to stay safe in an earthquake.

For a link to this website, go to **www.usborne-quicklinks.com**

Animal instincts

Scientists think that animals' highly developed senses may alert them to earthquakes before they happen. It is possible that they can detect slight vibrations, changes in electrical currents in rocks, or the release of gases. In San Francisco, U.S.A., zoo animals are monitored in case the way they behave gives warning of an earthquake.

If animals become unusually agitated, it may be a clue that an earthquake is about to happen.

Safe buildings

In areas where there is a high risk of earthquakes happening, more buildings are being designed so that minimum damage is caused if there is an earthquake. The foundations of some buildings are constructed to absorb vibrations and reduce the effects of shaking. Steel frames can be used to strengthen buildings, so that a building may sway but will not collapse when the ground trembles.

The Transamerica skyscraper in San Francisco, U.S.A., is designed to withstand tremors.

GIANT WAVES

An earthquake or a volcanic eruption under the sea or near the coast can cause giant waves called tsunami. These waves surge across the sea in all directions. Just before a tsunami crashes onto the shore, it may swell to an enormous height.

In 1998, a tsunami caused incredible devastation in Papua New Guinea. This is a still from a video taken there. It shows steel roofing wrapped around a tree by the force of the water.

Tsunami

Tsunami begin when an earthquake or volcano causes the water to shift and waves to form. Out at sea, tsunami are a similar height to ordinary waves, but the distance between one tsunami and the next can be more than 100km (62 miles). What makes tsunami so dangerous is their speed. They race across the sea at speeds of up to 800kph (500mph). Normally tsunami do not break like ordinary waves. As a tsunami enters shallow water, its height increases and it surges over the land. This is what causes the devastating flooding of coastal regions.

Internet links

See animated diagrams that show how a tsunami forms.

For a link to this website, go to
www.usborne-quicklinks.com

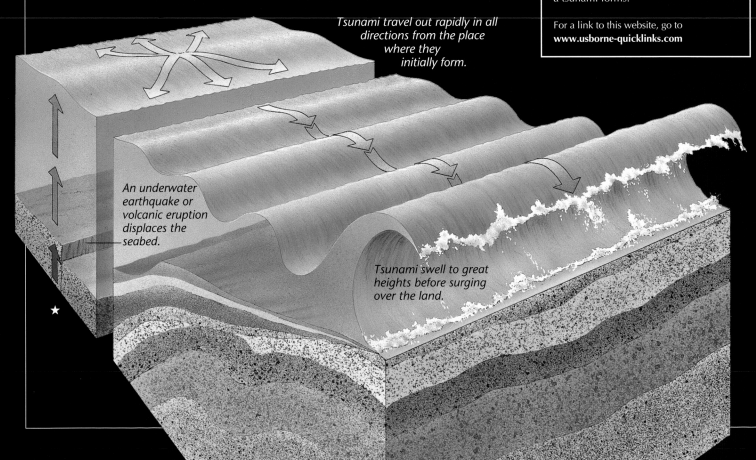

Tsunami travel out rapidly in all directions from the place where they initially form.

An underwater earthquake or volcanic eruption displaces the seabed.

Tsunami swell to great heights before surging over the land.

Tsunami warning system

Most tsunami occur in the Pacific Ocean. For this reason, there are observation stations throughout the Pacific to monitor earthquakes. If an earthquake is large enough to generate tsunami, warnings are issued to coastal towns, so that they can prepare for it. Tide stations along the coast then monitor the arrival of the tsunami.

Observation and tide stations in the Pacific monitor tsunami.

PACIFIC OCEAN

North America

South America

Central Pacific tsunami warning station

Australia

● Tide stations
● Observation stations

Tsunami look like a huge wall of water. They can reach heights of up to 50m (165ft).

A group of Atlantic salmon swimming

RIVERS AND OCEANS

RIVERS

The water in rivers comes from rainfall, from snow and ice melting, and from water inside the Earth, called groundwater. Rivers carry this water downhill to lakes and oceans.

Hippopotamuses live in and around slow, muddy rivers in Africa. This one has an egret on its head.

A river's course

A river changes as it flows downhill along its path, or course. Many rivers begin in mountain areas, where rain and melting ice run into steep, clear streams. Mountain streams cut narrow, deep valleys and join together as they flow downhill. Smaller streams and rivers that flow into a bigger river are called tributaries.

Mountain streams, like this one in Connecticut, U.S.A., form series of mini waterfalls as they tumble down over the steep, rocky slopes.

Away from the mountains, the water flows more smoothly in broader channels and larger valleys. As the land levels out, the river starts to form large bends, or meanders.

Finally, the river widens out into a broad estuary, or sometimes splits to form a delta*, before flowing into the sea (or sometimes into a large lake). The part of a river where it meets the sea is called the river mouth.

Internet links

Discover more facts about rivers, see aerial photographs showing the different stages of rivers and find out more about river creatures.

For a link to this website, go to
www.usborne-quicklinks.com

Stonefly larvae live in mountain streams. They cling to stones with their claws so they don't get swept away by the water.

Drainage

The area of land from which a river collects its water is called its drainage basin. When water drains into streams and rivers, it forms different patterns, depending on the shape of the land and the type of rock it is made of.

When there is only one type of rock, streams form a tree-like pattern like this. It is called a dendritic drainage pattern.

River records

The Manu River, a tributary of the Amazon, winding its way through the rainforests of Peru

The longest river in the world is the River Nile in Africa. It travels northward for 6,671km (4,145 miles) from its source in Burundi to its delta in Egypt, where it flows into the Mediterranean Sea. However, the world's biggest river, or the one that holds the most water, is the Amazon in South America. It is about 6,440km (4,000 miles) long, and flows across South America from west to east. Every single second, it pours about 94 million litres (20 million gallons) of water into the Atlantic Ocean. At its mouth, the Amazon is 240km (150 miles) wide.

A Nile crocodile stalks its prey by swimming silently along in the river, with most of its body underwater.

RIVERS AT WORK

R ivers can carve through solid rock and move huge boulders hundreds of miles. Over many years, rivers have eroded deep gorges and huge waterfalls, and carried vast amounts of rock, sand, soil and mud to the sea.

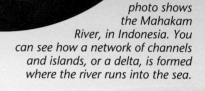

This satellite photo shows the Mahakam River, in Indonesia. You can see how a network of channels and islands, or a delta, is formed where the river runs into the sea.

How rivers erode

As a river flows, the water sweeps along any loose soil, sand or rocks in its way. As they roll, slide and bounce along, the rocks and pebbles chip away at the riverbed, making it deeper and wider. They also grind against each other, which wears them down and breaks them into smaller pieces.

The river forces water and air bubbles into cracks in the riverbed, breaking off more chunks of rock. Another reason that rivers erode is that river water is slightly acidic, because it comes from rain*. It gradually wears away some types of rocks by dissolving them.

These rocks have been smoothed and rounded by the action of the water in the river.

Deposition

In its upper stages, a river is very turbulent and has lots of large boulders and pebbles on its bed. As it flows downstream the riverbed becomes smoother, so the water flows slightly faster. It starts to drop, or deposit, sand, silt and then mud. This is why the lower sections of a river have muddy beds. Near the sea, the deposited sediment may build up to form whole islands. The river splits up and forms a network of channels called a delta. The rest of the sediment flows into the sea.

*Meander, 58; rainwater, 32

Changing course

Rivers flow faster around the outside of a meander* than on the inside. The outside edge is slowly eroded, while the river deposits debris on the inside edge. Eventually the two sides of the meander meet, and the river cuts through to form a new course.

Internet links

Take an interactive field trip and find out all about rivers and how they change their course.

For a link to this website, go to
www.usborne-quicklinks.com

★ *A river erodes the outside of a meander and deposits sediment on the inside, making a loop.*

The loop grows longer and narrower until the river finally breaks through.

The river flows past the ends of the loop and they slowly become silted up.

Eventually the loop gets cut off completely and forms a lake called an oxbow lake.

This is the Horseshoe Falls, part of Niagara Falls, which is a huge waterfall on the border between Canada and the U.S.A. The waterfall moves upstream by around 3m (11ft) per year.

Waterfalls

Waterfalls begin when a river flows from an area of hard rock onto soft rock. The river wears away the soft rock more quickly and creates a ledge. Water falling over the ledge erodes a hollow at the bottom called a plunge pool. The action of the water and pebbles churning in the plunge pool can undercut the hard rock, creating an overhanging ledge. Chunks of the overhanging rock break off and very gradually, over hundreds of years, the waterfall moves backward, cutting a deep valley called a gorge.

This diagram shows how a waterfall is formed.

Waterfall cutting back

Falling water cuts away at the soft rock below.

Hard rock

Plunge pool

Softer rock

Spray undercuts here.

USING RIVERS

Rivers are central to the way human civilization has developed. They have been used for thousands of years for drinking and washing and as transport routes. Farming and industry depend on the water they provide and we can convert their flowing force into useful energy.

This engraving shows London, England, in 1631, with large ships plying their trade up and down the River Thames.

Amsterdam in the Netherlands is not on the sea, but is an important port, with over 80km (50 miles) of canals dividing it into over 80 islands.

River ports

A port is a city where ships can load and unload. When most international transport was by sea, many large ports, such as Montreal in Canada, Manaus in Brazil, and London in England, grew up near navigable rivers, that is rivers that can be used by ships. For example, most of the Amazon is navigable, because it is so wide and deep.

Canals

Canals are artificial waterways built to replace or extend rivers. Irrigation canals divert water from rivers onto fields. Navigational canals are built for boats or ships to travel on. For example, the Suez Canal joins the Mediterranean Sea to the Red Sea, so that ships can take a short cut between Europe and the Indian Ocean. The beds and banks of canals are usually built of brick or concrete, so they suffer less erosion* than rivers.

Internet links
Read about the history of the Suez Canal, look at major river systems and learn how dams are built and how they affect the land around them.

For links to these websites, go to **www.usborne-quicklinks.com**

*River erosion, 60

Clean energy

Electrical energy from water power is called hydroelectric power or HEP. An HEP plant usually consists of a dam built on a river to create a large reservoir or lake. High-pressure jets of water are released from the lake through narrow channels, and used to spin turbines which produce electricity.

Water power is increasingly important as an energy source. Unlike fossil fuels, it is renewable (it won't run out). It also causes little pollution. But there can be problems when hydroelectric reservoirs take up precious land, or when dams collapse.

Part of the Shasta Hydroelectric Dam in California, U.S.A. The spillway in the picture releases water to stop the dam from overflowing.

Dam disasters

The present-day ruins of the Malpasset Dam, in France, which burst in 1959.

In the past, several large dams have caused disaster by breaking or overflowing. One example is the Malpasset Dam in Frejus, France. It collapsed in 1959, causing a flood which killed over 500 people. The dam failed because it was built on rock called schist, which cracks easily.

This small waterwheel generates electricity for a rural area of Washington State, U.S.A.

Water power

The energy in a river can be converted into electricity or other useful forms of energy. The earliest water power systems used a river or stream to turn a waterwheel. The turning force of the wheel was then used to drive machines, such as mills for grinding flour. Simple waterwheels like this are still used in many countries.

WATER IN THE GROUND

Water doesn't just flow over the surface of the Earth; it flows under it too. As well as the rivers and lakes that we can see, there is a huge amount of water, called groundwater, stored underground in rocks and caves.

Bottling mineral water and spring water to sell as drinking water is a major industry in some areas.

Groundwater

Many types of rocks are permeable, which means that water can soak through them. Water that has soaked into the ground and then been soaked up, or absorbed, into a layer of permeable rock is known as groundwater. Underground, the upper layers of rock press down on the lower layers, compressing them so that they are less permeable. So the amount of groundwater decreases farther down. The top level of the water-soaked layer is known as the water table.

Aquifers are layers of rock that can hold water. Some stretch for thousands of miles under the ground. In some places they are an important source of fresh water.

Springs

A spring is a stream of fresh water springing out of the ground. Springs form where a layer of water-filled rock meets the surface of the Earth, especially on a hillside. The groundwater flows out of the rock and forms a small pool or stream.

Spring water is often clean and sparkling because it has been filtered through layers of rock. Sometimes the water dissolves minerals from the rocks. Some of these minerals are thought to be good for your health.

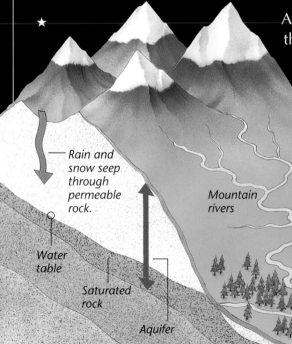

Rain and snow seep through permeable rock.

Water table

Saturated rock

Aquifer

Mountain rivers

Rivers, lakes and springs may appear where an aquifer meets the surface.

A spring emerges where saturated rock meets the surface.

Lake

Impermeable rock

Rivers under the ground

Water can also be found in underground rivers, waterfalls and even large lakes in caves and tunnels. These usually form in limestone. The water eats away at the rock through chemical weathering*.

Internet links

Take an interactive look at the water cycle, find out about water's journey under the ground and see how springs form.

For a link to this website, go to
www.usborne-quicklinks.com

Stalactites and stalagmites

In some caves, long columns of stone, called stalactites, hang from the ceiling, and columns called stalagmites rise up from the floor. They are formed when water full of dissolved minerals drips from the cave roof. With each drop, a tiny deposit of rock is left behind and over time this grows into a long column. As the drips hit the ground, they deposit more minerals, which build up into stalagmites.

These stalactites are constantly growing as more water drips off them, depositing a tiny amount of dissolved rock with each drip.

Inside this cave in Mexico, long stalactites have grown down from the ceiling, while water has gathered to form a still underground pool.

*Chemical weathering, 32

RIVERS OF ICE

Internet links

Learn more about the different stages of a glacier's life by taking a quick online tour, with historical photographs.

For a link to this website, go to
www.usborne-quicklinks.com

A glacier is a huge mass of ice that flows downhill, a little like a river. Glaciers flow much more slowly than rivers. But, because they are solid, they cut through the landscape more easily, gouging deep U-shaped valleys as they carry rocks and soil along with them.

This is a glacier in Glacier Bay National Park, Alaska, U.S.A.

Ice force

Glaciers are very heavy and powerful. As a glacier flows along, the ice and rocks caught in it scrape soil and rock from the sides and floor of the valley, carving a deep channel. When the ice melts, it deposits thick layers of debris, called moraine, and boulders, known as erratics, on the valley floor.

How glaciers form

Glaciers are found in cold places, such as high mountains. At the top of a glacier, known as the accumulation zone, layers of snow collect and become packed down into hard, solid ice. As more snow falls on top, the mass of ice gets heavier and heavier, until it starts to move down the mountain.

As the ice gradually flows downhill, it gets warmer, because the air is warmer lower down. At the lower end, called the ablation zone, the glacier melts and the icy-cold water, known as meltwater, flows into streams and rivers.

Fresh snow falls here.

Accumulation zone

As a glacier moves over bumps and around corners, it may develop cracks called crevasses.

Boulders carried along by the glacier scratch grooves in the rock below.

The glacier melts here.

Ablation zone

Meltwater

★

This diagram shows the different parts of a glacier and the way it moves downhill.

Glacial clues

If the climate gets warmer, glaciers sometimes melt, leaving behind a glacial valley. You can recognize a glacial valley by its deep, rounded U-shape and by debris, such as boulders and moraine hills, or drumlins, left on the valley floor. Sometimes, valleys called hanging valleys, that once joined the glacier, are left high above the main valley. At the coast, some glacial valleys are filled with seawater. They form narrow inlets called fjords.

This diagram shows some of the features that will help you to recognize a glacial valley. A glacial valley filled with seawater, like this, is called a fjord.

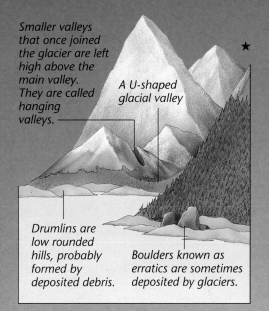

Smaller valleys that once joined the glacier are left high above the main valley. They are called hanging valleys.

A U-shaped glacial valley

Drumlins are low rounded hills, probably formed by deposited debris.

Boulders known as erratics are sometimes deposited by glaciers.

Ice sheets

Not all glaciers are found on mountains. They also form in very cold places near the poles, such as Greenland and Antarctica. There, ice collects in huge sheets, called continental ice sheets. The ice flows outward at the edges as more snow falls and more ice forms in the middle. Parts of the glacier can be pushed right into the sea and break off, forming icebergs.

Icebergs float away into the ocean, gradually melting as they reach warmer areas.

THE EDGE OF THE SEA

The coast, where the land meets the sea, is constantly being broken down and built up by the action of waves. The ebb and flow of the tide means that the environment at the seashore is always changing. Specially adapted animals and plants make their homes there.

Internet links

See different kinds of shorelines, find out more about how tides occur and learn about waves and currents.

For a link to this website, go to
www.usborne-quicklinks.com

Waves

Waves are formed far out at sea by the wind. Although they travel through water, they do not move the water itself forward. They make water particles move in circles under the surface. When a wave reaches shallow water, these circles are interrupted at the bottom and the wave breaks.

Out at sea, wind blows the surface of the ocean into waves.

The waves make particles of water move in circular patterns under the surface.

On a shallow, flat beach, waves break before they reach the shore.

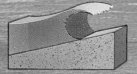
On a sloping coast, waves break at the shore and crash onto the beach.

On a very steep slope, waves do not break, but surge against the shore.

★

Coastal erosion

This archway in Dorset, England, is called Durdle Door. It was created over many years by the destructive action of waves. It started as a headland with caves on either side. The waves gradually eroded the caves until, eventually, they broke through, creating an arch.

Waves that crash onto the shore are known as destructive waves, because they gradually wear away, or erode, the coast. When they break onto beaches, they drag sand, pebbles and other debris out to sea. When they crash onto rocky cliffs, any debris they are carrying is flung against the rock, wearing it down. Waves force water and air into cracks in cliffs, carving out caves.

Destructive waves erode the coastline at different rates. Soft rock wears down quite fast, and is worn away into curved bays. Hard rock is left behind, forming cliffs and jutting pieces of land called headlands. Sometimes two caves form on either side of a headland, and the sea breaks through, leaving an arch. The arch may collapse, leaving a tower of rock called a stack.

Building beaches

While destructive waves wear away parts of the coast, other waves, called constructive waves, wash up debris onto the shore, forming beaches. When a wave breaks gently onto a flat coast, it slows down and loses energy. This makes it drop any debris it may be carrying, such as pebbles and grains of sand previously broken off into the sea from cliffs and rocky shores. Over time, this deposited material builds up into a beach.

Stones and pebbles in the sea are polished and rounded by the action of the waves.

Tides

Tides* are caused by the gravity, or pulling force, of the Moon. The Moon pulls the sea slightly towards it. So, as the Earth spins, the part nearest the Moon has a high tide. There are roughly two high tides each day.

Animals and plants that live on the seashore have to be able to survive in the water at high tide, and in the air at low tide. They also have to find ways to avoid being smashed to pieces or swept away by crashing waves.

Crabs, like this rock crab, can breathe in both water and air. They have hard shells to protect them from the sea, and can burrow into the sand to hide from predators.

Coastlines

Over many years, the action of the sea changes the shapes of countries, as it builds up the land in some places and wears it away in others. Buildings near the sea sometimes fall in or get washed away as the land is gradually eroded.

For example, the coast of Holderness in Lincolnshire, England, has worn away quickly. Over 50 coastal villages listed in a national survey of towns and villages called the Domesday Book in 1086 have since been washed into the sea.

SEAS AND OCEANS

More than two-thirds of the Earth's surface is covered with salt water. The Earth's five oceans and its seas are all connected, so sea water flows freely among them. The seas and oceans, and the creatures that live in them, still hold many mysteries for scientists to explore.

The ballan wrasse fish is found mainly near rocky shores in Europe.

Under the sea

Near the land, the seabed slopes gradually downhill, forming a wide shelf called the continental shelf. At the edge of the shelf, a cliff called the continental slope drops away to the deeper part of the ocean floor, which is called the abyssal plain.

A 3-D map of part of the floor of the Atlantic Ocean

Just like the land, the abyssal plain has valleys, hills, mountains and even volcanoes. It also has ridges* where new rock is pushed out from inside the Earth, and trenches* where the Earth's crust is swallowed up again.

Exploring the sea

By studying the seabed and the creatures that live there sea scientists, called oceanographers, can find out about how the Earth was formed and how life began. Oceanographers visit the seabed in mini-submarines called submersibles, or explore it from the surface using unmanned robots called remote operated vehicles (ROVs). They also map the seabed using sonar. This sends out sounds which are bounced back as echoes, showing how deep the seabed is.

This diver is retrieving a rock from a remote operated vehicle (ROV). The ROV has returned to shallow waters after collecting rock samples from the seabed.

*Ridges, 20; trenches, 20

Life in the oceans

Seas and oceans contain a huge variety of plant and animal life, from the surface all the way down to the deepest trenches.

The loggerhead turtle lives in warm, shallow seas and comes ashore to lay its eggs.

The main food source in the sea is phytoplankton, a type of microscopic plant. Billions of phytoplankton drift near the surface of the sea, making food from sunlight, water, gases and minerals.

Part of a coral reef in the Red Sea, which lies between Egypt and Saudi Arabia

Coral reefs

Coral reefs are amazing undersea structures made of the skeletons of tiny animals called coral polyps. When old polyps die, new ones grow on top of their bodies, and over many years a huge reef builds up.

Internet links

Explore seven different ocean environments and play an online game that takes you to the depths of the ocean.

For a link to this website, go to **www.usborne-quicklinks.com**

Ocean zones

The deeper down you go in the ocean, the darker and colder it is, and the fewer plants and animals are found.

Sunlit zone
Sea plants and many animals live here.

Down to 200m (650ft)

Twilight zone
Many fish, such as swordfish, survive here.

Down to 1,000m (3,300ft)

Sunless zone
Animals feed on dead food that falls from above.

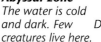

Down to 4,000m (13,100ft)

Abyssal zone
The water is cold and dark. Few creatures live here.

Down to 5,000m (16,400ft)

USING SEAS AND OCEANS

For thousands of years, the sea has provided people with food. We also carry passengers and goods by sea and go on trips to the coast. But the oceans are often used as a place to dump waste, which causes pollution and may endanger wildlife.

Above and top right: sea bass are the most common fish caught and eaten around the world. These were caught in Tokyo Bay, Japan.

Fishing

Most sea fish are still caught using nets. There are three main types of nets. Purse seine nets are drawn closed around schools of fish that swim near the surface. Otter trawl nets are dragged along the seabed to catch fish that live there, while drift or gill nets can be used near the surface or on the seabed. Fishing boats now find schools of fish by using sonar* and satellite* technology.

Overfishing

Because of advances in fishing technology, fishing boats are now able to catch more fish than ever before, and the number of fish in the sea is falling rapidly. International laws have now been passed to restrict the areas where fishing boats can fish and the numbers and types of fish that can be caught.

A Japanese fishing boat at work in Tokyo Bay, Japan, drawing a large net behind it.

Internet links

Watch an animation that explains the causes of oil pollution and how it is cleaned up.

For a link to this website, go to
www.usborne-quicklinks.com

CB3-50869

*Satellites, 252; sonar, 70

World travel

A century ago, if you wanted to travel across the sea, you had to go by boat. Huge ocean liners carried people around the world, and travel could take months.

Today, most people go long distances by plane, but boats such as ferries, hovercrafts and hydrofoils are still used for shorter distances. The only ocean liners left are cruise ships, which take people on long, relaxing sea journeys on vacations.

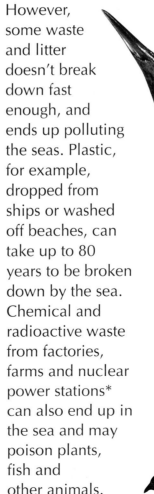

Container ships carry all kinds of goods in large metal boxes called containers. Cranes lift the containers off the ships and transfer them to trucks or trains.

Shipping

Millions of different products, from oil and bananas to books and computers, are transported around the world on cargo ships. Ships travel more slowly than planes, but they can carry a lot more goods at once and are much cheaper to use.

Sea pollution

The seas and oceans are huge and can absorb and break down a lot of the waste we pump into them. For example, a lot of sewage (waste from drains and toilets) goes into the sea and is broken down naturally into harmless chemicals.

However, some waste and litter doesn't break down fast enough, and ends up polluting the seas. Plastic, for example, dropped from ships or washed off beaches, can take up to 80 years to be broken down by the sea. Chemical and radioactive waste from factories, farms and nuclear power stations* can also end up in the sea and may poison plants, fish and other animals.

Oil tankers occasionally sink and spill the oil they are carrying. It can harm plants and animals, such as this seabird, by poisoning them or by coating them in oil so that they cannot breathe or move properly.

*Nuclear power, 27

Frost on a window

WEATHER

WHAT IS WEATHER?

W eather is the way the Earth's atmosphere* behaves, whether it is hot or cold, windy or still, raining, snowing or hailing. Climate* means the overall temperature and patterns of weather in a particular place.

The importance of weather

Weather affects everyone's life. Anything from crops to summer vacations can be ruined if the weather behaves unexpectedly. Weather is also a factor in many of the world's worst disasters, such as floods, droughts and famines.

For thousands of years, people have worshipped weather gods and used rituals to try to affect the weather. But, even with modern technology, it is almost impossible to control.

This Japanese dancer wears a special costume as part of a traditional dance which is meant to make the rain fall.

Internet links

Website 1 See pictures of dangerous types of weather, such as hurricanes and tornadoes, and find out what makes them happen.

Website 2 Watch a short animated movie about weather and try an online quiz.

Website 3 Simple weather animations and information.

For links to these websites, go to **www.usborne-quicklinks.com**

*Atmosphere, 94; climate, 100; cumulus clouds, 79; evaporation, 78

What weather is

Weather is made up of three main ingredients: temperature, the movement of the air, and the amount of water in the air.

Hot weather is caused by the Sun heating up the land and the atmosphere*. If the Sun is hidden by clouds, or if a cold wind is blowing, the temperature is cooler.

Wind is also caused by the Sun. As air gets hotter, it expands, gets less dense, and rises. A mass of colder, heavier air rushes in to replace it, making wind.

Finally, the Sun's heat makes water from plants, soil, rivers and seas evaporate* into the air. High up, this condenses into water droplets which form clouds, and may then fall as rain, snow or hail.

These factors are always changing and affecting each other. They combine to make complicated patterns, known as weather systems.

Umbrellas have been used for hundreds of years to protect people from the weather. These paper umbrellas, called parasols, help to protect people from the Sun.

Traditional signs

Cumulus clouds usually appear when the weather is warm and sunny.

The way bees behave could help us predict the weather.

Today, scientists can predict the weather using satellites and computers. But before these were invented, people predicted the weather by observing signs, such as the way the clouds look, and the way animals behave. For example, cumulus clouds* usually mean sunny weather, and bees usually go home to their hives before a storm.

Weather facts

• The heaviest hailstones, weighing up to 1kg (2lb 2oz), fell in Gopalganj, Bangladesh, in 1986.

• The wettest place in the world is Mawssynrma, India. It gets nearly 12m (40ft) of rain a year.

• The biggest recorded snowflakes were 38cm (15in) across and fell on Montana, U.S.A., in 1887.

• The driest place in the world is the Atacama Desert, Chile. In some spots, there has been no rain for 500 years.

WATER AND CLOUDS

The amount of water on Earth doesn't change, but water changes its state as it moves in a cycle. It exists as a liquid (water) in seas, rivers and cloud droplets, it freezes into a solid (ice) as snow and hail, and it exists as an invisible gas in the air.

Snowflakes form when water droplets freeze into ice crystals. These snowflakes have been tinted so you can see their six-sided shapes more clearly.

The water cycle

When water is heated up, it changes from a liquid into an invisible gas. This process is called evaporation.

The Sun's heat causes water to evaporate from rivers, lakes and seas. Plants suck up water from the ground and it escapes from their leaves as a gas. Similarly, people and animals breathe out water as a gas.

As the gas molecules rise, they get cooler. This makes the water condense, or turn into liquid again, to form tiny droplets which can be seen as clouds. As the cloud droplets move around they collide with each other and grow bigger. When they are heavy enough, they fall as rain, and the water flows back into rivers, lakes and seas. This process is known as the water cycle.

When cloud droplets become heavy, they fall as rain, snow or hail.

Water flows down to the sea in streams and rivers.

As the water that has evaporated rises, it cools down to form clouds.

Plants and animals take in water that has fallen as rain.

Water evaporates from rivers and seas in the heat of the Sun.

This diagram shows how the water cycle works.

Clouds

The way clouds look depends on how much the air is moving up and down and how much water is in them. When clouds form in calm air, they spread out in sheets. On hot days, they puff up into heaps, following the rising air. Clouds full of big droplets look darker.

Cumulus clouds look like white, puffy heaps. They often form high in the sky in warm sunny weather.

Stratus clouds form low, flat layers and often block out the sunshine.

Cirrus clouds are high and wispy. (The word cirrus *means "like wispy hair" in Latin.)*

These tall, piled-up cumulonimbus clouds were photographed over the Gulf of Mexico. A cumulonimbus cloud is freezing at the top, but warmer at the bottom.

Precipitation

Water that falls onto the Earth's surface is called precipitation. Rain is the most common kind. There are many types of rain, from light drizzle to monsoon rains*. In freezing weather, precipitation sometimes takes the form of snow or hail instead of raindrops.

This diagram shows how hailstones are formed.

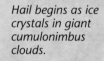

Hail begins as ice crystals in giant cumulonimbus clouds.

Air currents push the crystals up and around inside the cloud.

As they move, the crystals bump into water droplets, which freeze around them in layers, like the layers of an onion.

The layers of ice build up until they form heavy hailstones, which fall to Earth.

Internet links

See how the water cycle works, with animated diagrams, and see pictures of different types of clouds.

For a link to this website, go to **www.usborne-quicklinks.com**

*Monsoons, 120

THUNDERSTORMS

Sometimes in warm weather, huge storm clouds form very quickly. These clouds are full of water and fast-moving air currents. They can build up a store of electricity powerful enough to make lightning and thunder.

Internet links

See an interactive animation that explains what happens when lightning strikes and why the bright flash occurs.

For a link to this website, go to **www.usborne-quicklinks.com**

Electric clouds

In hot, damp weather, the evaporated water in the air rises very fast. When it hits the colder air above, tall, piled-up clouds called cumulonimbus clouds form.

Inside the cloud, water droplets and ice crystals rub together in the swirling air. This rubbing causes the crystals and droplets to build up a strong electric charge. Some have a negative charge (-) and some have a positive charge (+). Negative charges collect at the bottom of the cloud, making a huge energy difference between the cloud and the ground, which has a positive charge.

The difference builds up so much that it has to be equalized. A giant spark jumps between the bottom of the cloud and the ground, allowing the different charges to even out. The spark appears as a flash of lightning.

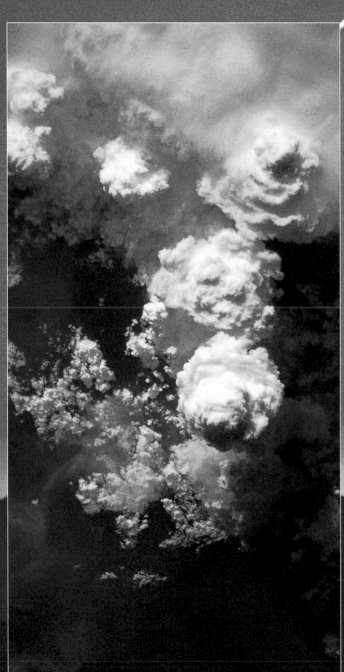

The satellite photograph on the left shows piled-up cumulonimbus storm clouds viewed from above.

Lightning zigzags through the air as it finds the easiest path from the cloud to the ground.

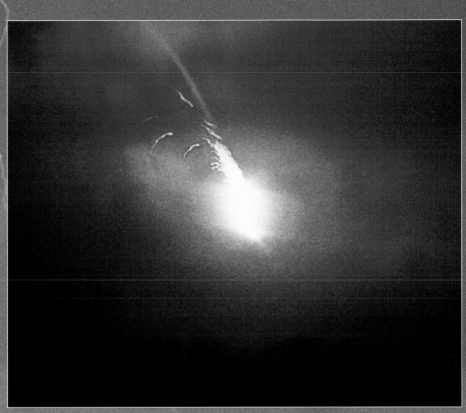

Ball lightning is a very rare kind of lightning which appears as a small, floating ball of bright light. It can travel through walls and has been seen inside buildings and aircraft.

Lightning

When lightning strikes, it travels first downward, then upward. The first stroke, called the leader stroke, is invisible. It jumps from the cloud to the ground. This creates a path for the main stroke, which sparks from the ground back up to the cloud.

The main stroke contains so much energy that it heats up the air around it. The heat makes the air expand quickly, causing an explosion. This is the loud noise of thunder.

Struck by lightning

Lightning always travels the shortest distance it can between a cloud and the ground. So it usually strikes high places, tall buildings or prominent objects such as trees or people.

Lightning quickly heats up whatever it strikes. When a tree is struck, the water in the tree boils instantly and turns into steam, which makes the trunk explode. But although lightning is dangerous, being struck is very rare. You can stay safe by avoiding trees and open spaces during storms.

WINDSTORMS

Because of the way the world spins, wind doesn't flow in straight lines, but swirls into spirals. Sometimes, wind spirals grow into terrifying storms, such as hurricanes and tornadoes, which contain the fastest wind speeds on Earth.

A satellite picture of the hurricane Typhoon Odessa

Coriolis effect

Winds are caused by high-pressure air rushing toward low-pressure areas, called cyclones. But instead of moving straight into the cyclone, the air circles around it in a spiral. This is called the Coriolis effect, and it happens because the spinning of the Earth always pushes winds to one side.

Hurricanes

Hurricanes are very powerful windstorms that can be hundreds of miles wide and last up to ten days. They only form in warm, wet conditions, usually over the sea in tropical areas near the Equator. No one knows exactly what makes a hurricane start.

The warm, wet air has a very low pressure, so cooler winds spiral toward it.

The damp air rises higher and condenses into thick clouds. They are blown into a spiral by the wind.

After hurricanes form, they sometimes hit land and cause massive damage. Winds of up to 240kph (150mph) destroy buildings and rip trees out of the ground. But hurricanes die down soon after they hit land, as there is not enough moisture to keep them going.

Tornadoes

Tornadoes are much smaller than hurricanes, but they can be even more dangerous. Tornadoes form during violent thunderstorms, when a hot, fast-moving upward air current meets a cold, downward air current. Because of the Coriolis effect, the hot and cold currents spiral around each other into a tight funnel of clouds.

The wind inside a tornado's funnel can be as fast as 480kph (300mph), the fastest wind speeds measured on Earth. Where the funnel touches the ground, it can be up to 500m (1,640ft) wide. It roars across the land, dragging people, animals and even cars into the air. Most tornadoes only last a few minutes.

Internet links

Create a tornado online, watch an animated guide that shows how a hurricane forms and browse a hurricane hunter's photo album packed with amazing storm pictures.

For a link to this website, go to
www.usborne-quicklinks.com

A tornado looks like a huge black or grey trunk, twisting from the thunderclouds down to the ground.

Tornado Alley

Some places have frequent thunderstorms and lots of tornadoes. Part of the U.S.A., between Texas and Illinois, has so many that it is known as Tornado Alley. The worst tornado ever recorded there hit Ellington, Missouri, on March 18, 1925. It lasted 3½ hours, destroyed four towns and killed 689 people.

Waterspouts

When a tornado moves over the sea a narrow column of swirling water droplets reaches into the clouds above. These tornadoes are called waterspouts (though not much water is actually sucked up from the sea). Sailors used to think they were sea monsters.

This 19th-century engraving shows monstrous waterspouts.

FLOODS AND DROUGHTS

Plants, animals and people need water to survive, and they rely on the weather to bring it to them. If there is too little rain, rivers dry up and crops fail. On the other hand, too much rain causes floods, which can damage crops and buildings and wash away precious soil.

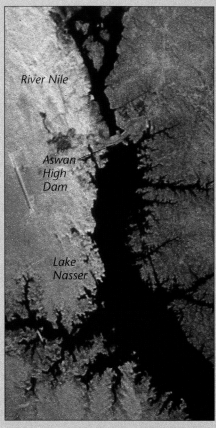

The Aswan High Dam enables people to control the flooding of the River Nile. When the river floods, it waters the land, making it fertile (good for growing crops) without causing destruction.

Wet and dry

Some parts of the world always have more rain than others, and many places have wet and dry seasons. Rainy and dry periods like these are not usually a problem if they are regular, but too much or too little rain can be dangerous when unexpected weather changes take people by surprise.

This picture shows terrible flooding in Vietnam. People are forced to use boats to get around.

Too much rain

Normally, rainfall soaks into the ground or flows away in streams and rivers. Floods happen when there is suddenly too much water for the ground to hold, and streams, rivers and drains overflow. The extra water can come from rain, brought by heavy storms, from ice and snow on mountains melting and flowing into streams and rivers, or even from the sea spilling onto the land.

Dirt and disease

Floods are very dangerous. As well as drowning people and animals and destroying homes and crops, floods can actually cause water shortages. They cover the land with dirty water, contaminating clean water supplies and helping diseases to spread.

Lack of rain can make soil harden, crack into lumps, and eventually crumble into dry dust.

This pump is an important source of clean water, but the dirty floodwater surrounding it could contaminate the water supply.

Not enough rain

A drought happens when there is less than the expected amount of rain. Droughts are often hard to predict, but they usually happen when winds change direction and no rain clouds are blown over the land. Droughts can happen in almost all climates. A bad drought may last several years and make the land completely infertile. The effects of drought can be much worse if the land has not been used carefully.

Internet links

Read an eyewitness account about the disastrous effects of the 1930s drought in the U.S., find out about Bangladesh's annual floods and discover the world's wettest town.

For a link to this website, go to **www.usborne-quicklinks.com**

FREEZING AND FRYING

This woman is carrying frozen milk home. It is so cold in Siberia, where she lives, that there's no danger of the milk melting.

The temperature on Earth can range from a bone-numbing -88°C (-127°F), measured at Vostok in Antarctica, to an unbearably hot 58°C (136°F), recorded at Al Aziziyah, Libya. Extreme hot and cold weather can be deadly, and often has strange effects on people and places.

World of ice

Ice storms are caused by rain falling onto very cold surfaces. They happen when a mass of warm air passes through a cold area in winter, bringing rain that falls in the form of liquid raindrops, instead of as snow or hail. But when the drops of water hit cold surfaces, they immediately freeze into a coating of solid ice. Ice storms are beautiful, but lethal. If enough rain falls, outdoor surfaces can get covered in a layer of ice up to 15cm (6in) thick. It makes roads hazardous to drive on and builds up on rooftops until they cave in.

The ice also weighs down power lines until they snap. People can freeze to death in their homes.

Blizzards

Blizzards are a combination of heavy snow, strong winds and cold temperatures. They are especially dangerous because blizzard victims are blinded by the swirling snow, as well as being caught in the freezing cold.

This branch was caught in an ice storm that hit Kingston, Canada, in 1998.

Internet links

Learn about the dangers of winter storms by taking an online challenge where you have to drive safely through a blizzard, making decisions based on weather reports.

For a link to this website, go to **www.usborne-quicklinks.com**

Heatwaves

A heatwave is a period of extra-hot weather. Heatwaves are caused by a combination of factors. Usually, a lack of wind and cloud allows the Sun to heat up the land and the atmosphere much more than normal. The hotter the air is, the more moisture it can hold as a gas. This makes the air very humid, which makes it feel "sticky".

In some hot places, people have siestas – they sleep during the hottest part of the day to avoid the Sun.

This Egyptian boy's white clothes reflect the Sun's heat and help to keep him cool in hot weather.

Heatstroke

Heatstroke is usually caused by staying out in the sun too long. Normally, if you get too hot, your body sweats. The sweat evaporating from your skin helps you cool down. But heatstroke stops your body from sweating so that you get much too hot, and may go into a coma.

Heatstroke can happen quickly, especially inside a car, where the windows act like a greenhouse and stop heat from escaping. This is why animals and babies should never be left inside cars on hot days.

Sun and skin

Although the Sun provides warmth and energy, direct sunlight can be bad for you. It can cause wrinkles, sunburn and even skin cancer.

A poster advising Australians to wear T-shirts, sunscreen and sunhats

Hot and bothered

Hot weather can affect how we behave. For example, statistics show that in New York, U.S.A., the murder rate rises as the temperature goes up, and most big riots start on hot, humid nights. No one is sure why heat makes people angry.

This riot took place in the hot city of Los Angeles, in western U.S.A., in 1992.

STRANGE WEATHER

U nusual, extreme weather, often called freak weather, can take people by surprise. Sometimes it can be so odd it doesn't seem like weather at all. Strange lights in the sky, clouds that look like UFOs, and even showers of frogs, are all natural weather phenomena.

Weather beliefs

When strange weather strikes, people often think they're seeing something magical or supernatural. Weather may lie behind many traditional beliefs in fairies and ghosts, and also behind sightings of UFOs. One type of cloud, called a lenticular cloud, looks exactly like a flying saucer.

Lenticular clouds are shaped by waves of wind blowing around mountaintops. This one was seen at Mauna Kea, Hawaii, U.S.A.

Strange lights

The aurora borealis and aurora australis light up the sky around the poles with blue, red, green and white patterns. They are caused by streams of electrical particles which come from the Sun. When they interact with the gases in the Earth's atmosphere, they release energy which lights up the sky.

A solar flare is a storm on the Sun that sends electrical particles out into space, causing auroras on Earth.

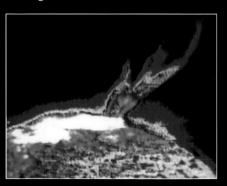

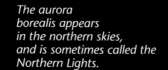

The aurora borealis appears in the northern skies, and is sometimes called the Northern Lights.

Raining frogs

"Rain" consisting of animals, fish or other objects has been reported many times through the centuries. The Roman historian Pliny reported a shower of frogs almost 2,000 years ago and in the fourth century, fish fell on a town in Greece for three days. During a storm in England in 1939, so many frogs fell that witnesses were afraid to walk around in case they squashed them.

Showers like this, also known as "skyfalls", are probably caused by tornadoes* sucking up animals from ponds and rivers. Frogs are most often reported, but there have also been showers of snails, maggots, worms, pebbles and even sheep.

The common frog, a species seen falling from the sky

This magazine from May 1958 shows a skyfall of frogs which had recently been reported.

Internet links

See video clips of auroras and find out why no two auroras are alike.

For a link to this website, go to **www.usborne-quicklinks.com**

Big waves

Freak waves are one of the most dangerous types of unusual weather, though not all big waves are freak waves. Freak waves can appear from nowhere, even in calm conditions. Scientists think big waves like this may form when several smaller waves merge together. These waves are especially dangerous because people are not prepared for them.

*Tornadoes, 83

WEATHER FORECASTING

Weather often seems random but, by careful observation, meteorologists (weather scientists) can learn how weather behaves and how to predict it. Radar and satellites* help them to track clouds and watch weather patterns from space.

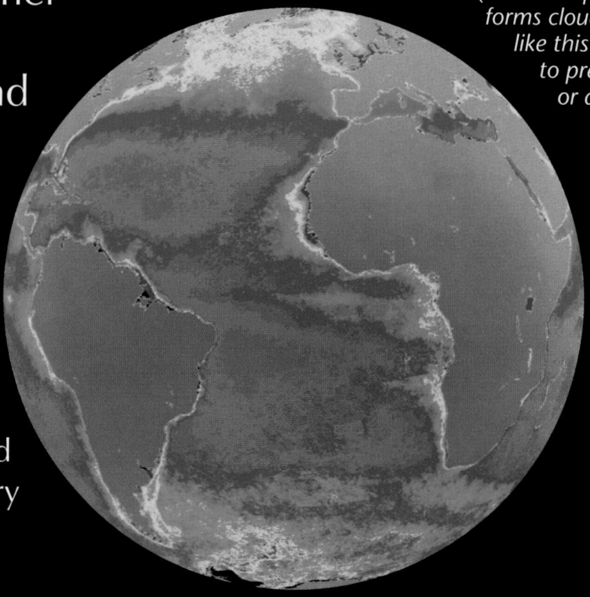

This satellite image shows the temperature of the sea. Water evaporates from warm areas (shown in pink) and forms clouds. Maps like this are used to predict rain or droughts.

Measuring weather

Meteorologists measure different aspects of the weather, such as temperature, atmospheric pressure* and the amount of rainfall, at weather stations around the world. Weather balloons and weather planes carry instruments into the sky, where they can track the movements of clouds and high-altitude winds.

Weather technology

Weather satellites have been used since about 1960 to record the Earth's weather from space. From their positions in orbit above the Earth, satellites can take photographs and measure the temperature of the Earth's surface.

Geostationary satellites, like the weather satellite shown here, hover 36,000km (22,370 miles) above the Equator.

On the ground, radar equipment is used to detect cloud patterns. Radar waves are sent out, bounce off raindrops and are collected by giant radar dishes. Computers collect the signals and create maps which show where rain clouds are heading.

90

*Atmospheric pressure, 96; satellites, 252

Predicting weather

To forecast weather, readings from weather stations and satellites are stored in powerful computers. The data can then be examined to detect patterns and make predictions. At the moment, meteorologists can only predict weather a few days in advance. Weather can change so quickly that the forecasts are sometimes wrong.

Internet links

Look up world weather forecasts or try to predict the weather in a fun online activity.

For a link to this website, go to
www.usborne-quicklinks.com

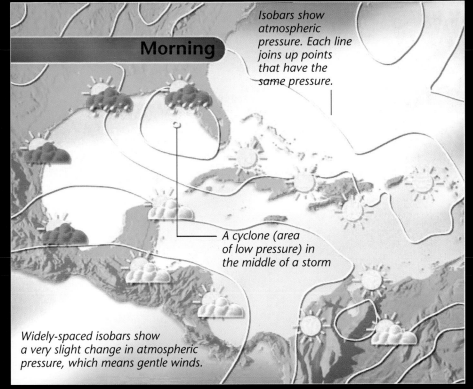

Isobars show atmospheric pressure. Each line joins up points that have the same pressure.

Morning

A cyclone (area of low pressure) in the middle of a storm

Widely-spaced isobars show a very slight change in atmospheric pressure, which means gentle winds.

Weather maps use lines called isobars to show differences in atmospheric pressure*, and symbols to indicate sunshine, rain and snow.

A satellite photograph of a hurricane over the Pacific Ocean

Autumn in the Cache National Forest, Idaho, U.S.A.

CLIMATE

THE EARTH'S ATMOSPHERE

Surrounding the Earth is a blanket of gases which makes up its atmosphere. The atmosphere contains the air we need to breathe. It also affects weather and climate and protects us from extremes of temperature and from the Sun's harmful rays.

The atmosphere's structure

The gases surrounding the Earth are held by its gravity, a force which attracts things to Earth. The atmosphere is divided into layers according to the temperature of these gases. The diagram below shows the different layers.

This diagram shows some of the layers in the Earth's atmosphere. The outermost layer, the exosphere, is not marked; it is around 500km (310 miles) from Earth.

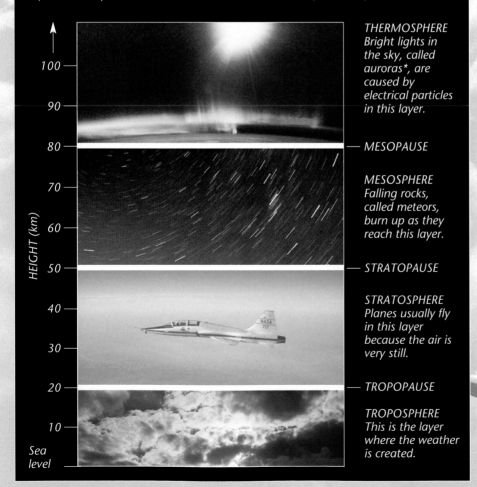

HEIGHT (km)

100
90
80
70
60
50
40
30
20
10
Sea level

THERMOSPHERE
Bright lights in the sky, called auroras*, are caused by electrical particles in this layer.

— MESOPAUSE

MESOSPHERE
Falling rocks, called meteors, burn up as they reach this layer.

— STRATOPAUSE

STRATOSPHERE
Planes usually fly in this layer because the air is very still.

— TROPOPAUSE

TROPOSPHERE
This is the layer where the weather is created.

The troposphere

The troposphere is the layer of the atmosphere nearest to the Earth's surface. As well as a mixture of gases, this layer contains clouds, dust and pollution. It extends to between 10km (6 miles) and 20km (12 miles) from the Earth. Temperatures are high near the Earth because the air is heated from below by the Earth's surface, which is warmed by the Sun. Higher up, the air is thinner and can't hold as much heat, so temperatures decrease.

The troposphere is the layer where the weather is produced. It gets its name from the Greek word *tropos* which means "a turn". This is because the air there is constantly circulating*.

*Air currents, 96; auroras, 88

The stratosphere

The upper limit of the stratosphere is around 50km (30 miles) from the Earth's surface. The stratosphere contains a concentration of ozone gas. This layer of ozone gas is very important, as it absorbs ultraviolet rays from the Sun which can cause skin cancer.

The mesosphere

The mesosphere reaches to a height of around 80km (50 miles). Temperatures there are the coolest in the atmosphere because there is very little ozone or dust and few clouds to absorb energy from the Sun. It is warmer at the bottom as there is more ozone there.

The thermosphere

Temperatures in the thermosphere can be extremely high, reaching up to 1,500°C (2,732°F). This is because there is a high proportion of a gas called atomic oxygen. This gets warmed as it absorbs energy from the Sun.

The ozone layer

The layer of ozone gas in the stratosphere is being damaged by chemicals called chlorofluorocarbons (CFCs), which are used in some spray cans and refrigerators. At certain times of year, a hole in the ozone layer appears over Antarctica, and in other areas the ozone layer becomes very thin. This damage means that more of the Sun's harmful ultraviolet rays reach the Earth's surface.

The bright pink areas in this picture show a hole in the layer of ozone gas over Antarctica.

Internet links

Find out more about the ozone layer, why we need it and how we can stop damaging it.

For a link to this website, go to
www.usborne-quicklinks.com

When you fly in a plane in the stratosphere you can often see the clouds in the troposphere below.

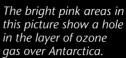

AIR AND OCEAN CURRENTS

As the Sun heats the Earth, it causes air and water to move around in the form of currents. As particles of air and water are heated, they first expand and rise and then they cool and fall, producing patterns of circulating air and water, which are crucial in determining climate.

The circular shapes on the satellite image in the background are called spiral eddies. They are swirls of water that have separated from the main band, or current, of water.

Moving air

The air around us is constantly pushing in every direction. The force that it exerts is known as atmospheric pressure.

The movement of air is affected by temperature. The Sun heats up the land and oceans, which in turn heat the air directly above in the troposphere*. As the air is heated, it rises and so leaves behind an area of low pressure. When the air cools, it sinks down on the Earth's surface in a different area, causing high pressure.

Because the Sun doesn't heat up the world evenly, there are differences of pressure. Where there is a difference, air flows from high to low pressure areas in order to even out the pressure. This moving air is wind. As the air moves, the spinning of the Earth causes it to be deflected sideways. This deflection is known as the Coriolis effect*.

Global winds

Air is constantly circulating between the tropics and the poles as global winds. Warm air flows from the tropics and displaces the cold air at the poles, which then flows back toward the tropics. Global winds form because areas near the Equator receive more heat from the Sun than other areas. As the air is heated, it rises and spreads out. When it cools, it sinks at around 30° north and south of the Equator. This increases pressure at the Earth's surface and air at the base of the atmosphere is forced outward in the direction of both the Equator and the poles. The surface air currents moving toward the Equator are called the trade winds.

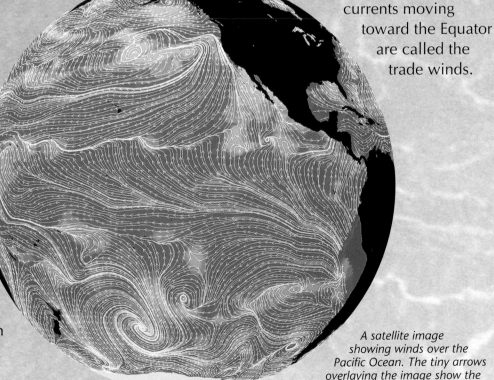

A satellite image showing winds over the Pacific Ocean. The tiny arrows overlaying the image show the direction of the winds.

*Coriolis effect, 82; troposphere, 94

Moving water

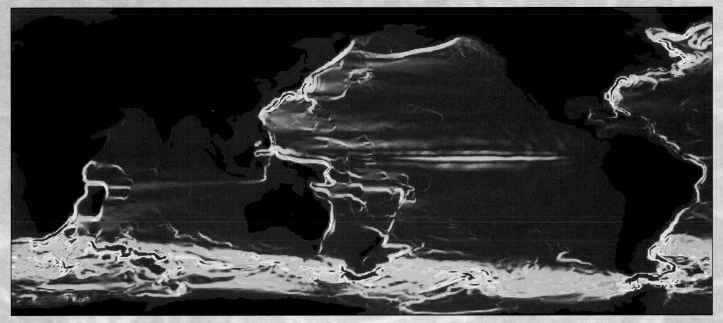

This image shows ocean currents around the world. The red areas are fast currents and the light blue areas are slow currents.

Ocean currents are wide bands of water, like rivers that flow in the world's oceans. They sweep around the oceans, moving water between hot and cold places.

Heat from the Sun also causes the movement of water in the form of currents. However, in the oceans, the temperature difference between the poles and the Equator is greater than it is on land. Near the Equator, the Sun's rays penetrate far below the ocean's surface. At the poles, the Sun's rays hit the water at a shallow angle. This causes the water to act like a mirror, reflecting rather than absorbing the Sun's rays.

A satellite picture of part of the Gulf Stream, a current of warm water that flows in the Atlantic Ocean

Internet links

Find out exactly what El Niño is, how it can wreak havoc around the world and how it could affect the area where you live.

For a link to this website, go to **www.usborne-quicklinks.com**

Effects of currents

Currents vary in temperature and move at different speeds. If a current is much warmer or cooler than the surrounding water, it can dramatically affect the climates of the nearby coastal areas. A warm current called the Gulf Stream, which runs between the Gulf of Mexico and Europe, brings a mild climate to northwest Europe.

El Niño

The incredible effect that the warming of the ocean can have on weather and climate is illustrated by a phenomenon known as El Niño. Every few years, a current of water in the Pacific, off the northwest coast of South America, suddenly becomes warmer. Scientists are not sure why it happens, but it causes a chain of climatic changes around the world, including floods and severe storms.

NATURAL CYCLES

S ome substances, such as nitrogen and carbon, are constantly changing form as they move around in huge cycles. This exchange of substances is essential to life on Earth. The air, land, water, plants, animals, and even your own body, all form a part of these cycles.

This magnified part of a pea plant contains bacteria which convert nitrogen from the air into a form the plant can use.

Keeping a balance

Living things take in substances such as oxygen, nitrogen, carbon and water from the world around them through food, soil and air. They use them to live and grow. When a plant or animal dies and decays, its body is broken down and gases are released into the air. The cycle continues, with these substances being used again and again. This process maintains the balance of gases in the air.

The nitrogen cycle

This diagram shows some of the different forms that nitrogen takes.

Plants take in nitrogen from the air.

Plants are eaten by animals.

Bacteria convert ammonia in the soil into nitrates, which are then taken in by plants.

As dead plants and animals decay, nitrogen is released into the soil.

Nitrogen (chemical symbol – N) makes up 78% of the air. Plants and animals need it for growth. Plants take in nitrogen from the air and the soil. Bacteria convert the substance into a form the plants can use. Animals obtain nitrogen by eating plants or by eating animals that have eaten plants. When plants and animals die and decay, fungi and bacteria break down their remains and nitrogen is released back into the soil.

This dung beetle is feeding on animal dung. Insects like this help to break down plant and animal matter.

One form that carbon can take is charcoal, as shown here. Charcoal can be burned as a fuel. When it is burned, it gives out carbon dioxide.

Upsetting cycles

Left alone, these cycles create a natural balance of gases. However, human activities interfere with this balance by adding waste and pollution to the atmosphere. The effects of human disruption on the carbon cycle are described on pages 102 to 103.

When farmers harvest crops, they break the nitrogen cycle because the plants are not allowed to decay naturally. Farmers often use a chemical fertilizer* to replace nitrates in soil. If too much is added, it can seep through the soil into rivers, where it can affect plants and animals.

The carbon cycle

Carbon forms part of the gases in the air, mainly as carbon dioxide (chemical symbol – CO_2), which is a compound of carbon and oxygen. Plants take in CO_2 from the air and use it to make food. At night, they give out CO_2.

Animals obtain carbon by eating plants. They release carbon in their waste and when they breathe out. CO_2 is also released when plants and animals die and decay. Carbon can be stored in the form of fossilized remains. Eventually these form fossil fuels* such as coal and oil, which release CO_2 when burned.

The algae in this canal are thriving because of excess nitrates running into the canal from fertilizer used on nearby farmland.

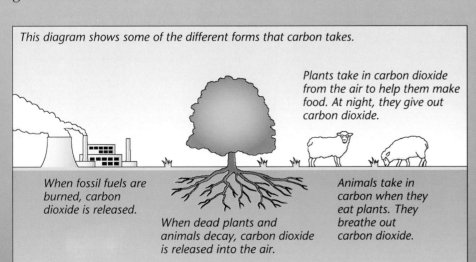

This diagram shows some of the different forms that carbon takes.

Plants take in carbon dioxide from the air to help them make food. At night, they give out carbon dioxide.

When fossil fuels are burned, carbon dioxide is released.

When dead plants and animals decay, carbon dioxide is released into the air.

Animals take in carbon when they eat plants. They breathe out carbon dioxide.

Internet links

Explore animated scenes that explain how the carbon cycle works and where carbon is found then test your knowledge with an online quiz.

For a link to this website, go to
www.usborne-quicklinks.com

*Fertilizer, 30; fossil fuels, 26

WORLD CLIMATES

The long-term or typical pattern of weather in a particular area is known as its climate. Climates vary enormously in different parts of the world. They determine the character of an area, affecting the plants, animals and people that live there.

This map of the Earth's surface contains information from several different satellites*. It shows some of the main climate types around the world.

Maple trees grow in temperate regions.

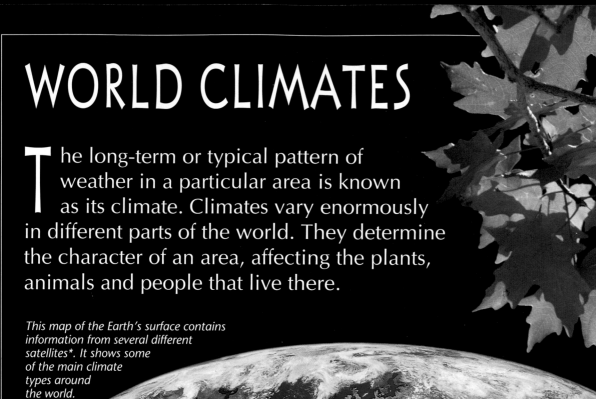

Temperate and tropical regions are green. They contain lots of vegetation.

Tropical grasslands and deserts are yellow and brown. They are dry, with little vegetation.

Snowy regions are light blue or white. The swirling white masses are clouds.

Climate types

Areas can be grouped into several main climate types, such as polar, temperate and tropical. These are also known as biomes*. The most important factor in determining an area's climate is its latitude*, because this affects the amount of heat received from the Sun. This in turn has a crucial effect on the vegetation and animals which give each climate zone its distinctive characteristics.

The map above shows how areas at the same latitude share broadly similar climates. The different climate zones are described in more detail on pages 116–131.

Other factors, such as height and distance from the ocean, are also very important in determining the climate of a particular area.

*Biomes, 113; latitude, 250; satellites, 252

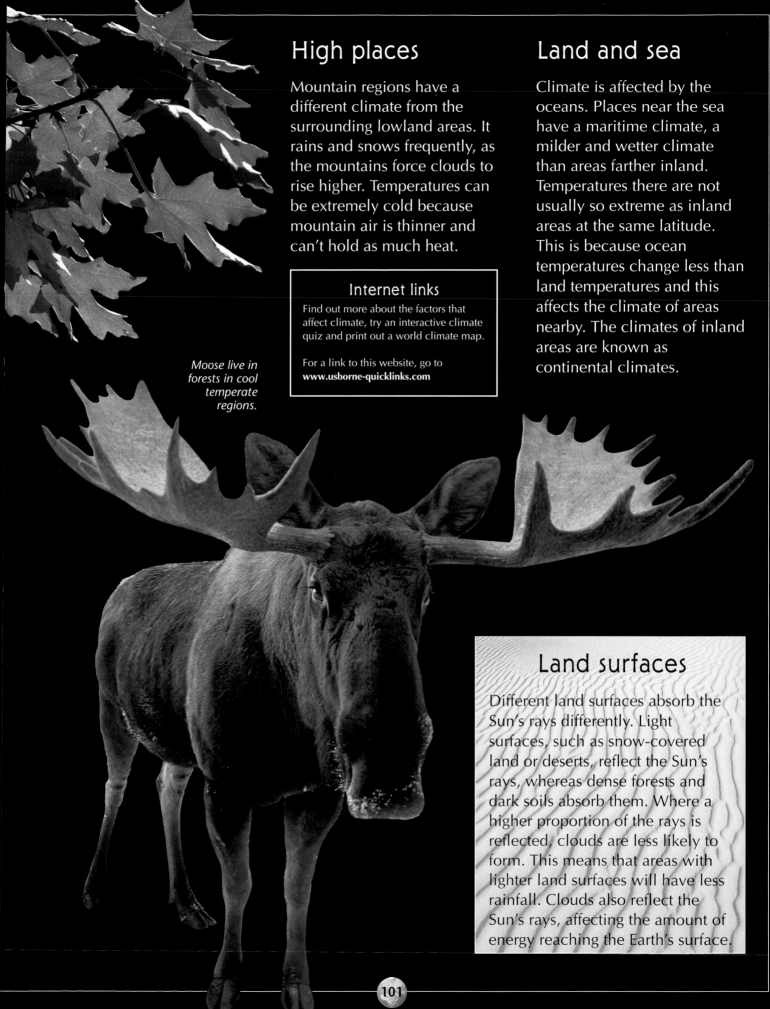

High places

Mountain regions have a different climate from the surrounding lowland areas. It rains and snows frequently, as the mountains force clouds to rise higher. Temperatures can be extremely cold because mountain air is thinner and can't hold as much heat.

Moose live in forests in cool temperate regions.

Internet links

Find out more about the factors that affect climate, try an interactive climate quiz and print out a world climate map.

For a link to this website, go to **www.usborne-quicklinks.com**

Land and sea

Climate is affected by the oceans. Places near the sea have a maritime climate, a milder and wetter climate than areas farther inland. Temperatures there are not usually so extreme as inland areas at the same latitude. This is because ocean temperatures change less than land temperatures and this affects the climate of areas nearby. The climates of inland areas are known as continental climates.

Land surfaces

Different land surfaces absorb the Sun's rays differently. Light surfaces, such as snow-covered land or deserts, reflect the Sun's rays, whereas dense forests and dark soils absorb them. Where a higher proportion of the rays is reflected, clouds are less likely to form. This means that areas with lighter land surfaces will have less rainfall. Clouds also reflect the Sun's rays, affecting the amount of energy reaching the Earth's surface.

GLOBAL WARMING

Some of the gases in the atmosphere help to keep the Earth warm. They trap heat from the Sun in the same way that a greenhouse traps heat. This process is known as the greenhouse effect. But, as these gases increase, the Earth might be getting too warm.

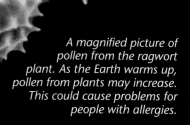

A magnified picture of pollen from the ragwort plant. As the Earth warms up, pollen from plants may increase. This could cause problems for people with allergies.

Greenhouse gases

The Earth's surface absorbs much of the heat from the Sun. This is then given off as heat energy into the atmosphere. It gets trapped there by gases, such as carbon dioxide, which are known as greenhouse gases. As the amount of greenhouse gases increases, more heat is trapped.

Most greenhouse gases occur naturally, but industrial processes and other pollution are increasing the amount of greenhouse gases in the atmosphere. Scientists think that this may be causing the Earth to become warmer. This process is known as global warming.

Plants are important for the balance of greenhouse gases because they take in carbon dioxide.

Balance of gases

Whenever we burn oil, coal or wood, carbon dioxide is released. For example, when forests are burned to make room for farming, they release carbon dioxide. This also reduces the number of plants available to absorb carbon dioxide, upsetting the natural balance of the carbon cycle*. Factories, power stations and cars also give out pollution which may contribute to global warming.

Huge roads, like this one, are useful for car drivers, but the pollution from cars could be contributing to global warming.

cArthur Blvd
n Wayne Airport
NEXT EXIT

Venice, Italy, is a city built on over 100 tiny islands in the Lagoon of Venice. If the sea level rises, it may eventually disappear under the sea.

Rising sea level

As atmospheric temperatures rise, so does the sea level. This will eventually result in the flooding of low-lying areas. Scientists estimate that the sea level is rising at a rate of 1–2mm (0.04–0.08in) each year. It may rise by another 0.25–1m (0.8–3.3ft) by the year 2100. There are two main reasons for the increased volume of water. First, as the oceans heat up, the water expands. The sea level rises because the water takes up more space. Secondly, the higher temperatures may cause glaciers and icecaps on land to melt. This water will then flood into the sea.

Changing climate

Scientists predict the average atmospheric temperature will increase by around 2°C (3.6°F) this century. Extreme weather may become more common. Climate change will affect the habitats* of plants and animals. Some species may thrive, but others may struggle to survive.

Internet links

Find out more about global warming and the greenhouse effect, test your knowledge with games and quizzes, and find out how you can make a difference.

For a link to this website, go to
www.usborne-quicklinks.com

Shifting the balance

People have already begun to take steps to reduce the emission of gases that contribute to global warming. The main ways that this can be achieved are by looking at alternative energy sources and reducing pollution levels.

*Carbon cycle, 99; habitats, 112

CHANGING CLIMATES

E ver since the Earth was formed, its climate has been changing. Volcanic eruptions, collisions with asteroids, and the path of the Solar System through space may all have caused climate changes that affected the atmosphere, the landscape and living things.

The red outline on this map shows the areas of the Earth that were covered in ice during the last Ice age. The white areas are those places that are still covered in ice today.

Long ago, widespread volcanic activity could have caused fires which damaged habitats, wiping out various species.

Ice ages

Throughout its history, the Earth has gone through several Ice ages, when the climate was colder than it is now, and glaciers* and ice sheets spread across much of the globe. Sea levels were lower as well, because so much of the water was frozen into ice on land.

Ice ages have several causes. As the galaxy spins, the Earth may enter the magnetic fields which shield it from the Sun's heat. Earth may also sometimes change its orbit, move away from the Sun and get cooler. There may be another Ice age in the future.

Internet links

Explore an interactive geological timeline to find out what fossils can tell us about the geological period they came from. There are also maps showing how the world has changed.

For a link to this website, go to **www.usborne-quicklinks.com**

Explosions

Long-term climate patterns can be affected by sudden events, such as huge volcanic eruptions, or asteroids* hitting the Earth. Events like this in the past could have filled Earth's atmosphere with smoke and dust which blocked out the sunlight, making the climate cold and dark and killing plants and animals.

*Asteroids, 11; glaciers, 66

Geological evidence

We can tell the Earth's climate has changed by looking at rocks and fossils. Many rocks form gradually in layers. These layers provide a record of what happened, called the fossil record. In warmer periods of the Earth's history, more plants and animals were alive and more fossils were preserved. Layers with fewer fossils show colder periods, when there were fewer living things.

Landscapes also hold clues about the past. For example, a U-shaped valley shows where a glacier gouged out a huge channel during an Ice age.

Fossils found in stone, such as this well-preserved bird fossil, can reveal which types of animals lived in which places long ago.

As well as blocking out vital sunlight with smoke and ash, volcanic eruptions can destroy plant life by smothering the land with lava, hot molten rock that burns everything in its path.

Moving continents

As the plates* that make up the Earth's crust have slowly changed position, the climate of each continent has altered. For example, what is now West Africa was once at the South Pole. As it got nearer the Equator, its climate warmed up as it received more sunlight. Climates are also affected by ocean currents*. As the continents separated from each other, currents could flow between them, bringing cold or warm water from other parts of the Earth.

*Ocean currents, 97; plates, 20

WORLD ECOSYSTEMS

PLANT LIFE ON EARTH

The Earth is the only planet so far discovered whose land looks green from space.

The Earth is the only planet known to support living things, or organisms. There are millions of different kinds of living things on Earth. They fall into two main groups: animals and plants. To survive, nearly all of them need light and heat from the Sun, food, water and air.

The green planet

Most plants are green because they contain a green substance called chlorophyll, which helps them to make their food. From space, the Earth's land looks mainly green, because of the billions of plants on its surface.

Plant food

Plants feed themselves by turning sunlight into food chemicals. This process is called photosynthesis, which means "building with light". For this to happen, plants also need water and nutrients* from the soil, and carbon dioxide from the air. They then use all these things to make glucose, a kind of sugar, which they can feed on.

Internet links

Learn more about plant life by finding clues, doing experiments and solving problems in this online mystery game.

For a link to this website, go to **www.usborne-quicklinks.com**

The Sun provides energy, in the form of light.

A plant's flowers contain parts that make seeds. These grow into new plants.

This part of the underside of a leaf has been magnified.

Leaves convert water and carbon dioxide into glucose and oxygen.

The stalk carries water and nutrients from roots to the leaves and flower.

Leaf stalk

Tiny holes called stomata let carbon dioxide in, and water and oxygen out.

*Nutrients, 28

Why we need plants

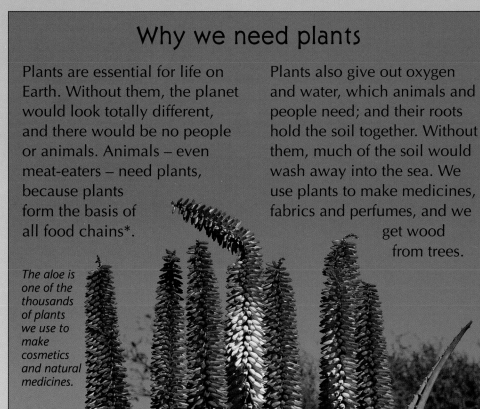

Plants are essential for life on Earth. Without them, the planet would look totally different, and there would be no people or animals. Animals – even meat-eaters – need plants, because plants form the basis of all food chains*.

Plants also give out oxygen and water, which animals and people need; and their roots hold the soil together. Without them, much of the soil would wash away into the sea. We use plants to make medicines, fabrics and perfumes, and we get wood from trees.

The aloe is one of the thousands of plants we use to make cosmetics and natural medicines.

Plant babies

Like all living things, plants reproduce (make new versions of themselves). Most do this by making seeds. The seeds usually form inside the flower. They may then be carried a long way by the wind before falling to the ground and beginning to grow.

A sunflower contains hundreds of seeds like these. Like the seeds of many plants, they are an important source of food for people and animals.

Types of plants

Different types of living things are called species. There are millions of species of plants, from tiny flowers to enormous trees called giant sequoias, which are the biggest living things on Earth. Different species are suited, or adapted, to living in different parts of the world. In deserts, for example, where water is scarce, cactuses grow thick stems for storing water.

A giant sequoia tree. These are found mainly in California, U.S.A.

*Food chains, 112

ANIMAL LIFE ON EARTH

There are millions of types, or species, of animals living on Earth. They include insects, fish, birds, reptiles, amphibians and mammals, such as humans. Unlike plants, animals can move around to find food and water.

The bald eagle is a carnivore. It feeds mainly on fish, swooping down and snatching its prey from lakes and rivers.

How animals live

All animals have to eat in order to survive. Herbivores eat plants and carnivores eat animals. There are some animals, such as giant pandas, that eat both plants and animals. These are called omnivores. Most humans are also omnivores.

Honeyeaters are herbivores. They feed on nectar, a sweet juice found inside flowers.

Many animals have to watch out for predators, which are other animals that want to eat them. Their bodies have to be adapted for running fast or hiding. Some animals, such as zebras, are camouflaged, which means they are patterned so that they blend in with their background and are harder for predators to see. But some predators are also camouflaged, so they can creep up on their prey.

Tools for eating

Animals' bodies are adapted to suit the kind of food they eat. Herbivores usually have flat, broad teeth designed for munching plants, while most carnivores have sharp teeth to help them grab and grip their prey (the animals they eat) and tear raw flesh.

You can see the long, sharp teeth in this badger's skull. They are good for gripping and slicing through flesh.

In this roe deer's skull, you can see the long front teeth which are suited to biting off pieces of plants and flat molar teeth which are good for chewing plants.

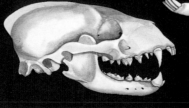

Natural selection

Why are animals and plants so well adapted to their way of life? One answer might be that they have gradually changed, or evolved, over a very long time to suit the places they live in and the food that is available to them. In the 19th century, a scientist named Charles Darwin (1809–1882) put forward a theory, which he called "natural selection", to explain how these changes might happen.

According to Darwin, individual animals and plants sometimes have qualities that help them to survive. For example, in a green forest, a green bug would probably survive longer than a brown bug, because its appearance would help it to avoid being seen and eaten.

The individuals that survive the longest are likely to have more babies, and will pass on their useful qualities to them. Over a very long time, each species will gradually develop all the most useful qualities for surviving in its own habitat.

Internet links

Play interactive games to find out more about some of the amazing animals around the world.

For a link to this website, go to
www.usborne-quicklinks.com

Breathing

As well as eating food, animals need to breathe oxygen, a gas which is found in air and water. All animals take oxygen into their bodies, in a variety of different ways.

Fish have gills, which filter oxygen from the water as it flows through them.

Gills

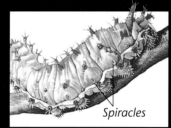

Spiracles

Insects take in oxygen through tiny holes in their bodies, called spiracles.

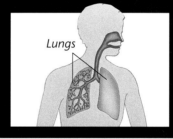

Lungs

Humans and many other animals have lungs, which extract oxygen from the air.

Useful animals

Animals are very useful to humans, providing meat, milk, eggs, wool, silk, leather and even medicines. Many animals are farmed carefully, but some species are in danger of dying out and becoming extinct, because humans have killed too many of them. You can find out about these endangered species on page 115.

Guanacos are hunted for their long, thick wool.

ECOSYSTEMS

A place where a plant or animal lives is called its habitat. For example, seas, rivers, mountains, forests and deserts are all habitats. Together, a habitat and the group, or community, of plants and animals that live in it form a whole system, called an ecosystem.

Snowy owls and lemmings are part of the ecosystem in the Arctic.

Meat-eaters survive by eating other animals found in their habitat. These cheetahs are chasing a Thomson's gazelle.

Food webs

In an ecosystem, many different food chains intertwine to make up a complicated system known as a food web. Each animal in the web may eat many different species and be hunted by several others. The diagram below shows part of a food web in a mountain forest in a northern country, such as Canada. Each blue arrow points from a species that is eaten to a species that eats it. (This is a simplified diagram. In fact, there would be many more species than this in one ecosystem, and the whole food web would be too complicated to fit on the page.)

Food chains

The animals and plants in an ecosystem depend on each other for food. One species eats another, and is in turn eaten by another. This is called a food chain. Plants form the first link in a food chain, because they make their own food from sunlight, using a process called photosynthesis*. Plant-eating animals (herbivores) eat plants, and meat-eating animals (carnivores) eat herbivores and other carnivores.

As in all ecosystems, plants form the basis of this food web.

*Photosynthesis, 108; soil, 28

Trophic levels

A food web has several layers, known as trophic levels. There are different kinds of plants or animals on each level.

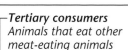

The Sun provides light and energy for plants.

Tertiary consumers
Animals that eat other meat-eating animals

Secondary consumers
Animals that eat plant-eating animals

Primary consumers
Animals that eat plants

Producers
Plants that use the Sun's energy to manufacture food

Decomposers
Organisms that feed on dead plants and animals and break them down in the soil*

The energy cycle

Plants and animals use food to make energy, which helps them grow, move, keep warm, make seeds and have babies. When plants or animals die, they are broken down by decomposers, such as fungi, and the energy goes back into the soil in the form of chemicals. These help plants to grow, and the cycle begins again.

Internet links

Discover more about food chains and webs, the different methods predators use to hunt their prey and unusual ways of eating, with video clips, animations and photographs.

For a link to this website, go to
www.usborne-quicklinks.com

Competition

Each type of plant or animal has a unique place in its ecosystem, known as a niche. If two different species try to compete for the same food, the stronger one survives, and the other dies out or has to move away. Different species in an ecosystem can survive side by side by eating slightly different types of food. For example, in African grasslands, elephants reach up to eat the higher branches of trees and bushes, gerenuks eat leaves lower down and warthogs nibble grasses on the ground.

Biomes

The Earth has several climate types, or biomes, such as rainforests and deserts. Each biome supports many ecosystems, but can also be seen as one big ecosystem. Together, all the biomes combine to form the biggest ecosystem of all, the Earth itself.

An elephant's long trunk allows it to reach to the tops of trees to collect food, while other animals eat the leaves lower down.

PEOPLE AND ECOSYSTEMS

Like every other plant and animal on Earth, you are part of an ecosystem. But there are now so many humans that we need more energy and make more waste than our ecosystem can deal with.

Using up energy

The first humans were suited to the ecosystems of the places they lived in. They ate the food that was available and used only as much energy as they needed to survive.

Now, though, we use up lots more energy than we really need to survive, because of all the things that modern humans do, such as running factories, getting around in cars and planes, and using electric lights and machines. We get most of our energy by burning fossil fuels*. This creates waste gases which can't be broken down quickly enough, so they build up around us as pollution.

Pollution

Pollution is any waste product that nature can't easily process and recycle. Things such as exhaust from cars, smoke from factories, and plastic packaging are all pollution.

Some pollution is just ugly, but some can be dangerous. For example, exhaust fumes that build up in the air can cause asthma, and chemicals that leak from farms into rivers can kill fish and upset the local food web*.

Smog is a kind of pollution caused when fossil fuels are burned and give off waste gases.*

Upsetting ecosystems

Each part of an ecosystem depends on all the other parts, making a natural balance. If one part is damaged or destroyed, it affects all the others.

If the plants in this food chain were destroyed, the animals farther up the chain might starve.*

*Food chains, 112; food webs, 112; fossil fuels, 26

Using up space

Our farms, cities, roads and airports all need space. We use space that used to be the habitats of plants and animals. Without its habitat, an ecosystem can't work, and animals and plants die. If this happens too often, some species become extinct, which means they die out completely.

Extinction is sometimes caused by natural disasters, such as volcanic eruptions, but often it is brought about by people. Pollution, hunting and introducing animals into new areas can all cause extinctions. For example, several species of flightless birds were wiped out when humans brought dogs and cats to Australia and New Zealand.

Wind turbines like these convert the energy of the wind into electricity. This causes less pollution than burning fuel.

The dodo, which lived on the island of Mauritius, died out in about 1680 after it was hunted to extinction by Dutch settlers.

Internet links

See what it would cost to replace some of the Earth's natural resources if we continue to consume resources faster than the Earth can replenish them.

For a link to this website, go to
www.usborne-quicklinks.com

Conserving the Earth

Conservation means trying to reduce the damage done to the Earth and its species by pollution and other human activities. We can begin to conserve the Earth by using less energy, making less waste, and replacing as much as possible of the resources we use up. This is sometimes called sustainable living.

We cannot bring back plants and animals that are already extinct, but endangered species (those that are in danger of dying out) can be protected. Conservationists work to save natural habitats and protect rare wild animals from being hunted, so that they can build up their numbers.

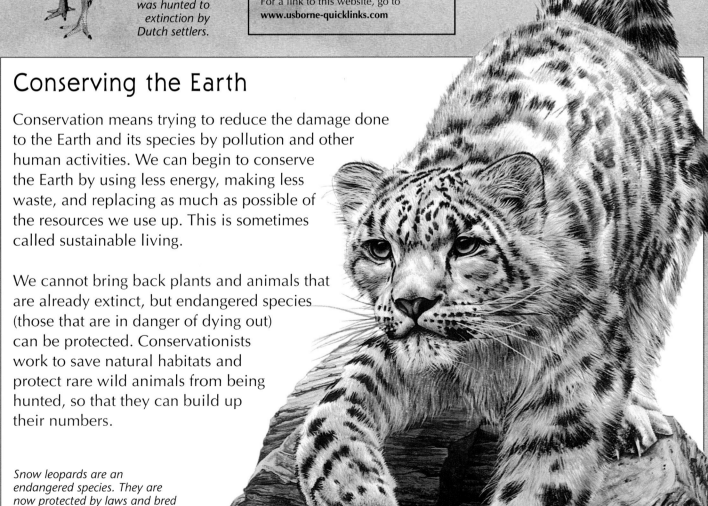

Snow leopards are an endangered species. They are now protected by laws and bred in zoos to try to save them.

RAINFORESTS

In the tropics*, it rains nearly every day and is hot throughout the year. Large areas are covered in thick, lush forests called tropical rainforests.

Rainy places

Tropical rainforests receive more than 2,000mm (80in) of rain each year. The intense heat causes water to evaporate quickly, making the air very moist, or humid.

Internet links

Discover the threats to rainforests around the world and read some of the strategies used to protect them.

For a link to this website, go to **www.usborne-quicklinks.com**

This is a tropical rainforest in Bali, Indonesia. The trees grow quickly as they compete to reach the light.

This map shows where the tropical rainforests are.

Rainforest trees spread out their branches to absorb the light, forming a canopy which can be up to 7m (23ft) thick.

*Tropics, 250

Rainforest people

Many small ethnic groups living in tropical rainforests survive by hunting animals and gathering plants, or by small-scale farming. However, their lifestyle has been threatened by people who have moved to these areas for commercial reasons. They chop down trees and burn them in order to clear land for farming and mining.

These rainforest trees are being burned to create space for farming.

Animal life

Rainforests are home to over half the world's plant and animal species. Different kinds of animals have adapted to living at different levels in the rainforest. Many animals live in the branches of trees. They need to be good at climbing and able to move easily from tree to tree by swinging, jumping or gliding.

On the forest floor, it is dark and the tangled vegetation makes it difficult for some animals to move around. The larger animals tend to be sturdy so they can easily force their way through. There are also many insects.

Colugos climb trees for food. They use the flaps of skin between their arms and legs to help them glide between trees.

Forests in danger

Every year, huge areas of rainforest are chopped down or burned. The disappearance of so many trees affects the balance of gases in the atmosphere. This may cause an increase in global warming*. Due to the destruction of their natural habitat, many rainforest plants and animals have died out and many others are endangered.

Golden lion tamarins are an endangered species of monkey.

117

*Global warming, 102

TROPICAL GRASSLANDS

The tropical grasslands are flat, open plains in the central parts of continents. They occur between 5° and 15° north and south of the Equator and get their name from the grasses that make up the majority of their vegetation.

This map shows where the tropical grasslands are.

Acacia trees in the Taragire National Park, Tanzania, Africa. Acacias are among the few trees that can survive in the dry tropical grasslands.

Two seasons

The tropical grasslands have two seasons: a dry season, when the vegetation is dry and brown, and a rainy season, when the grasses become tall and green.

The rainy season occurs when the Sun is directly overhead and the trade winds* meet and cause rainfall. As the Sun moves, so does the point where the trade winds meet until the dry season begins.

Vegetation

Only a few trees grow in the tropical grasslands, for example the acacia tree whose thick trunk is resistant to the fires that sometimes rage during the dry season. However, there are around 8,000 species of grasses, which are suited to dry conditions. They have long roots which can reach downward and sideways in search of water.

Internet links

Read more about grassland vegetation, learn the different names for grasslands in different parts of the world and find information on grassland animals.

For a link to this website, go to
www.usborne-quicklinks.com

118

Grassland animals

The tropical grasslands are home to large numbers of herbivores (plant-eating animals). These attract large hunting animals, such as lions and cheetahs, that feed on them. Because the land is so exposed, many animals live in large groups, so that some animals can watch out for predators while others feed or rest.

Some of the fastest animals, such as cheetahs, gazelles and ostriches, live in grasslands. Speed is important for survival, both for the hunters and the hunted. With so few hiding places, a hunt for food often results in a chase.

During the dry season, wildebeest move away, or migrate, to find food and water. Many thousands of wildebeest migrate together for protection.

Cheetahs are the fastest land mammals, reaching speeds of up to 110kph (68mph).

The tsetse fly

Many grassland areas are now used for farming. However, the largest grasslands, in Africa, are almost untouched. This is because of a parasite, carried by an insect called the tsetse fly, which infects humans and animals. In humans, it causes sleeping sickness, the effects of which are sluggishness, fever and sometimes death. In animals, it causes a similar disease called nagana.

A close-up of a tsetse fly feeding on a human arm

MONSOONS

At certain times of year, some areas of the tropics have a period of torrential rain and another period of drier weather. This strong seasonal change is known as a monsoon. The rain can cause severe flooding, but people also rely on it for survival.

Three seasons

Monsoons occur in certain parts of the tropics, particularly in Southeast Asia. Monsoon regions have three seasons – a long, cool dry season, a hot humid season when the land is very dry and a rainy season when there are thunderstorms on most days.

During the rainy season, it rains very heavily and there are strong winds. You can see how strong the winds are by the way the trees are blowing.

Changing winds

The word *monsoon* is from an Arabic word meaning "season". It refers to the seasonal reversal of the wind direction. During the cooler season, the land is cooler than the ocean, and so winds blow from the land to the ocean, giving dry weather over the land. The warm season occurs when the midday Sun is almost directly overhead. The land is hotter than the ocean, so moist winds rush in from the ocean and shed their moisture on the land as heavy rain.

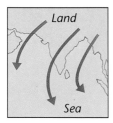

In the dry season, winds blow from the land to the sea.

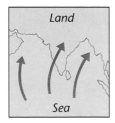

In the rainy season, moist winds rush in from the sea.

Farming

Around a quarter of the world's people live in monsoon areas. Many of them rely on growing their own food. The main crops are rice and tea, which grow well in wet conditions.

Rice in particular needs lots of water to grow. The seedlings are planted during the wet monsoon season in flooded fields called paddy fields. Rice is an important food for many poor nations, because it can be grown cheaply and in large quantities. If there is too little rain, it can be disastrous, resulting in crop failure which may in turn cause famine.

A rice farm in China. The field has been flooded with water, as rice plants grow well in waterlogged soils.

Internet links

Find out more about monsoons in Asia and Australia, and their impact on people's lives and agriculture, or build a virtual rice paddy.

For links to these websites, go to **www.usborne-quicklinks.com**

Diseases

A mosquito magnified. These insects thrive in monsoon regions.

A number of serious diseases spread easily after the monsoon season, because stagnant floodwater provides an ideal breeding ground for the bacteria that cause them. Typhoid and cholera are particularly common. Mosquitoes, insects which can carry diseases such as malaria and yellow fever, also thrive in the warm, wet conditions of monsoon regions.

TROPICAL DESERTS

The tropical deserts are the hottest and driest places in the world. With so little water or shelter, only a few animals and plants are able to survive in the burning heat of the day. Very few people live in tropical deserts.

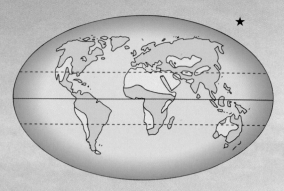

Tropical deserts exist mainly between 15° and 30° north and south of the Equator.

This is a fertile area, called an oasis, in the Thar Desert, Rajasthan, India. The people are collecting water.

Desert climate

Most deserts are hot during the day and cold at night. During the day, the heat is intense because the Sun is high in the sky and there are few clouds to block the Sun's rays. Temperatures can reach over 52°C (126°F). At night, the lack of clouds allows heat to escape, so temperatures can drop to below freezing. Less than 250mm (10in) of rain falls on deserts each year. When it rains, it is usually in short, violent storms. If the land has been baked by the heat of the Sun, these brief rainstorms can cause floods because the rain is not absorbed quickly enough by the dry ground.

Oases

There is water in the desert, but most of it is located underground in rocks that are porous, which means they can hold water like a sponge. In a few places, where these rocks are at the surface, moist areas called oases are formed. Birds, animals and people gather at oases to drink.

Desert landscapes

Only 25% of the world's deserts are sandy. Most deserts consist of bare rock or stone. Some even have dramatic rocky mountains. In sandy deserts, sand often collects together to form hills called dunes, which move and change shape as the wind blows the sand across the desert.

Strong winds sometimes sweep across deserts, causing sand-storms which can wear away the rocks in their path. Over many years, this "sand-blasting" effect can produce some unusually-shaped rocks. The process of wearing away rocks in this way is a type of erosion*.

This is a sand dune in the Sahara Desert, Africa, the biggest desert in the world. The man is one of the Tuareg, a group of people who live in the Sahara.

Internet links

Explore the vast and mysterious Sahara Desert, where less than 125mm (5in) of rain falls each year, and find out about its wildlife, landscape and peoples.

For a link to this website, go to
www.usborne-quicklinks.com

Adaptation

In order to survive in the desert, those plants and animals that live there have adapted so that they are able to cope with the heat and limited supplies of water. Some desert plants can store water in their stems or can access water deep in the ground through long roots. Many desert animals have dry droppings to help them save water.

Camels can drink gallons of water in a few minutes and then last days without any.

Desert expansion

The world's deserts are increasing in size. This process, known as desertification, is caused by the destruction of the vegetation near the edges of deserts. People living in these dry areas need grass for their animals to eat and wood from trees to burn as fuel. This destruction of vegetation means that the soil is easily washed or blown away and the water cycle* is disrupted. Once this has happened, it is very difficult for vegetation to grow there.

Erosion, 34; water cycle, 78

MEDITERRANEAN CLIMATES

Mediterranean climates are warm temperate* climates. They get their name from the regions bordering the Mediterranean Sea. However, other parts of the world, such as small areas around Cape Town (South Africa), Perth (Australia), San Francisco (U.S.A.) and Valparaiso (Chile) also have Mediterranean climates.

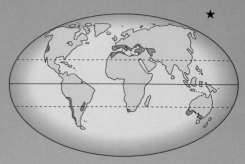

This map shows those areas with a Mediterranean climate.

Warm and dry

Mediterranean climates cover only a small part of the world. They are found on the west coasts of continents between 30° and 40° north and south of the Equator.

In summer in the Mediterranean, descending air usually causes hot, cloudless weather. In winter, the westerly winds bring moist air from the Atlantic, causing wetter weather.

In the Mediterranean region itself, the Mediterranean Sea (an inland sea with a narrow link to the Atlantic Ocean) has a moderating influence on the climate of the surrounding countries, making the winters milder than they would be otherwise.

In other parts of the world that have Mediterranean climates, cold offshore currents* have a similar effect on the local climate as the Mediterranean Sea has on southern Europe.

This town in the south of France overlooks the Cote d'Azur, a stretch of coastline by the Mediterranean Sea which is a popular spot for tourists.

Oranges grow well in Mediterranean climates.

Vegetation

There are two main types of vegetation in Mediterranean regions: trees such as cork oaks and olives, and low woody plants, or scrub. The vegetation is well adapted to the dry summer climate. Plants have thick, waxy leaves which reduce the amount of water they lose, and long roots which enable them to reach water deep underground.

Farming

Those places with Mediterranean climates are home to some of the world's most important wine producers. Grape vines are particularly well adapted to the climate, as they have long roots and tough bark.

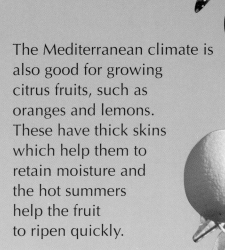

Tourism

People sunbathing on a beach in the Cote d'Azur, southern France

The hot, dry summers in Mediterranean countries such as Greece, Spain, Italy and southern France have made them popular destinations for tourists from cooler climates searching for summer sunshine. This has meant that tourism has become an important part of the economies of these countries. Resorts tend to be developed in strips along the coast, where closeness to the sea and pleasant beaches are also major attractions for people.

A vineyard in the Douro Valley, Portugal. The grapes are being hand-picked to make wine.

The Mediterranean climate is also good for growing citrus fruits, such as oranges and lemons. These have thick skins which help them to retain moisture and the hot summers help the fruit to ripen quickly.

Internet links

Read about Greek climate and weather and discover how the Greeks have adapted to the extremes of their Mediterranean climate.

For a link to this website, go to **www.usborne-quicklinks.com**

*Ocean currents, 97; temperate climates, 126

TEMPERATE CLIMATES

The areas of the globe between the Arctic and Antarctic Circles and the tropics have a temperate climate. As the term temperate suggests, temperatures there are never very extreme. This vast area contains a wide range of landscapes.

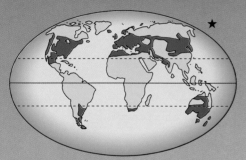

The dark blue areas of this map show the parts of the world with temperate climates.

Varied climates

The vegetation in temperate regions ranges from forests to dry grasslands. However, all the different areas have four seasons*: spring, summer, autumn and winter. This is because of the Earth's tilt and the way that each hemisphere faces the Sun in one season and then faces away from it in another.

Green lands

The mid-latitudes (between 40° and 60° north and south of the Equator) have a rainy climate, which is usually described as cool temperate. The steady rain throughout the year is the result of cool air from the poles meeting warm air from the tropics. The warm air is forced upward, causing swirling patterns of clouds and rain known as depressions.

The moderate temperatures in cool temperate regions mean that vegetation has a long period of uninterrupted growth, so the landscape is very green. Most trees are deciduous, which means that they lose their leaves in winter.

This region, which includes most of Europe, contains the richest farmland areas. The fertile soil and rainfall throughout the year make it suitable for a wide variety of crops, including grains, green vegetables and deciduous fruits.

Before the leaves on deciduous trees fall, they change from green to orange, red and yellow.

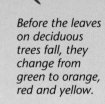

Grasslands

A view of the huge grasslands, or prairies, of North America

The prairies of North America and the steppes of Russia are huge temperate grasslands which lie in the middle of continents. Their summers are hot and sunny, but their winters can be quite harsh because they are away from the warming effects of the ocean*.

These areas receive too little rainfall for trees to grow, so the main vegetation is grasses. In the vast, treeless prairies of North America, winter frosts break up the rich soils, but summer days are long and warm. Wheat is suited to these conditions and is grown extensively.

Seasonal life

The lives of many animals and plants in temperate regions follow the cycle of the seasons. Annual plants complete their life's cycle in a year. They begin growing from seeds in spring and then flower in summer. In autumn, they produce their own seeds and fruit. At the end of the year the plants die.

Internet links

Explore an autumn leaf scrapbook to find out more about deciduous forests, or build a virtual prairie.

For a link to this website, go to **www.usborne-quicklinks.com**

Many animals prepare for the winter by storing up food. Some, such as the dormouse, cope with the lack of food by going into a deep sleep known as hibernation. During hibernation, an animal's breathing and heartbeat slow down and it does not need to eat. There are also animals that avoid the cold weather altogether by moving, or migrating, to warmer places.

A dormouse hibernating in its nest during the winter months

POLAR REGIONS

The Arctic, the area around the North Pole, and the Antarctic, the area around the South Pole, are known as the polar regions. The temperatures there are usually below freezing and huge expanses of land and sea are covered in ice and snow.

Antarctic

In the middle of the Antarctic Ocean is a land mass, or continent, known as Antarctica, which is covered in a thick layer of ice. Temperatures there are so low that when snow falls it doesn't melt, but builds up with each snowfall. The weight of the snow on top presses down on the lower layers to form ice.

No land mammals live permanently in Antarctica because it is so cold, but some animals, such as seals, go there to breed. A number of seabirds, including penguins, live there permanently.

Young penguin chicks sit on their parents' feet and snuggle under a special flap of skin to keep warm. This one is a little too big for this, but it still huddles up close for warmth.

Arctic

The Arctic is mainly made up of the Arctic Ocean, but several countries, including Canada, jut into it. The land there, called tundra, is warm enough for animals and plants to survive.

In summer, the ice on the tundra melts and the surface of the ground thaws. The ground often becomes boggy, because deeper down it is still frozen and the water can't seep through. The frozen layer is called permafrost.

Keeping warm

Some polar animals, such as penguins and seals, have adapted to living in the sea, away from icy winds. Other animals have different ways of coping with the cold. Polar bears have a thick layer of fat under their skin and musk oxen have thick, shaggy coats. Many polar animals have small ears, which help to reduce heat loss.

Blending in

Many polar animals have white coats, which enable them to blend in with the snowy landscape. This is called camouflage. It helps them to hide from predators or to stalk their prey without being seen. A few animals, such as arctic foxes and snowshoe hares, have different winter and summer coats. During the summer they have brown coats which blend in easily with rocks and plants. Then, as the snow falls in the winter, their coats change and become white, so they don't stand out.

This polar bear's shaggy white coat blends in with the snow and protects it from the cold. It has fur all over its body except for on its nose and the pads on its feet.

Arctic shelters

Some animals that live in the Arctic build burrows or dens in the snow to protect themselves from the cold winds. For example, polar bears build dens with chambers in the snow for their cubs to take shelter.

Hole for air

Entrance tunnel

Cubs' chamber

Main chamber

Some dens have a lower chamber.

This cutaway picture shows the inside of a polar bear's den.

MOUNTAINS

About 5% of the world's land surface is covered by high mountains and mountain ranges. Mountain areas have more than one type of climate because, as you go up a mountain, there are fewer particles in the air and the temperature falls.

The Great Basin Desert in Nevada, U.S.A., lies on the sheltered side, or rain shadow, of the Sierra Nevada mountains.

Mountain ranges

Most mountains are formed when the plates that make up the lithosphere* push together, forcing the land into fold mountains*. This is why mountains often occur in long lines, or ranges.

When air flows from the sea onto a mountain range, it is forced to rise. Clouds form as a result of condensation and rain or snow then falls on the mountainside. The sheltered land on the other side of the mountain, called the rain shadow, gets very little rain, and may become a desert.

Mountain peaks in the Andes, on the border between Chile and Argentina

Mountain levels

The higher up a mountain you go, the colder it gets. This is because the air higher up is thinner, so it can store less heat. There are different types of weather, vegetation and animal life at different heights up the mountain. Few species live on the windy peaks, but mountain goats and sheep graze on the grassy, rocky slopes below. Farther down, below a line called the treeline, it is warm enough for trees to grow. Animals such as cougars and hares live in mountain forests.

Internet links

Take an interactive tour of Everest, from base camp to the summit of the world's highest mountain.

For a link to this website, go to
www.usborne-quicklinks.com

The Alpine forget-me-not flower is adapted to mountain climates. It has shorter, thicker stems and deeper roots than the common forget-me-not.

This shepherd from the Basque region of France is holding two baby goats. Goats are suited to the mountain climate.

Mountain dwellers

Both animals and people living in high mountain areas have bigger lungs to help them breathe more easily in the thin air. Animals need thick fur and people need thick coats to keep them warm. Mountain people may be cut off from other cultures. For example, the Basque people, who have lived in the Pyrenees mountains between France and Spain for thousands of years, have a very unusual language which is unlike any other on Earth. This is because, for centuries, they rarely mixed with other peoples.

*Fold mountains, 21; lithosphere, 18

These tourists riding on dromedaries in Rajasthan, India, cast huge shadows on the desert sand.

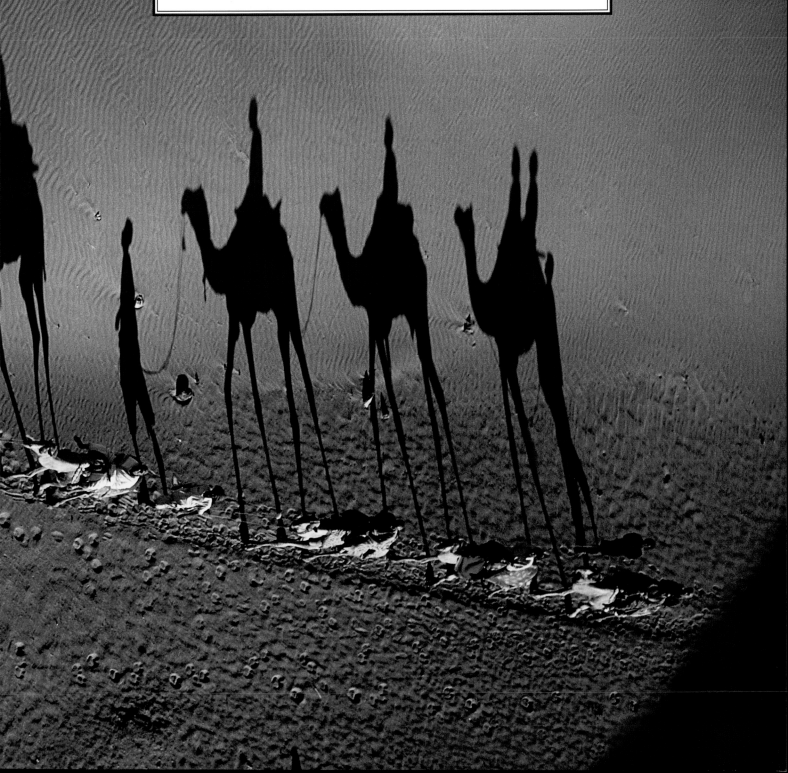

PEOPLE AND
THE WORLD

FARMING

F arming means growing plants or raising animals to meet human needs. It is the biggest industry in the world and produces much of what you eat, wear and use.

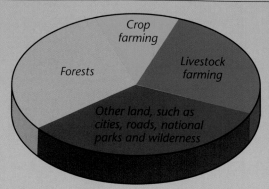

This pie chart shows how the world's land is used. Livestock farming uses more space than crop farming, but produces less food.

Types of farming

Growing plants is called crop farming or arable farming, and keeping animals is called livestock farming or pastoral farming. A mixture of both is called mixed farming. Farmers choose what to farm according to the type of land they have, the soil and the climate.

Internet links

Meet farmers from around the world and learn about different types of farms and farming methods, with photographs and maps.

For a link to this website, go to **www.usborne-quicklinks.com**

Yaks are adapted to surviving in high mountain areas. Farmers in the Himalayas keep them for milk and wool.

World industry

Around 45% of the world's workforce are farmers. Instead of just growing their own food, many farmers grow cash crops – crops grown specially to be sold and exported around the world. This is why, in some countries, you can buy different kinds of foods from all over the world in one supermarket.

Wet soil and a warm climate are ideal for growing rice. In hilly areas, farmers build steps of land, or terraces, to hold the water and soil in place. This picture shows rice terraces in China.

Growing crops

Combine harvesters are used to gather all kinds of crops. This one is gathering wheat. It is much quicker than harvesting crops by hand.

Crop farming uses up around 11% of the world's land. It is the best way of producing as much food as possible from the soil, so poor countries usually grow a greater proportion of crops than rich countries do. Planting, protecting and harvesting (collecting) crops is hard work, but many farmers use machinery to do these tasks.

Animal care

Like crops, livestock has to be looked after carefully. The animals need food, water, shelter and protection from predators and diseases. Animal products also have to be "harvested", which means collecting the animals' milk, wool or eggs, or killing them for their meat.

Farm animals often have more than one use. We may use their wool or skins as well as meat. In many countries they also work, pulling carts or farm machinery.

★

Ostriches are farmed for meat, eggs and leather, and their feathers are used in fashion accessories.

FARMING METHODS

Farmers want to get as much as they can from their land. There are various ways of improving the yield, or amount of produce that comes from the land.

Choosing the best

An important part of farming is selective breeding, which involves choosing the best plants and animals and developing them to make more useful varieties. For instance, wheat started off as a type of grass called einkorn. When replanting, early farmers chose the einkorn with the biggest seeds because these would provide more food. Gradually, einkorn developed into modern wheat, which has lots of large seeds on each stalk.

Helicopters like this are used by intensive farmers to spray fertilizers or pesticides onto their crops.

A grass called einkorn

★

Modern farmed wheat, developed from einkorn

Internet links

Compare fascinating photographs and information about different types of farms.

For a link to this website, go to **www.usborne-quicklinks.com**

Modern farm pigs, such as Landrace pigs (right), are descended from wild boar (below).

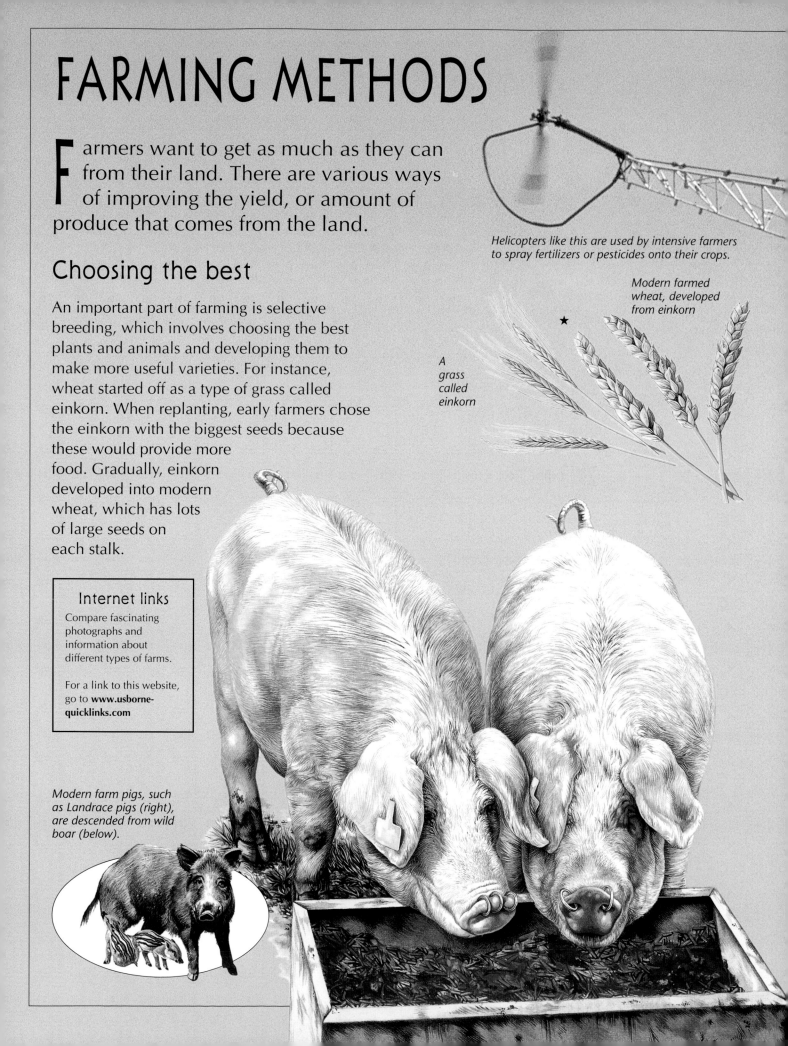

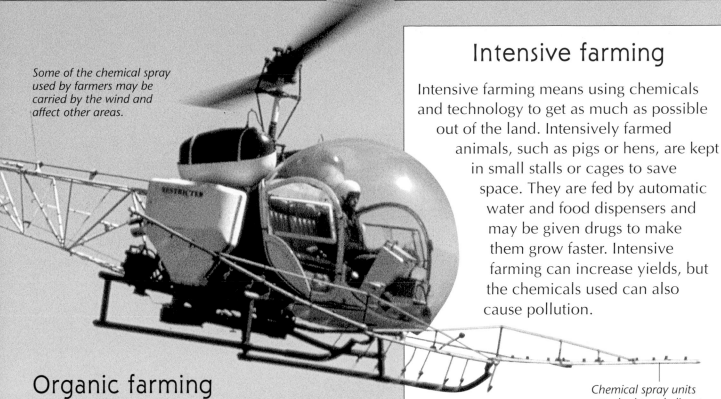

Some of the chemical spray used by farmers may be carried by the wind and affect other areas.

Intensive farming

Intensive farming means using chemicals and technology to get as much as possible out of the land. Intensively farmed animals, such as pigs or hens, are kept in small stalls or cages to save space. They are fed by automatic water and food dispensers and may be given drugs to make them grow faster. Intensive farming can increase yields, but the chemicals used can also cause pollution.

Chemical spray units attached to a helicopter

Organic farming

Organic farming means farming without using artificial chemicals or processes. Organic farmers use animal dung or compost instead of artificial fertilizer, and don't give animals drugs to make them grow faster. Organic food is expensive, because without drugs and artificial chemicals, diseases are harder to control and yields fall. However, there is a demand for organic products from people who are worried about their health, pollution and animal welfare.

Some people think intensive farming is cruel, because the animals are kept in unnatural conditions. "Free range" animals live in more natural conditions and are allowed to move around, or range freely.

Bug warfare

Insects and other bugs that eat farm crops can be a big problem. Intensive farmers (see right) often spray crops to kill insects, but organic farmers do not use chemical sprays. Instead, they sometimes try biological pest control. They change the ecosystem* in their fields by introducing another species to feed on the pest species.

These tiny aphids damage many crops. Instead of spraying, some farmers release ladybirds (ladybugs) to eat them.

Intensively farmed battery hens live in small cages and are usually fed by machines. The eggs they lay roll into a tray and are carried away on a conveyor belt.

*Ecosystems, 112

SCIENCE AND FARMING

Farming has always made use of science and technology, in the form of machinery and selective breeding. But today, more complex science is being used. Computers can make farms more efficient, while genetic engineering is being used to create new crop species.

Big fields

Some modern farm machines, such as combine harvesters, are hard to use in small fields. So, in the last 100 years, fields in many parts of the world have been made bigger and bigger. They are more efficient than small fields because less space is taken up with walls and paths. However, large fields can also be harder to manage, as one field can contain several types of farmland and soil can be eroded more easily*.

The picture below shows a huge wheat field on a modern farm in Sweden.

Precision farming

Precision farming is a new way of using science and technology to manage farms, especially those with very large fields.

For example, some combine harvesters have recording systems that measure how much yield is being collected. At the same time, the farmer uses a Global Positioning System, linked to a satellite* in space, to record where the harvester is in the field. This information is used to make a yield map.

Computer power

Computer maps are used to compare the yield with other factors, such as the acidity or dampness of the soil. The computer then calculates how much fertilizer or water is needed. This saves time and money, and helps farmers avoid using unnecessary fertilizer or water.

This computerized map shows which parts of a field are the most fertile. Darker areas show the highest yield, and pale areas show the lowest yield.

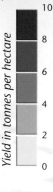

Yield in tonnes per hectare

10
8
6
4
2
0

*Satellites, 252; soil erosion, 31

The tomatoes above are covered in a type of fungus, but the plant that produced the ones on the left was genetically engineered so that its tomatoes would be resistant to the fungus.

Instead of being grown from seeds, the plant shoots in this tub have been "cloned" from fragments of a parent plant to make sure they have exactly the same DNA.

Genetic engineering

Scientists have recently learned how to make changes to DNA, the code inside cells that tells living things how to grow. This is called genetic engineering and it is very important for farming. By altering DNA, we can now change plant species to make them work better as crops.

For example, cotton plants have been genetically engineered to resist a type of weedkiller called Roundup®, which kills all other plants. When the farmer applies the weedkiller, all the weeds die, but the crop stays alive.

Genetically modified foods

Many food crops are being genetically changed, or modified, to make them grow faster or resist pests. GM (genetically modified) foods are tested before they can be sold, but some people worry that they may be bad for us. Nobody yet knows what long-term problems they may cause. GM crops may also damage the environment, for example, by encouraging farmers to use more weedkiller which could harm animals. On the other hand, GM crops could be good news for farmers and consumers in places where crops often fail.

Internet links

Learn more about the issues surrounding GM foods and try an online activity.

For a link to this website, go to
www.usborne-quicklinks.com

POPULATION

Population is the number of people who live in a particular area. The population of the world has been rising for thousands of years, and is now going up faster than ever. In very crowded areas, it can sometimes be hard for people to get enough work, food or housing.

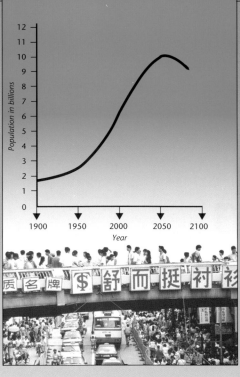

This graph shows how population is predicted to rise and then start falling.

Counting people

With thousands of people being born and dying every day, it can be hard to measure population. Many countries hold a census, or population count, every ten years. Each household fills in a questionnaire, saying how many people live there. Experts use the results to estimate the population of a country at any one time, and to calculate the total population of the world.

Rising numbers

The world's population began to rise quickly in the 17th century, when there were about 500 million people on Earth. There are now over six billion. Population is shooting up because the birth rate (the number of people being born in every 1,000) is higher than the death rate (the number of people dying in every 1,000). The death rate has dropped dramatically with advances in medicine and technology.

Predicting a fall

Population scientists, called demographers, predict that attempts to control population will soon have an effect. They suggest the world's population total will peak at around ten billion people in the 21st century and then begin to fall.

Over and under

The world's population is not spread out evenly. Some areas are overpopulated, with not enough food, water or work for everyone. Other areas, such as the French countryside, are underpopulated, as young people leave the towns and villages for the big cities.

This map shows the average population density by country.

Population density

Population density is the number of people living in a given amount of space. It is measured in people per sq km or sq mile. For example, Mongolia (a big country with a small population) has a low population density of less than two people per sq km (five people per sq mile).

Internet links

Website 1 See video clips and image galleries that explore the impact the growth of the world's population has had on the Earth.

Website 2 See UN predictions for world population growth by the year 2050 and learn more about efforts to manage population growth in different countries.

For links to these websites, go to **www.usborne-quicklinks.com**

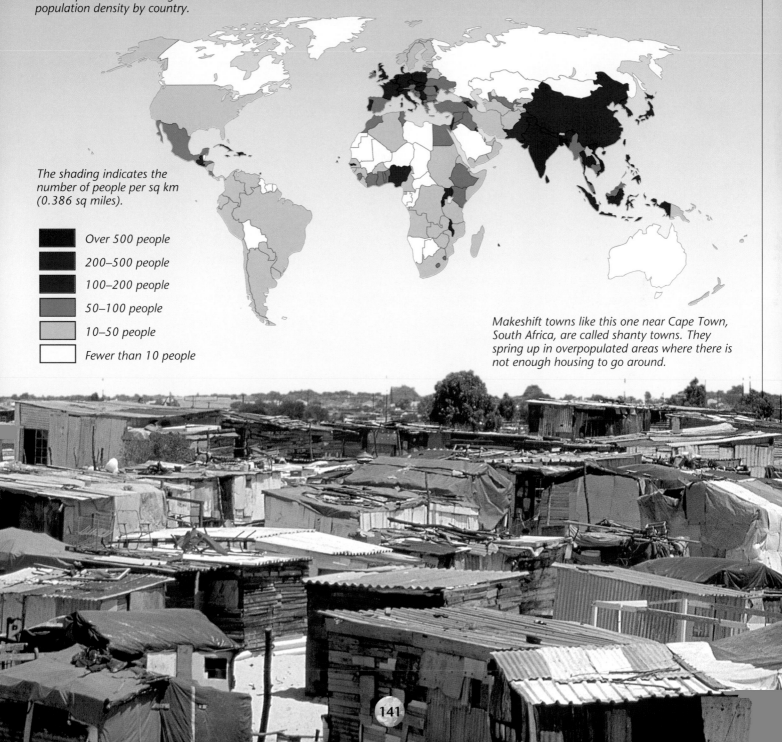

The shading indicates the number of people per sq km (0.386 sq miles).

- Over 500 people
- 200–500 people
- 100–200 people
- 50–100 people
- 10–50 people
- Fewer than 10 people

Makeshift towns like this one near Cape Town, South Africa, are called shanty towns. They spring up in overpopulated areas where there is not enough housing to go around.

MOVING AROUND

P eople have been moving from one part of the world to another for thousands of years. We travel for relaxation, to find food or better jobs, to escape from danger and poverty, and to transport goods around the globe.

This picture shows Haitian refugees sailing on a rickety boat to the U.S.A. They are fleeing Haiti for economic and political reasons, and hope that the U.S.A. will let them in.

Migration

A large number of people moving from one place to another is called a migration. The word migration is usually used to describe a permanent change of home, but it can also refer to seasonal and daily journeys. People may move within a city or country, or between countries. Many people migrate to places that have better jobs and opportunities, better schools for their children, or a better climate. Advantages like these are known as pull factors.

Forced to move

Sometimes people leave their homes because of negative factors, or push factors, such as war or low wages. People may be forced out because they are being attacked for their ethnic origin or political views. People who have been forced to find a new place to live are often called refugees (because they are seeking refuge, or safety).

Nomads

Some groups of people have a lifestyle which involves constantly moving around. This is called a nomadic lifestyle. Traditional nomads make their living from hunting and gathering or herding. For example, the !Kung San* people of southern Africa move around to find food and water, while the Sami* people of Lapland follow the seasonal migrations of the reindeer. There are also commercial nomads who make a living from trade and entertainment.

A family of Bella nomads from Burkina Faso using donkeys to transport themselves and their belongings

Right to enter

Most people have an identity card or passport showing which country they belong to. A passport allows you to travel out of and back into your country. Some countries will only let you cross their border if you also have a visa, which shows you have been given permission to be there for a certain period of time.

These children are descendants of American soldiers in Vietnam. They are waiting for visas so that they can travel to the U.S.A.

Internet links

Website 1 Read personal stories of people becoming refugees and take a virtual tour of a refugee camp.

Website 2 Explore a world map that reveals refugee hotspots and find facts, personal stories and photographs about refugee lives.

For links to these websites, go to **www.usborne-quicklinks.com**

*!Kung San, 243; Sami, 225

SETTLEMENTS

Most people in the world live in groups of houses, apartments, huts or tents. These groups are known as settlements. There are two main kinds of settlements: rural settlements, such as farms, hamlets and villages, and urban settlements, which are towns and cities.

A satellite view of Washington D.C., capital of the U.S.A., which began as a small settlement by the Potomac River

Choosing a site

When people first looked for permanent places to settle, it was very important to choose a site that had nearby water and fuel supplies, fertile land and shelter from strong winds. Today, people also choose sites for political, social or economic reasons.

Good situations

Whether or not a settlement grows can depend on its situation in the surrounding area. Good situations for growth have tended to be near river mouths, in gaps in ranges of hills and at crossroads. In these areas it is easy for people to meet and trade with one another, so settlements in such places usually do well.

Fulfilling functions

Every settlement fulfils certain functions for the people who live there, and for those who live in the surrounding area. A settlement's functions can include providing housing, employment and services such as hospitals, schools and public transportation.

The site of this village in Sudan, East Africa, may have been chosen because it has nearby wood supplies for cooking and building.

Rural and urban

Rural settlements usually have smaller populations than urban settlements and cover smaller areas. Most of the people who live in rural settlements are employed in rural activities, such as farming or forestry, whereas people in urban settlements have a wider variety of jobs. Urban settlements are also more likely to be on good transportation routes.

Services

Urban settlements usually provide more goods and services than rural settlements. A village is likely to have only very basic services and will probably only serve the few hundred people living there. Geographers call small settlements with few services low-order settlements.

A town usually has many stores, businesses and special services such as banks and hospitals. As well as serving the thousands of people living there, it may serve people in surrounding rural areas. Large settlements with lots of services are known as high-order settlements.

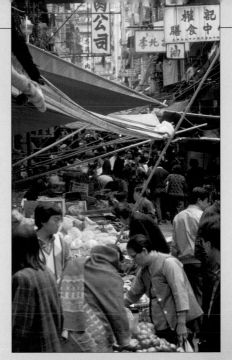

Many urban settlements have shops and markets which offer a wide range of goods. This food market is in Hong Kong.

Internet links

Find diagrams and information about different kinds of settlements.

For a link to this website, go to **www.usborne-quicklinks.com**

TOWNS AND CITIES

Today, more people live in towns and cities than in the countryside and the numbers are increasing all the time as people move in search of jobs. This process of city growth is called urbanization.

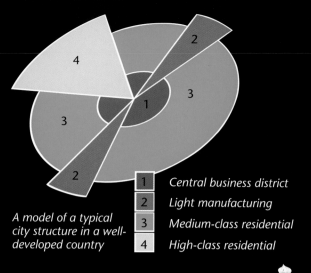

A model of a typical city structure in a well-developed country

1 Central business district
2 Light manufacturing
3 Medium-class residential
4 High-class residential

Megacities

Some cities have so many people living in them that they are known as megacities. Megacities have populations of more than ten million people. They are formed when people from rural areas move to one or two urban areas in their country.

Geographers predict that these megacities will continue to grow. Mexico City, for example, has an estimated population of around 18 million people, although it's difficult to get accurate figures and the population changes rapidly. Most of the world's biggest cities are in less developed countries*.

Growing cities

As the population of a city grows, so does the size of the city itself. Eventually, towns and cities may merge and become one huge urban area, called a conurbation.

*Less developed countries, 152

146

City structure

Different parts of towns and cities usually have different functions. For example, in one part of a town you may find shopping areas, offices and banks. This is called the central business district (CBD), and is generally found in the middle of a city.

Another part of town may be mainly made up of housing, and yet another may be industrial. Many cities have industrial areas lining the major roads that lead out of the city.

This view of Atlanta, U.S.A., shows the busy roads leading in and out of the city.

Problems in cities

As urban populations continue to grow, towns and cities are faced with problems such as overcrowding, homelessness and pollution from industry and traffic. Housing shortages are a particular problem in poorer countries. Many people who move from the countryside to cities cannot find anywhere to live. They build huts from whatever they can find, usually on the outskirts of cities. Whole makeshift towns, called shanty towns, have grown up in this way. Some governments have tried to improve shanty towns by adding electricity, running water and sewage systems.

This shanty town in the Philippines has been improved by building a children's playground.

Internet links

Website 1 Find out about the inhabitants, histories and customs of five of the world's most famous megacities.

Website 2 Read about how three cities (Alexandria, Cordoba and New York) developed in different periods of history.

For links to these websites, go to **www.usborne-quicklinks.com**

EARNING A LIVING

Most of the people in the world have to work to survive and support their families. As well as providing an income for their own families, the jobs most people do create wealth for their countries through taxes.

Working the land

Billions of people live by growing crops or raising animals. Some have small farms, while others move around with their herds of animals. They usually keep some of their produce for themselves, and sell the rest to make money to buy other things.

Working for wages

As the world becomes more industrialized and modern technology develops, more and more people are employed in paid jobs on big farms, in factories and mines, or in service industries* such as banking. Others are self-employed, which means they have their own businesses selling goods or services to other people.

A worker in a steel factory in Germany. Steel is important in industry because it is used to make tools, machinery and vehicles. Jobs like this that involve processing steel or other materials are called secondary jobs.

Internet links

Find out about the problems facing children around the world who work for a living, and read about some possible solutions.

For a link to this website, go to **www.usborne-quicklinks.com**

*Service industries, 151

In small factories, like this glass factory in Bangladesh, people still do many tasks by hand that would be done by machines in larger factories. This woman is inspecting glass containers.

Types of jobs

Geographers divide jobs into four main types:
Primary jobs involve obtaining raw materials from the Earth, e.g. mining, farming, fishing.
Secondary jobs involve making things out of raw materials, e.g. building, making cloth in a factory.
Tertiary jobs provide services for people, business and industry, e.g. hotel management, transporting goods.
Quaternary jobs provide information resources, e.g. accountancy, computing, property-development.

Working conditions

Most countries have laws to protect workers. For example, they make sure workplaces are safe and make it illegal for young children to work. Some places have a minimum wage and maximum working hours. However, millions of people are very poor because they are paid too little for their work. In some parts of the world, children still work in factories and down mines to make enough money for their families to survive.

This mechanic is checking the engine of a jet plane to ensure that it is in good working order. Jobs like this that involve servicing products, transporting them or helping other people are called tertiary jobs.

MANUFACTURING AND SERVICES

Making new products is called manufacturing. There are many different kinds of manufacturing industries, such as making clothes and making cars. People who work in service industries are doing or supplying something for other people, such as teaching and providing banking services.

Energy production is an example of a manufacturing industry. This power plant produces energy for homes and factories.

Heavy and light industries

The materials that are used to make new products are called raw materials. If an industry uses a large amount of heavy raw materials, such as coal and iron ore, it is known as a heavy industry. For example, ship-building is a heavy industry. Light industries use fewer raw materials and make products that are easy to transport.

This machine is being used to mine lignite, which will be used as fuel by industries close to the mining site.

Choosing a location

Today, most manufacturing companies make goods in factories. When a company builds a new factory, it has to choose its location carefully. Most factories are built near transportation links, so that they are accessible for workers and goods, and raw materials can be moved easily. Heavy industries tend to have factories near ports, as it is cheaper to transport heavy goods by ship. Heavy industries also need to be close to the source of their bulky raw materials, to reduce transport costs.

Footloose industries

Light industries, such as electronics companies, are often located near airports or major roads, so that they can transport their goods easily.

However, unlike heavy industries, they do not have to be close to their raw materials. Because light industries are more flexible about where they locate, they are also sometimes known as footloose industries.

Services

There are many different kinds of services, such as healthcare, transportation, tourism and retail. Many of these services are located in the central zones of towns and cities, where they are easily accessible to their customers and workers. However, if the land in a town becomes too expensive, people may build out-of-town shopping areas.

This is the sign for a motel in the U.S.A. Many of the people who work in the service industry have jobs in hotels, motels and restaurants.

Service jobs

In richer countries, many more people work in services than in manufacturing. This is because most of the work in manufacturing is now done by machines. However, service industries still need huge numbers of people. In poorer countries there are often only a few basic services available, so people have to do most things for themselves.

Computers at work

Many service jobs are now being done with the help of computers. For example, more and more train tickets are sold by computerized machines instead of by people. Computers speed things up and make people's jobs easier to do.

Internet links

Explore the world of manufacturing and find out about the different methods used to make everyday products, from cars and airplanes to chocolate and jelly beans, with lots of video clips.

For a link to this website, go to **www.usborne-quicklinks.com**

RICH AND POOR

Standards of living vary greatly around the world. Over 80% of the world's wealth is owned by less than 20% of its people. Most of this wealth is concentrated in Europe and North America. By contrast, many people in southern African countries live in total poverty.

There is poverty in wealthy countries as well as poorer ones. These people are homeless. They are sheltering under a bridge in Hamburg, Germany.

A Vietnamese businessman talking on a mobile phone and standing beside an expensive car. Ownership of cars and phones is often used as a measure of wealth.

Development

Development is about improving the conditions in a country or region. Poorer countries are known as less developed countries and richer countries as more developed countries. The less developed countries are mostly in the tropics and southern hemisphere.

Some poorer countries, such as Brazil, Mexico and Argentina, have recently increased wealth and improved standards of living through the development of modern industries. These are called newly industrialized countries.

Living in poverty

Poverty isn't just about having little money. In some countries many people lack basic resources such as food and safe drinking water. They may not be able to get a job or an education and may only have access to the most basic healthcare, so life expectancy is low. Many richer countries have some people living in poverty too.

Measuring development

Development can be measured in different ways. Sometimes a country's GNP, or gross national product, is used. This is the value of goods and services produced by a country. However, this only gives an indication of a country's wealth. An organization called the United Nations has studied the standard of living in different countries and has devised a system called the Human Development Index which considers other factors, such as life expectancy and education. These give us an idea of people's quality of life.

Internet links

Website 1 Find out about the United Nations (U.N.), an international organization working for peace and development around the world.

Website 2 Read about the current food crises around the world and the U.N.'s efforts to alleviate poverty and hunger.

For links to these websites, go to **www.usborne-quicklinks.com**

Causes of poverty

Regions can be poor for many reasons. One main cause of poverty is the exploitation of certain countries by more powerful countries. Wars can also increase poverty. As well as killing and injuring people, they lead to the destruction of buildings and resources and interrupt food production and distribution.

Some countries have problems transporting people, food and goods, because of the long distances to remote places. Others suffer from natural hazards like floods and droughts. All these things can increase poverty.

This porter, in India, is carrying a tourist up a mountain. In some countries, jobs in tourism pay better than other jobs, but many people are still not paid fair wages or fees for their work.

A SMALL WORLD

With the invention of new, fast forms of transportation and communication, people often say that the world is getting smaller. This is because getting from place to place and sending messages is quicker and easier than ever before.

Satellites in space have greatly improved communication speed. This is the DIRECTV 1-R satellite. It picks up radio, TV and telephone signals from one part of the Earth and relays them to other parts of the globe.

Like many forms of transportation, trains are becoming faster. This is a magnetic suspension train developed in Germany. It uses magnetic forces to travel at high speeds.

Transportation and trade

Moving people and things from place to place is now one of the world's biggest industries. Millions of people have jobs building cars, planes, trains, trucks and ships, and transporting goods from one country to another.

If people want to transport things over long distances, the quickest way is usually by plane. However, heavy or bulky goods are generally carried by truck, train or boat. This takes longer but is much cheaper.

Globalization

People are now able to organize industry on a worldwide scale. This is called globalization. It means that companies in one part of the world can get materials or employ workers in another part of the world, often because they are cheaper or there are specialist skills or facilities there.

This may enable poorer countries to attract investment. But it can lead to exploitation, with companies profiting from the workforces and resources of poorer countries without paying a fair price.

Communication

With satellite communication and the Internet, information can be relayed quickly to a huge number of people. People can work from home via online computers and have video conferences with people on the other side of the world. Some people argue that a negative effect of this is that certain cultures become dominant and that local traditions are lost as people follow similar lifestyles.

Global tourism

Tourism is one of the world's fastest-growing industries. Over 600 million trips abroad are made by tourists each year. The sudden growth of tourism can damage the environment and culture of an area, and benefits may not be spread evenly. However, in some places people are developing sustainable tourism which addresses these problems.

Isolated areas

People around the world are not affected equally by improvements in transportation and communication. Africa has less than 1% of the world's online computers, while North America has over 40%. In poorer countries, the roads are often in bad repair and few people have cars. Physical isolation often causes poverty because it makes trade and development difficult.

Internet links

Website 1 Find out about telecommunications, the growth of the industry and everyday objects that were once considered incredible.

Website 2 Follow a special cargo container around the world and find out how goods are transported.

For links to these websites, go to **www.usborne-quicklinks.com**

Hong Kong's port, shown here with the Central Island district in the background, is very important to the city's success in international trade.

In many parts of the world people use animals to transport heavy loads. This is a bullock cart in Thailand.

GLOBAL CITIZENSHIP

Global citizenship is about being interested in the wider world and thinking about the ways that different countries affect one another. It involves people everywhere becoming aware of global issues, such as poverty, the environment and human rights.

This boy is collecting safe water from a pump funded by a charity called Wateraid.

Giving aid

An important part of being a global citizen is wanting to help people in other countries. People in richer countries sometimes try to help poorer countries to develop by giving aid. This may be money, food, equipment or expert help from engineers and teachers.

However, it is not only richer countries that give aid. Poorer countries often help other countries in times of emergency, such as after a flood or an earthquake.

Kinds of aid

There are two main kinds of aid. Short-term aid may involve sending supplies to help a country after an emergency. Long-term aid aims to improve the quality of life of people in poorer countries, for example, through building and healthcare projects.

There can be problems with giving aid, such as countries becoming dependent on aid, or money not reaching the people who need help. Sometimes, in return for aid, rich countries make poorer countries promise to buy goods from them, even if they could buy them more cheaply elsewhere.

These children are protesting against the killing of whales. They are part of an international action group called "Kids for Whales", organized by Greenpeace.

Internet links

Website 1 Find out about the lives of children around the world.

Website 2 Read about some of the latest global issues.

For links to these websites, go to
www.usborne-quicklinks.com

Human rights

A vital part of being a global citizen is believing that everyone has the same right to food, water, education, health, security and justice. People may choose to work for human rights by campaigning about a particular issue. However, it's important that they are well informed about the complexities of the situation and the effects of their actions.

The environment

Environmental problems not only affect the country which causes them, they can affect the whole world. For example, burning fossil fuels or chopping down trees in one country can lead to global warming*.

Being a global citizen is about learning how to take care of the world. Many people do this by joining environmental organizations, or by changing their lifestyles to help the environment, for example by using trains or buses instead of cars, or recycling household waste.

This boy is protesting against French nuclear tests on Cook Island, in the Pacific.

*Global warming, 102

American football fans wave pom-poms at the Rose Bowl stadium, Los Angeles, California

PEOPLES OF
NORTH AMERICA

NORTH AMERICA

The name "North America" can be used to mean several different things. In this book, the northern part of the American continent begins with Panama in the south and stretches up to Canada and Greenland in the north. It includes the U.S.A., Mexico, Central America and the Caribbean.

This carved, painted pillar is part of a totem pole. Some Native American groups used these as community symbols or in memory of someone who had died.

Native Americans

Native Americans are the people who lived in North America before European explorers arrived. Each Native American group had its own lifestyles and customs and was governed by a chief.

In the 19th century, the European settlers forced Native Americans to live on areas of land called reservations and tried to force them to adopt European lifestyles. Many Native American traditions were forgotten. Now languages are being revived and Native Americans make and sell traditional pottery, baskets or textiles. However, people also lead modern lifestyles – for example some groups run casinos.

This modern Native American is wearing traditional clothes, reflecting the interest in reviving traditional culture. But the Christian monument he is leaning against is a sign of the influence of European culture.

Internet links

Website 1 Gain further insight into the traditions, culture and music of Native Americans by following a fascinating audio slide show.

Website 2 Find out how different Native American communities lived.

For links to these websites, go to
www.usborne-quicklinks.com

Different lands

The landscape and climate of North America is extremely varied. Greenland and Alaska in the far north are cold, icy and sparsely populated, Arizona in the U.S.A. has vast stretches of desert, and Central America is dominated by hot, humid rainforests. Cities such as New York and Mexico City are among the biggest in the world and are filled with towering skyscrapers.

This is the Chrysler building in New York. When it was built in 1930, it was the tallest building in the world. Now, tall skyscrapers dominate the skylines of many cities in the U.S.A.

Living in America

North America is home to some of the world's richest and poorest countries. The wealthy U.S.A. (often known simply as America) is one of the world's most powerful nations, while Guatemala has been bankrupted by years of war and is extremely poor.

THE U.S.A.

The United States of America, also known as the U.S.A. or America, is a huge country, although it's not much more than half the size of Russia, the biggest country. The U.S.A. is very rich and has immense political and cultural influence worldwide.

Land and law

The U.S.A. has hundreds of large theme parks with huge rides like this roller coaster.

The U.S.A. is divided into 50 states. Power is shared between state governments and a central federal government based in the capital, Washington D.C. The southern states are warm, green and rich in oil, while the main farming areas are in the western states. The northeast is the main business region. Manufacturing has moved more to the southern states in recent years. Many computer companies are located in Silicon Valley in California.

The 'American Dream'

People from all over the world have moved to the U.S.A., and a million new immigrants arrive each year. Many are following the 'American Dream': the belief that, in America, anyone can become rich and successful. However, many Americans are still very poor.

The mixture of peoples gives the U.S.A. a rich, diverse culture. Jazz and blues music, for instance, developed out of rhythms brought to the U.S.A. from Africa, while cheesecake and bagels were originally Jewish foods.

Dr. Martin Luther King Jr., the leader of the 1960s Civil Rights movement for equality for black Americans, speaks at a "March against Fear" rally in 1966.

The crowned figure in the background is the Statue of Liberty in New York. It is a symbol of the political freedom enshrined in the Constitution of the U.S.A.

Internet links

Website 1 Learn more about America's history by watching video clips, listening to songs and exploring different states.

Website 2 Read about historical events in the U.S.A. that have their anniversaries today, and browse through the archive.

Website 3 Find out about the structure of the U.S. government.

For links to these websites, go to **www.usborne-quicklinks.com**

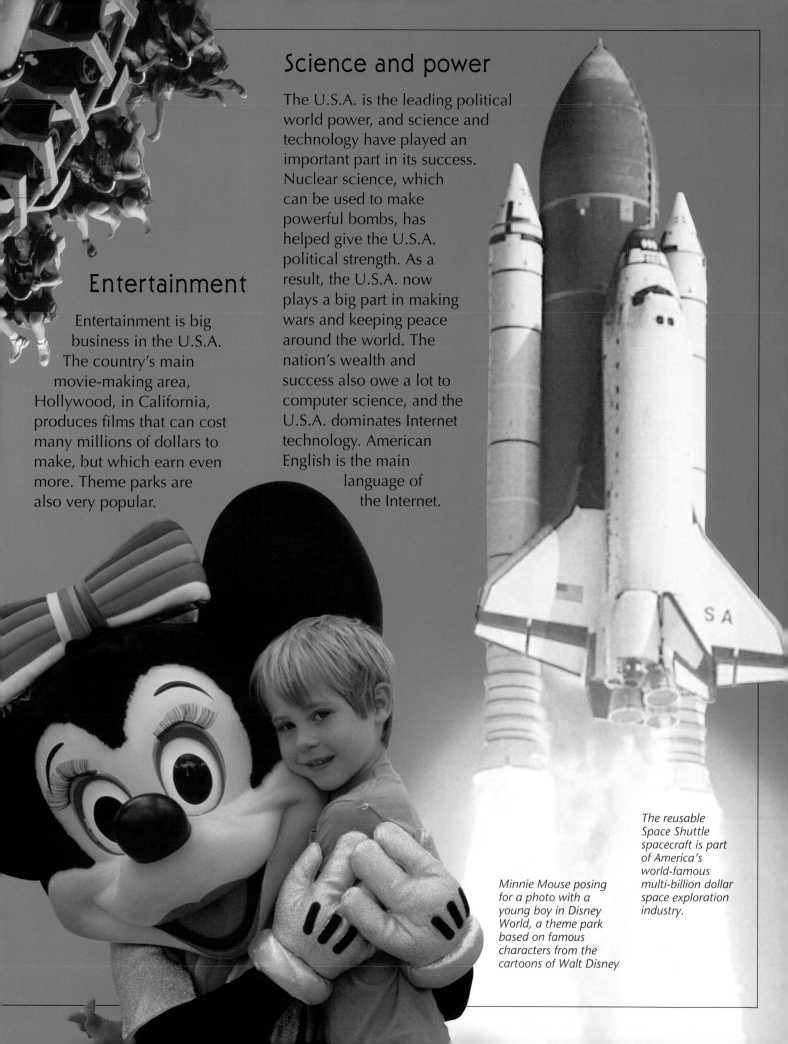

Entertainment

Entertainment is big business in the U.S.A. The country's main movie-making area, Hollywood, in California, produces films that can cost many millions of dollars to make, but which earn even more. Theme parks are also very popular.

Science and power

The U.S.A. is the leading political world power, and science and technology have played an important part in its success. Nuclear science, which can be used to make powerful bombs, has helped give the U.S.A. political strength. As a result, the U.S.A. now plays a big part in making wars and keeping peace around the world. The nation's wealth and success also owe a lot to computer science, and the U.S.A. dominates Internet technology. American English is the main language of the Internet.

Minnie Mouse posing for a photo with a young boy in Disney World, a theme park based on famous characters from the cartoons of Walt Disney

The reusable Space Shuttle spacecraft is part of America's world-famous multi-billion dollar space exploration industry.

THE FAR NORTH

The far north of North America is taken up by Greenland, Canada and Alaska (part of the U.S.A.). This is a vast area: Canada is the second largest country in the world, and Greenland is the world's biggest island.

In Canada, people ski in resorts where there are ski lifts and other facilities, but people also ski cross country just to get from place to place.

Many cultures

Canada is divided into ten provinces and three territories: the Yukon, Nunavut and the Northwest Territories.

Many Canadians have British, French or Native American ancestors and the offical languages are English and French. French culture is strong in the province of Quebec where cafes and shops reflect its influence.

Skiers swoop down a slope in Banff National Park, Alberta, Canada. Many tourists visit Canada for its natural beauty and outdoor activities.

Natural resources

Most Canadians live in large cities along the border with the U.S.A. The rest of the country has a varied landscape, including lakes, mountains, forests and grasslands, or prairies. These provide rich natural resources such as timber, water power, gas, oil and minerals. Outside the cities, many people's jobs are based around mining and forestry.

Winter sports

Outdoor sports and activities such as canoeing, riding horses and rafting are popular in Canada. But the country is particularly known for its winter sports, especially ice hockey which can be played on frozen ponds and lakes.

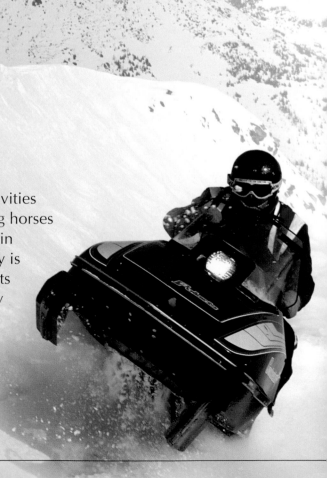

Snowmobiling at a winter sports festival in Canada

Greenland

Although Greenland is the world's largest island, its population is very small because conditions there are so harsh. Most of Greenland lies within the Arctic Circle, and its central region is covered by a layer of ice that never melts.

The island has a small road network, but planes and dog sleds provide a flexible and reliable way of getting around. The majority of Greenlanders live along the coast, where the climate is mildest, making a living from catching fish, shrimps and seals.

Inuit people

The Inuit are the native people of northern Canada. In 1999, the Canadian government made part of the Northwest Territories into a new Inuit territory, giving back land which the Inuit had lost to settlers. The new territory is called Nunavut, which means "our land" in Inuktitut, the Inuit language.

The Inuit keep their traditions alive by speaking Inuktitut, hunting for food, and making wood and bone carvings. They also take advantage of modern technology, using snowmobiles, telephones and computers.

Villages in Greenland are small. This one has about 500 human residents and 2,000 sled dogs, which are used for hunting and transportation.

These Inuit people are wearing heavy animal-skin coats to keep warm.

Internet links

Website 1 Discover more about Nunavut and Inuit history and culture then listen to some words in Inuktitut.

Website 2 See the varied landscape of Canada by exploring a clickable map.

For links to these websites, go to **www.usborne-quicklinks.com**

MEXICO

Mexico is a big country between the U.S.A. and Central America. It is very mountainous, but most Mexicans live in towns and cities in the middle of the country, where the land is flat.

A reconstruction of the Aztec calendar, on display in the National Museum of Anthropology in Mexico City

The Aztecs

From the early-14th century, Mexico was ruled by the Aztecs, a Native American people. They built an empire with a capital city called Tenochtitlan and ruled over many Native American peoples. The empire ended when the Spanish conquered Mexico in 1521. Today's Mexicans are mainly *mestizos*, of mixed Spanish and Native American descent.

Hot and spicy

Mexican food is popular all over the world. *Guacamole* (mashed avocados), *tortillas* (flat bread), and meat and beans cooked in tomato sauce with hot chillies* are typical Mexican dishes. Over 60 different kinds of chillies are grown in Mexico. In some areas, people eat salads made out of cactus plants.

Corn tortilla chips are eaten with Mexican-style dips around the world.

Mexico City

Mexico City, the capital of Mexico, was built directly over the ruins of the Aztec capital. Today, it is one of the world's biggest cities, with around 18 million people. The majority of the country's business is there, and the city is extremely busy, with lots of noise and traffic. It lies in a valley overlooked by volcanoes, and is regularly affected by earthquakes. The soil beneath it is so soft and swampy that the city sinks a little each year.

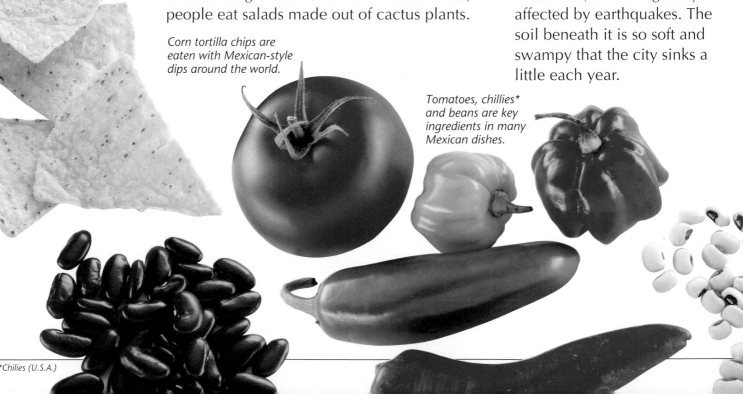

Tomatoes, chillies and beans are key ingredients in many Mexican dishes.*

*Chilies (U.S.A.)

Day of the Dead

The Day of the Dead is a joyous celebration that takes place on November 2 each year. All over Mexico, markets and shops sell skeletons and skulls made out of sugar or bread. People also dress up as skeletons and dance in huge parades. At home, families make small altars which they use to pray for and remember their dead friends and relatives. They decorate the altars with flowers, candles, food and photographs of those they want to remember.

Internet links

Website 1 Find out about the history of the Day of the Dead festival, see what items traditionally make up the altars and discover how to bake the "bread of the dead".

Website 2 Discover more about the religion, culture and everyday life of the ancient Aztecs.

For links to these websites, go to **www.usborne-quicklinks.com**

This skeleton model has been made from papier-mâché for a Day of the Dead parade.

CENTRAL AMERICA

C entral America is the narrow strip of land, or isthmus, connecting North and South America. The landscape of Central America is mainly made up of mountains and volcanoes and people's lives are affected by frequent earthquakes and volcanic eruptions.

These girls are dressed as angels to take part in a religious procession in El Salvador. Religious festivals are common in Central America.

Takeover

The Spanish arrived in Central America 500 years ago, and many people living there today are of mixed Spanish and Native American descent. But each country has its own mix of peoples. As well as Native Americans and people of European descent, there are people of African descent along the Caribbean coast.

Land of the Maya

The Maya had a powerful empire around AD200–900, when they built great cities. The empire covered most of Guatemala, and parts of Belize, Mexico, Honduras and El Salvador. Ruined cities can still be found in the jungles of Guatemala. The Maya are no longer powerful, but they still make up nearly half of Guatemala's population.

This Mayan girl in Guatemala is carrying a younger child on her back, wrapped in a traditional Mayan shawl.

Internet links

Website 1 Learn how to make a worry doll and find games played by children in Central America.

Website 2 Embark on a Mayan adventure, exploring ancient sites and carrying out

experiments. There's a log book where you can record details of your journey and find pictures to look at along the way.

For links to these websites, go to **www.usborne-quicklinks.com**

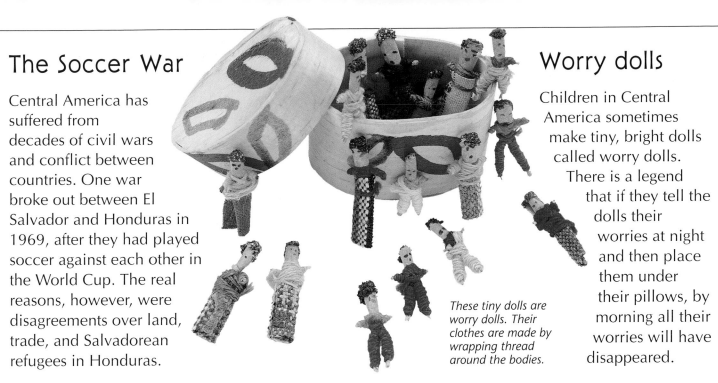

The Soccer War

Central America has suffered from decades of civil wars and conflict between countries. One war broke out between El Salvador and Honduras in 1969, after they had played soccer against each other in the World Cup. The real reasons, however, were disagreements over land, trade, and Salvadorean refugees in Honduras.

Worry dolls

Children in Central America sometimes make tiny, bright dolls called worry dolls. There is a legend that if they tell the dolls their worries at night and then place them under their pillows, by morning all their worries will have disappeared.

These tiny dolls are worry dolls. Their clothes are made by wrapping thread around the bodies.

The Panama Canal

The Panama Canal is one of the most important waterways in the world. It is a channel of water around 65km (40 miles) long that cuts through Panama, linking the Atlantic Ocean with the Pacific Ocean. Each vessel that uses the canal must pay a fee according to its weight. This means that while ships pay thousands of dollars, Richard Halliburton, who swam through the canal in 1928, only paid 36 cents.

A thatched bohio, or hut, in a rainforest clearing in Panama. Huts like these are the homes of the Guaymi people, who live on the border between Panama and Costa Rica.

Rainforest life

A large area of Central America is covered by rainforest, which is home to a huge variety of plants and animals. But the rainforest is being devastated and many plants and animals may die out as trees are cut down to make timber for export, and to clear land for farming.

THE CARIBBEAN

A rich variety of fruit is grown on the tropical islands of the Caribbean.

Pineapple

The Caribbean is the name given to the chain of hundreds of tropical islands stretching from North America to South America across the Caribbean Sea.

Plantains are green fruits which belong to the same family as bananas.

Slavery

From around 1500, Europeans fought with each other over possession of the Caribbean islands. They brought slaves from Africa, the Middle East, the Far East and India to work on sugar, tobacco and cocoa plantations. Many of today's inhabitants are descendants of these slaves. Languages from around the world have combined to form unique regional dialects known as *creoles*.

Mango

Papaya

Tourism

The Caribbean islands are known for their white sandy beaches, clear blue sea and tropical sunshine. Their beauty and isolation has given them a reputation of being a "paradise on earth". As a result, tourism is one of the Caribbean's most important industries.

Tourists often go diving in the clear blue sea of the Caribbean. This boy is looking at a shell he has found while diving at Virgin Gorda, in the British Virgin Islands.

Hard work

Although the Caribbean may be seen as a paradise by people who go there as tourists, life is not always easy for its inhabitants. Many of those who do not work in the tourist industry make a living growing sugar cane, the Caribbean's main export, and other crops such as bananas, coffee and tobacco. Some of the poorest countries, such as Haiti, suffer from severe unemployment. Many Haitians have to cross the border into the wealthier Dominican Republic to find work.

Music

Africa has had an important influence on the music of the Caribbean. Many Caribbean musical styles, such as reggae, conga, cha-cha-cha, plena and calypso, have African roots. Calypso, which originated in Trinidad, is the music style most associated with the Caribbean. Calypso songs are often improvised and tend to focus on social and political subjects.

Street parties

Carnivals held to mark religious festivals are an important part of island life. The main carnival season takes place before Lent (the period of 40 days leading up to Easter in the Christian calendar). The streets are filled with parades, loud music, and people singing and dancing in bright costumes.

Junkanoo is a huge festival in the Bahamas. People make flamboyant costumes like this to take part in parades.

Internet links

Travel to the islands of the Caribbean and discover more about the people, animals, climate and geography, with fun online activities.

For a link to this website, go to
www.usborne-quicklinks.com

A busy outdoor market in Zumbahua, Ecuador

PEOPLES OF
SOUTH AMERICA

SOUTH AMERICA

The people of South America have a huge range of origins. Over the centuries, settlers have arrived from Europe, Africa and Asia to join the Native Americans who have lived there for thousands of years.

A pair condors flying high in the Andes, the mountain range that runs most of the length of South America

Empty and crowded

Much of South America is covered in rainforest, mountains and deserts where it can be hard to survive. Many people live in small villages and work as farmers. Yet along the coast are some of the world's biggest cities, with towering skyscrapers and crowded shanty towns.

Internet links

Website 1 Find out about the lifestyles of modern Inca people.

Website 2 Look at the influences of the past that have shaped Latin America's culture and landscapes of today.

Website 3 See amazing pictures of the Inca ruins at Machu Picchu.

For links to these websites, go to **www.usborne-quicklinks.com**

The Inca people had a powerful empire in South America around 500 years ago. This watchtower is part of Inca ruins at Machu Picchu, in the Andes mountains.

Native Americans

Experts think the first South Americans came from Asia. They probably walked across a strip of land in the north that once joined what are now Russia and Alaska. Their descendants now live mostly in South America's mountainous countries, such as Colombia, Bolivia, Ecuador and Peru.

Religions

Over 90% of the people in South America are Roman Catholics. This form of Christianity was introduced by Spanish and Portuguese invaders who took control of the continent in the 1500s.

Many South Americans also worship traditional Native American or African gods and spirits. Some traditional religions have priests called shamans, who are believed to have magical powers.

Latin languages

South America is sometimes called Latin America, because most South Americans speak the Latin-based languages Spanish and Portuguese. These were brought by the European invaders. However, many people speak Native American languages, such as Quechua and Aymara.

Christian festivals are important to many South Americans. This Brazilian pilgrim is carrying a cross in an Easter procession in Jerusalem.

IN THE MOUNTAINS

The vast Andes mountain range snakes down the western side of South America, through Colombia, Ecuador, Peru, Bolivia, Chile and Argentina. Despite dangers from volcanoes and earthquakes, the Andes are home to millions of miners, farmers, craftspeople and city-dwellers.

This young boy from Ecuador is harnessing a llama to lead it to market.

Fertile farms

The peaks of the Andes are covered in snow, but the lower slopes are good for growing crops. Mountain farmers grow corn, coffee and other crops on small plots of land, sometimes with terraces to stop the soil from being washed away. If the land is not good enough for crops, they keep herds of mountain animals, such as llamas and alpacas, which provide milk and wool, and which may also be used to transport goods.

Craft work

Many Native Americans live in villages in the Andes. Some earn a living from traditional crafts. They weave brightly striped shawls, blankets and hats. These are used by local people as well as being sold to tourists and exported around the world.

A traditional mountain folk band playing for tourists in Machu Picchu, Peru

Internet links

Take an interactive tour through the Andes, starting at the southern tip of South America, see Peru's most famous sites or go on a virtual dig of the Inca Empire.

For links to these websites, go to
www.usborne-quicklinks.com

This is a view over La Paz, Bolivia. At over 3,650m (12,000ft), it is the world's highest capital city.

Cities

The Andes has some large cities, including Colombia's capital, Bogota, and La Paz, one of Bolivia's two capitals (the other is Sucre). Most city-dwellers work in factories or mines. In the mountains there are huge deposits of gold, copper, tin, coal and jewels, especially emeralds. The biggest emerald mines are in Muzo, Colombia. While mine workers use modern machinery to extract the emeralds, poor *Guaqueros* (or "treasure hunters") sift through the dust and rubble, hoping to find leftover gems.

Inca influence

The Tahuantinsuyo, also known as the Incas, once ruled a large area of western South America. Their reign ended 400 years ago, but they still influence the Andean countries today.

Quechua, the Inca language, is spoken by about 13 million people. Mountain farmers use terraces that were built by the Incas, and ruined Inca cities, such as Machu Picchu in Peru, are tourist attractions.

This Peruvian girl in traditional costume is one of the Quechua people, who are descended from the Incas.

RAINFOREST PEOPLES

South America's huge Amazon valley is covered in millions of square miles of thick, humid rainforest. The Amazon rainforest is so big that it contains over a third of the world's trees. For thousands of years, it has also been the home of Native American peoples.

Leaders of the Kayapo people of Brazil sometimes wear lip-plates like this which emphasize their roles as public speakers.

Traditional lives

The rainforest is so vast that groups of people living in it have been cut off from the rest of the world for centuries. Some have only recently been discovered by outsiders. There may be others who have never had contact with the outside world. Rainforest peoples such as the Jivaro, Txikao and Kayapo have their own languages and customs. But many of them share similar lifestyles, surviving by hunting animals, gathering fruits and nuts, and growing crops in forest clearings.

Losing lifestyles

As new roads are built into the rainforest, the people who live there have more contact with outsiders. They may even lose their homes when parts of the rainforest are cut down. To make a living, they may have to learn more widely spoken languages or move away from the forest into towns and cities, leaving their old traditions and lifestyles behind.

Internet links

Website 1 Discover the unique lifestyles and cultures of some of the peoples of the Venezuelan Amazon.

Website 2 Explore the Amazon rainforest and play an interactive game where you try to run an ecotourism project.

For links to these websites, go to
www.usborne-quicklinks.com

This man playing a wooden flute is one of the Jivaro people of the Amazon.

Clearing the forest

Rainforest trees provide all kinds of useful products, such as brazil nuts, cashew nuts, wax and rubber. At one time these things were simply collected from the forest, but now they are mostly farmed on plantations.

Traditionally, rainforest peoples cleared small areas of land to grow crops, and moved on after a few years. Because the cleared areas were tiny, this method, called shifting agriculture, did not harm much of the forest, and the trees eventually grew back. But since the 1960s, more rainforest has been cut down, for timber and to make space for farms, mines and factories. So the amount of rainforest is decreasing.

These are rainforest plants in Ecuador. Many rainforest plants can be used to make medicines.

Forest food

Although most rainforest peoples grow crops, they can also find food in the rainforest. Hunting and fishing provide them with a wide range of meat, including monkeys, toucans and caimans, which are reptiles similar to alligators. The Piaroa people of Venezuela sometimes eat tarantulas (a type of spider), cooking them by squeezing their insides onto a leaf and baking it over a fire.

Many rainforest peoples grow just enough food to supply their village. This woman is processing locally-grown manioc (a plant a little like a potato) to make flour.

COMBINED CULTURES

South American culture is influenced by the traditions of the different types of people who live there. For example, many South Americans love soccer, which came from Europe; samba music from Africa; and foods that combine Spanish, African and Native American influences.

Party!

Carnivals and costume parades take place frequently all over South America. Most of them celebrate Christian festivals, such as Lent, Easter and Christmas. They are lively occasions, with plenty of loud music, dancing, dressing up, eating and drinking. Many cities, towns and villages also hold their own local religious or historical celebrations.

Delicious dishes

All kinds of foods are eaten in South America. Argentinians and Uruguayans eat lots of meat, and Bolivians have dozens of varieties of potatoes. A typical meal in the Andes consists of fried beef, beans, a fried egg, rice and a slice of avocado. This type of dish is called *churrasco* in Ecuador and *bandeja paisa* in Colombia. Local delicacies include *cuy* (guinea pig) and *hormiga culona* (fried ants) in Colombia, and iguana (a type of lizard) in Guyana.

This Peruvian woman is preparing guinea pigs for roasting.

These costumed dancers are taking part in a parade in Venezuela, held to mark the Catholic feast of Corpus Christi.

Soccer fever

Soccer is the biggest sport in South America, and national team members are heroes. Uruguay hosted and won the first ever soccer World Cup in 1930 and Argentina and Brazil have since won it several times. Children play soccer in the streets all over South America. Most towns and villages have local teams, and even rainforest-dwellers have a patch of land set aside for soccer games.

Internet links

Listen to South American music and find out about South American teams preparing for the FIFA World Cup.

For links to these websites, go to
www.usborne-quicklinks.com

These children are playing informal games of soccer by an old fort at Sacsahuaman, near Cusco in Peru.

African influence

Culture along the east coast of South America has a strong African element. People from West Africa arrived as slaves hundreds of years ago, to work in mines and on sugar plantations for the area's European rulers. Their beliefs, music and culture had an important influence, which is still present today. African rhythms blended with Spanish, Portuguese and Native American sounds to produce musical styles such as samba and salsa. Many Brazilians follow a spiritual religion called Candomblé, which is based on African traditions.

This dancer represents the God of Medicine in the Candomblé religion.

BRAZIL

Brazil is the biggest country in South America. It contains most of the Amazon rainforest and also has some of the world's largest cities. In many ways it is a very modern country, with futuristic buildings and high-tech industries, but a lot of its people are still poor.

This 30m (100ft) high statue of Christ stands on Corcovado Hill above Rio de Janeiro. Its shape can be seen from far out at sea.

Portugal and Brazil

Unlike the rest of South America, Brazil was once ruled by Portugal, and its main language is Portuguese. This happened because just before 1500, news reached Europe that the Spanish had discovered lands not previously known to Europeans, which they called the "New World". Portugal wanted some of the land for itself, so the two countries agreed that Portugal could take over the eastern side of the continent. Brazil has been independent from Portugal since 1822.

Carnaval

Brazil is famous for its festivals, music and nightclubs. The most famous event is Carnaval (the Brazilian spelling of "carnival"). Carnaval celebrations are held all over Brazil every February or March, to mark the start of Lent.

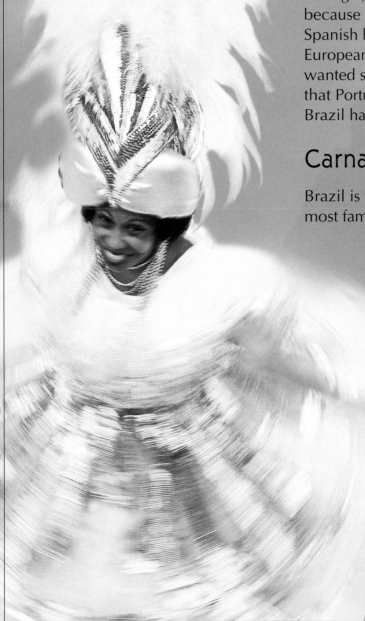

The celebrations go on for five days, with feasting, dancing, a huge costume parade and samba competitions. Samba is a type of percussion music popular in Brazil. There are special samba schools where people can learn samba music and dancing.

A samba dancer twirls at Rio's famous Carnaval.

A new capital

In 1956 the Brazilian government began to build a new capital city, Brasilia. Brasilia was planned as a modern, hi-tech city and it is still known for its space-age buildings. It was designed to be fast and easy to drive around, so it had no traffic lights. But when people moved in, they complained that it was too hard to cross the roads, so the design was changed.

Internet links

Find out more about the history, culture and geography of Brazil, and see a slide show of some famous Brazilian sites.

For a link to this website, go to
www.usborne-quicklinks.com

This is the Metropolitan Cathedral in Brasilia. It is a good example of the city's modern architecture.

Cities out of control

The populations of many of Brazil's cities, such as Sao Paulo and Rio de Janeiro, are rising fast as more and more people from rural areas arrive, looking for jobs and homes.

Often there is not enough housing for the new arrivals, and so shanty towns develop on the outskirts of cities. These are made up of makeshift houses built out of scrap metal and junk. The shanty towns are nicknamed *favelas* after a type of hillside flower.

Shanty towns, like this one in Sao Paulo, often develop on hillsides, where the land is too steep to build bigger houses.

ARGENTINA

Argentina is the second biggest country in South America. It ranges from lakes and glaciers in the south, across flat grasslands, known as the Pampas, to mountains in the west and rainforest in the north. However, more than a third of the population lives in or around the capital city, Buenos Aires.

This is the Avenida 9 de Julio, Buenos Aires. It is the widest street in the world.

Invaders

The first people to live in Argentina were Native American groups who farmed the land. But then in 1516 a Spanish explorer named Juan de Solis arrived and claimed the land for the Spanish. The Spanish named the country Argentina, which means "Land of Silver", and ruled there until 1810.

This is La Boca, a district in Buenos Aires made up of brightly painted metal houses.

Buenos Aires

Around 12 million people live in Buenos Aires, making it one of the largest cities in the world. It is also Argentina's main port, and its inhabitants are known as *porteños*, or port people.

Buenos Aires is sometimes called the "Paris of South America", as its architecture is very European. In the 19th and 20th centuries people from all over Europe moved to Argentina, and most settled in Buenos Aires. Many of the immigrants lived together in districts called *barrios*. Today, you can still see these districts and each one has its own individual style and character.

Gauchos

Gauchos are Argentinian cowboys. The first gauchos lived in the 18th century and worked on the Pampas, taming wild horses and using them to catch cattle. Then, in the 1800s, Argentina's cattle industry began to develop. The Pampas were fenced into huge cattle ranches called *estancias* and gauchos became farmhands.

Internet links

Explore the mountains, beaches and parks of Patagonia then test your knowledge with a quiz, or take a tour of Argentina's famous sites.

For a link to this website, go to **www.usborne-quicklinks.com**

The tango

Argentina is famous for the dance and music known as the tango. It began in the mid-19th century in the poor immigrant areas of Buenos Aires, as a mixture of Italian, Spanish and African music. At first, people found the tango shocking because the dancers' bodies were very close together, but by the 1900s it had become a craze in fashionable European circles. The tango is still danced today in many parts of the world. Finland has more than 2,000 tango clubs.

Professional dancers perform the tango in a street in Argentina.

Patagonia

With 90% of Argentinians living in cities, much of the country is wilderness. Patagonia, in the south, is one of the least populated regions in the world. It is home to many kinds of animals, such as elephant seals and some of the world's rarest birds.

Two girls in front of their thatched house in Samoa

PEOPLES OF AUSTRALASIA AND OCEANIA

AUSTRALASIA AND OCEANIA

The definitions of what makes up Australasia and Oceania vary, but Australasia usually refers to Australia and New Zealand and Oceania to the three main groups of Pacific Islands: Melanesia, Micronesia and Polynesia.

Small populations

Australasia and Oceania are not very heavily populated. The Pacific islands, including Papua New Guinea, are home to around eight million people, 20 million people live in Australia and four million in New Zealand.

Land masses

Australia is more than three times the size of Greenland, the world's largest island. It is too large to be called an island, so it is usually described as a continent, or land mass. It is home to many unusual animals, such as kangaroos, wombats and koalas. There are thousands of tiny islands in the Pacific. Many have been formed by erupting volcanoes under the sea*.

Kangaroos belong to a group of animals called marsupials, most of which carry their young in pouches like this. Most marsupials live in Australasia and Oceania.

This tiny islet is part of the group of Pacific islands known as Micronesia.

This is part of a wooden pillar of Maori carvings. Traditionally, the Maoris often used carvings to record details of real events.

Europeans arrive

In 1606, a Dutchman named Willem Jantszoon became the first European in Australia. In 1642, his countryman Abel Tasman was the first European to see New Zealand.

An English explorer, James Cook, landed at Botany Bay, on the east coast of Australia in 1770. Eighteen years later the British established a colony there for prisoners. During the 19th century, many parts of the Pacific were colonized by European countries. Today, most Pacific nations have gained independence.

Internet links

Delve into the history of the Aborigines and Torres Strait Islanders and find out more about the European settlements in Australia in the early 19th century.

For a link to this website, go to **www.usborne-quicklinks.com**

This man from Papua New Guinea is holding the paddle of a traditional wooden canoe.

Early explorers

The first people to explore and inhabit Australasia and Oceania came originally from Southeast Asia. They include the Aborigines, who arrived in Australia between 40,000 and 60,000 years ago, the peoples who arrived on the Pacific islands about 7,000 years ago, and the Maoris, who arrived in New Zealand a little over 1,000 years ago.

AUSTRALIA

Australia is bordered by the Pacific Ocean on one side and the Indian Ocean on the other. It is almost as big as Europe, yet has less than 3% of the population Europe has. Most Australians live on the country's eastern and southeastern coasts.

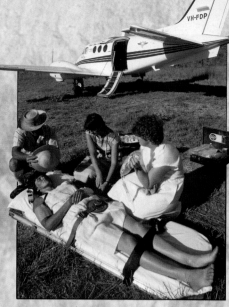

Many people in the outback live a long way from a hospital, so a medical service known as the Flying Doctors rescues sick people by plane.

Australia's people

For many thousands of years the Aborigines and Torres Strait islanders were the only inhabitants of Australia. British colonists arrived in Australia in the 18th century, and in the 1850s gold was discovered. This brought a rush of people from Europe, China and the U.S.A., all hoping to make their fortunes by mining. In 1901 Australia ceased to be a set of colonies and became a federation.

City life

Over 80% of Australia's population lives in cities and towns along the coast, as this is where jobs are to be found. Canberra is the capital, but Sydney is the biggest city. Around four million people, a fifth of Australia's total population, live there. The other major Australian cities are Melbourne, Perth, Brisbane, Adelaide, Hobart and Darwin.

The outback

The vast desert area in the middle of Australia, known as the outback, is one of the hottest, driest places in the world. The soil is too dry for crops, but farmers keep sheep and cattle on enormous farms called stations, which can have 15,000 sq km (5,800 sq miles) or more of land. With farms and towns so far apart, people living in the outback can lead isolated lives. Children often live so far from the nearest school that lessons have to be held via the Internet, or transmitted by TV or radio.

Sydney's opera house sits on the edge of Sydney Harbour. Its roof mirrors the shape of the boats that sail past.

The first Australians

When the Aboriginal peoples came to Australia, they spread gradually across the country in large, nomadic groups, hunting animals and gathering plants. Sometimes they settled for quite long periods in some places. They believed that the land and its wildlife were sacred. When Europeans arrived, they seized much of the land for themselves, destroying many Aboriginal sacred places.

Today, less than 2% of the Australian population is Aboriginal, and many no longer have a traditional lifestyle. They are just as likely to live in cities and have modern jobs. However, most Aboriginal peoples want to preserve their culture and, after years of campaigning, some traditional lands are now being returned to their original owners.

The coral reefs that make up the Great Barrier Reef support a huge variety of underwater life.

This Aboriginal man has painted his body and face as Aboriginal peoples have done for thousands of years. Body painting is a group activity and is usually done for special ceremonies.

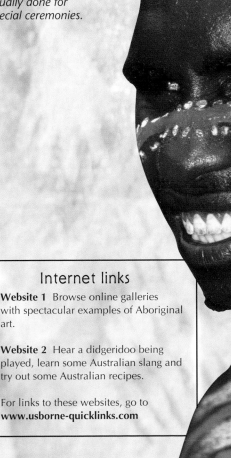

Sun, sea and sports

Australians enjoy their warm, sunny climate and spend a lot of time outdoors, playing sports, swimming, surfing and sailing. The climate and range of outdoor activities available also make Australia attractive as a tourist destination. Swimming and diving at Australia's Great Barrier Reef are especially popular, although scientists are concerned that too much tourism will damage the wildlife living around the reef.

Internet links

Website 1 Browse online galleries with spectacular examples of Aboriginal art.

Website 2 Hear a didgeridoo being played, learn some Australian slang and try out some Australian recipes.

For links to these websites, go to **www.usborne-quicklinks.com**

NEW ZEALAND

New Zealand lies in the South Pacific, about 1,500km (1,000 miles) southeast of Australia. The country is made up of two main islands, known as the North Island and the South Island, and several smaller ones. Much of New Zealand is wild and mountainous, and the country is sparsely populated, with fewer than four million people.

A young nation

New Zealand was one of the last places in the world to be inhabited. The first settlers, the Maoris, arrived just over 1,000 years ago, migrating from islands farther north. Europeans started to arrive in the late 18th century, and in 1840 New Zealand came under British rule. Today, it is an independent state. The majority of New Zealanders are still of British descent. The rest are mostly Maoris and South Sea islanders.

An experienced shearer can shear a sheep in just a few minutes. Wool is one of New Zealand's most important exports.

Important industries

Many New Zealanders make their living from farming. Over half the land is used for sheep farming and this is the country's biggest industry. Wool and lamb are major exports. Other exports include dairy products, wine, vegetables and fruit, such as oranges, lemons, grapefruits and kiwi fruit. New Zealand used to trade mainly with Britain, but today much of its trade is with Australia and Asian countries. Non-agricultural exports include wood and paper products, textiles and machinery.

This is a typical New Zealand sheep farm, stretching over a vast area.

These tourists are photographing a geyser spouting hot water in Waiotapua Thermal Park.

Clean and green

New Zealand does not use nuclear power, and has little heavy industry and relatively small towns and cities. As a result, it is one of the world's least polluted countries. Its beautiful scenery attracts many tourists. In the North Island, active volcanoes and spouting geysers can be seen, and in the South Island, there are spectacular mountains with huge glaciers.

Internet links

See traditional Maori instruments and listen to the sounds they make. You can also read about the legends behind the music and hear sound clips of some Maori songs.

For a link to this website, go to **www.usborne-quicklinks.com**

The Maoris

When they first arrived in New Zealand, the Maoris lived a traditional lifestyle. They hunted, fished and grew crops, and lived in small ethnic groups ruled by chiefs. Then in the 18th century, British colonists arrived. Battles raged over who owned the land and many Maoris were killed. Most of those that were left were forced to move to the new towns and cities.

This Maori man has tattoos known as Ta Moko on his face. He is carrying a club called a wahaika, to take part in a traditional dance.

Modern Maoris

Today, Maoris make up about 10% of the population of New Zealand and their culture is being re-established. The Maori language is taught in schools and traditional arts such as tattooing (*Ta Moko*) have been revived. But many Maoris are still campaigning for the return of lands they lost. Their name for New Zealand is *Aotearoa*, which means "land of the long white clouds".

PAPUA NEW GUINEA

N ew Guinea, the world's second largest island after Greenland, lies in the Pacific Ocean, to the north of Australia. Its western half, called Irian Jaya, is part of Indonesia*. Its eastern half, together with around 600 small islands, makes up the country of Papua New Guinea.

Internet links

Browse some photographs of masks from Papua New Guinea and see other kinds of art from different areas of the country.

For a link to this website, go to
www.usborne-quicklinks.com

Peoples of Papua

Most Papua New Guineans are of Papuan or Melanesian* origin, although there are also people of European, Polynesian* and Chinese origin. The first inhabitants migrated from Southeast Asia over 40,000 years ago. They lived in small groups and found food by hunting and gathering.

The country is dominated by mountains and thick rainforests. This has meant that groups often became isolated. Today, there are still hundreds of different ethnic groups living in Papua New Guinea.

Languages

Because there are so many separate groups, many different languages have developed in Papua New Guinea. There are more than 700 in total, a huge number of languages for a population of less than five million. The different groups communicate with each other in a language called Hiri Motu, or in pidgin English, which is a mixture of English and local languages. The official language is English, but in fact only 2% of the population can speak it.

This Waghi boy, from the eastern mountains of Papua New Guinea, is wearing a traditional feather headdress for a festival at his high school.

*Indonesia, 213; Melanesia, 196; Polynesia, 196

Village life

About a fifth of Papua New Guinea's people live in towns, where many have moved to find work. The rest still have a traditional lifestyle, similar to that of their ancestors. They live in villages, grow fruit and vegetables, catch fish and keep pigs and poultry. Some farmers sell their produce at local markets. Villagers eat a diet based on starchy crops such as sweet potatoes in the highland areas, and sago in the lowlands.

A father and son display their catch of fish for sale to passers-by.

These are men from a village called Asaro. They are wearing mud masks and their bodies are covered in mud too. Warriors of Asaro are said to have once dressed like this in order to win a battle, and villagers still sometimes dress like this today for tourists.

Art and life

The art of Papua New Guinea is a key part of local life, history and culture. Traditions vary from region to region and most forms of art have a practical or religious function.

In Malangan culture, people make wooden masks to commemorate a death. The people of Kambot carve wooden story boards showing incidents from village life. Around the Gulf Province, shield-like objects called gope boards are hung outside houses. They are said to contain protective spirits which ward off sickness and evil. Many Papuan peoples also carve elaborate prows for canoes.

OCEANIA

Scattered over the vast Pacific Ocean are more than 20,000 islands, which are collectively known as Oceania. Some, such as New Guinea, are huge, but many are little more than specks in the ocean. Only a few thousand of the islands are inhabited.

This brightly-painted building is a Hindu temple in Nadi, Fiji.

Pacific peoples

The original inhabitants of the Pacific islands migrated from Southeast Asia about 7,000 years ago. They made long sea journeys and, over many generations, settled one group of islands after another. Later, in the 16th century, European explorers started to discover the Pacific islands. Colonists began to arrive, and by the 1800s many islands were under the control of other countries. Today, some Pacific islands are independent and others are still ruled by states such as the U.S.A., France and New Zealand.

Island groups

There are three main Pacific island groups: Melanesia, Polynesia and Micronesia. Polynesia means "many islands" and Micronesia means "small islands". Melanesia means "black islands"; it got its name because the people there tend to have darker skin than elsewhere in the Pacific.

These French Polynesian girls are wearing traditional flower garlands, known as leis.

Tourism

Some of the Pacific islands, such as those that make up Fiji, Tonga and Samoa, are among the most beautiful in the world. This, together with their tropical climate, makes them popular tourist destinations. Tourism brings money to the islands but too many tourists can also damage the environment.

Internet links

Website 1 Find out about the history, culture and lifestyles of the people of the Federated States of Micronesia.

Website 2 Browse photo galleries of the Pacific islands of Tonga, Fiji and Samoa.

For links to these websites, go to **www.usborne-quicklinks.com**

Huts cluster along the beach on Mana Island, one of the many islands that make up Fiji.

Island life

On more developed Pacific islands, many people live in urban areas and work in mining and tourism. However, traditional village life is still strong. Fishing is common, crops such as cassava, yams and sweet potatoes are grown and families often keep livestock – for example, chickens and pigs. On some islands, people live in large, extended families, and community and religious life is often important.

Testing weapons

Because of their remote locations, the Pacific islands have been used by a number of countries, including the U.K. and the U.S.A., for testing nuclear weapons. For example, in 1946, an atom bomb was detonated on Bikini, one of the Marshall Islands in Micronesia. Nuclear testing has damaged coral reefs, forced some islanders to move home and caused concern about the effects of radiation on local people's health.

This man is fishing by standing on a ledge jutting out just over the water and stabbing at fish with his spear.

Children carry balloons and flowers at the opening ceremony of a school in Hanoi, Vietnam

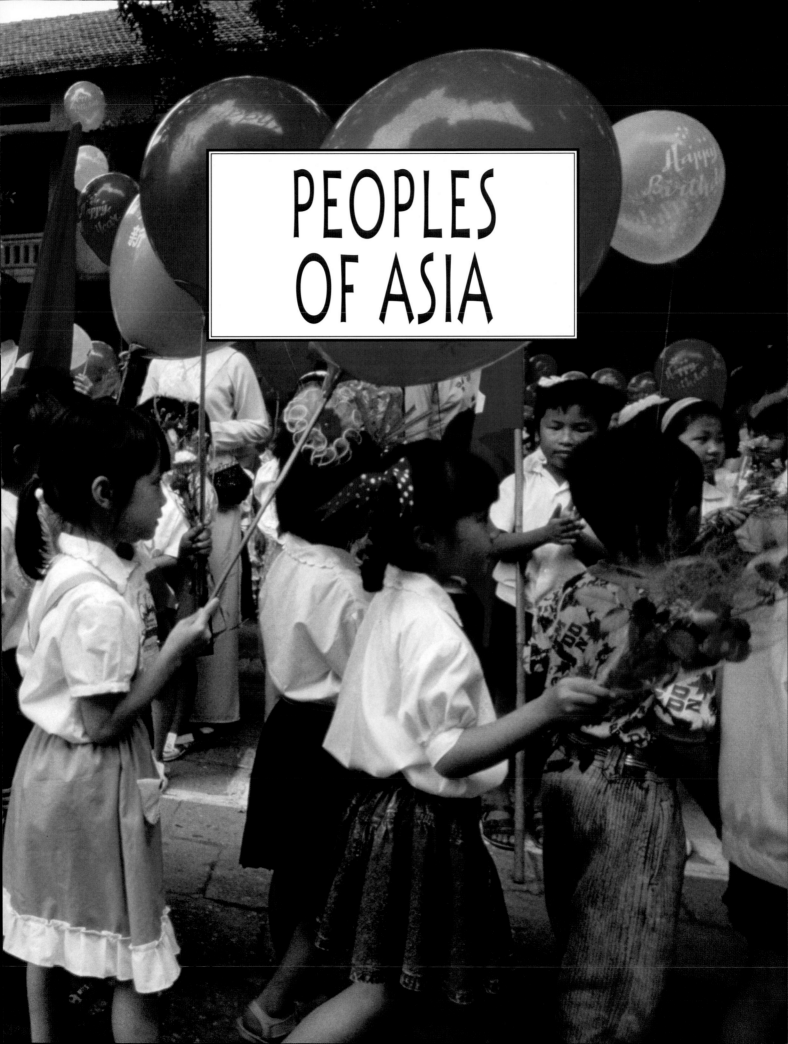

PEOPLES OF ASIA

ASIA

Asia is the world's biggest continent. It covers almost a third of the Earth's land surface, and over 60% of the world's people live there. Asian peoples are very diverse, with many different cultures, lifestyles, religions and political systems.

A farm worker picking tea leaves in Malaysia. Tea is an important crop in Asia.

New states

Since 1991, Asia has gained several new states, including Tajikistan, Kyrgyzstan and Kazakhstan. These were once part of the U.S.S.R. (Union of Soviet Socialist Republics), a huge country governed from Moscow. In 1991 the U.S.S.R. dissolved into a number of independent states, including Russia.

Fishing and farming

Asia has thousands and thousands of miles of coastline, especially in the southeast, where there are over 15,000 islands. Because of this, fishing is a vital source of food and work for millions of Asians.

The continent also has vast areas of fertile farmland, with millions of tiny farms where poor families grow food for their own use. But Asia also has large farms that export crops such as rice, rubber, tea and coffee.

Trade and industry

Asia is also home to some of the world's biggest banking, manufacturing and trading nations. Wealthy cities such as Hong Kong, Singapore, Tokyo and Dubai tower with gleaming skyscrapers.

Many of the things you own, especially clothes, computers, toys, phones and CDs, have probably been made in Asia. Millions of factory workers in countries such as China, Taiwan and Japan make goods to be exported and sold all over the world.

Trade is important for many Asian nations. Here you can see people trading in the stock exchange in Malaysia.

Internet links

Website 1 Read about some of the diverse countries of Asia.

Website 2 Find out the latest news in Asia and compare statistics on different Asian countries.

Website 3 Discover the importance of rice for the people of Asia, with fascinating facts and photographs.

For links to these websites, go to **www.usborne-quicklinks.com**

The Buddhist religion plays a central role in the lives of many people throughout Southeast Asia and boys are encouraged to spend some time as monks. These boys are young Buddhist monks.

A RANGE OF RELIGIONS

All the world's major religions started in Asia. The continent still has a wide range of religions and many of them, such as Christianity, Islam and Judaism, have also spread around the world. For billions of Asians, religious rituals are an essential everyday activity.

Holy places

Important holy sites are found all over Asia. They include places where prophets were born or died, places where religions began, and cities, mountains and rivers that are believed to be sacred. Millions of people from all over the world make religious journeys, or pilgrimages, to these sites every year.

Holy water

The Ganges River in northern India is sacred to Hindus, who make up more than 80% of India's population. Pilgrims visit the Ganges to purify themselves by bathing in its waters, and religious ceremonies are held on its banks.

These women are bathing at dawn in the Ganges River at Varanasi, India. Steps have been built there so pilgrims can get in and out of the water safely.

A trip to Mecca

All Muslims are expected to make a pilgrimage (or *Hajj*) to the holy city of Mecca, in Saudi Arabia, at least once in their lives. It is the birthplace of Mohammed, the prophet of Islam. When they arrive, the pilgrims walk around a shrine called the Ka'bah, which is said to have been built by the prophet Ibrahim.

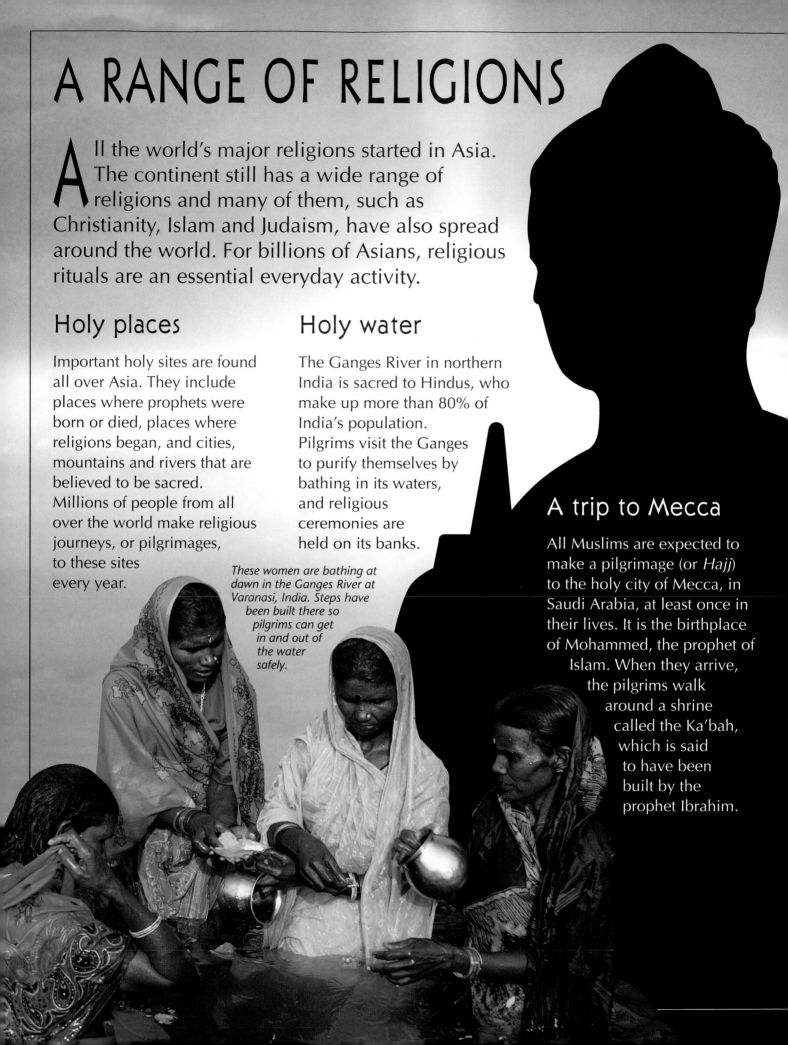

Jerusalem

Jerusalem, which is now the capital of Israel, is a holy city for Jews, Christians and Muslims. It contains the Western Wall, the remains of a Jewish temple, and the Dome of the Rock, a Muslim shrine marking the spot where the prophet Mohammed is said to have risen into heaven. Also, Jesus Christ, the central figure of Christianity, was crucified just outside the ancient city walls.

Internet links

Make your own virtual *Hajj* (pilgrimage) to Mecca and see amazing photographs of the customs and the rituals that pilgrims make on their journeys.

For a link to this website, go to
www.usborne-quicklinks.com

The silhouette in the background is part of the huge Borobudur Buddhist temple in Java, Indonesia.

Jewish pilgrims visit the Western Wall to mourn the destruction of their temple, and to insert prayers into cracks in the wall. In the background is the Dome of the Rock, part of a Muslim shrine.

Beautiful buildings

There are beautiful religious buildings all over Asia: Muslim mosques, Sikh gurdwaras, Christian churches, Hindu temples, and Buddhist pagodas. Many of these holy buildings have been created by the very best craftspeople, using expensive and gorgeous materials. Their impressive shapes often dominate cities' skylines.

Spiritual sounds

In Asia, many people take part in regular religious chanting, praying or singing. For example, Muslims are called to prayer five times a day, many Buddhists chant verses every day, and dancing and singing are an important part of Hindu ceremonies.

This man is calling Muslims to prayer. An official who does this is called a muezzin.

RUSSIA

Russia is the world's biggest country. It covers 11% of the Earth's land surface, is divided into 11 time zones and straddles two continents: Europe and Asia. It takes over a week to travel by train from St. Petersburg in the west to Vladivostok in the east.

City culture

Russia's cities are famous across the world for their art and culture. Moscow and St. Petersburg (which are both in European Russia) have dozens of beautiful museums and palaces. Russia is also home to world-famous orchestras and ballet companies such as Moscow's Bolshoi Ballet.

This is St. Basil's Cathedral, Moscow. The beautiful onion-shaped domes are characteristic of Russian church architecture.

These are matryoshka dolls, which open up into halves so that several dolls can fit one inside the other. The word matryoshka means mother in Russian.

Big changes

The independent country of Russia, officially known as the Russian Federation, has only existed since 1991. Before that, it belonged to the U.S.S.R. This was an even bigger country, created in 1917 when a Communist revolution overthrew the Russian czar, or king. For most of the 20th century, Communists ran the U.S.S.R.

Communism

Communism is a way of running a country. Under Communism, the state owns everything, including railways, roads, factories and houses, and it distributes things like food, money and medicine among the people. It is the opposite of Capitalism, in which people can own their own houses and run their own businesses. The government which ruled the U.S.S.R. from 1917 to 1991 was the world's best-known Communist system.

This girl is playing outside the tent where her family lives, in Chukchi, in the far northeast of Russia.

Size matters

Russia stretches 7,700km (4,800 miles) along the Arctic Circle. When it's bedtime in the west, people in the east are just waking up. People in different parts of the country have very different lifestyles, depending on the climate and landscape where they live, and the influence of nearby countries. In the north, Russia extends beyond the Arctic Circle, but few people live there because it's too cold. There is a central government in Moscow, but many regions have their own laws, parliaments and languages.

In some parts of Russia it can be extremely cold. These children live in the Kamchatka region where the average temperature is -40°C (-40°F).

New freedoms

Under Communism there were strict rules. Books and newspapers were tightly regulated, religion was suppressed and it was hard to leave the country. In 1991, the Communists were ousted and the U.S.S.R. broke up into 15 new countries. Many of the old rules were relaxed. However, the new freedoms also meant that crime increased. Many people are poorer than they were under Communism, because the state no longer looks after everyone.

Varied literature

Russian literature is well-known around the world. Russia's most famous writers include Dostoevsky, Tolstoy and Pushkin; they wrote realist novels. However Russia also has a rich tradition of magical folk tales and fairy tales, which have been passed down orally for centuries.

Internet links

Website 1 Take a virtual journey of Russia with a clickable map, travel through Russia's past and listen to common phrases in Russian.

Website 2 Travel back through Russia's remarkable history using an interactive timeline. You can find out about icon painting, the founding of Moscow, Ivan the Terrible and much more.

For links to these websites, go to **www.usborne-quicklinks.com**

THE MIDDLE EAST

The Middle East is famous for its beautiful old buildings and wealthy modern cities, and the hospitality of its peoples. It was where Sumer, the home of the first civilization, was; and it is the nucleus of the world's oil industry. It is sometimes seen as a trouble spot, because of the many wars and revolutions that have taken place there.

These are Marsh Arabs, a people from Iraq who live in houses built on floating platforms of reeds. They are loading mats made from reeds onto a truck.

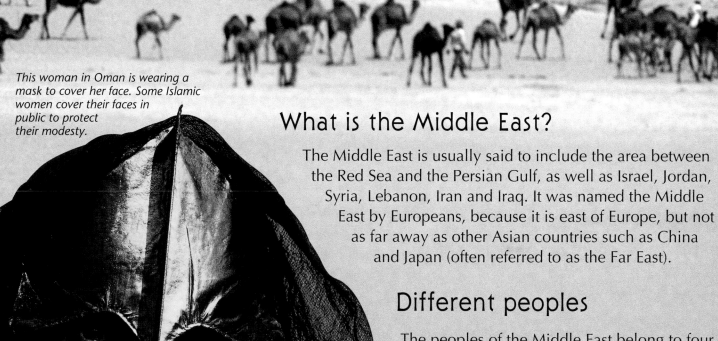

This woman in Oman is wearing a mask to cover her face. Some Islamic women cover their faces in public to protect their modesty.

What is the Middle East?

The Middle East is usually said to include the area between the Red Sea and the Persian Gulf, as well as Israel, Jordan, Syria, Lebanon, Iran and Iraq. It was named the Middle East by Europeans, because it is east of Europe, but not as far away as other Asian countries such as China and Japan (often referred to as the Far East).

Different peoples

The peoples of the Middle East belong to four main groups: Arabs, Persians, Turks and Jews. The area's Arabic countries (Bahrain, Saudi Arabia, Yemen, Oman, Qatar, Kuwait and United Arab Emirates) lie in and around the peninsula of Arabia. Their people are Muslims and speak Arabic languages. But Iran, once known as Persia, is not Arabic, and nor is Turkey, although they too are mainly Muslim. Israel is a Jewish state which was created in 1948. Many Arabs claim that Israel's land belongs to an Arabic people, the Palestinians.

Desert life

Stretching across the Middle East are vast deserts which contain important oil reserves. Few people live in these areas. However, some Bedouin herders still travel across the desert from one oasis to the next with their animals. They use either camels or four-wheel-drive vehicles to carry their tents and possessions.

Bedouin people are nomads who traditionally live in the desert. These Bedouins are leading a train of camels.

Ancient and modern

When oil was discovered in the Middle East, it made many nations rich. They were able to rebuild their cities with new apartments and skyscrapers, and to provide for new banks and businesses. But most cities still have old areas with narrow streets and traditional markets, called souks.

These huge towers in Kuwait are for water storage. Kuwait is a desert nation with no rivers or lakes, so sea water has to be processed to make it safe to drink, then stored.

Coffee and small talk

Coffee probably first came from Yemen, in southern Arabia, and it is still an important part of life in the Middle East. When Middle Eastern people have visitors, they usually offer them coffee, along with dates or pieces of cake called baklava. Then, even if there is something important to discuss, it is polite to make small talk over coffee before getting down to business.

This is the traditional Middle Eastern way of pouring coffee, holding the pot up high to create a long, fine flow.

Internet links

Find out more about the histories and languages of Middle Eastern peoples.

For a link to this website, go to **www.usborne-quicklinks.com**

CHINA

Nearly a quarter of the people on Earth are Chinese, and China is one of the world's oldest nations. It has existed for about 2,000 years, and had one of the earliest civilizations. The ancient Chinese invented paper, silk, gunpowder and seismology, the science of predicting earthquakes.

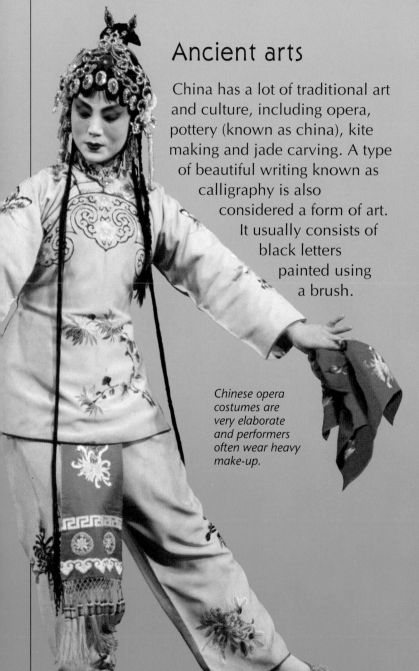

In Chinese cities people often use pedal power to get around. These children are riding in a wooden trailer on the back of a tricycle.

Ancient arts

China has a lot of traditional art and culture, including opera, pottery (known as china), kite making and jade carving. A type of beautiful writing known as calligraphy is also considered a form of art. It usually consists of black letters painted using a brush.

Chinese opera costumes are very elaborate and performers often wear heavy make-up.

Population explosion

In 1982, China became the first country to have over a billion people. It now has around 1.2 billion. It is hard for China to provide enough food, schools and doctors for all its people. Since the 1950s, the government has tried to slow down the population increase. Couples are encouraged to get married later in life, and to have only one child.

Farming nation

Even though China has a lot of big cities, nearly three-quarters of its people live in the countryside and survive by farming. Their main crops are rice, wheat and millet.

China is mountainous, and only about 10% of its land is fertile, so all the soil has to be used carefully. Terraces built into hillsides allow farmers to grow crops on steep slopes. Throughout China, farmland is irrigated, or watered, using systems of canals and streams.

Chinese beliefs

Many people in China follow Confucianism, a way of behaving based on the ideas of Confucius, who lived in the area 2,500 years ago. He taught that people should be polite and considerate and obey their elders.

The ancient Chinese worshipped their ancestors and various gods. These old beliefs are remembered at certain times of the year. For example, many families keep a picture of the kitchen god next to the kitchen stove. Just before the New Year, they take it down and smear honey and wine on the god's lips to keep him happy. When the New Year arrives, a new picture is put up.

This is a holder for burning incense sticks. Incense gives off a scent which is said to attract the attention of the gods.

New Year

The start of the Chinese year, which is usually in February, is marked with celebrations, including fireworks, parades and feasts. People decorate their homes with symbols of good fortune and unmarried people receive red envelopes containing money for good luck.

Internet links

Website 1 Get a Chinese name based on your name and personal characteristics.

Website 2 Take a photo tour of China and see a timeline of China's history.

For links to these websites, go to **www.usborne-quicklinks.com**

Spellings

Chinese writing uses symbols, or characters, to represent words. In other languages, Chinese words have to be written down as they sound. Recently these spellings have been changed to make them more consistent, so you might see different spellings in different books.

The Chinese characters on the right spell out the phrase "Peoples of the World".

The final day of Chinese New Year celebrations culminates in the Lantern Festival, where elaborate lanterns like this dragon lantern are carried along in a night-time procession.

*Chinese writing, 25; Communism, 102

INDIA AND PAKISTAN

India and Pakistan straddle the area where, around 4,500 years ago, a complex ancient society began in and around the Indus Valley. The two countries are now both modern states, but many of their people also follow ancient traditions and beliefs.

Pakistani truck, van and bus drivers are proud of their hand-decorated vehicles, like this truck covered in patterns and symbols.

Dividing into states

India and Pakistan used to be one country, which was ruled by Britain in the 19th century. Britain agreed to grant India its independence in 1947, but Hindus and Muslims wanted their own separate states. So the country was divided into two parts: Pakistan for the Muslims, and India for the more numerous Hindus. At first, Bangladesh was part of Pakistan, but it too became independent in 1971.

East and West

Britain's influence can be seen all over India and Pakistan. European-style buildings from the time of British rule stand among mosques and temples. Cricket, originally an English game, is an important sport in both India and Pakistan.

Indians and Pakistanis wear a mixture of European-style clothes and traditional dress, such as the *shalwar kameez* (baggy shirt and trousers) in Pakistan and the sari, a wrap-around gown, in India.

Women from Rajasthan, in India, carrying heavy loads on their heads

The building in the background is the Taj Mahal, near the city of Agra. It is an elaborate tomb built by a 17th-century Indian emperor, Shah Jahan, for his wife.

Film fanatics

India has the world's biggest film industry, based in Mumbai (Bombay) and known as "Bollywood". Bollywood films are usually love stories or historical dramas, with lots of songs and dance routines. The top film stars and singers are incredibly rich and famous.

Posters advertising Bollywood films.

Getting around

In crowded cities such as Lahore and Calcutta, the streets are full of buses, trams, taxis, rickshaws and bikes jostling for space with pedestrians and market stalls. In India, cows wander the streets as well. Hindus regard cows as sacred animals and no one is allowed to harm them, so they slow down the traffic as everyone tries to keep out of their way.

Internet links

Website 1 Take an interactive photo tour of India's regions.

Website 2 Find out how to wear a sari by following this step-by-step guide.

For links to these websites, go to **www.usborne-quicklinks.com**

A rickshaw is a kind of open-air taxi. Rickshaws can be motorized or driven by pedal power. When a pedal rickshaw comes to a hill, the passengers get out and push it.

Caste

In Indian tradition, most people are born with a *Jati*, or caste, an inherited status. In ancient India, it determined the job you did, and you could only marry someone from the same group. *Jati* is still important to many people and people of the same *Jati* support each other. But some of the old laws have been abolished, so that Indians from all levels of society can hold positions of power.

Curry craze

Spicy food from Pakistan and India is popular across the globe. Its name "curry" comes from *kari*, from the Tamil language of southern India. Curry is usually vegetables or meat with a sauce, eaten with rice or bread. Hindus avoid eating meat, so Indian food is often vegetarian.

SOUTHEAST ASIA

Southeast Asia stretches out into the sea to the south of China and Japan. The countries there, including Thailand, Vietnam, Laos, Malaysia and Indonesia, are spread out over a long peninsula and a series of hilly, forested islands.

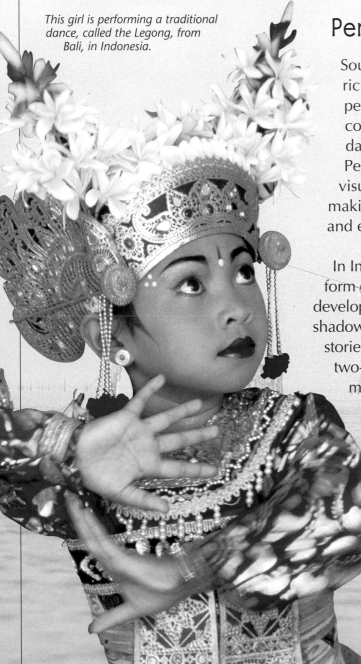

This girl is performing a traditional dance, called the Legong, from Bali, in Indonesia.

This is an Indonesian shadow puppet. It is moved using the rods attached to its arms and head.

Performing arts

Southeast Asia has a rich tradition of performing arts, often combining music, dance and drama. Performances are visually stunning, making use of masks and elaborate costumes.

In Indonesia, an unusual form of storytelling has developed which uses shadow puppets to tell the stories. The puppets are two-dimensional figures moved using rods. During a show, a light and a screen are placed behind them, so you can just see their silhouettes. A puppet's features reveal its character and status, so the audience is able to recognize key character types.

Temples and mosques

In Southeast Asia, many different religions exist side by side, usually peacefully. Some countries, such as Burma, are mainly Buddhist; others, such as Indonesia, are mainly Muslim; but other religions such as Christianity and Hinduism are also common. Temples, mosques and churches are found everywhere. There are also many ruined temples which have now been abandoned.

Internet links

Watch short video clips of shadow puppets in Bali, and slide shows about modern life in the Philippines and Vietnam.

For links to these websites, go to **www.usborne-quicklinks.com**

Nations in pieces

Malaysia, Indonesia and the Philippines stretch across a vast archipelago (a network of islands) southeast of the Asian mainland. Even within the same country, different islands can be very unlike each other.

For example, Bali, one of Indonesia's most populated islands, is small and crowded, with farms, towns and a big tourist industry. Its main religion is a type of Hinduism, and it has thousands of temples.

Irian Jaya, part of the much bigger island of New Guinea, is very remote, with thick forests. Most of its peoples live by farming, fishing and hunting. Some have converted to Christianity, while others worship the spirits of their ancestors.

On the marshy eastern coast of Sumatra in Indonesia, men and boys spend part of the year fishing from huts on tall stilts built up to 10km (6 miles) out at sea.

Rice and spice

Although Southeast Asia has some big cities, most of its people are farmers and live in the countryside. Rice is their main crop and it forms a part of almost every meal.

Thailand and Indonesia are famous for their spicy food. Spices are not a major crop now, but hundreds of years ago they made this part of the world rich. Merchants came from India, Arabia, Europe and China to buy cloves, mace and nutmeg, which were more valuable than gold.

Elephant work

On the Southeast Asian mainland, elephants are used to transport people and for moving heavy loads, such as logs. Sometimes they are also dressed up in glittery costumes for parades and special occasions.

In Laos (which was once known as the Land of a Million Elephants) and Thailand, each working elephant has its own trainer, or mahout. One mahout may spend his whole life caring for the same animal.

A mahout starts working with an elephant while it is still young. Over the years they build up a close relationship. These baby elephants are just starting to be trained.

BIG BUSINESS

Although many Asians are poor and live by farming, Asia is also home to some of the world's biggest banking, trading and manufacturing nations.

A farm worker in India gathers crocuses to collect saffron from them. Saffron is added to food and can be used as a yellow dye.

Trading history

Some of the reasons for the success of Asian cities are historical. Hong Kong, Singapore and Dubai are ancient ports on trading routes that have been used for centuries. The Chinese, in particular, have a long history of trading. They invented paper money in the 9th century.

New resources

As the population of Asia has risen, some countries have been unable to make enough money from traditional industries such as farming, so they have turned to business and services instead. For example, Japan has very little fertile land, but banking and manufacturing have allowed it to become rich without relying on its natural resources.

These are banknotes from Singapore. Singapore is one of Asia's "Four Tigers" – countries which became known for their fast-growing economies.

Money from oil

In some parts of Asia, especially the Middle East, a lot of wealth comes from selling oil. The money can then be lent to other businesses and used to build hotels, restaurants and new apartments. This type of financial service is provided by banks called merchant banks, which can become very rich in the process. In this way, these countries provide for when the oil runs out.

Ways of working

Some people suggest that business in Asia is successful because the culture places a positive emphasis on working hard, giving Asian peoples a strong "work ethic".

For example, many Japanese people have a strong work ethic, believing you should work long hours if necessary, and be loyal to your company. Singapore, meanwhile, is famous for its culture of honesty, making it a popular place for other countries to trade with.

Internet links

Website 1 Discover more about Petronas Towers, the world's tallest building.

Website 2 Explore the Middle East's past and its modern-day role as a major oil producer.

For links to these websites, go to **www.usborne-quicklinks.com**

This robot was developed by a Japanese electronics company. Japan is one of the world leaders in developing new technology.

Big buildings

Big businesses need big office blocks, and the money they make means they can afford to build new, expensive skyscrapers. Asian countries compete with each other to create the most amazing modern architecture and the tallest skyscrapers. The Petronas Towers building in Kuala Lumpur, Malaysia, is currently the tallest building in the world.

This is a view of Kuala Lumpur, in Malaysia. In the middle, you can see the impressive twin towers of the Petronas Towers building. They are 452m (1,483ft) high.

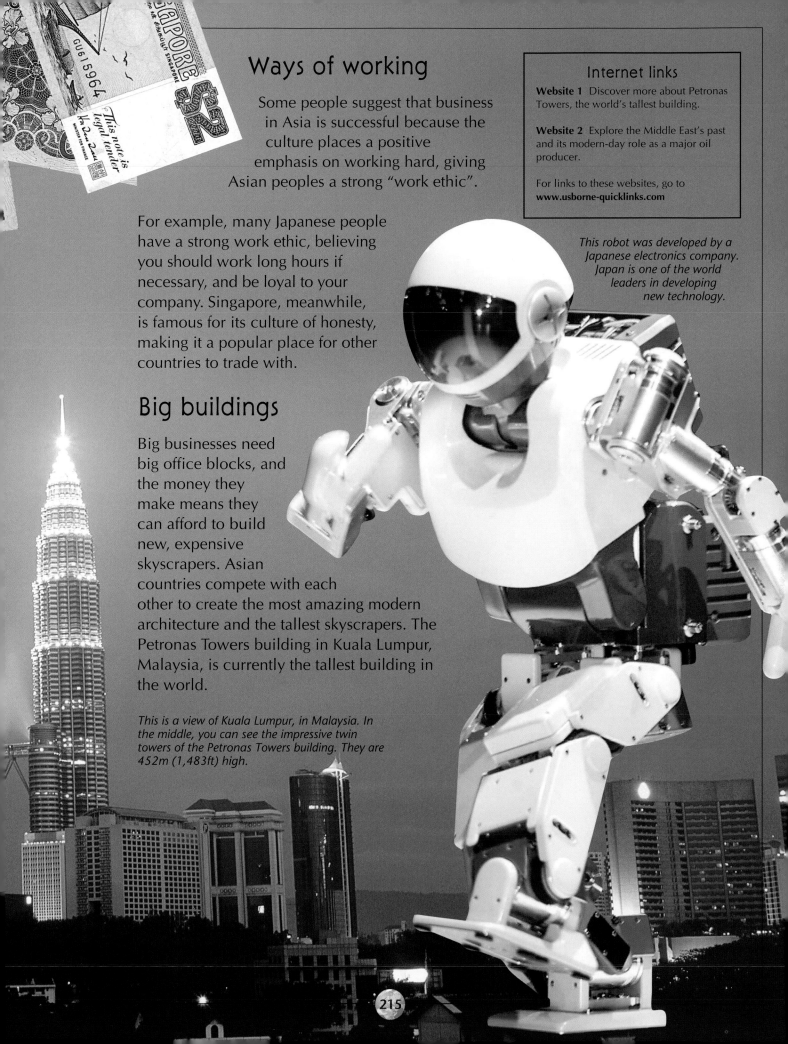

Masked partygoers at the Venice Carnival in Italy

PEOPLES OF EUROPE

This is a picture of St. John from a 12th century Christian manuscript.

EUROPE

Although Europe is the second smallest continent in the world, it contains over 40 countries, and its peoples speak more than 50 different languages. Throughout history there have been many migrations* within, to and from Europe.

Ancient Europe

For nearly six centuries, until around 1,500 years ago, the Romans ruled much of Europe. Today, there are similarities in law, language, architecture and education across the continent that date back to the Romans. You can still see the ruins of Roman towns throughout Europe. The Romans took many of their ideas from the Greeks, who had their own powerful empire and culture.

Christianity

Christianity has been the main religion in Europe since the days of the Roman Empire. Today, many Europeans do not go to church regularly, and many others follow different religions. Yet the influence of Christianity on art, architecture and culture can be seen all over Europe.

Internet links

See documentary footage of the Berlin Wall being erected, and read about the people who tried to cross it.

For a link to this website, go to **www.usborne-quicklinks.com**

---

*Migrations, 142; U.S.S.R., 204

People climbing on the Berlin Wall in 1989

European arts

Europe has produced many great artists, composers and writers. The ancient Greek poet Homer and the English playwright Shakespeare, composers like Bach, Mozart and Beethoven, and artists such as Michelangelo and Picasso are famous around the world. Europe also attracts millions of tourists every year to see its ancient ruins, beautiful architecture and fine art galleries.

Europe divided

After the Second World War, much of eastern Europe was under the control of the Communist U.S.S.R.* Political differences between the U.S.S.R. and the non-Communist west increased until Europe split in two. In 1961, East German authorities built a wall in the German city of Berlin to prevent people fleeing from east to west. The wall was guarded by armed soldiers. In 1989, protests against the lack of freedom led to the destruction of the Berlin Wall.

As well as having a great history of art, Europe still produces a wide range of art today. This is a modern sculpture, known as the "Angel of the North", in the north of England. Its huge steel structure is 20m (65ft) tall.

WESTERN EUROPE

In western Europe, most people live in cities or towns. City life can be fast and exciting and most western European cities have lots of stores, restaurants, cinemas, concert halls and museums. But many cities are also crowded and polluted.

Pasta is popular around the world, but it is particularly associated with Italy. Here are some of the different pasta shapes.

Food culture

The food of western Europe is extremely varied and many countries are known for particular foods or ways of eating. For example, Italy is known for pizzas and pasta, Germany for sausages, Greece for kebabs and France for breads and cheeses. Many Spanish bars serve small snacks called tapas with drinks. These foods are popular in other countries around the world, too.

Work in industry

Many western Europeans have jobs in manufacturing industries, designing and making products such as cars and clothes. However, as more factories use machines and computers to make their products, more people are getting jobs in service industries. These are jobs which involve doing things for other people. Hotel staff, bank managers and TV presenters are examples of service jobs.

Rural life

In a few parts of western Europe, farmers still use oxen to pull farm machinery, and harvest their crops by hand. But in most areas, only large, industrialized modern farms can survive, so smaller farms are disappearing.

The Mediterranean

The northern coast of the Mediterranean Sea forms the southern border of Europe. People who live there enjoy long, hot, dry summers, which make the Mediterranean area a popular tourist destination. Many of the people living around the coast work in the tourist industry.

Internet links

Website 1 See famous Italian sites, find out about Italy's key events in history and listen to everyday phrases in Italian.

Website 2 Discover the Spanish traditions of flamenco dancing and bullfighting, and find out more about Spanish fiestas and folklore.

Website 3 Read about the unusual cheese rolling festival held every year at Cooper's Hill in Gloucestershire, England, and see video clips of the event.

For links to these websites, go to **www.usborne-quicklinks.com**

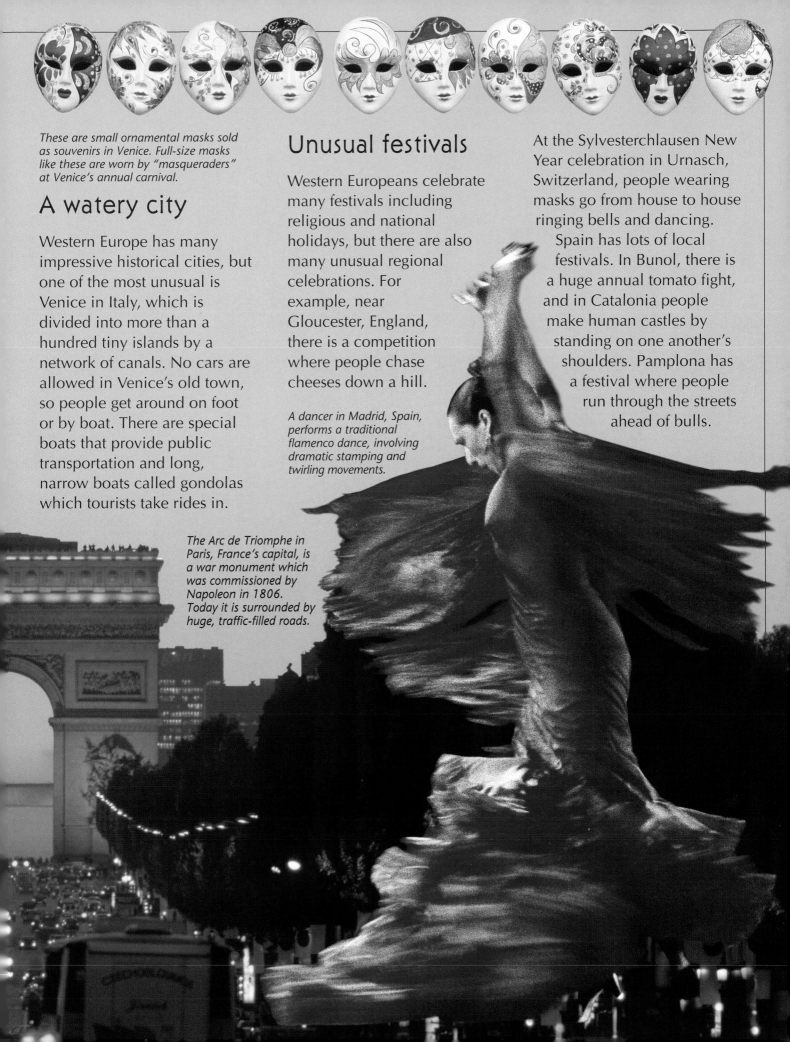

These are small ornamental masks sold as souvenirs in Venice. Full-size masks like these are worn by "masqueraders" at Venice's annual carnival.

A watery city

Western Europe has many impressive historical cities, but one of the most unusual is Venice in Italy, which is divided into more than a hundred tiny islands by a network of canals. No cars are allowed in Venice's old town, so people get around on foot or by boat. There are special boats that provide public transportation and long, narrow boats called gondolas which tourists take rides in.

The Arc de Triomphe in Paris, France's capital, is a war monument which was commissioned by Napoleon in 1806. Today it is surrounded by huge, traffic-filled roads.

Unusual festivals

Western Europeans celebrate many festivals including religious and national holidays, but there are also many unusual regional celebrations. For example, near Gloucester, England, there is a competition where people chase cheeses down a hill.

A dancer in Madrid, Spain, performs a traditional flamenco dance, involving dramatic stamping and twirling movements.

At the Sylvesterchlausen New Year celebration in Urnasch, Switzerland, people wearing masks go from house to house ringing bells and dancing. Spain has lots of local festivals. In Bunol, there is a huge annual tomato fight, and in Catalonia people make human castles by standing on one another's shoulders. Pamplona has a festival where people run through the streets ahead of bulls.

EASTERN EUROPE

Until the 1990s much of eastern Europe was ruled by the former Communist power the U.S.S.R.* But in the late 1980s and the 1990s, people rebelled against their Communist leaders, and today the area is a patchwork of independent states.

This is a corridor in a school near Chernobyl which was evacuated after a nuclear disaster.

Peoples at war

Over the centuries, eastern Europe has seen many wars. In recent years, fighting broke out when small ethnic groups demanded more freedom from the people who ruled over them. For example, Yugoslavia, now called Serbia and Montenegro, was once much bigger. It contained many peoples: Serbs, Bosnians, Croats, Slovenes, Montenegrins, Albanians and Macedonians. Since the Communist collapse in 1990, wars have raged in the area as ethnic groups have fought to set up their own states.

Pollution

Pollution is a big problem in eastern Europe. Many factories, set up under Communism, still use old-fashioned fuels and methods which allow toxic gases to escape. In 1986, an accident at a nuclear power station in Chernobyl, Ukraine, sent radioactive dust into the air, polluting large areas of Europe. Hundreds of people had to leave their villages and the radiation made many people ill.

Trade links

The collapse of the U.S.S.R. and Communism has led to an explosion of trade between eastern Europe and the rest of the world. As well as selling products such as wine and factory goods, eastern European countries have become major buyers of new technology such as computing systems and mobile phones.

This is a statue from Statue Park, in Hungary. The park contains Communist statues that once stood in public places.

*Communism, U.S.S.R., 204

Spa towns

Spas are springs containing minerals. During the 19th century, it became fashionable throughout Europe to drink and bathe in spa waters. Many resorts were developed to cater for visitors. There are numerous spas throughout eastern Europe which remain popular today, such as those in Budapest in Hungary, and Karlovy Vary and Marianske Lazne in the Czech Republic. People can still go to these places to drink the waters.

Internet links

Website 1 Discover the architectural diversity of Prague as you view these beautiful panoramic pictures.

Website 2 See photographs of the statues of former Communist leaders in Statue Park, Budapest.

For links to these websites, go to **www.usborne-quicklinks.com**

Old age record

Georgia has more people who live to be over 100 than any other country. Many Georgians suggest this is due to their outdoor lifestyle, gentle climate and fertile farmland. According to Georgian legend, when God created the Georgians, he didn't have any land left for them to live on. So he had to give them the piece of land he had saved for himself, which was the best in the world.

Architecture

Many cities of eastern Europe, such as Prague, Krakow and Budapest, have well-preserved old towns. These have winding cobbled streets and a wide variety of architecture, including impressive churches and castles. Some houses are made from wood and many larger houses have distinctive painted facades, or fronts. However, some cities, such as Warsaw in Poland, which had to be heavily rebuilt after the Second World War, are dominated by modern apartment buildings.

This modern building in Prague was designed by an architect named Frank Gehry. It is nicknamed "Ginger and Fred" after the dancers Ginger Rogers and Fred Astaire, because its shape looks a little like a dancing couple.

NORTHERN EUROPE

Denmark, Sweden, Norway and Finland form the area known as Scandinavia. Together with the volcanic island of Iceland, they make up northern Europe. There is very little poverty in Scandinavia and Iceland, and their clean cities and countryside are envied by many.

People bathing in the Blue Lagoon, a warm spring near Keflavik in Iceland

Land of the Midnight Sun

The northern part of Scandinavia juts far into the Arctic, the area around the North Pole. In midwinter, for about a month, the people who live there see no daylight at all, while from the end of May until the end of July the Sun never sets. Because of this, it is sometimes known as the Land of the Midnight Sun.

This hotel in Sweden is made entirely of ice. Every summer it melts and has to be rebuilt the following winter. Even the glasses people drink from are made of ice.

Skiing is a popular leisure activity in Scandinavia. In winter, it's also a way of getting to and from school and work.

Winter months

During the winter, much of northern Europe is covered in snow. In many places, skiing becomes the easiest way of getting around. Children often learn to ski as soon as they can walk, and some ski to school every morning. Many places hold annual ski competitions.

The environment

Many children and adults in Scandinavia belong to "green" groups that try to protect the environment by looking after the countryside and preventing pollution. Governments run recycling projects to collect reusable products from people's homes, and Scandinavia leads the way in building eco-friendly homes which use solar panels and insulation to save energy.

Lapland

Lapland, in the far north of Scandinavia, is one of the last areas of wilderness in Europe. It stretches from northern Russia across the north of Finland, and through parts of Sweden and Norway. It is home to the Sami, a people with their own language and culture. Some of the Sami still live a traditional lifestyle and herd reindeer. Their traditional homes are conical tents called *kota*. But these days most Sami live in houses, grouped together in small villages.

A Sami reindeer herder in northern Norway tends a newborn reindeer calf.

Internet links

Website 1 See more photographs of the amazing Ice Hotel in Sweden.

Website 2 Look at pictures of modern Sami people herding reindeer and read about their culture and traditions.

For links to these websites, go to **www.usborne-quicklinks.com**

Daring design

Scandinavia is famous for its exciting design styles. Scandinavian companies are renowned for making everyday objects, like chairs, tables and cars, that are simple to use yet beautiful to look at. The Scandinavian style is now copied all over the world.

A UNITING EUROPE

Most of Europe's countries belong to organizations such as the European Union and the Council of Europe, in which several states band together to support each other. Many Europeans feel this has major advantages, although others worry that countries may lose their individuality.

Representatives of E.U. states meet in Strasbourg, France.

What is the E.U.?

The E.U., or European Union, is the most important European organization. It dates from 1957, when Belgium, France, Italy, Germany, Luxembourg and the Netherlands formed the E.E.C. (European Economic Community) to improve trade and cooperation between their countries. The group changed over the years, and in 1993 it became known as the European Union. By the year 2000 it had 15 members, with more applying to join.

Internet links

Website 1 Find out how the European Union (E.U.) works, with online activities.

Website 2 Discover which countries are in the E.U. and find out more about how the E.U. works and what it does.

For links to these websites, go to **www.usborne-quicklinks.com**

Free trade

The E.U. has set up laws to allow its member states to trade with each other easily. The E.U. also has laws to regulate measuring systems and safety standards for its workers, and workers from any E.U. state can work in any other without a visa or work permit.

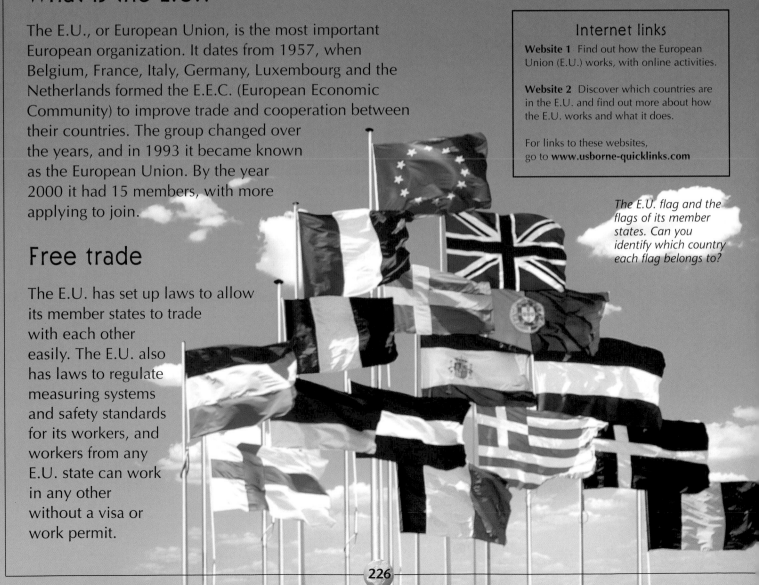

The E.U. flag and the flags of its member states. Can you identify which country each flag belongs to?

226

Single currency

In the 1990s, the European Union began to introduce a single currency called the Euro. Eventually it is intended to replace the national currencies of all the member states. However, some countries did not join the single currency immediately. It was launched on January 1, 1999, with 11 member states taking part.

These are 50-cent coins, part of the new Euro currency. There are 100 cents in one Euro.

The Council of Europe

The Council of Europe is not part of the E.U. It is a European organization that exists to protect human rights in Europe. It has 41 members, many more than the E.U. The citizens of any of its member states can appeal to the European Court, run by the Council of Europe, if they feel they are not being treated fairly by the legal system in their own country.

The E.U. flag has 12 stars representing the 12 states which were members when the E.U. was named in 1993.

Euro-skeptics

Although belonging to European organizations brings benefits, it may also have disadvantages. Some people in Europe are worried that the increasing power of European organizations could threaten the unique culture of individual countries. In several countries, political activists, sometimes called Euro-skeptics, campaign to stop their governments from signing up to European laws and joining the single currency.

These are farmers from all over Europe protesting in Strasbourg against some of the European Union's agricultural policies.

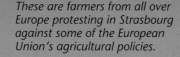

EUROPE AND THE WORLD

Over the centuries, European countries have explored and dominated many other lands, imposing their languages, customs and cultures. Europe itself has also been greatly influenced by the cultures it has come into contact with.

Internet links

Find photographs and short articles about the Second World War.

For a link to this website, go to
www.usborne-quicklinks.com

This cloud was produced by the atomic bomb that was dropped on Nagasaki, in Japan, on August 9, 1945. Five days later Japan surrendered, ending the Second World War.

Two world wars

The First and Second World Wars of the 20th century both began in Europe. They grew larger as nations around the world became involved. Both wars spread as far as Africa and the Far East.

The Second World War in particular had a huge impact on the world. It began in 1939 after German troops, under the leadership of Adolf Hitler, began invading other European countries. Nations worldwide took sides in the conflict, and the war only ended in 1945, after the U.S.A. used newly invented nuclear weapons against two Japanese cities, Hiroshima and Nagasaki.

Science

Europe's inventors and scientists have changed the world. The idea that the world was round and not flat began in ancient Greece. When it was finally proved in the 15th century, it spurred European explorers to discover and colonize other continents.

Europeans also invented machines such as the steam engine, which led to the Industrial Revolution in the 18th century. This meant goods began to be mass-produced in factories instead of being made by individual craftspeople. Colonization ensured that European-style factories soon spread around the world.

Cultural exchanges

In the past, many Europeans saw it as their right to spread European culture in the places they colonized. For example, Spanish missionaries spread Catholicism in South America, and British educational and political systems were put in place in India. Most former European colonies are now independent, but some aspects of European culture, such as religions and clothes styles, remain behind. These former colonies have also had an influence on European culture and some people from them have moved to Europe.

This is the Royal Pavilion in Brighton, in the south of England. The design of the building was influenced by architecture in India, a former British colony.

These young Indian boys are learning to play cricket, which was brought to India from Britain.

Colonization

Like other peoples around the world, Europeans have been exploring for thousands of years. On many expeditions, European explorers also attempted to colonize the places they found, and bring them under European control.

From the 1500s onwards, Spain and Portugal ruled much of South America, Britain colonized India, and several European nations claimed parts of Africa. During the 18th and 19th centuries, European countries ruled over more than half the people in the world.

Zulu men wearing traditional headdresses for a celebration in Durban, South Africa

PEOPLES OF
AFRICA

AFRICA

Africa is a huge continent, the second biggest in the world. It contains more than 50 countries, many hundreds of peoples and many different religions and ways of life. Yet many Africans also have a sense of belonging together as one big group, especially in the part of the continent south of the Sahara Desert.

These women are collecting water from a village well in Burkina Faso.

Freedom

In the 15th century, Europeans began to transport people from West Africa to Europe and North and South America to work as slaves.

Slavery was abolished in the 19th century, but European countries then began to take over Africa for themselves. Most of the continent was divided into colonies ruled by Portugal, Belgium, Italy, France, Britain and Germany. The African peoples resisted foreign rule, and most African countries became independent in the 1960s and 1970s.

1,000 languages

Over 1,000 languages are spoken in Africa. Countries with lots of languages usually have an official language as well, so that everyone can communicate with each other easily.

Most people learn the official language for use at work and at school, but may speak other languages at home and with their friends.

Internet links

Website 1 Click on an interactive timeline to take a journey through the history of Africa. You'll find fascinating audio recordings of Africans talking about their lives and cultures.

Website 2 Tour the African continent and discover more about its peoples, culture and countries, with photos, facts and sound clips.

For links to these websites, go to **www.usborne-quicklinks.com**

Two Masai* women, wearing traditional dress, talk together. The language they speak is also called Masai. The Masai people live in Kenya and Tanzania.

A Herero woman milks a cow in her village in Botswana. Herero women wear bright dresses with full skirts, and skilfully arranged headscarves called taku or distinctive hats.

Africa's peoples

Africa's largest populations are mainly in its capital cities, but Africa as a whole is sparsely populated and many of its people lead rural lives. Around three thousand different ethnic groups have been classified. One country can contain many different peoples, while a single ethnic group can spread across several countries.

PEOPLES AND POWER

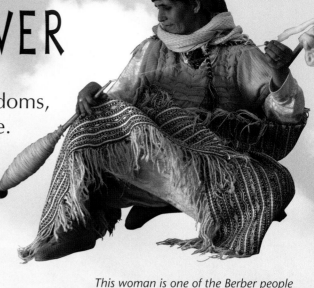

A frica was once made up of ethnic kingdoms, each with its own language and culture. But when European powers split Africa into countries, the new borders ran across the kingdoms of peoples such as the Tuareg and the Masai, dividing up their homelands.

This woman is one of the Berber people of northern Africa. She is spinning wool in the traditional way.

Ethnic emphasis

Africans often feel that their ethnic group is just as important as their nationality. Instead of just being Ghanaian or Kenyan, for example, Africans may introduce themselves as Yoruba, Bantu, Mundani, !Kung San, Berber, or one of hundreds of other groups.

Wars and civil wars

After countries such as Chad, Nigeria and Angola gained independence from Europe, different ethnic groups began to fight for power. Many of the wars still going on in Africa are based on ethnic disagreements. Often, as in the conflict between Hutu and Tutsi peoples in Rwanda and Burundi in the 1990s,

people on the losing side are forced to flee across borders to nearby countries for safety. These people are called refugees*. When there are large numbers of refugees they may have to live in temporary refugee camps.

This is a refugee camp in Rwanda. It provided a temporary shelter for thousands of people who were forced to leave home by the war there in 1994.

*Refugees, 142

Local leaders

Although African countries are ruled by their governments, many villages and ethnic groups also have their own local leaders, or chiefs. A chief has the power to settle disputes, and presides over ceremonies and official celebrations. The role of chief is usually passed from father to son.

This is a leader of the Anlo-Ewe people of Ghana, dressed in ceremonial clothing.

Internet links

Website 1 Read how Uganda's efforts to recognize its ethnic groups is leading the country towards a more peaceful future.

Website 2 Follow the histories of Africa's great civilizations.

Website 3 Everyday life for children in Africa's countries.

For links to these websites, go to **www.usborne-quicklinks.com**

The Nanas Benz of Togo

Women rarely gain political power in African governments. But some African peoples have matriarchal societies. This means that power is passed from mother to daughter. In parts of Togo, for example, rich female cloth traders called "Nanas Benz" are the most powerful people in their communities. They pass on their businesses and their wealth to their daughters. If they only have sons, they pass everything to their nieces instead.

DESERT LANDS

The Sahara, the world's biggest desert, divides northern Africa from the rest of the continent. The Mediterranean countries (Morocco, Algeria, Tunisia, Libya and Egypt) are Muslim nations. They tend to have more in common with the Middle East than with the rest of Africa.

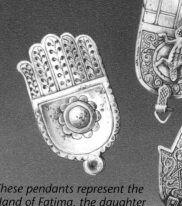

These pendants represent the Hand of Fatima, the daughter of Mohammed who is the main prophet of Islam.

Life in the desert

The Sahara takes up most of northern Africa, though only a few people live there. These include the Tuareg, a nomadic people who looked after trade routes in the desert in ancient times. Because of severe droughts in the last few decades, many desert people have had to abandon their old lifestyles and move to the cities.

Fatima's hand

In Northern Africa, the Muslim religion is very important. Most people pray several times each day. They also protect themselves from bad luck with images of a patterned hand, called the Hand of Fatima. It is said to ward off the "evil eye", which means a curse caused by a jealous glance.

Traditionally, Tuareg men wear veils like these, which show only the eyes, in the presence of women and strangers.

Walled cities

In some modern northern African cities, such as Marrakesh in Morocco and Tunis in Tunisia, there are still old medieval towns, or *medinas*. Surrounded by tall, thick walls, these old towns are crammed with tiny winding streets, along which markets, or *souks,* are held. Different kinds of goods are sold or made in different areas of the town. For example, noisy or smelly trades such as leather-making take place near the edge of the town, while crafts such as bookbinding are close to the main mosque.

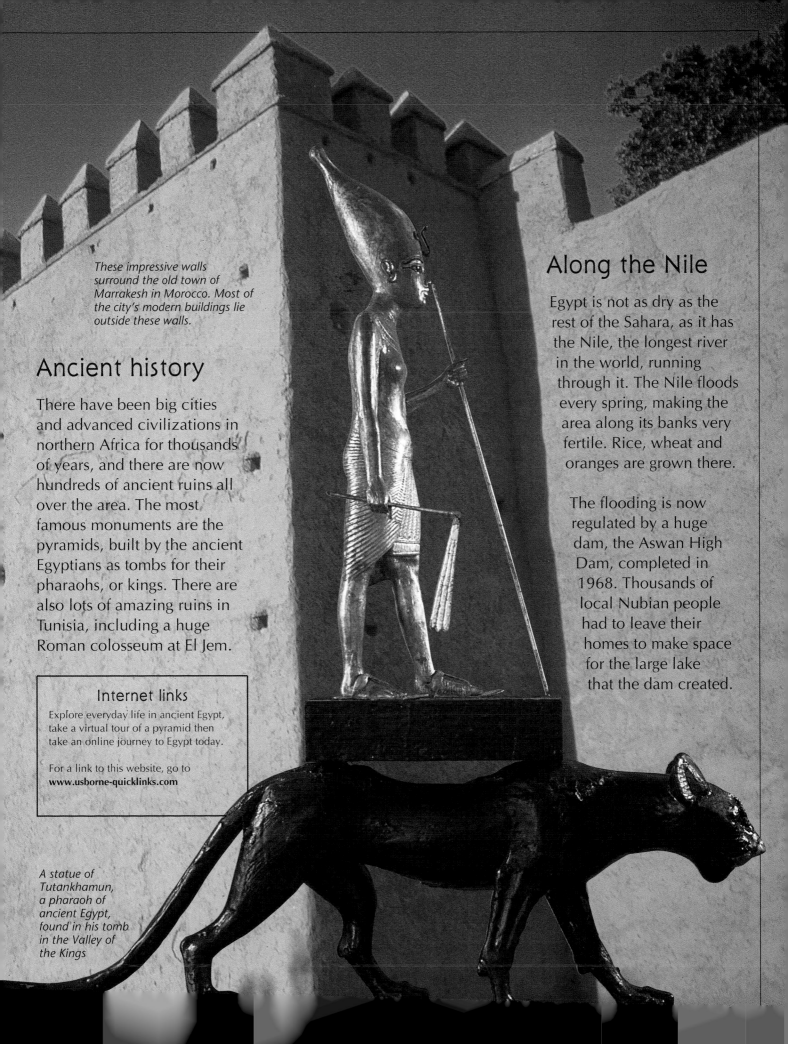

These impressive walls surround the old town of Marrakesh in Morocco. Most of the city's modern buildings lie outside these walls.

Ancient history

There have been big cities and advanced civilizations in northern Africa for thousands of years, and there are now hundreds of ancient ruins all over the area. The most famous monuments are the pyramids, built by the ancient Egyptians as tombs for their pharaohs, or kings. There are also lots of amazing ruins in Tunisia, including a huge Roman colosseum at El Jem.

Internet links

Explore everyday life in ancient Egypt, take a virtual tour of a pyramid then take an online journey to Egypt today.

For a link to this website, go to
www.usborne-quicklinks.com

A statue of Tutankhamun, a pharaoh of ancient Egypt, found in his tomb in the Valley of the Kings

Along the Nile

Egypt is not as dry as the rest of the Sahara, as it has the Nile, the longest river in the world, running through it. The Nile floods every spring, making the area along its banks very fertile. Rice, wheat and oranges are grown there.

The flooding is now regulated by a huge dam, the Aswan High Dam, completed in 1968. Thousands of local Nubian people had to leave their homes to make space for the large lake that the dam created.

WEST AND CENTRAL AFRICA

The countries of West and Central Africa are tightly packed around a huge bay known as the Gulf of Guinea. Nigeria, right in the middle of this region, is Africa's most populous country. This part of the world is characterized by its diversity of peoples, cultures and religions, and its thriving art and music scene.

The Sahel

The Sahel is a strip of dry land south of the Sahara Desert. Countries there, such as Chad, Niger and Mali, are cut off from the coast and have little fertile land. Bad droughts happen every few years. Nomadic herders, such as the Tuareg, live in the north of the Sahel. In the south, the land is greener and people live by farming and fishing.

Left: Dogon people dance on stilts at a traditional celebration in the village of Sangha, Mali.

Along the coast

The small countries along the western African coast, such as Ghana and Senegal, are among Africa's wealthier nations. As well as farming and fishing, many of them mine valuable deposits of iron ore, diamonds and gold. Having been ruled by Europe, these countries gained their independence in the mid-20th century. But some, such as Sierra Leone, have been damaged by wars between groups battling for power.

Nigeria

Nigeria is a land of huge diversity, from the high-rise coastal city of Lagos to tropical forests in the east, and dusty plains and mud-walled villages in the central regions. Nigeria also has many different peoples, belonging to over 250 ethnic groups. The biggest groups are the mainly-Muslim Hausa and Fulani peoples of the north, the Christian Igbo of the south, and the southwestern Yoruba people, most of whom follow traditional local religions.

This statue is part of a Yoruba shrine in Oshogbo, southwestern Nigeria, dedicated to a river goddess called Oshun.

Internet links

Explore a Web site where you can take virtual tours of Togo, Ghana, Burkina Faso and Mali. View photographs, try out recipes, listen to music and find out about the sports, arts and daily life of their peoples.

For a link to this website, go to **www.usborne-quicklinks.com**

Diverse religions

Across Africa, many ancient, local belief systems are still strong. They often involve animism, a belief in spirits belonging to plants or animals. The spirit world is believed to exist alongside the physical world and to be able to affect it in various ways.

A street in Lagos, Nigeria's biggest city, crammed with cars, buses, pedestrians and busy markets

These Buduma people are fishing from a papyrus reed boat. The Buduma live on a series of islands in Lake Chad, which is bordered by Chad, Niger, Nigeria and Cameroon.

LANDSCAPES OF THE EAST

Africa's most famous landscapes are found along its eastern side, where deserts in the north give way to grasslands, lakes and wildlife reserves in the Great Rift Valley. This region has been influenced by many peoples, including Indians, Arabs, and local ethnic groups such as the Masai.

Eastern Africa has huge expanses of open grasslands which are home to many large animals, such as lions.

The Horn of Africa

The Horn of Africa is a hook-shaped piece of land sticking out into the sea just south of Arabia. The countries there, such as Ethiopia, Djibouti and Somalia, are hot and dry, and most people live by herding cattle from place to place.

Recently Ethiopia and Somalia have suffered from famines, triggered by droughts which have killed crops and farm animals. Money has often been spent on wars instead of food, and areas have become so dangerous that aid workers are unable to reach them.

Ecotourism

In Kenya and Tanzania, the Great Rift Valley's grassy plains teem with leopards, lions, antelopes and other wildlife. These countries have set aside huge national parks and reserves, which not only protect the animals, but also make money from tourism. In the past, people paid to hunt these animals, but now tourists go on safaris to spot and photograph them.

The round, thatched huts in this farming village near Belet Weyne, Somalia, are typical traditional East African homes. There is also a pen for the cattle.

Losing a lake

The peoples who live around Lake Victoria, which straddles Uganda, Tanzania and Kenya, have fished in the lake and used it as a way to get around for centuries. But recently Lake Victoria has been polluted by fertilizers running into it from coffee and tea fields, and the amount of fish in it has fallen.

Great Rift Valley

The Great Rift Valley is made up of a huge series of valleys and lakes which stretch all the way down East Africa. The lakes and fertile hillsides make this a good area for fishing and farming. Archaeologists searching there have found skulls and tools which suggest that East Africa was the home of the first ever human beings.

The Masai

East Africa is home to many local ethnic groups. The Masai, who live in Tanzania and Kenya, are proud of their nomadic cattle-herding lifestyle. They rarely slaughter their cattle for food. Instead, they get protein by drinking milk and blood drawn from the cattle.

Today, Masai people also visit towns to sell their cattle and buy goods. Some also make money by selling their famous beadwork and posing in traditional dress for tourists.

Internet links

Website 1 See some photographs and read about everyday life in an East African village.

Website 2 Watch a fascinating photo-essay about a coming of age ceremony for Masai warriors.

For links to these websites, go to **www.usborne-quicklinks.com**

A young Masai woman dressed up in a traditional beadwork headdress, necklaces and earrings

SOUTHERN AFRICA

Southern Africa is a region of rich farmland, dusty deserts, beautiful coasts and steamy swamps. It is dominated by South Africa, Africa's richest country. South Africa's mines, farms and factories provide work for many people from other southern African countries. Yet South Africa itself is in the midst of huge changes.

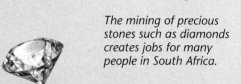

The mining of precious stones such as diamonds creates jobs for many people in South Africa.

Divisions and inequality

In 1994, South Africa held its first free election after more than 40 years of a regime known as apartheid. Under apartheid (which means "apartness"), only white people could vote. They ruled the country, and the main ethnic groups were forced to live separately from each other.

At the election, a party called the African National Congress was voted into power and things began to change. People of all ethnic groups can now live and work together. But there are big inequalities, and many South Africans still struggle with poverty, violence and a high crime rate.

Nelson Mandela was a leading member of South Africa's anti-apartheid movement. He was the country's president from 1994 to 1999.

Diamonds and gold

A lot of southern Africa's wealth comes from its rich deposits of valuable minerals. The world's biggest goldfield is in Witwatersrand, near Johannesburg in South Africa, and thousands of people across southern Africa work in mines extracting precious stones and metals.

Internet links

Visit South Africa's famous places with an online sightseeing guide and read an interview with Nelson Mandela, South Africa's first democratically elected president.

For a link to this website, go to **www.usborne-quicklinks.com**

!Kung San

The Kalahari is a stony desert which occupies parts of Botswana, South Africa and Namibia. It has been home to the !Kung San people for several thousand years. Many have moved to the cities, but a few still live as hunter-gatherers. The men hunt wild animals, while the women and children collect nuts, fruit and honey.

The !Kung San, along with many other southern African peoples, speak a language belonging to a group called Khoisan languages. As well as vowels and consonants, these languages include clicking noises made with the tongue. The ! sign stands for just one of many different types of click.

Hunter-gatherers, like these !Kung San picking berries in the Kalahari, have one of the world's oldest lifestyles.

Island life

Two young boys from Madagascar carrying a fishing net. Fishing is an important part of island life.

To the east of southern Africa lie the islands of Madagascar, Mauritius, Comoros and the Seychelles. The first people to live there came from Southeast Asia, over 4,000km (2,500 miles) away across the Indian Ocean. Today, the people are a mix of African, south Asian and Arabic ethnic groups. They make a living from fishing and tourism, and from growing spices.

AFRICAN ART

Africa is famous for its arts and crafts of all kinds: sculpture and mask-making, painting, beadwork, pottery and carving. Traditionally, African artworks were used in religious ceremonies or worn on special occasions. Today, they are also sold to tourists, exported, or shown in art galleries.

Prehistoric pictures

8,000-year-old rock paintings and engravings found in the Sahara Desert are the earliest examples of African art. The hunting scenes in these pictures suggest that the Sahara was once much greener than it is today, with more people and wildlife living in it.

A prehistoric rock painting found in Tassili, Algeria, showing people with a herd of cattle.

Masks and statues

Masks and statues are much more common in African art than pictures of landscapes or objects. This is because African art is often designed for use in ceremonies. Masks and statues can show gods, spirits, or images of perfect beauty, and can also be used for good luck. Some Ashanti women in Ghana, for example, carry a figure of a baby as a charm to help them have healthy children.

This mask is from Zimbabwe. It is part of a ceremonial dancing costume.

Symbolic coffins

In Accra, Ghana's capital city, an unusual art form has developed. Those who can afford it can be buried in special coffins built to represent their lifestyles. For example, a businessman might have a car-shaped coffin or a fisherman could have a fish or boat-shaped coffin.

This chicken-shaped coffin was probably built for a farmer.

Internet links

Website 1 See many different examples of traditional African art, including masks, statues, carpets and other objects.

Website 2 View online museum collections of textiles,

musical instruments, furniture and weapons, and find out about the diverse uses of African art.

For links to these websites, go to **www.usborne-quicklinks.com**

Body art

Earrings and nose rings, face painting and elaborate hairstyles are vital elements of many traditional ceremonies. Some peoples also use tattooing and scarification (marking the skin with scars) to create a kind of body art.

Women of the Nuer people of southern Sudan have their faces patterned with scars to mark their passage into adulthood.

Ancient Egyptian artworks, like this carving in Saqqara, attract many tourists to Africa every year.

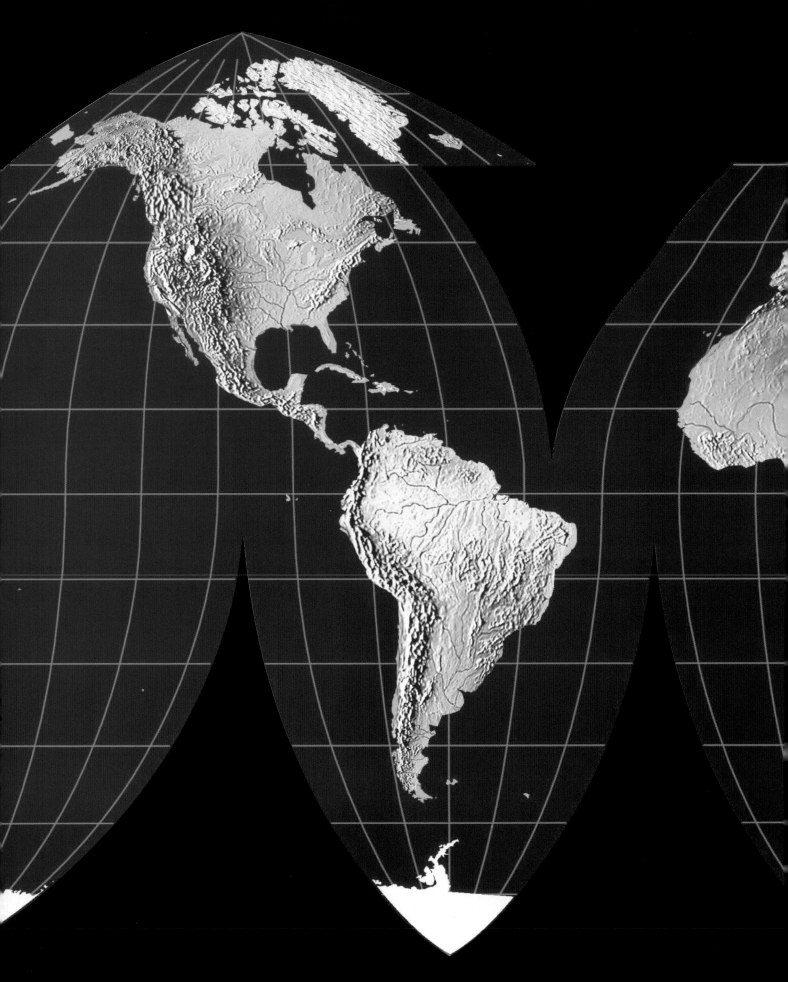

This map projection is called Boggs Eumorphic. It is a modified cylindrical projection. This type of map reduces the distortion of land areas.

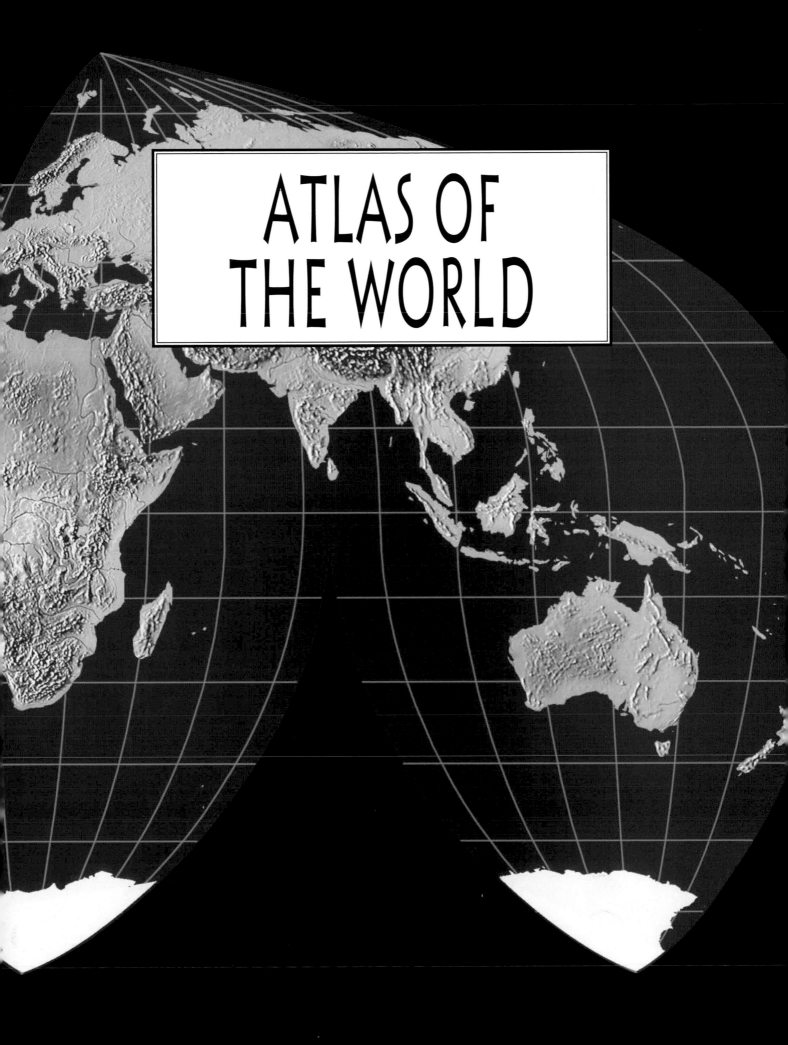

ATLAS OF
THE WORLD

WHAT IS A MAP?

A map is an image that represents a particular area of the Earth's surface, usually from above and at a reduced size. A map can show the whole world or just a street. There can be many kinds of maps of the same place, each giving different types of information.

What maps show

Unlike an aerial photograph, which shows exactly what an area looks like from above, a map can show features of the area in a clearer, simplified way. It can also give different kinds of information about the area, such as the names of places, the position of borders between countries, or the types of crops that grow there.

This map was drawn in 1584. Although people at this time knew much less about the shapes and locations of countries, they still created many maps of the world.

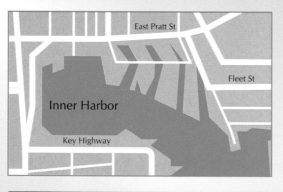

On the left is a simple map of Baltimore Harbor, U.S.A. It just shows the area's main streets.

On this aerial photograph of the same area it's difficult to see the streets.

Internet links

Website 1 Look at physical and political maps of different countries.

Website 2 Find street maps of any town or city in the world.

For links to these websites, go to **www.usborne-quicklinks.com**

Map features

Maps are designed to be clear, so most of them use conventions to help us recognize certain features. Land is often shown as green, and seas, rivers and lakes are usually shown as blue. Symbols can also be used to represent features. The meanings of the symbols are usually explained in a key.

- Mountain vegetation
- Coniferous forest
- Deciduous forest
- Grassland
- Scrubland

This is a thematic map that shows Europe's natural vegetation. The key above indicates the type of land that the different shading represents.

Kinds of maps

There are many different kinds of maps. Physical maps focus on natural features such as mountains, rivers and lakes. Political maps focus on the division of the Earth's surface into separate states*. Some maps are thematic. This means that only certain information, such as climate types or population, is represented. Thematic maps can help us make comparisons between the features of different areas.

Which way is up?

Although the Earth doesn't have a top and a bottom, north is usually at the top of maps. But it is sometimes more convenient to reposition a map, so north might not necessarily be at the top. Some maps have a compass symbol that indicates where north lies.

Scale

The size of a map in relation to the area it shows is called its scale. Some maps have a scale bar, which is a rule with measurements. It tells you how many miles or km are represented by a certain distance on the map. Other maps show this ratio in numbers. The figure 1:100 may mean, for example, that 1cm on the map represents 100cm on the Earth's surface. The scale of a map depends on its purpose. A map showing the whole world is on a very small scale, but a town plan is on a much larger scale so that features, such as roads and buildings, can be shown clearly.

1:80,000,000

| 0 | 1,000 | 2,000 | 3,000km |

| 0 | 1,000 | 2,000 miles |

This map of Europe is on a small scale so that it all fits onto one small map.

1:7,000,000

| 0 | 100 | 200 | 300km |

| 0 | 100 | 200 miles |

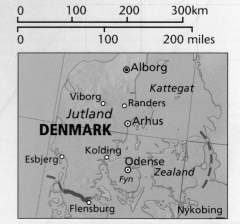

This map of Denmark is on a larger scale to show more detail.

*States, 256

DIVIDING LINES

We divide up the Earth with imaginary lines to help us measure distances and find where places are. There are two sets of lines, called latitude and longitude.

This arctic fox lives in northern Canada, very near the Arctic Circle line of latitude.

Latitude lines

Lines of latitude run around the globe. They are parallel to each other and get shorter the closer they are to the two poles. The latitude line that runs around the middle of the Earth is called the Equator. It is the most important line of latitude as all other lines are measured north or south of it.

Longitude lines

Lines of longitude run from the North Pole to the South Pole. All the lines are the same length, and they all meet at the North and South Poles.

The most important line of longitude is the Prime Meridian Line, which runs through Greenwich, in England. All other lines of longitude are measured east or west of this line.

Other lines

The Equator is not the only named latitude line. The Tropic of Cancer is a line north of the Equator. The Tropic of Capricorn is at the same distance south of the Equator. Between these lines is the hottest, stormiest part of the world. It is called the tropics.

The Arctic Circle is a latitude line far north of the Equator. The area north of this includes the North Pole and is called the Arctic. On the other side of the globe is the Antarctic Circle. The area south of this includes the South Pole and is known as the Antarctic.

Latitude lines   *Longitude lines*

Here is a drawing of the Earth, showing the main lines of latitude and longitude.

North Pole

Arctic Circle (66°30′N)

Prime Meridian Line (0°)

Tropic of Cancer (23°27′N)

Equator (0°)

Lines of longitude

Lines of latitude

Tropic of Capricorn (23°27′S)

South Pole

Internet links

Find out more about lines of latitude and longitude, then see if you can work out the latitude and longitude of where you live.

For a link to this website, go to **www.usborne-quicklinks.com**

Using the lines

Lines of latitude and longitude are measured in degrees (°). We describe the positions of places according to which lines of latitude and longitude are nearest to them. For example, a place with a location of 50°S and 100°E has a latitude 50 degrees south of the Equator, and a longitude 100 degrees east of the Prime Meridian Line.

Exact locations

The distance between degrees is divided up to give even more precise measurements. Each degree is divided into 60 minutes ('), and each minute is divided into 60 seconds ("). The subdivisions allow us to locate any place on Earth. For example, the city of New York, U.S.A., is at 40°42'51"N and 74°00'23"W.

The steamy rainforests of Malaysia lie near the Equator. Many orang-utans, like the one shown here, live in these rainforests.

This is a map of New Zealand, with a grid formed by lines of latitude and longitude.

Using a grid

Lines of latitude and longitude form grids on maps. The maps in this book look similar to the one on the left. The vertical columns formed by lines of longitude are marked with letters, and the horizontal rows formed by lines of latitude are numbered.

All the places listed in the map index on page 376 have a letter and a number reference that tell you where to find them on a particular page. For example, on the map on the left, the city of Christchurch would have a grid reference of C3.

LOOKING AT THE EARTH

Modern technology has enabled scientists to make more accurate maps of the world than ever before. Even remote places, such as deserts, ocean floors and mountain ranges, have been mapped in detail using information from satellites that observe the Earth from space.

What is a satellite?

Artificial satellites are machines that orbit, or travel around, the Earth. They observe the Earth using a technique called remote sensing. Instruments on the satellite monitor the Earth without touching it, and send back pictures of its surface. Satellites also monitor moons and other planets.

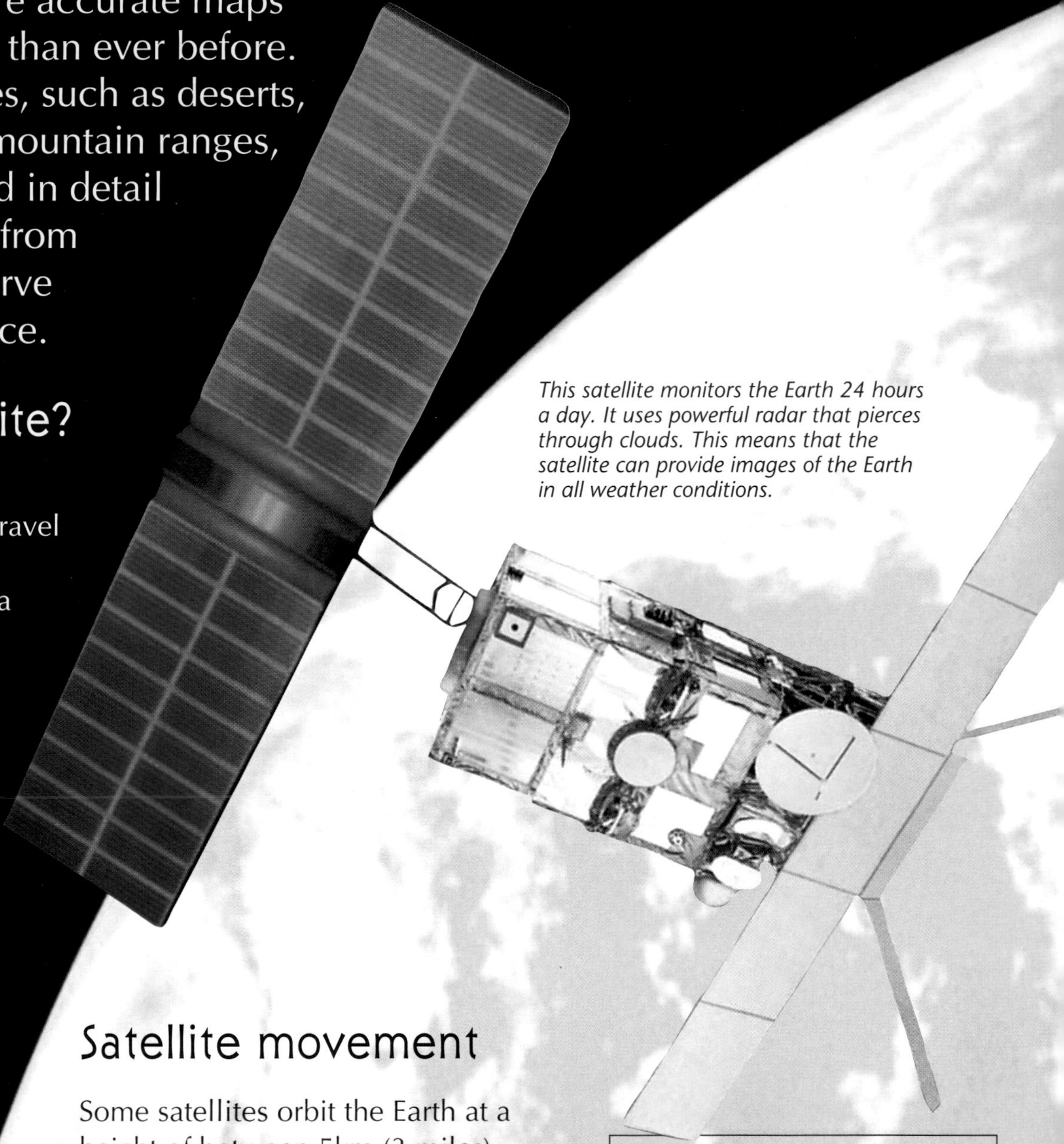

This satellite monitors the Earth 24 hours a day. It uses powerful radar that pierces through clouds. This means that the satellite can provide images of the Earth in all weather conditions.

Satellite movement

Some satellites orbit the Earth at a height of between 5km (3 miles) and 1,500km (930 miles), providing views of different parts of the planet. Others stay above the same place all the time, moving at the same speed as the Earth rotates to give a constant view of a particular area. These are called geostationary satellites. They travel at a height of around 36,000km (22,370 miles).

Internet links

Website 1 Look at detailed satellite pictures from NASA of any part of the world.

Website 2 See more amazing satellite images, and find out how they can show the way land changes over time.

For links to these websites, go to **www.usborne-quicklinks.com**

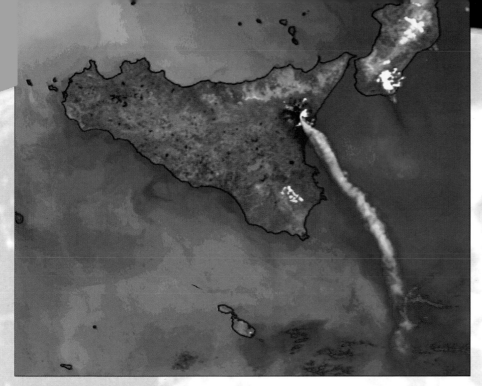

This satellite image of Sicily was taken in July 2001. It shows the volcano Mount Etna erupting. You can see smoke from the volcano on the right of the picture.

Satellite uses

The information provided by satellites helps scientists to produce accurate maps. Satellite pictures can also be used to help predict and monitor natural hazards such as volcanic eruptions or earthquakes. Some satellites monitor the weather*. Satellite images can also show the effects that people have on their environment, for example the destruction of rainforests in South America.

Remote sensing

Satellites use a range of remote sensing techniques. One type is radar, which can provide images of the Earth even when it is dark or cloudy. Radar works by reflecting radio waves off a target object. The time it takes for a wave to bounce back indicates how far away the object is.

Powerful cameras provide pictures of the Earth's surface. Often, infrared cameras are used. Different surfaces reflect the infrared rays differently, so infrared images of the Earth are able to show its various types of land surfaces, such as deserts, grasslands and forests.

This satellite image of the Earth shows different types of land. Deserts and other dry regions are red, and areas with lots of vegetation are orange and yellow.

*Weather satellites, 90

HOW MAPS ARE MADE

The process of making maps is called cartography. Map-makers, or cartographers, compile each map by gathering information about the area and then representing it as an image as accurately as possible.

Internet links

Find out more about map projections and how cartographers make maps, with interactive diagrams.

For a link to this website, go to
www.usborne-quicklinks.com

Creating maps

Many sources are used to create maps. These include satellite images and aerial photographs. Cartographers often visit the area to be mapped, where they take many extra measurements.

In addition, cartographers use statistics, such as population figures, from censuses* and other documents. As the maps are being made, many people check them to make sure they are accurate and up-to-date.

Map projections

Cartographers can't draw maps that show the world exactly as it is, because it is impossible to show a curved surface on a flat map without distorting (stretching or squashing) some areas. A representation of the Earth on a map is called a projection. Projections are worked out using complex mathematics.

There are three basic types of projections – cylindrical, conical and azimuthal, but there are also variations on these. They all distort the Earth's surface in some way, either by altering the shapes or sizes of areas of land or the distance between places.

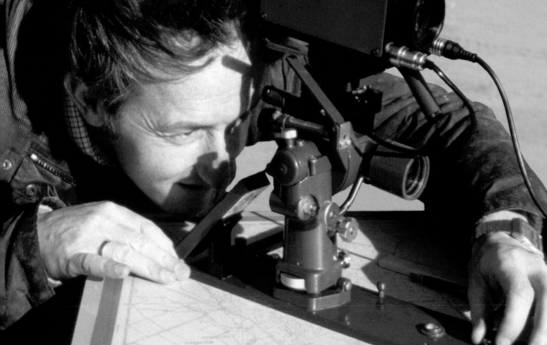

A cartographer uses an electronic distance measurer to check the measurements of an area of land.

Cylindrical projections

A cylindrical projection is similar to what you would get if you wrapped a piece of paper around a globe to form a cylinder and then shone a light inside the globe. The shapes of countries would be projected onto the paper. Near the middle they would be accurate, but farther away they would be distorted.

Cartographers often alter the basic cylindrical projection to make the distortion less obvious in certain areas, but they can never make a map that is completely accurate.

This picture of a piece of paper wrapped around a globe illustrates how a cylindrical projection is made.

Below is a type of cylindrical projection called the Mercator projection, which was invented in 1596 by a cartographer called Gerardus Mercator. It makes countries the right shape, but makes those near the poles too big.

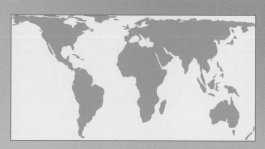

This cylindrical projection makes countries the right size in relation to each other, but some parts are too long. The projection was created in 1973 by Arno Peters. It is called the Peters Projection.

Conical projections

A conical projection is similar to the image you would get if you wrapped a cone of paper around part of a globe, then shone a light inside the globe. Where the cone touches the globe, the projection will be most accurate.

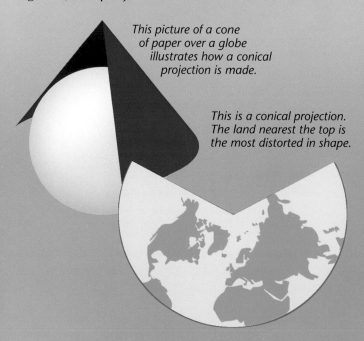

This picture of a cone of paper over a globe illustrates how a conical projection is made.

This is a conical projection. The land nearest the top is the most distorted in shape.

Azimuthal projections

An azimuthal projection is like an image made by holding paper in front of a globe, and shining a light through it. Land projected onto the middle of the paper would be accurate, but areas farther away would be distorted.

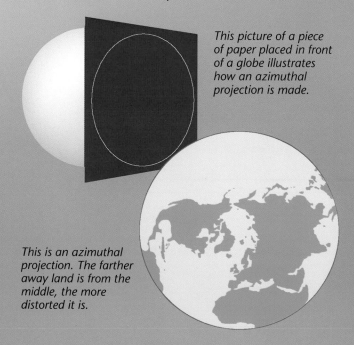

This picture of a piece of paper placed in front of a globe illustrates how an azimuthal projection is made.

This is an azimuthal projection. The farther away land is from the middle, the more distorted it is.

STATES AND BORDERS

The world's main land masses, which are called continents, are divided into independent states and dependent territories. The different areas are separated by borders.

What is a state?

A state is an area of land that has its own government* and is fully independent. Independent states are also known as countries.

Some large countries, such as the U.S.A., are split into several regions. Each region has its own government, which is responsible for the affairs of that region. In the U.S.A. these regions are also known as states.

Changing states

States don't always stay the same. They can divide or merge. For example, Germany was split into two states after the Second World War, and was then reunited in 1990. Sometimes an area becomes independent and a new state is formed. For example, Georgia was once part of the USSR but became a separate state when the USSR dissolved in 1991.

The picture above shows people sitting on the Berlin Wall. The wall formed a border between East and West Berlin when East and West Germany were separate states. It has now been pulled down.

What is a territory?

A dependent territory is an area of land that has a very limited government or no government at all. Instead, the land is owned and governed by a separate, independent state. For example, French Guiana in South America is a dependent territory of France.

*Governments, 353

Border disputes

Sometimes states disagree about where the border between them should be. This can lead to long conflicts, such as the war between Eritrea and Ethiopia. Eritrea was once part of Ethiopia but became an independent state in 1993. The two countries are still disputing the position of the border between them. Thousands of people have been killed in the conflict.

Borders often follow natural features such as rivers or mountain ranges. The Danube River separates several countries. Above, it is shown separating Serbia (left) and Romania (right).

Internet links

Try quizzes to test your knowledge of different states around the world.

For a link to this website, go to **www.usborne-quicklinks.com**

Some borders are marked by barriers. Guards check that anyone crossing from one state to another is permitted to do so. This barrier marks the border between Belarus and Poland.

HOW TO USE THE MAPS

The maps in this book are divided up by continent. At the beginning of each section there is a political map showing the whole continent. The rest of the maps are larger scale maps showing more detailed views of the region.

Political maps

The shading on the political maps in this book is there to help you see clearly the different countries that make up each continent. The main purpose of these maps is to show country borders and capital cities. Alongside them there are facts and figures about the continents and their features.

This is a section of the political map of South America. You can see the whole map on pages 276–7.

Environmental maps

The majority of the maps in this book are environmental maps, like the one on the right. The shading on these maps shows different types of land, or environments, such as desert, mountain or wetland.

The main key on the opposite page shows what the different shading means. It also shows the symbols used to represent towns, cities and other features. There is a smaller key on each environmental map repeating the most important information from this key.

Finding places

To find a particular place or feature on the environmental maps, look up its name in the index on pages 376–389. Its page number and grid reference is given next to the name. You can find out how to use the grid on page 251.

The map on the right is part of the environmental map of the U.S.A. The numbered labels at the top explain some important features of these maps.

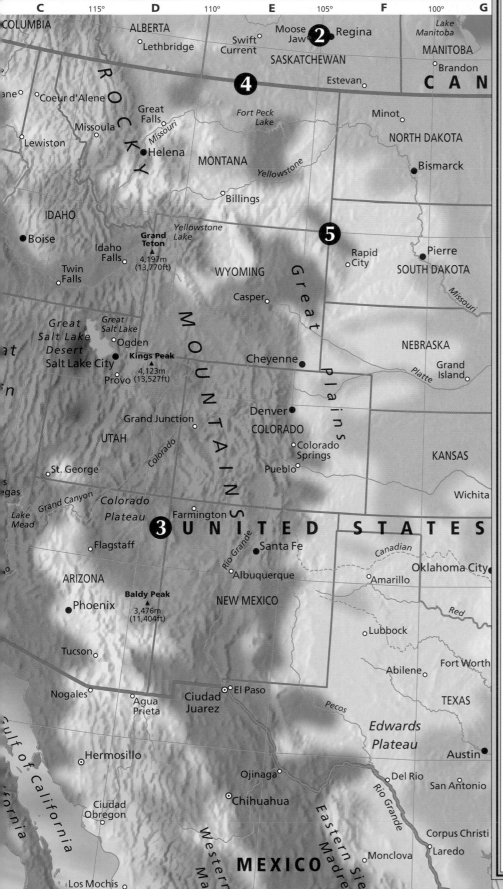

❶ *The letters and numbers in the border help you to find a place you have looked up in the index.*

❷ *Lines of latitude and longitude are shown as thin blue lines.*

❸ *The names of countries are shown in large, bold type with capital letters.*

❹ *The thick purple lines are country boundaries.*
❺ *The thinner purple lines are boundaries of internal regions within a country.*

Main key

Land cover:
- Boreal forest
- Temperate forest
- Tropical forest
- Temperate grassland
- Savanna
- Semi-desert and scrub
- Hot desert
- Wetland
- Mountain (Only high mountains are marked.)
- Tundra
- Ice
- Cultivation
- Urban

Cities and towns:
- ■ National capital
- ● Internal capital
- ⊙ Major city or town
- ○ Other town

Boundaries:
- ── International boundary
- --- International boundary through water
- ── Internal boundary
- --- Internal boundary through water

Water features:
- Sea
- Lake or reservoir
- Seasonal lake
- Dry lake/salt pan
- River
- Seasonal river
- Waterfall/dam

Other features:
- ▲ 2,490m (7,988ft) Height above or below sea level (Only a selection of elevation points are given. Places below sea level have a minus sign in front of the height.)
- ⁂ Ruin or other place of interest
- ⊓⊓⊓ Ancient wall

Scale:
This tells you the size of the map in relation to the area it represents. For example:

1:12,000,000

0	200	400km

0	100	200	300 miles

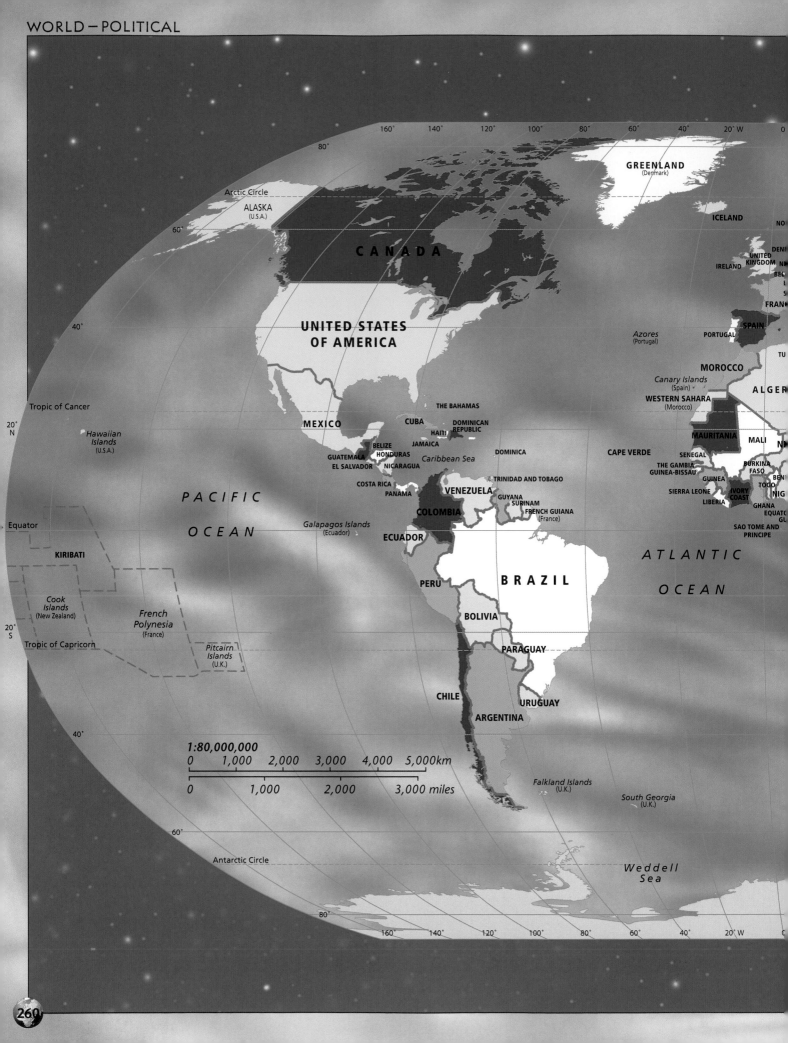

GREENLAND
(Denmark)

ICELAND

Arctic Circle

ALASKA
(U.S.A.)

NOR...

CANADA

UNITED
KINGDOM

DEN...

IRELAND

BEL...

FRAN...

SPAIN

PORTUGAL

Azores
(Portugal)

UNITED STATES
OF AMERICA

TU...

MOROCCO

Canary Islands
(Spain)

Tropic of Cancer

WESTERN SAHARA
(Morocco)

ALGER...

Hawaiian
Islands
(U.S.A.)

20°
N

MEXICO

THE BAHAMAS

CUBA

DOMINICAN
REPUBLIC

HAITI

MAURITANIA

MALI

BELIZE

HONDURAS

JAMAICA

CAPE VERDE

SENEGAL

BURKINA
FASO

GUATEMALA

EL SALVADOR

NICARAGUA

Caribbean Sea

DOMINICA

THE GAMBIA

GUINEA-BISSAU

BEN...

TOGO

COSTA RICA

PANAMA

TRINIDAD AND TOBAGO

GUINEA

SIERRA LEONE

IVORY
COAST

NIG...

VENEZUELA

GUYANA

LIBERIA

GHANA

PACIFIC

SURINAM

EQUATO...

GL...

COLOMBIA

FRENCH GUIANA
(France)

SAO TOME AND
PRINCIPE

OCEAN

Galapagos Islands
(Ecuador)

ECUADOR

Equator

ATLANTIC

KIRIBATI

PERU

BRAZIL

OCEAN

Cook
Islands
(New Zealand)

French
Polynesia
(France)

BOLIVIA

20°
S

Tropic of Capricorn

Pitcairn
Islands
(U.K.)

PARAGUAY

CHILE

URUGUAY

ARGENTINA

40°

1:80,000,000

0   1,000   2,000   3,000   4,000   5,000km

0   1,000   2,000   3,000 miles

Falkland Islands
(U.K.)

South Georgia
(U.K.)

60°

Antarctic Circle

Weddell
Sea

80°

40° 60° 80° 100° 120° 140° 160° 180°

80°

Abbreviations used on map:

ARM.   ARMENIA
AUST.   AUSTRIA
AZER.   AZERBAIJAN
BELG.   BELGIUM
B.H.   BOSNIA AND HERZEGOVINA
CRO.   CROATIA
CZECH REP. CZECH REPUBLIC
LEB.   LEBANON
LUX.   LUXEMBOURG
MAC.   MACEDONIA
NETH.   NETHERLANDS
SLOV.   SLOVENIA
S.M.   SERBIA & MONTENEGRO
SWITZ.   SWITZERLAND
U.A.E.   UNITED ARAB EMIRATES

Svalbard
(Norway)

Arctic Circle

RUSSIA

FINLAND
ESTONIA
LATVIA
SWEDEN
LITHUANIA
GERMANY
BELARUS
POLAND
CZ REP
SLOVAKIA
UKRAINE
MOLDOVA
HUNGARY
ROMANIA
B.H.
S.M.
BULGARIA
Black Sea
ALBANIA MAC.
GREECE
TURKEY
GEORGIA
ARM.
AZER.
Caspian
Sea
KAZAKHSTAN
MONGOLIA
60°

UZBEKISTAN
KYRGYZSTAN
TURKMENISTAN
TAJIKISTAN
40°

NORTH
KOREA
SOUTH
KOREA
JAPAN

Mediterranean Sea
CYPRUS
LEB
ISRAEL
SYRIA
JORDAN
IRAQ
IRAN
AFGHANISTAN
PAKISTAN
CHINA
PACIFIC

OCEAN

LIBYA
EGYPT
SAUDI
ARABIA
KUWAIT
BAHRAIN
QATAR
U.A.E.
OMAN
NEPAL
BHUTAN
BANGLA-
DESH
INDIA
BURMA
(MYANMAR)
LAOS
TAIWAN
Tropic of Cancer

20°
N
Northern
Mariana
Islands
(U.S.A.)

CHAD
SUDAN
ERITREA
YEMEN
DJIBOUTI
ETHIOPIA
THAILAND
VIETNAM
CAMBODIA
PHILIPPINES
MARSHALL
ISLANDS

CENTRAL
AFRICAN
REPUBLIC
CAMEROON
UGANDA
SOMALIA
SRI LANKA
BRUNEI
MALAYSIA
SINGAPORE
FEDERATED STATES
OF MICRONESIA
PALAU

CONGO
(DEMOCRATIC
REPUBLIC)
KENYA
RWANDA
BURUNDI
MALDIVES
INDONESIA
PAPUA
NEW GUINEA
NAURU
KIRIBATI
Equator

SEYCHELLES
INDIAN
TANZANIA
SOLOMON
ISLANDS
TUVALU

ANGOLA
ZAMBIA
MALAWI
COMOROS
OCEAN
SAMOA

ZIMBABWE
MADAGASCAR
MAURITIUS
Coral Sea
Islands
Territory
(Australia)
VANUATU
New
Caledonia
(France)
FIJI TONGA
20°
S

NAMIBIA
BOTSWANA
MOZAMBIQUE
Reunion
(France)
Tropic of Capricorn

SWAZILAND
AUSTRALIA

LESOTHO
SOUTH AFRICA

40°

NEW
ZEALAND

Kerguelen Islands
(France)

60°

Antarctic Circle

The shading on this map is there to help
you see the different countries clearly.

ANTARCTICA

40° 60° 80° 100° 120° 140° 160° 180°
80°

261

Beaufort
Sea

Victoria
Island

Queen
Elizabeth
Islands

Ellesmere
Island

Baffin
Bay

Greenland

Greenland
Sea

80°

Baffin
Island

Iceland

Arctic Circle

Alaska

Mount McKinley
▲
6,194m
(20,321ft)

Yukon

60°

Hudson
Bay

Labrador
Sea

British
Isles

Gulf of Alaska

Aleutian Islands

Newfoundland

**NORTH
AMERICA**

Rocky Mountains

Great Plains

*Great
Lakes*

Appalachian Mountains

40°

Azores

Mississippi

Atlas Moun

Tropic of Cancer

Gulf of
Mexico

Canary
Islands

20°
N

Hawaiian
Islands

Cuba

West Indies

Greater Antilles

Caribbean
Sea

Cape Verde
Islands

*Lesser
Antilles*

Guiana
Highlands

Equator

PACIFIC

Galapagos
Islands

Amazon
Basin

Amazon

ATLANTIC

Polynesia

OCEAN

Selvas

**SOUTH
AMERICA**

OCEAN

Tahiti

Andes

20°
S

Tropic of Capricorn

Easter Island

Atacama Desert

Aconcagua
▲
6,959m
(22,831ft)

Pampas

1:80,000,000

0   1,000   2,000   3,000   4,000   5,000km

40°

Patagonia

Falkland Islands

0   1,000   2,000   3,000 miles

South Georgia

Cape Horn

60°

Antarctic Circle

Antarctic
Peninsula

*Weddell
Sea*

80°

160°   140°   120°   100°   80°   60°   40°   20° W

ARCTIC OCEAN

Svalbard
Novaya Zemlya
North Cape
Barents Sea
Severnaya Zemlya
Kara Sea
Laptev Sea
New Siberia Islands
East Siberian Sea
Arctic Circle

andinavia
orth European Plain
Ob
Yenisey
Siberia
Verkhoyansk Range
Kamchatka Peninsula
60°

EUROPE
Volga
Ural Mountains
ASIA
Lake Baikal
Altai Mountains
Sea of Okhotsk
Hokkaido
40°

Danube
Black Sea
Mount Elbrus
5,642m (18,510ft)
Aral Sea
Caspian Sea
Gobi Desert
Huang He (Yellow)
Sea of Japan
Honshu

editerranean Sea
Zagros Mountains
Himalayas
Yellow Sea
East China Sea
Tropic of Cancer

ara
Nile
Red Sea
Arabian Peninsula
Ganges
Mount Everest
8,850m (29,035ft)
Chang Jiang (Yangtze)
Taiwan
20° N

el
Deccan Plateau
Bay of Bengal
Mekong
South China Sea
Philippine Islands
Micronesia
PACIFIC

FRICA
Ethiopian Highlands
Arabian Sea
Celebes Sea
OCEAN

Lake Victoria
Sri Lanka
Equator

Congo Basin
Kilimanjaro
5,895m (19,340ft)
Seychelles
Sumatra
Borneo
Melanesia

INDIAN
Greater Sunda Islands
New Guinea
Mount Wilhelm
4,509m (14,793ft)
Solomon Islands

Comoro Islands
Java
Lesser Sunda Islands
Arafura Sea

Rift Valley
OCEAN
Madagascar
Mauritius
Reunion
Coral Sea
New Caledonia
Fiji Islands
20° S

ib Desert
Kalahari Desert
Great Sandy Desert
Great Barrier Reef
Tropic of Capricorn

Drakensberg
AUSTRALASIA AND OCEANIA
Great Dividing Range

e of Good Hope
Great Victoria Desert
Tasman Sea
North Island
40°

Tasmania
South Island

SOUTHERN OCEAN
60°

Kerguelen Islands
Antarctic Circle

See page 259 for key.

ANTARCTICA
80°

E 40° 60° 80° 100° 120° 140° 160° 180°

This is a satellite picture of North America. The large islands to the right are Cuba and Haiti.

MAPS OF
NORTH AMERICA

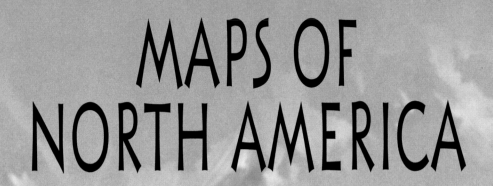

A bald eagle flying over the glaciers of Alaska, U.S.A.

n this atlas, North America includes Canada, the U.S.A., the Caribbean, and the countries of Central America, which run along the narrow strip of land between the U.S.A. and South America. This large continent contains over 20 countries, ranging from Canada, the world's second largest state, to tiny islands such as Grenada and Saint Lucia.

Arctic Circle

ARCTIC OCEAN

Beaufort Sea

Bering Sea

Yukon

ALASKA (U.S.A.)

Anchorage

Victoria Island

CANADA

These are columns of rock called hoodoos in Bryce Canyon National Park, U.S.A.

Vancouver

Columbia

PACIFIC OCEAN

Hawaiian Islands (U.S.A.)

UNITED STATE

Colorado

Los Angeles

Rio Grande

Tropic of Cancer

MEXICO

Mexico Ci

The shading on this map is there to help you see clearly the different countries that make up the continent.

GREENLAND
(Denmark)

Ellesmere Island

Queen Elizabeth Islands

Baffin Island

Godthab

Arctic Circle

Hudson Bay

Newfoundland

St. Lawrence

Montreal
Ottawa

Great Lakes

Chicago

New York

Washington D.C.

AMERICA

Mississippi

ATLANTIC OCEAN

Tropic of Cancer

Houston

THE BAHAMAS

Gulf of Mexico

Havana
CUBA

Puerto Rico
(U.S.A.)

Guadeloupe
(France)

HAITI
DOMINICAN REPUBLIC

DOMINICA
Martinique (France)

BARBADOS

JAMAICA

TRINIDAD AND TOBAGO

BELIZE
HONDURAS

Caribbean Sea

GUATEMALA

EL SALVADOR

NICARAGUA

COSTA RICA
PANAMA

Facts

Total land area 22,656,190 sq km (8,745,289 sq miles)

Total population 487 million

Biggest city Mexico City, Mexico

Biggest country Canada 9,970,610 sq km *(3,849,653 sq miles)*

Smallest country Saint Kitts and Nevis 269 sq km *(104 sq miles)*

Highest mountain Mount McKinley, Alaska, U.S.A. 6,194m *(20,321ft)*

Longest river Mississippi/Missouri, U.S.A. 6,019km *(3,741 miles)*

Biggest lake Lake Superior, between the U.S.A. and Canada 82,414 sq km *(31,820 sq miles)*

Highest waterfall Yosemite Falls, on the Yosemite Creek, California, U.S.A. 739m *(2,425ft)*

Biggest desert Great Basin Desert, U.S.A. 492,000 sq km *(190,000 sq miles)*

Biggest island Greenland 2,175,600 sq km *(840,000 sq miles)*

Main mineral deposits Silver, gold, copper, lead, zinc, graphite, molybdenum, nickel

Main fuel deposits Oil, coal, natural gas, uranium

The bald eagle is the national bird of the U.S.A. It is not really bald, but has white feathers on its head.

267

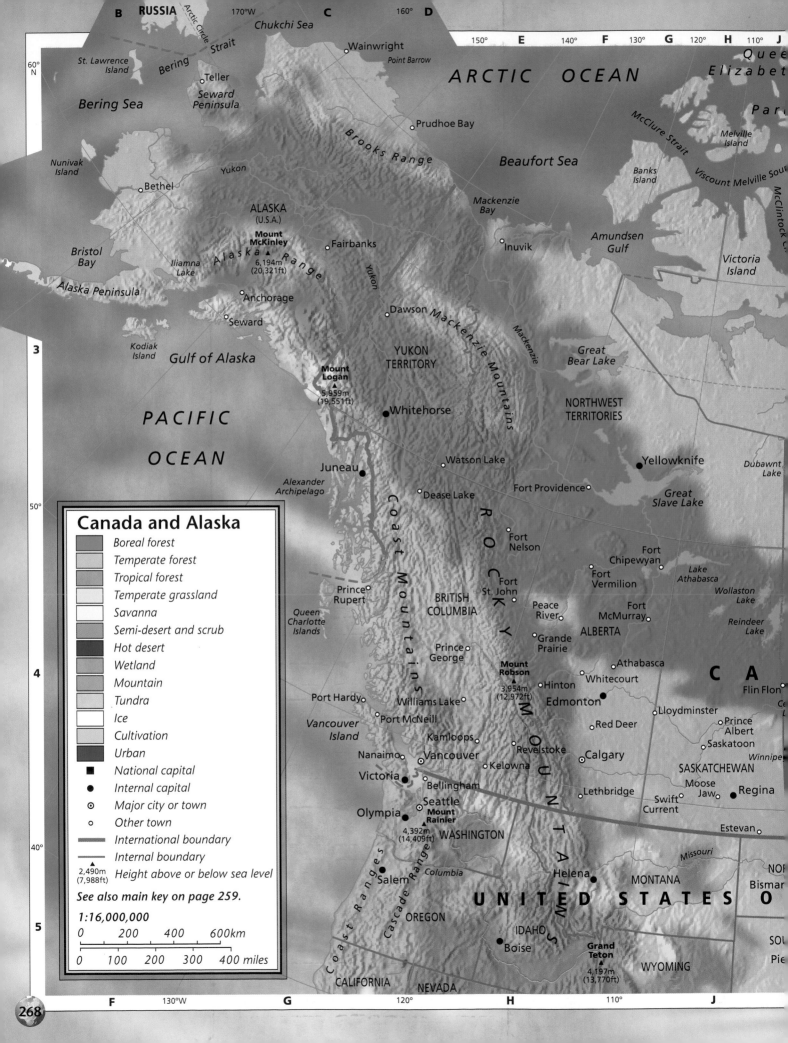

Canada and Alaska

Boreal forest
Temperate forest
Tropical forest
Temperate grassland
Savanna
Semi-desert and scrub
Hot desert
Wetland
Mountain
Tundra
Ice
Cultivation
Urban

■ National capital
● Internal capital
◉ Major city or town
○ Other town
━━━ International boundary
━━━ Internal boundary
▲ 2,490m (7,988ft) Height above or below sea level

See also main key on page 259.

1:16,000,000

0   200   400   600km
0   100   200   300   400 miles

Arctic Circle
170°W   160°   150°   140°   130°   120°   110°

Chukchi Sea

Bering Strait

60°N

St. Lawrence Island

Bering Sea

●Teller

Seward Peninsula

ARCTIC OCEAN

●Wainwright

Point Barrow

●Prudhoe Bay

Beaufort Sea

Nunivak Island

Bering

○Bethel

Yukon

ALASKA (U.S.A.)

Mount McKinley ▲ 6,194m (20,321ft)

●Fairbanks

Mackenzie Bay

●Inuvik

McClure Strait

Melville Island

Banks Island

Viscount Melville Sound

Queen Elizabeth Par

Amundsen Gulf

Bristol Bay

Iliamna Lake

Alaska Range

Yukon

●Anchorage

○Seward

Alaska Peninsula

Kodiak Island

Gulf of Alaska

○Dawson

YUKON TERRITORY

Mackenzie Mountains

Mackenzie

Victoria Island

Great Bear Lake

NORTHWEST TERRITORIES

3

Mount Logan ▲ 5,959m (19,551ft)

●Whitehorse

PACIFIC OCEAN

○Juneau

●Watson Lake

●Yellowknife

Dubawnt Lake

50°

Alexander Archipelago

○Dease Lake

●Fort Providence

Great Slave Lake

R O C K Y

○Fort Nelson

Coast Mountains

○Prince Rupert

Queen Charlotte Islands

BRITISH COLUMBIA

○Fort St. John

●Fort Chipewyan

○Fort Vermilion

Lake Athabasca

Wollaston Lake

○Peace River

ALBERTA

Reindeer Lake

○Grande Prairie

○Fort McMurray

4

○Prince George

Mount Robson ▲ 3,954m (12,972ft)

○Hinton

○Whitecourt

●Athabasca

C A

Flin Flon

○Williams Lake

●Edmonton

○Lloydminster

Port Hardy

○Port McNeill

○Red Deer

●Prince Albert

Saskatoon

Winnipe

Vancouver Island

○Kamloops

○Revelstoke

●Calgary

SASKATCHEWAN

○Nanaimo

○Vancouver

○Kelowna

Moose Jaw

●Regina

○Victoria

○Bellingham

○Lethbridge

Swift Current

○Seattle

Mount Rainier ▲ 4,392m (14,409ft)

Estevan

○Olympia

WASHINGTON

40°

○Salem

Cascade Range

Columbia

Missouri

●Helena

MONTANA

NOR Bismar

Coast Ranges

OREGON

UNITED STATES

O

●Boise

IDAHO

Grand Teton ▲ 4,197m (13,770ft)

WYOMING

Pie

5

CALIFORNIA   NEVADA

268

F   130°W   G   120°   H   110°   J

Ellesmere
Island
Devon Island
Lancaster Sound
Somerset
Island
Gulf of
Boothia
Boothia
Peninsula

Baffin
Bay

Baffin
Island

Cumberland
Peninsula

Melville
Peninsula

Foxe
Basin

Nettilling
Lake

Foxe
Peninsula

Amadjuak
Lake

Iqaluit

Hudson Strait

Cape Chidley

NUNAVUT

Southampton
Island

Ivujivik

Ungava
Peninsula

Ungava
Bay

Nain

Makkovik

Cartwright

Kuujjuaq

NEWFOUNDLAND

All islands within Hudson Bay,
James Bay and Ungava Bay lie
within Nunavut.

Inukjuak

Happy Valley-
Goose Bay

Smallwood
Reservoir

Churchill Falls

Hudson Bay

Churchill

Belcher
Islands

La Grande
Reservoir

Labrador
City

Fort Severn

NITOBA

Thompson

James
Bay

Radisson

QUEBEC

Manicouagan
Reservoir

Anticosti
Island

Gander

St. John's

Newfoundland

Corner Brook

St. Pierre
and Miquelon
(France)

Lake
Winnipeg

Fort Albany

Waskaganish

Baie-
Comeau

Gaspe

Gulf of
St. Lawrence

Sydney

Lake
Mistassini

PRINCE
EDWARD
ISLAND

Chicoutimi

Edmundston

NEW
BRUNSWICK

Bathurst

Moncton

Charlottetown

ONTARIO

Val-d'Or

Quebec

Trois-Rivieres

Fredericton

Saint
John

NOVA
SCOTIA

Halifax

ipeg

Dryden

Lake
Nipigon

Kirkland Lake

St. Lawrence

Montreal

MAINE

Yarmouth

on

Kenora

Lake
of the
Woods

Marathon

Thunder Bay

Augusta

nipeg

Sudbury

North Bay

Ottawa

Montpelier

Lake Superior

Sault
Ste. Marie

Huntsville

Kingston

VERMONT

Concord

Boston

MINNESOTA

Owen
Sound

Lake
Ontario

Albany

MASSACHUSETTS

Providence

MICHIGAN

Toronto

NEW YORK

Hartford

RHODE ISLAND

St. Paul

WISCONSIN

Hamilton

Niagara
Falls

Buffalo

CONNECTICUT

Minneapolis

Mississippi

Madison

Lansing

London

Detroit

Lake Erie

Erie

PENNSYLVANIA

New York

Trenton

NEW JERSEY

Windsor

Cleveland

Harrisburg

Philadelphia

Dover

Chicago

Pittsburgh

Annapolis

DELAWARE

ILLINOIS

INDIANA

OHIO

Columbus

Washington D.C.

MERICA

Lake Michigan

Lake Huron

Bering Sea

Aleutian Islands

Attu
Island

Near
Islands

Shishaldin
Volcano

2,857m
(9,372ft)

Unimak
Island

Fox Islands

Unalaska
Island

Rat
Islands

Andreanof Islands

Atka
Island

Umnak
Island

Same scale as main map

GREENLAND
(Denmark)

Cape Farewell

Davis Strait

Labrador Sea

ATLANTIC

OCEAN

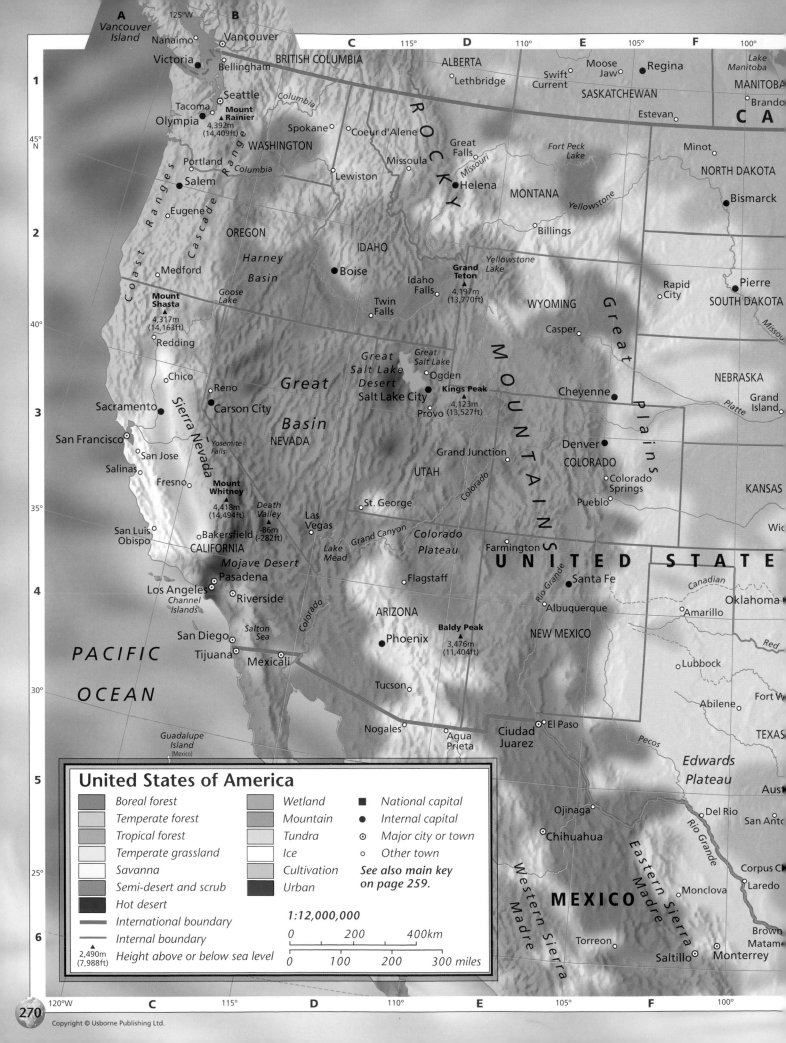

120°W A 115° B 110° C 105° D 100° E 95° F 90°

CALIFORNIA
San Diego
Tijuana
Mexicali
Phoenix
ARIZONA
Tucson
NEW MEXICO
UNITED STATES OF AMERICA
Lubbock
OKLAHOMA
Little Rock
ARKANSAS
Tupelo
MISSISSIPPI

1

30°N
Nogales
Agua Prieta
El Paso
Ciudad Juarez
Fort Worth
Texarkana
Dallas
Abilene
TEXAS
Shreveport
Jackson
Hattiesburg
LOUISIANA

Guadalupe Island (Mexico)

2
Hermosillo
Ojinaga
Chihuahua
Edwards Plateau
Waco
Austin
Houston
San Antonio
Baton Rouge
New Orleans

Cedros Island
Point Eugenia
Ciudad Obregon
Pecos
Rio Grande
Galveston
Mississippi Delta

25°N
Los Mochis
Laredo
Corpus Christi
Monclova

Tropic of Cancer
La Paz
Culiacan
Plateau of Mexico
Torreon
Saltillo
Monterrey
Brownsville
Matamoros
Gulf of Mexico

3
Durango
4,054m (13,300ft)
Ciudad Victoria

Cape San Lucas
Mazatlan
MEXICO
Matehuala
San Luis Potosi
Eastern Sierra Madre
Tampico

Lower California
Gulf of California
Western Sierra Madre

20°N
Aguascalientes
Leon
Puerto Vallarta
Celaya
Bay of Campeche
Merida
Yucatan Peninsula

Revillagigedo Islands (Mexico)
Guadalajara
Morelia
Teotihuacan
Mexico City
Veracruz
Campeche

4
Colima
Uruapan
Puebla
Orizaba 5,610m (18,405ft)
Tehuacan
Coatzacoalcos
Ciudad del Carmen

Southern Sierra Madre
Oaxaca
Isthmus of Tehuantepec
Villahermosa
Belmopa
BEL

15°N
Acapulco
Juchitan
Tuxtla Gutierrez
Tikal

Tajumulco 4,220m (13,845ft)
Gulf of Tehuantepec
GUATEMALA

Tapachula
Quezaltenan

PACIFIC OCEAN
Guatemala City
San Salvador
EL SALVA

Inset map:

L 65°W M 60° N

Virgin Islands (U.K.)
Anguilla (U.K.)
ATLANTIC OCEAN

San Juan
Virgin Islands (U.S.A.)
St. Martin (France and Netherlands)
ANTIGUA AND BARBUDA
St. John's

Puerto Rico (U.S.A.)
Basseterre
ST. KITTS AND NEVIS
Leeward Islands

4

Montserrat (U.K.)
Guadeloupe (France)

1:8,000,000
0 100 200km
0 50 100 miles

Basse-Terre

Roseau
DOMINICA
Windward Islands

15°N

6

Martinique (France)
Fort-de-France

Caribbean Sea
Castries
ST. LUCIA

5°N
Kingstown
BARBADOS

Lesser Antilles
ST. VINCENT AND THE GRENADINES
Bridgetown

7

St. George's
GRENADA

5

Margarita Island
Tobago
Porlamar
Port-of-Spain
TRINIDAD AND TOBAGO

8
Cumana
VENEZUELA
Trinidad
Equator

L 65°W M N 60°

Galapagos Islands (Ecuador)
Puerto Ayora

115°W B 110° C 105° D 100° E 95°

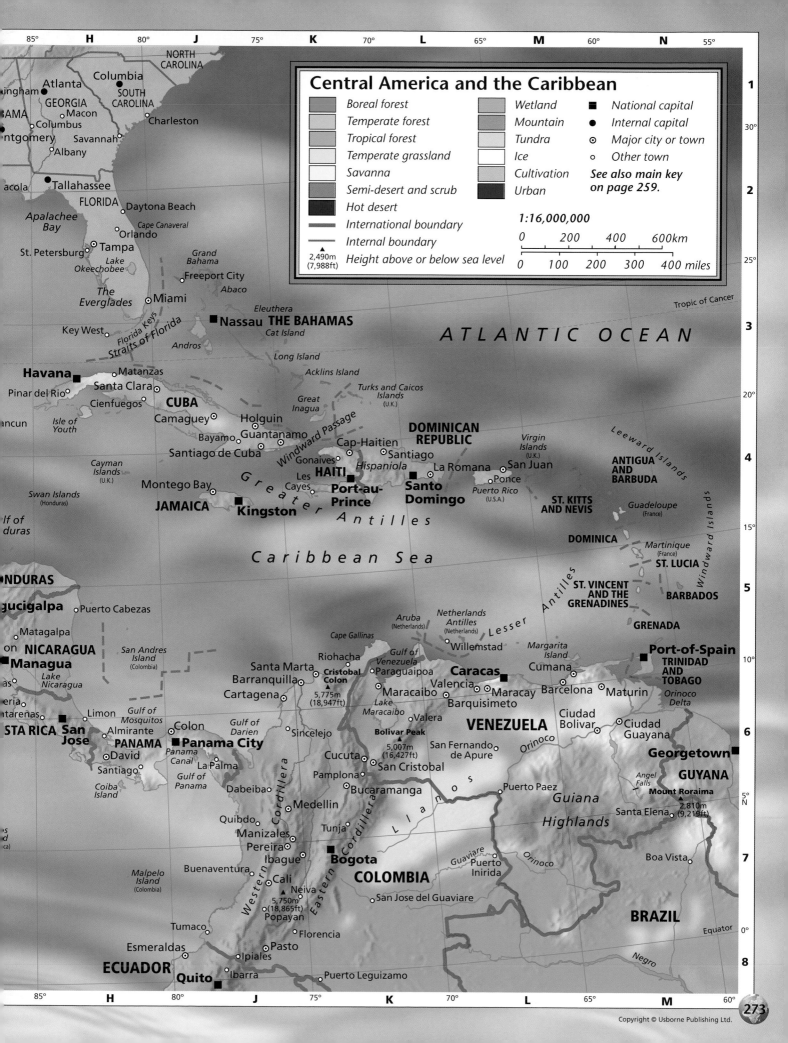

Central America and the Caribbean

Boreal forest	Wetland
Temperate forest	Mountain
Tropical forest	Tundra
Temperate grassland	Ice
Savanna	Cultivation
Semi-desert and scrub	Urban
Hot desert	

■ National capital
● Internal capital
⊙ Major city or town
○ Other town

See also main key on page 259.

International boundary
Internal boundary

▲ 2,490m (7,988ft) Height above or below sea level

1:16,000,000

0   200   400   600km
0   100   200   300   400 miles

NORTH CAROLINA

Atlanta Columbia
GEORGIA SOUTH CAROLINA
Macon Charleston
Columbus
Savannah
Albany
Tallahassee
FLORIDA Daytona Beach
Apalachee Bay Cape Canaveral
Orlando
St. Petersburg Tampa
Lake Okeechobee Grand Bahama
Abaco
The Everglades Miami Freeport City
Key West Tropic of Cancer
Straits of Florida Eleuthera
■ Nassau THE BAHAMAS
Andros Cat Island
Long Island ATLANTIC OCEAN
Havana ■ Matanzas
Pinar del Rio Santa Clara Acklins Island
CUBA Great Inagua Turks and Caicos Islands (U.K.)
Cienfuegos Camaguey Holguin
Isle of Youth Bayamo Guantanamo DOMINICAN REPUBLIC
Santiago de Cuba Cap-Haitien Santiago Virgin Islands (U.K.) Leeward Islands
Cayman Islands (U.K.) Gonaives Hispaniola San Juan ANTIGUA AND BARBUDA
Montego Bay HAITI La Romana Ponce Guadeloupe (France)
Swan Islands (Honduras) Les Cayes Port-au-Prince Santo Domingo Puerto Rico (U.S.A.) ST. KITTS AND NEVIS
JAMAICA ■ Kingston Greater Antilles DOMINICA
Caribbean Sea Martinique (France)
ST. LUCIA
BARBADOS
Lesser Antilles ST. VINCENT AND THE GRENADINES
HONDURAS Puerto Cabezas GRENADA
Matagalpa San Andres Island (Colombia) Aruba (Netherlands) Netherlands Antilles (Netherlands) Willemstad Margarita Island Port-of-Spain ■
NICARAGUA Cape Gallinas TRINIDAD AND TOBAGO
■ Managua Riohacha Gulf of Venezuela Cumana
Lake Nicaragua Santa Marta Paraguaipoa Caracas Barcelona
Limon Barranquilla Cristobal Colon Valencia Maracay Maturin
STA RICA San Jose Cartagena 5,775m (18,947ft) Maracaibo Barquisimeto Orinoco Delta
Almirante Colon Lake Maracaibo Valera
PANAMA ■ Panama City Gulf of Darien Ciudad Bolivar Ciudad Guayana
David Santiago Sincelejo Bolivar Peak VENEZUELA Georgetown ■
Panama Canal La Palma 5,007m (16,427ft) San Fernando de Apure
Coiba Island Gulf of Panama Cucuta San Cristobal GUYANA
Dabeibao Pamplona Puerto Paez Angel Falls
Malpelo Island (Colombia) Medellin Bucaramanga Guiana Highlands Mount Roraima 2,810m (9,219ft)
Quibdo Orinoco Santa Elena
Manizales Tunja Llanos Puerto Inirida Boa Vista
Pereira Ibague Guaviare
Buenaventura Bogota ■ Puerto Inirida
Cali COLOMBIA San Jose del Guaviare BRAZIL
Neiva Orinoco
Tumaco 5,750m (18,865ft) Popayan Equator
Esmeraldas Florencia
Ipiales Pasto Negro
ECUADOR Puerto Leguizamo
■ Quito Ibarra

A parrot snake

MAPS OF SOUTH AMERICA

This is a satellite image of South America. The brown, mottled streak along the west coast is the Andes mountain range.

Triangle-shaped South America is made up of only 12 independent countries, along with French Guiana, which belongs to France. A huge part of this continent is taken up with the Amazon rainforest, which covers the Amazon basin with over a third of the world's trees. South America also has dusty deserts, towering mountains and, in Venezuela, the world's highest waterfall - Angel Falls.

This is a guanaco. Guanacos are members of the camel family that live in South America. Guanaco hair is used to make textiles.

Caribbean Sea

Caracas

VENEZUELA

Medellin○ Bogota

COLOMBIA

Orinoco

Equator

Quito

ECUADOR

Galapagos
Islands
(Ecuador)

Guayaquil○

Mar

PERU

Lima

BOLIVIA

La Paz

Sucr

Tropic of Capricorn

CHILE

PACIFIC

OCEAN

Santiago ○Mendoza

ARGENTI

Cape Hor

Drake Pas.

The shading on this map is there to help you see clearly the different countries that make up the continent.

Georgetown
Paramaribo
Cayenne
ANA
URINAM FRENCH
GUIANA
(France)

Equator

azon

BRAZIL

Recife

Brasilia

Parana

Belo Horizonte

RAGUAY
Sao Paulo
Rio de Janeiro

Asuncion

Tropic of Capricorn

Porto Alegre

ATLANTIC
OCEAN

UGUAY
Montevideo
enos Aires

kland Islands
(U.K.)

This is a red-eyed tree frog. These frogs live in rainforests in South and Central America.

Facts

Total land area 17,866,130 sq km (6,898,113 sq miles)

Total population 346 million

Biggest city Sao Paulo, Brazil

Biggest country Brazil *8,547,400 sq km (3,300,151 sq miles)*

Smallest country Surinam *163,270 sq km (63,039 sq miles)*

Highest mountain Aconcagua, Argentina *6,959m (22,831ft)*

Longest river Amazon, mainly in Brazil *6,440km (4,000 miles)*

Biggest lake Lake Maracaibo, Venezuela *13,312 sq km (5,140 sq miles)*

Highest waterfall Angel Falls, on the Churun River, Venezuela *979m (3,212ft)*

Biggest desert Patagonian Desert, Argentina *673,000 sq km (260,000 sq miles)*

Biggest island Tierra del Fuego *46,360 sq km (17,900 sq miles)*

Main mineral deposits Copper, tin, molybdenum, bauxite, emeralds

Main fuel deposits Oil, coal

A 85°W   B   80°   C

Liberia
Puntarenas
Limon
San Jose
COSTA
RICA
Almirante
David
Santiago
Puerto
Armuelles
PANAMA
Coiba
Island

Riohacha
Cape Gallinas
Aruba 70° Netherlands Antilles 65° **GRENADA**
(Netherlands) (Netherlands) Lesser Antilles
Santa Marta **Cristobal** Paraguaipoa Coro Tortuga Margarita **TRINIDAD**
Barranquilla **Colon** Maracaibo Willemstad Island Island **AND TOBAGO**
Cartagena 5,775m Lagunillas Maracay **Caracas** Cumana **Port-**
(18,947ft) Lake Barquisimeto Valencia Barcelona Guiria **Spain**
Sincelejo Maracaibo Valera Araure Zaraza Maturin
Magangue Caceres **Bolivar Peak** Barinas Tucupita
Turbo Pamplona 5,007m San Fernando **VENEZUELA** Ciudad
Dabeiba **Bucaramanga** (16,427ft) de Apure Bolivar Ciudad
Nuqui Duitama Cravo Caicara Orinoco Guayana
Quibdo Tunja Norte Puerto Angel
Pereira **Manizales** Paez Falls
Bogota **Mount Rora**
Buga Ibague **COLOMBIA** Guaviare Puerto 2,810m
Buenaventura Cali Inirida Orinoco (9,219ft)
Neiva Santa Elena
5,750m San Jose del Guaviare Boa Vist
Tumaco Popayan (18,865ft)
Florencia _Guiana_
Highlands

Malpelo Island
(Colombia)

Colon
Panama City
Panama
Canal
Penonome
La Palma
Gulf of
Panama

Gulf of
Mosquitos

Gulf of
Darien

Western Cordillera

Eastern Cordillera

Llanos

Esmeraldas
Cape
San Francisco
Ibarra
Ipiales
Pasto
Equator
Quito
Santo Domingo de los Colorados
Nueva Loja
Puerto Leguizamo
La Chorrera
Negro
Manta
Quevedo
ECUADOR
Ambato
6,310m
(20,702ft)
Montalvo
Japura
Babahoyo
La Libertad
Guayaquil
Gulf of
Guayaquil
Cuenca
Iquitos
Amazon
Amazon
Tumbes
Machala
Talara
Loja
Leticia
Sullana
Zumba
Maranon
Atalaia do Norte
Piura
Chulucanas
Yurimaguas
Ucayali
_S e l v a s_
Cape Negro
Moyobamba
Chiclayo
PERU
Jurua
Pacasmayo
Cajamarca
Purus
Madeira
Trujillo
Huacrachuco
Pucallpa
Chimbote
Cruzeiro do Sul
Porto Velho
Mount Huascaran
6,746m
(22,132ft)
Huanuco
Rio Branco
PACIFIC
Cerro de Pasco
OCEAN
La Oroya
Riberalta
Central Cordillera
Lima
Huancayo
Puerto Cobija
Mala
Quillabamba Maldonado
Chincha Alta
Ayacucho
Machu Picchu
Magdalena
Western Cordillera
Ica
Cusco
Rurrenabaque
_A N D E S_
Eastern Cordillera
Sicuani
Trinidad
Nazca
Mount
Coropuna
Juliaca
Lake
Titicaca
Chala
6,425m Puno
Concepcion
(1,079ft)
La Paz
BOLIVIA
Mollendo Arequipa **Mount Illimani** Cochabamba
6,402m Oruro San Jose
(21,004ft) Santa Chiqu
Cruz
Gulf of _Lake_ Challapata
Arica _Poopo_ **Sucre**
CHILE Potosi Charagua
Camiri

Inset — Galapagos Islands:
N   90°W   P
Same scale as main map
9   9
Galapagos Islands
(Ecuador)
0° Equator 0°
San Salvador
Santa Cruz
Fernandina San Salvador
Isabela Puerto
Ayora San Cristobal
10   10
PACIFIC OCEAN
N   90°W   P

278

A 85°W   B 80°   C   75°   D 70°   E   F 65°

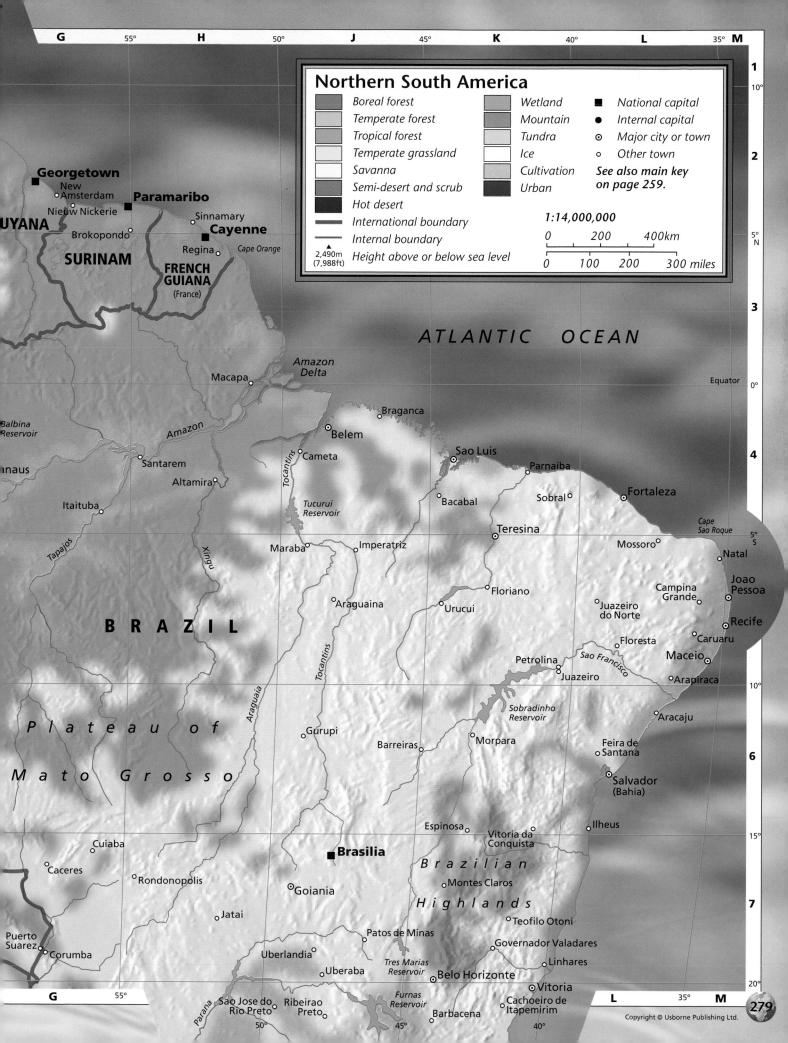

Northern South America

Boreal forest	Wetland	■ National capital
Temperate forest	Mountain	● Internal capital
Tropical forest	Tundra	⊙ Major city or town
Temperate grassland	Ice	○ Other town
Savanna	Cultivation	**See also main key**
Semi-desert and scrub	Urban	**on page 259.**
Hot desert		

International boundary

Internal boundary

▲ 2,490m (7,988ft) Height above or below sea level

1:14,000,000

0 200 400km

0 100 200 300 miles

ATLANTIC OCEAN

Georgetown
New Amsterdam
Nieuw Nickerie
Brokopondo
GUYANA
SURINAM
Paramaribo
Sinnamary
Cayenne
Regina
Cape Orange
FRENCH GUIANA
(France)

Balbina Reservoir
anaus
Amazon
Santarem
Itaituba
Tapajos

Macapa
Amazon Delta
Braganca
Belem
Cameta
Altamira
Tucurui Reservoir
Maraba
Araguaina

B R A Z I L

Xingu
Tocantins
Tocantins
Araguaia

Imperatriz
Floriano
Urucui
Gurupi
Barreiras
Morpara

Sao Luis
Parnaiba
Bacabal
Sobral
Teresina
Fortaleza
Cape Sao Roque
Mossoro
Natal
Campina Grande
Joao Pessoa
Juazeiro do Norte
Recife
Floresta
Caruaru
Maceio
Petrolina
Sao Francisco
Juazeiro
Arapiraca
Aracaju

Sobradinho Reservoir

Feira de Santana

Salvador (Bahia)

P l a t e a u   o f

M a t o   G r o s s o

Cuiaba
Caceres
Rondonopolis
Puerto Suarez
Corumba
Jatai
Goiania
■ **Brasilia**

Espinosa
Vitoria da Conquista
Ilheus

B r a z i l i a n
Montes Claros
H i g h l a n d s
Teofilo Otoni

Patos de Minas
Governador Valadares
Linhares
Uberlandia
Uberaba
Tres Marias Reservoir
Belo Horizonte
Vitoria
Parana
Furnas Reservoir
Cachoeiro de Itapemirim
Sao Jose do Rio Preto
Ribeirao Preto
Barbacena

Equator 0°

5° S

10°

15°

20°

PERU

BOLIVIA

BRAZIL

PARAGUAY

URUGUAY

CHILE

Plateau of Mato Grosso

Brazilian Highlands

Gran Chaco

A N D E S

Rio Branco
Cobija
Puerto Maldonado
Riberalta
Rurrenabaque
Trinidad
Magdalena
Juliaca
Puno
Arica
Tacna
Iquique
Pica
Ollague
Lake Titicaca
La Paz
Mount Illimani 6,402m (21,004ft)
Oruro
Challapata
Lake Poopo
Potosi
Uyuni
Tupiza
San Pedro de Atacama
Calama
Antofagasta
Taltal
Chanaral
Copiapo
Vallenar
Coquimbo
Ovalle
Illapelo
Valparaiso
Santiago
Rancagua
Mount Ojos del Salado 6,908m (22,664ft)
Mount Aconcagua 6,959m (22,831ft)
San Juan
Mendoza
Merlo
San Luis
Villa Mercedes
La Rioja
Catamarca
Salta
San Salvador de Jujuy
San Miguel de Tucuman
Santiago del Estero
Cordoba
San Francisco
Rio Cuarto
Villa Maria
Rufino
Rosario
Venado Tuerto
San Nicolas de los Arroyos
Santa Fe
Parana
Concordia
Gualeguaychu
Salto
Paysandu
Tacuarembo
Rivera
Durazno
Melo
Mirim Lake
Rio Grande
Pelotas
Bage
Porto Alegre
Caxias do Sul
Patos Lagoon
Santa Maria
Criciuma
Passo Fundo
Florianopolis
Itajai
Curitiba
Paranagua
Guarapuava
Cascavel
Foz do Iguacu
Iguacu Falls
Ciudad del Este
Eldorado
Posadas
Encarnacion
Corrientes
Reconquista
Uruguaiana
Formosa
Asuncion
Villarrica
Concepcion
Pedro Juan Caballero
Paraguay
Pilcomayo
Salado
Salado
Tartagal
San Ramon
Camiri
Charagua
Tarija
Sucre
Cochabamba
Santa Cruz
Concepcion
San Jose de Chiquitos
Puerto Suarez
Corumba
Caceres
Cuiaba
Rondonopolis
Campo Grande
Sao Jose do Rio Preto
Dourados
Ponta Pora
Jatai
Uberlandia
Uberaba
Presidente Prudente
Marilia
Londrina
Araraquara
Ribeirao Preto
Campinas
Itapetininga
Sao Paulo
Pocos de Caldas
Mount Agulhas Negras 2,787m (9,144ft)
Furnas Reservoir
Nova Iguacu
Rio de Janeiro
Macae
Campos
Juiz de Fora
Barbacena
Cachoeiro de Itapemirim
Vitoria
Governador Valadares
Teofilo Otoni
Linhares
Belo Horizonte
Patos de Minas
Tres Marias Reservoir
Montes Claros
Espinosa
Vitoria da Conquista
Ilheus
Feira de Santana
Morpara
Barreiras
Sobradinho Reservoir
Goiania
Brasilia

Tocantins
Araguaia
Gurupi
Parana
Parana

Tropic of Capricorn

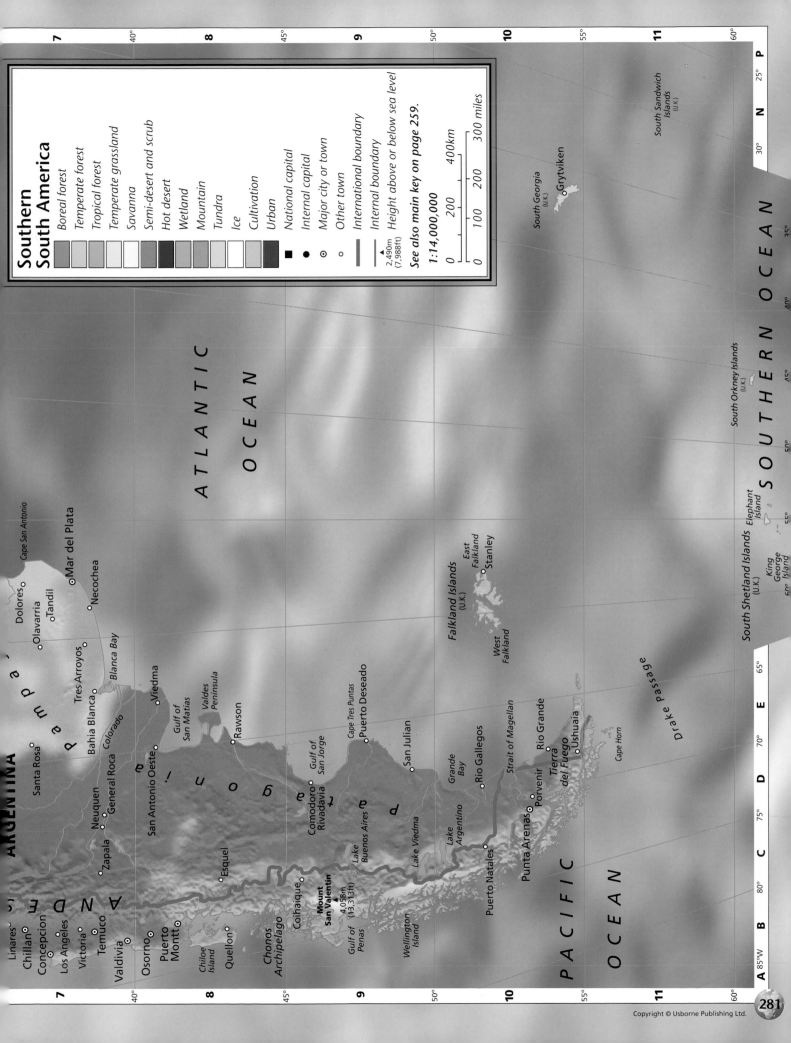

Key

Boreal forest
Temperate forest
Tropical forest
Temperate grassland
Savanna
Semi-desert and scrub
Hot desert
Wetland
Mountain
Tundra
Ice
Cultivation
Urban

■ National capital
● Internal capital
◉ Major city or town
○ Other town

— International boundary
— Internal boundary

▲ 2,490m (7,988ft) Height above or below sea level

See also main key on page 259.

1:14,000,000

0   100   200   300   400km
0   100   200   300 miles

ARGENTINA

Linares
Chillán
Concepción
Los Angeles
Victoria
Temuco
Valdivia
Osorno
Puerto Montt
Santa Rosa
Dolores
Olavarria
Tandil
Necochea
Cape San Antonio
Mar del Plata
Tres Arroyos
Bahia Blanca
Blanca Bay
Viedma
Neuquen
General Roca
Colorado
San Antonio Oeste
Gulf of San Matias
Valdes Peninsula
Rawson
Zapala
Pampas
Esquel
Coihaique
Mount San Valentin
4,058m (13,313ft)
Chonos Archipelago
Chiloe Island
Quellon
Gulf of Penas
Wellington Island
Comodoro Rivadavia
Gulf of San Jorge
Cape Tres Puntas
Puerto Deseado
San Julian
Lake Buenos Aires
Lake Viedma
Lake Argentino
Puerto Natales
Grande Bay
Rio Gallegos
Punta Arenas
Porvenir
Strait of Magellan
Tierra del Fuego
Rio Grande
Ushuaia
Cape Horn
Drake Passage

ATLANTIC OCEAN

PACIFIC OCEAN

SOUTHERN OCEAN

Falkland Islands (U.K.)
East Falkland
West Falkland
Stanley

South Georgia (U.K.)
Grytviken
South Sandwich Islands (U.K.)

South Orkney Islands (U.K.)

South Shetland Islands (U.K.)
Elephant Island
King George Island

MAPS OF
AUSTRALASIA
AND OCEANIA

A school of barracuda fish

This is a satellite image of Australasia, which includes Australia and New Zealand, and Oceania, which is the name given to the other islands in the Pacific Ocean.

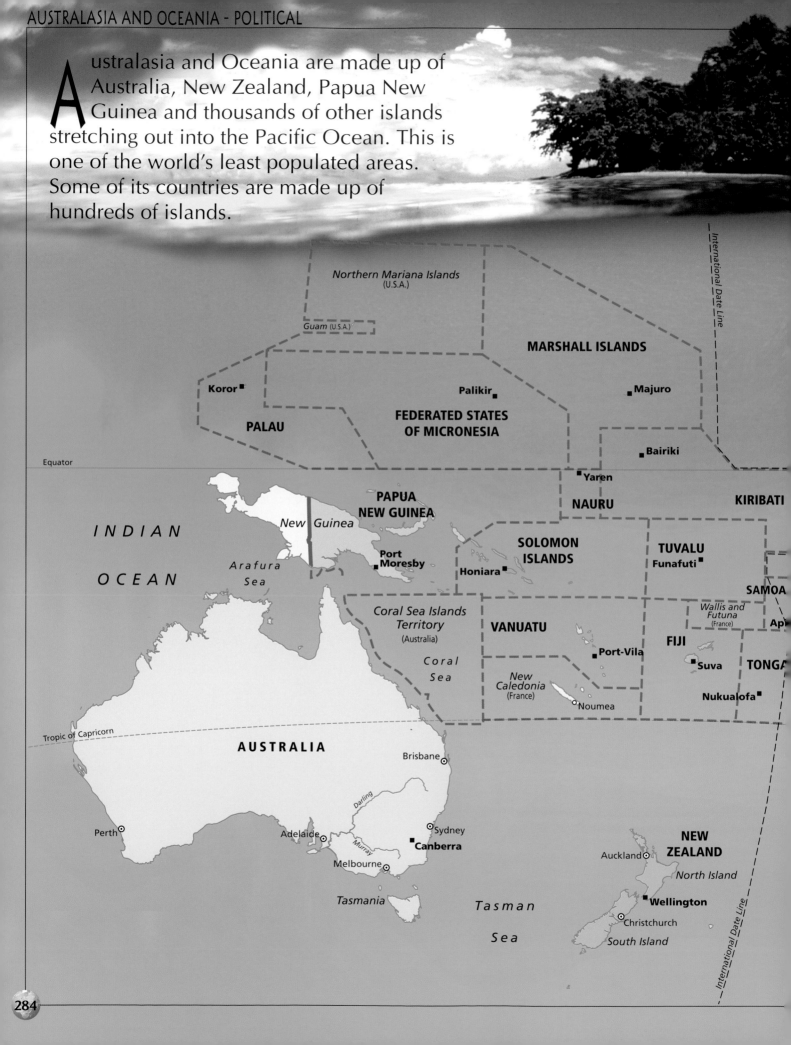

Australasia and Oceania

Australasia and Oceania are made up of Australia, New Zealand, Papua New Guinea and thousands of other islands stretching out into the Pacific Ocean. This is one of the world's least populated areas. Some of its countries are made up of hundreds of islands.

International Date Line

Northern Mariana Islands
(U.S.A.)

Guam (U.S.A.)

MARSHALL ISLANDS

Koror ■

Palikir ■

Majuro ■

PALAU

FEDERATED STATES
OF MICRONESIA

Bairiki ■

Equator

Yaren ■

NAURU

KIRIBATI

INDIAN

PAPUA
NEW GUINEA

New Guinea

SOLOMON
ISLANDS

TUVALU
Funafuti ■

Arafura
Sea

Port
Moresby ■

Honiara ■

SAMOA

OCEAN

Wallis and
Futuna
(France)

Ap

Coral Sea Islands
Territory
(Australia)

VANUATU

FIJI

Port-Vila ■

Coral
Sea

TONGA

New
Caledonia
(France)

Suva ■

Noumea ◉

Nukualofa ■

Tropic of Capricorn

AUSTRALIA

Brisbane ◉

Perth ◉

Sydney ◉

Adelaide ◉

Canberra ■

NEW
ZEALAND

Auckland ◉

Murray

Melbourne ◉

North Island

Darling

Tasmania

Tasman

Wellington ■

Sea

Christchurch ◉

South Island

International Date Line

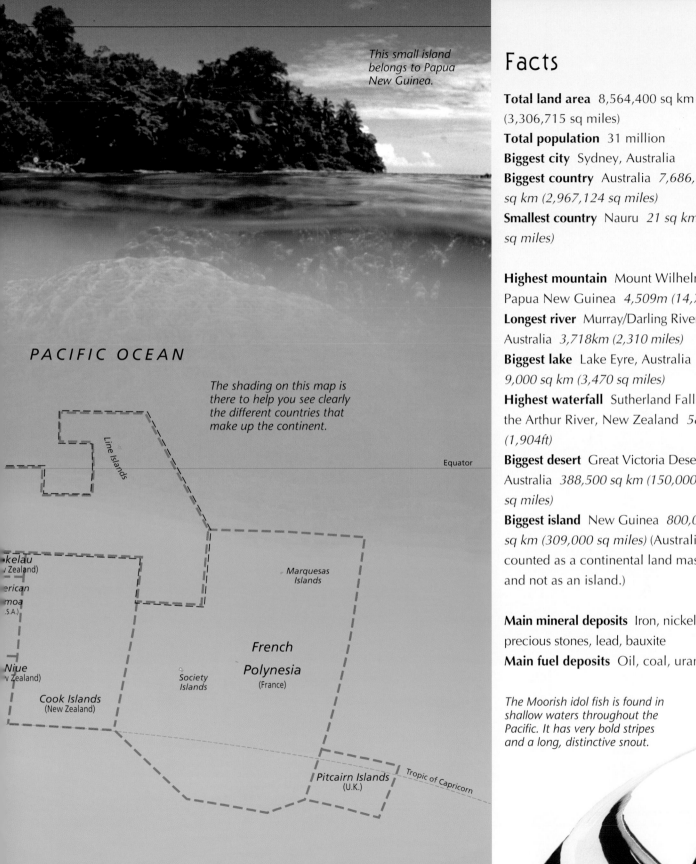

This small island belongs to Papua New Guinea.

PACIFIC OCEAN

The shading on this map is there to help you see clearly the different countries that make up the continent.

Line Islands

Equator

kelau
Zealand)

erican
moa
S.A.)

Niue
v Zealand)

Cook Islands
(New Zealand)

Society
Islands

Marquesas
Islands

French
Polynesia
(France)

Pitcairn Islands
(U.K.)

Tropic of Capricorn

Facts

Total land area 8,564,400 sq km (3,306,715 sq miles)

Total population 31 million

Biggest city Sydney, Australia

Biggest country Australia 7,686,850 sq km (2,967,124 sq miles)

Smallest country Nauru 21 sq km (8 sq miles)

Highest mountain Mount Wilhelm, Papua New Guinea 4,509m (14,793ft)

Longest river Murray/Darling River, Australia 3,718km (2,310 miles)

Biggest lake Lake Eyre, Australia 9,000 sq km (3,470 sq miles)

Highest waterfall Sutherland Falls, on the Arthur River, New Zealand 580m (1,904ft)

Biggest desert Great Victoria Desert, Australia 388,500 sq km (150,000 sq miles)

Biggest island New Guinea 800,000 sq km (309,000 sq miles) (Australia is counted as a continental land mass and not as an island.)

Main mineral deposits Iron, nickel, precious stones, lead, bauxite

Main fuel deposits Oil, coal, uranium

The Moorish idol fish is found in shallow waters throughout the Pacific. It has very bold stripes and a long, distinctive snout.

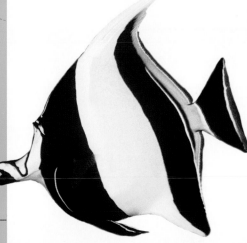

285

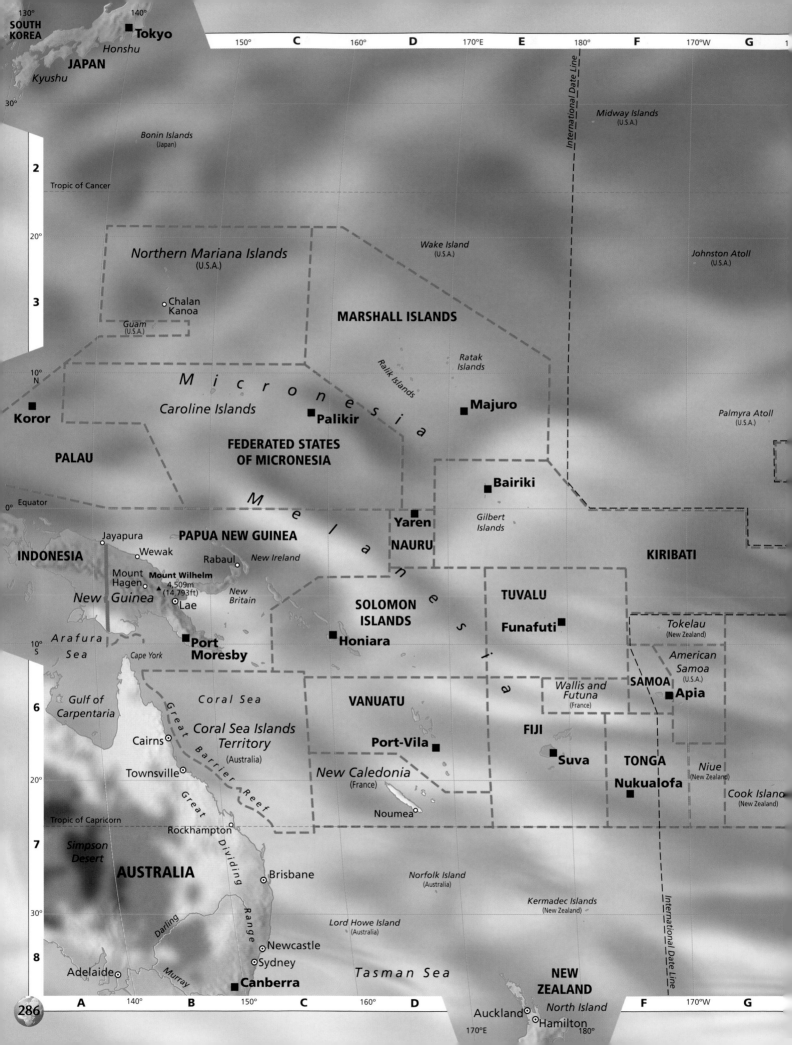

SOUTH KOREA

JAPAN

Honshu

Tokyo

Kyushu

130°　140°

Tropic of Cancer

Bonin Islands
(Japan)

Northern Mariana Islands
(U.S.A.)

Chalan
Kanoa

Guam
(U.S.A.)

Wake Island
(U.S.A.)

Midway Islands
(U.S.A.)

Johnston Atoll
(U.S.A.)

MARSHALL ISLANDS

M i c r o n e s i a

Ralik Islands

Ratak Islands

Caroline Islands

Palikir

Majuro

Palmyra Atoll
(U.S.A.)

Koror

PALAU

FEDERATED STATES
OF MICRONESIA

Bairiki

Equator

M e l a n e s i a

Yaren

NAURU

Gilbert Islands

KIRIBATI

INDONESIA

Jayapura

PAPUA NEW GUINEA

Wewak

Rabaul

New Ireland

Mount
Hagen

Mount Wilhelm
▲ 4,509m
(14,793ft)

Lae

New Guinea

New Britain

SOLOMON
ISLANDS

Honiara

TUVALU

Funafuti

Tokelau
(New Zealand)

American
Samoa
(U.S.A.)

SAMOA

Arafura
Sea

Cape York

Port
Moresby

Coral Sea

VANUATU

n e s i a

Wallis and
Futuna
(France)

FIJI

Apia

Gulf of
Carpentaria

Cairns

Coral Sea Islands
Territory
(Australia)

Port-Vila

Suva

TONGA

Niue
(New Zealand)

Townsville

Great Barrier Reef

Great Dividing Range

New Caledonia
(France)

Noumea

Nukualofa

Cook Island
(New Zealand)

Tropic of Capricorn

Rockhampton

Simpson
Desert

AUSTRALIA

Brisbane

Norfolk Island
(Australia)

Kermadec Islands
(New Zealand)

Darling

Murray

Adelaide

Newcastle

Sydney

Canberra

Lord Howe Island
(Australia)

Tasman Sea

NEW
ZEALAND

Auckland

North Island

Hamilton

A　140°　B　150°　C　160°　D　170°E　180°　F　170°W　G

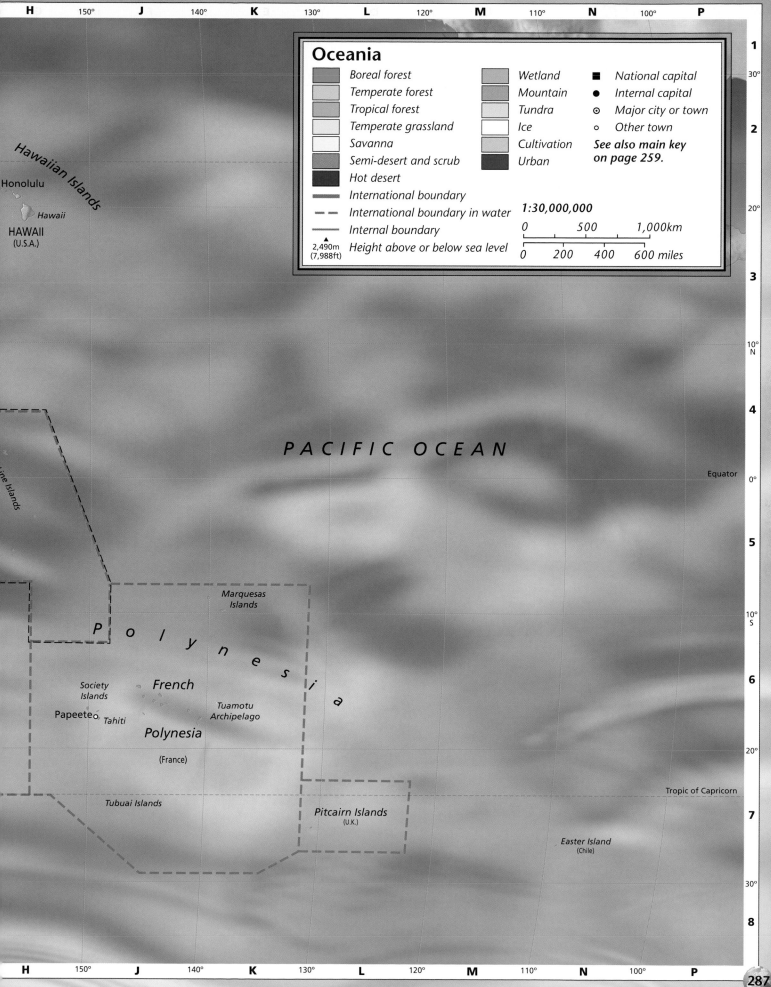

H 150° J 140° K 130° L 120° M 110° N 100° P

1
30°

Oceania

	Boreal forest		Wetland	■ National capital
	Temperate forest		Mountain	● Internal capital
	Tropical forest		Tundra	◉ Major city or town
	Temperate grassland		Ice	○ Other town
	Savanna		Cultivation	**See also main key**
	Semi-desert and scrub		Urban	**on page 259.**
	Hot desert			

International boundary

- - - International boundary in water

International boundary

▲
2,490m
(7,988ft) Height above or below sea level

1:30,000,000

0   500   1,000km

0   200   400   600 miles

2
20°

Hawaiian Islands

Honolulu

Hawaii

HAWAII
(U.S.A.)

3

10°
N

4

P A C I F I C   O C E A N

Equator 0°

ine Islands

5

*Marquesas
Islands*

10°
S

P o l y n e s i a

Society
Islands

French

*Tuamotu
Archipelago*

6

Papeete ○ *Tahiti*

Polynesia

(France)

20°

Tubuai Islands

Tropic of Capricorn

Pitcairn Islands
(U.K.)

7

Easter Island
(Chile)

30°

8

H 150° J 140° K 130° L 120° M 110° N 100° P

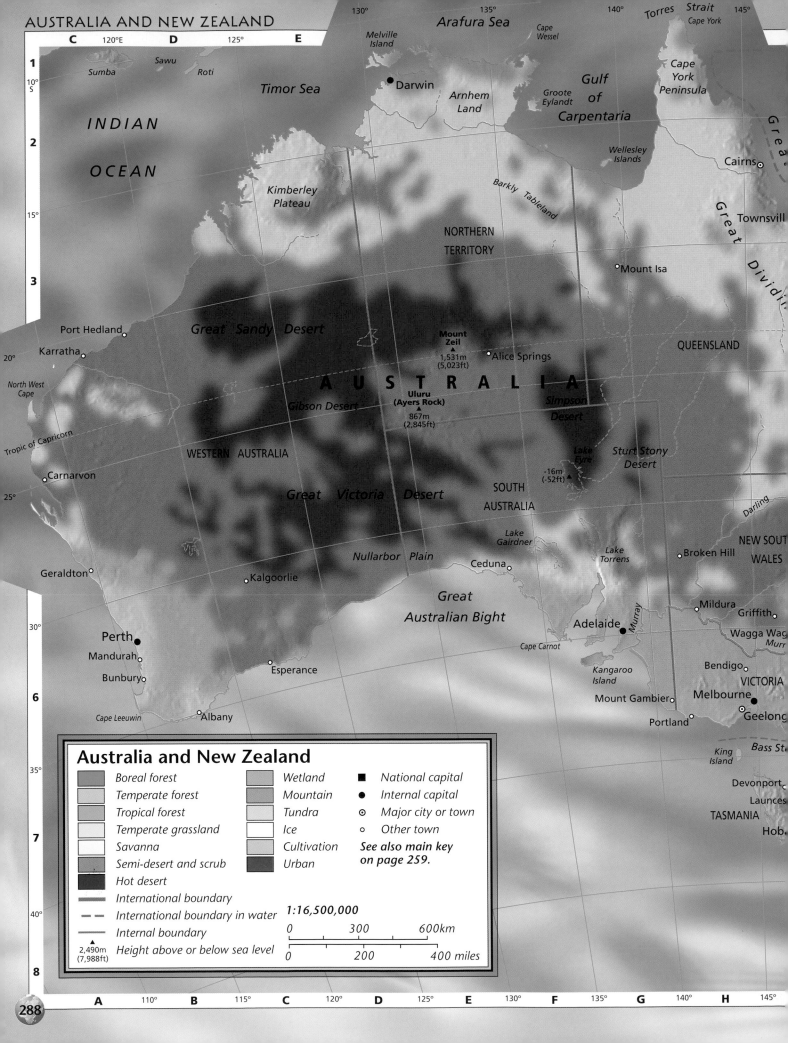

C 120°E D 125° E

1

10°S

Sumba *Sawu* *Roti*

INDIAN

OCEAN

Timor Sea

Melville
Island

● Darwin

Arnhem
Land

Arafura Sea

Cape
Wessel

Groote
Eylandt

Gulf
of
Carpentaria

Torres Strait
Cape York

Cape
York
Peninsula

130° 135° 140° 145°

2

Kimberley
Plateau

Wellesley
Islands

Cairns ◉

Great

15°

NORTHERN
TERRITORY

Barkly Tableland

Townsvill

Great Dividing

3

Port Hedland ◦

Karratha ◦

Great   Sandy   Desert

Mount
Zeil
▲
1,531m
(5,023ft)

Alice Springs ◉

Simpson

QUEENSLAND

20°

North West
Cape

Gibson Desert

Uluru
(Ayers Rock)
▲
867m
(2,845ft)

A U S T R A L I A

Desert

Tropic of Capricorn

Carnarvon ◦

WESTERN   AUSTRALIA

Sturt Stony
Desert

25°

Great   Victoria   Desert

Lake
Eyre

-16m
(-52ft) ▲

SOUTH
AUSTRALIA

Darling

Lake
Gairdner

NEW SOUT
WALES

Geraldton ◦

Nullarbor   Plain

Kalgoorlie ◦

Lake
Torrens

Broken Hill ◦

Ceduna ◦

30°

Perth ■

Mandurah ◦

Bunbury ◦

Esperance ◦

*Great
Australian Bight*

Cape Carnot

Adelaide ●

Murray

Mildura ◦

Griffith ◦

Wagga Wag
Murr

Bendigo ◦

VICTORIA

Kangaroo
Island

6

Cape Leeuwin

Albany ◦

Mount Gambier ◦

Melbourne ●

Geelong ◉

Portland ◦

King
Island

Bass St

35°

Devonport

Launces

Australia and New Zealand

▨ Boreal forest	▨ Wetland	■	National capital
▨ Temperate forest	▨ Mountain	●	Internal capital
▨ Tropical forest	▨ Tundra	◉	Major city or town
▨ Temperate grassland	▢ Ice	◦	Other town
▨ Savanna	▨ Cultivation		**See also main key**
▨ Semi-desert and scrub	▨ Urban		**on page 259.**
▨ Hot desert			

――― International boundary

‐ ‐ ‐ International boundary in water

――― Internal boundary

▲ 2,490m
(7,988ft) Height above or below sea level

1:16,500,000

0   300   600km

0   200   400 miles

TASMANIA

Hob

A 110° B 115° C 120° D 125° E 130° F 135° G 140° H 145°

1

Rennell Island

SOLOMON ISLANDS

Santa Cruz Islands

10°S

Coral Sea

TUVALU

Coral Sea Islands Territory (Australia)

2

Banks Islands

VANUATU

Espiritu Santo

○ Luganville

Malakula

15°

Efate ■ **Port-Vila**

FIJI

Vanua Levu

Lautoka ○

Viti Levu ■ **Suva**

arrier Reef

○ Mackay

Chesterfield Islands

New Caledonia (France)

hampton ○

Gladstone ○

20°

Bundaberg ○

Fraser Island

Noumea ○

Loyalty Islands

Gympie ○

nge

PACIFIC OCEAN

4

Toowoomba ○

● Brisbane

○ **Tropic of Capricorn**

Brisbane ● Gold Coast

oree ○

○ Grafton

25°

Norfolk Island (Australia)

Great Dividing Range

Armidale ○

Lord Howe Island (Australia)

Dubbo ○

○ Port Macquarie

5

○ Newcastle

● Sydney

Kermadec Islands (New Zealand)

○ Wollongong

■ **Canberra**

30°

AUSTRALIAN CAPITAL TERRITORY

ount iuszko

9m 3ft)

North Cape

6

Tasman Sea

○ Whangarei

○ Auckland

North Island

35°

Hamilton ○

East Cape

New Plymouth ○

Rotorua ○

nders nd

Lake Taupo

Cape Farewell

Napier ○

7

Nelson ○

Cook Strait

■ **Wellington**

South Island

NEW ZEALAND

Aoraki (Mount Cook) ▲ 3,754m (12,316ft)

○ Christchurch

Sutherland Falls

40°

Cape Providence

Invercargill ○

○ Dunedin

Chatham Islands (New Zealand)

Stewart Island

South West Cape

8

A satellite image of Earth, focusing on Asia. You can also see the Arctic at the top, the Indian Ocean (lower middle), Pacific Ocean (right) and some of the Pacific islands.

MAPS OF ASIA

A Bengal tiger

Asia is the world's largest continent and has over 40 countries, including Russia, the biggest country in the world. As well as large land masses, it has thousands of islands and inlets, giving it over 160,000km (100,000 miles) of coastline. Asia also contains the Himalayas, the world's highest mountain range. Turkey and Russia are part in Europe and part in Asia, but both are shown in full on this map.

The shading on this map is there to help you see clearly the different countries that make up the continent.

A type of Chinese sailing boat called a junk in the port at Singapore

ARCTIC OCEAN

Franz Josef Land

Novaya Zemlya

Barents Sea

Kara Sea

Ob

Moscow

R U S

Volga

Black Sea

Ankara

TURKEY

GEORGIA

Astana

KAZAKHSTAN

CYPRUS

ARMENIA

Caspian Sea

Aral Sea

AZERBAIJAN

UZBEKISTAN

LEBANON

SYRIA

Beirut

Damascus

TURKMENISTAN

Bishkek

Ashgabat

Tashkent

KYRGYZSTAN

Jerusalem

Amman

ISRAEL

JORDAN

Baghdad

Tehran

Dushanbe

TAJIKISTAN

IRAQ

IRAN

Kabul

Islamabad

Tropic of Cancer

KUWAIT

AFGHANISTAN

SAUDI ARABIA

BAHRAIN

QATAR

PAKISTAN

Riyadh

Doha

Indus

New Delhi

NEPAL

Kathmandu

Abu Dhabi

UNITED ARAB EMIRATES

Muscat

Ganges

Thim

BANGLAD.

Sana

OMAN

Arabian Sea

INDIA

YEMEN

Socotra (Yemen)

Bay o. Benga

INDIAN OCEAN

SRI LANKA

Sri Jayewardenepura Kotte

Equator

Colombo

MALDIVES

Male

Wrangel
Island

Bering Sea

East
Siberian
Sea

New Siberia
Islands

Severnaya
Zemlya

Laptev
Sea

Sea of
Okhotsk

A

Lena

Lake
Baikal

Hokkaido

Ulan Bator ■

Sea of
Japan

JAPAN
Tokyo ■

MONGOLIA

NORTH
KOREA

Pyongyang ■

Seoul ■

Beijing ■

Honshu

SOUTH
KOREA

Huang He (Yellow)

East China
Sea

C H I N A

Tropic of Cancer

Chang Jiang (Yangtze)

Taipei ■

TAIWAN

PACIFIC

OCEAN

TAN

Irrawaddy

ka

BURMA
(MYANMAR)

Hanoi ■

LAOS

South China
Sea

PHILIPPINES

Vientiane ■

goon

THAILAND

Mekong

VIETNAM

Manila ■

Philippine
Sea

Bangkok ■

CAMBODIA

Andaman
Islands
(India)

Phnom
Penh ■

Nicobar
Islands
(India)

Equator

BRUNEI

M A L A Y S I A

New Guinea

Kuala Lumpur ■

SINGAPORE

Borneo

Celebes

Sumatra

I N D O N E S I A

Dili ■

Arafura Sea

Jakarta ■

EAST
TIMOR

Java

Facts

Total land area 44,537,920 sq km
(17,196,090 sq miles)
Total population 3.8 billion
(including all of Russia)
Biggest city Tokyo, Japan
Biggest country Russia *Total area:*
17,075,200 sq km (6,592,735 sq
miles) Area of Asiatic Russia:
12,780,800 sq km (4,934,667 sq miles)
Smallest country Maldives *300 sq km*
(116 sq miles)

Highest mountain Mount Everest,
Nepal/China border *8,850m (29,035ft)*
Longest river Chang Jiang (Yangtze),
China *6,380km (3,964 miles)*
Biggest lake Caspian Sea, western
Asia *370,999 sq km (143,243 sq miles)*
Highest waterfall Jog Falls, on the
Sharavati River, India *253m (830ft)*
Biggest desert Arabian Desert, in and
around Saudi Arabia *2,230,000 sq km*
(900,000 sq miles)
Biggest island Borneo *751,100 sq km*
(290,000 sq miles)

Main mineral deposits Zinc, mica, tin,
chromium, iron, nickel
Main fuel deposits Oil, coal,
uranium, natural gas

*These are lotus flowers, Asian water
lilies known for their beauty. In China
they are associated with purity and
for Buddhists they are sacred.*

293

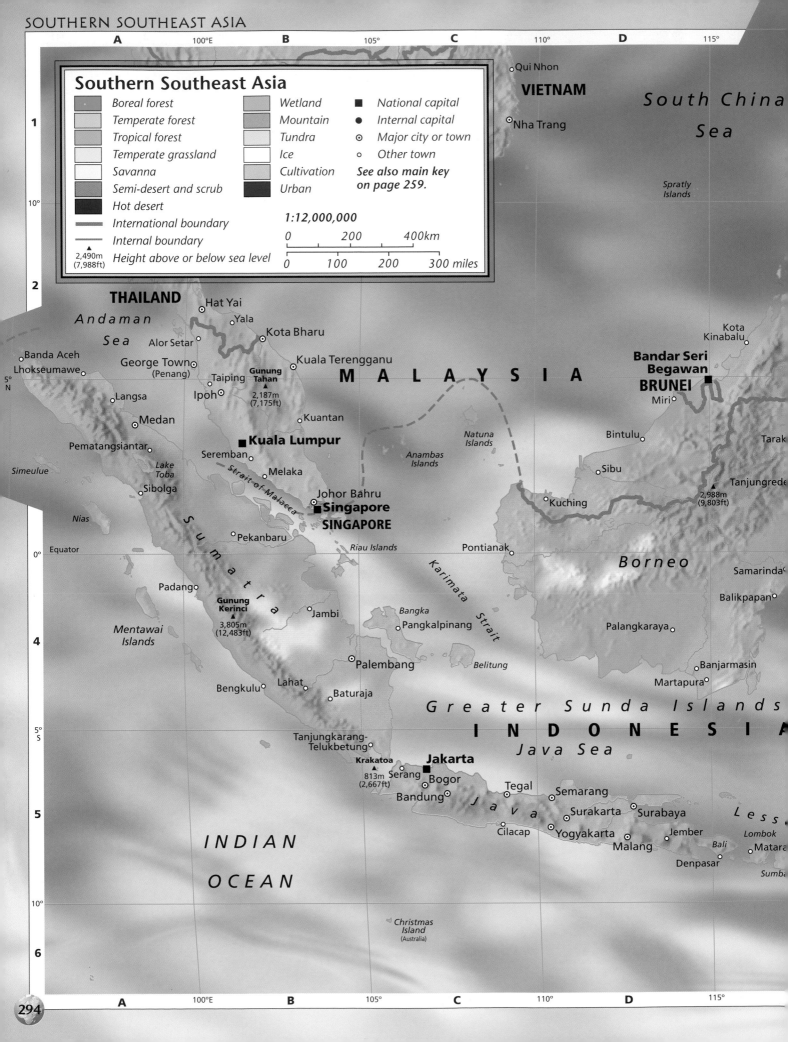

Southern Southeast Asia

	Boreal forest		Wetland
	Temperate forest		Mountain
	Tropical forest		Tundra
	Temperate grassland		Ice
	Savanna		Cultivation
	Semi-desert and scrub		Urban
	Hot desert		

■ National capital
● Internal capital
⊙ Major city or town
○ Other town

See also main key on page 259.

International boundary
Internal boundary

▲ 2,490m (7,988ft) Height above or below sea level

1:12,000,000

0   200   400km
0 100 200 300 miles

VIETNAM
Qui Nhon
Nha Trang

South China Sea

Spratly Islands

THAILAND
Andaman Sea
Hat Yai
Yala
Kota Bharu
Alor Setar
Banda Aceh
Lhokseumawe
George Town (Penang)
Taiping
Kuala Terengganu
Gunung Tahan ▲ 2,187m (7,175ft)
Ipoh
Kuantan
Langsa
Medan
Pematangsiantar
Lake Toba
Kuala Lumpur
Seremban
Melaka
Simeulue
Sibolga
Strait of Malacca
Nias
Johor Bahru
Singapore
SINGAPORE

MALAYSIA

Natuna Islands
Anambas Islands

Kota Kinabalu
Bandar Seri Begawan
BRUNEI
Miri
Bintulu
Tarak
Sibu
Kuching
Tanjungrede ▲ 2,988m (9,803ft)

Riau Islands
Pekanbaru
Pontianak
Borneo
Samarinda
Balikpapan

Equator

Padang
Gunung Kerinci ▲ 3,805m (12,483ft)
Mentawai Islands
Jambi
Bangka
Pangkalpinang
Karimata Strait
Palangkaraya
Sumatra
Palembang
Belitung
Banjarmasin
Lahat
Martapura
Bengkulu
Baturaja

Greater Sunda Islands
INDONESIA
Java Sea

Tanjungkarang-Telukbetung
Krakatoa ▲ 813m (2,667ft)
Serang
Jakarta
Bogor
Tegal
Semarang
Bandung
Surakarta
Surabaya
Less
Java
Cilacap
Yogyakarta
Jember
Lombok
Malang
Bali
Matara
Denpasar
Sumba

INDIAN OCEAN

Christmas Island (Australia)

G
H
J
F
120°
125°
130°
135°
140°
Cabanatuan
Luzon
Olongapo
Quezon City
Manila
Lucena
Naga
Calapan
Legaspi
Mindoro
PHILIPPINES
Masbate
Masbate
Calbayog
Calamian Group
Roxas
Samar
Panay
Tacloban
Taytay
Philippine Sea
Iloilo
Bacolod
Cebu
Negros
Puerto Princesa
Bohol
Surigao
Dumaguete
Butuan
Cagayan de Oro
Sulu Sea
Pagadian
Iligan
Mindanao
Davao
Zamboanga
Jolo
General Santos
Sulu Archipelago
Talaud Islands
Celebes Sea
PACIFIC OCEAN
PALAU
Sangihe Islands
Morotai
Manado
Ternate
Halmahera
Gorontalo
Makassar Strait
Molucca Sea
Equator
Palu
Sorong
Biak
Peleng
Obi
Misool
Yapen
Celebes
Sula Islands
Ceram Sea
Jayapura
Palopo
Fakfak
Ceram
Buru
Maoke Range
Puncak Jaya
5,030m (16,502ft)
Ambon
Kendari
New Guinea
Watampone
Buton
Ujung Pandang
Banda Sea
Aru Islands
Flores Sea
Wetar
Tanimbar Islands
Dolak
Flores
Dili
Ende
EAST TIMOR
Sumba
Sawu Sea
Timor
Arafura Sea
Torres Strait
Sawu
Kupang
Roti
Timor Sea
AUSTRALIA
Darwin
NORTHERN TERRITORY
1
2
3
6
10°
5° N
0°
5° S
10°
J 140°E K 145° L 150° M Equator 155° N
0°
PACIFIC OCEAN
Admiralty Islands
Jayapura
Wewak
Bismarck Sea
New Ireland
Rabaul
Mount Wilhelm
4,509m (14,793ft)
Madang
Mount Hagen
New Britain
New Guinea
Lae
PAPUA NEW GUINEA
Kerema
Solomon Sea
Gulf of Papua
D'Entrecasteaux Islands
Port Moresby
Torres Strait
Cape York
1:18,000,000
0 400km
0 200 miles
Cape York Peninsula
AUSTRALIA
4
5
6
5° S
10°

A 90°E B 95° C 100° D 105° E

Brahmaputra Lhasa

H i m a l a y a s

Mount Everest
8,850m
(29,035ft)

Thimphu

INDIA

NEPAL BHUTAN

Darjeeling

Biratnagar Dibrugarh

Darbhanga *Brahmaputra* Jorhat

Bhagalpur Rangpur Guwahati

Asansol Rajshahi Sylhet Shillong

BANGLADESH Imphal

Jamshedpur **Dhaka** Aizawl

Kolkata Khulna
(Calcutta)

Chittagong Monywa Mandalay

Mouths of the Ganges Mount Lashio
Victoria
3,053m BURMA
(10,016ft) (MYANMAR)

Sittwe Meiktila Taunggyi

Bay of Bengal Pyinmana

Sandoway Pye *Salween*

Henzada *Irrawaddy*

Pathein Pegu

Thaton
Rangoon Moulmein

*Mouths of the
Irrawaddy*

INDIAN

OCEAN Tavoy

Andaman *Andaman*
Islands *Sea*
(India) Mergui

Port Blair *Mergui
Archipelago* Prachuap
Khiri Khan
Little
Andaman

Ten Degree Channel Chumphon

Gongga Shan Chengdu Wanxian

Leshan Chongqing
7,556m
(24,790ft) Neijiang Ensh

Xichang Luzhou C H
Yibin

Zhaotong Zunyi Huaih

Panzhihua Guiyang

Dali Anshun

Baoshan Kunming Liuzho

Red Kaiyuan Nanni

Simao Gejiu

Phongsali Ha Giang

Lao Cai Qinzhou
Son La Thai Nguyen

Hanoi

Mekong Louangphrabang Hai Phong

LAOS Thanh Hoa

Chiang Mai *Gulf of
Tonkin*
Vientiane Vinh

Sany
Udon Thani

Phitsanulok Savannakhet Hue

Khon Da Nar
Kaen

Nakhon Sawan Ubon
Ratchathani Pakxe

THAILAND Nakhon Ratchasima Attapu

VIETNA

Bangkok Qui Nhon

Angkor *Tonle Sap* Stoeng Treng Buon Me
Pattaya Thuot
Batdambang CAMBODIA
Da Lat N
Kampong Tra
Chhnang Kampong
Cham
Krong **Phnom
Kaoh Kong Penh** Bien Hoa

Kampong Saom Ho Chi Minh Cit
Long Xuyen (Saigon)

Gulf of Thailand Can Tho

Nakhon Si Bac Lieu
Thammarat *Con Son*

Nicobar Islands
(India) Hat Yai

Yala

Alor Setar Kota Bharu

Banda Aceh Kuala Terengganu

Lhokseumawe George Town
(Penang) Gunung
Tahan
Sumatra Langsa Taiping Ipoh 2,187m MALAYSIA *Natuna
Islands*
INDONESIA (7,175ft) (Indonesia)

A 90°E B 95° C 100° D 105° E

Northern Southeast Asia

	Boreal forest
	Temperate forest
	Tropical forest
	Temperate grassland
	Savanna
	Semi-desert and scrub
	Hot desert
	Wetland
	Mountain
	Tundra
	Ice
	Cultivation
	Urban
■	National capital
●	Internal capital
⊙	Major city or town
○	Other town
	International boundary
	Internal boundary
▲ 2,490m (7,988ft)	Height above or below sea level

See also main key on page 259.

1:12,000,000

| 0 | 200 | 400km |
| 0 | 100 | 200 | 300 miles |

Yichang
Huangshi
Wuhan
Luan
Hefei
Nanjing
Nantong
Wuxi
Shanghai
120°
115°
G
Chang Jiang (Yangtze)
Anqing
Wuhu
Tai Lake
Hangzhou
angde
Yueyang
Dongting Lake
Poyang Lake
Ningbo
A
Changsha
Nanchang
Jinhua
East China Sea
Zhuzhou
Linchuan
Wenzhou
Shaoyang
Hengyang
Nanping
25°N
Chenzhou
Ganzhou
Yongan
Fuzhou
Ryukyu Islands (Japan)
uilin
Shaoguan
Zhangzhou
Xiamen
Chilung
Taipei
Sakishima Islands
Wuzhou
Canton (Guangzhou)
Shantou
Changhua
Taichung
TAIWAN
Tropic of Cancer
3
Xi Jiang
Yu Shan 3,997m (13,113ft)
in
Macau
Hong Kong (Xianggang)
Tainan
Kaohsiung
20°
anjiang
Batan Islands
Luzon Strait
aikou
Babuyan Islands
4
Hainan
Laoag
Aparri
Paracel Islands
Tuguegarao
Ilagan
Mount Pulog 2,930m (9,613ft)
15°
Dagupan
Cabanatuan
Luzon
Philippine Sea
PACIFIC OCEAN
Olongapo
Quezon City
South China Sea
Manila
Lucena
Naga
Legaspi
PHILIPPINES
5
Calapan
Mindoro
Masbate
Calbayog
Samar
Masbate
Tacloban
Roxas
Calamian Group
Panay
Iloilo
Bacolod
Cebu
10°
Taytay
Negros
Surigao
Sprenly Islands
Palawan
Puerto Princesa
Dumaguete
Bohol
Butuan
Cagayan de Oro
6
Iligan
Sulu Sea
Pagadian
Mindanao
Davao
MALAYSIA
Zamboanga
General Santos
Jolo
5°
Bandar Seri Begawan
Kota Kinabalu
Sandakan
Sulu Archipelago
Celebes Sea
Talaud Islands
7
BRUNEI
Miri
Tawau
INDONESIA
Borneo
Bintulu
Tarakan
120°
H
125°
J
130°
K

A 80°E B 85° C 90° D 95° E 100° F 105° G 110°

KAZAKHSTAN

Karamay

Bulgan

■ **Ulan Bator**

Almaty

Yining

Dzungarian Basin

Altay

2

Lake Issyk

Kuytun

Altai Mountains

MONGOLIA

KYRGYZSTAN

Shihezi

Urumqi

Pik Pobedy 7,439m (24,406ft)

T i e n   S h a n

Aksu

Turpan

Hami

Erenh

40° N

Korla

Bosten Lake

-154m (-505ft)

Turpan Depression

G o b i   D e s e r t

Lop Lake

Mogao Caves

3

Hotan

Tarim Basin

Taklimakan Desert

Altun Mountains

Yumen

The Great Wall of China

Baotou

Hohhot

35°

5,547m (18,199ft)

Wuhai

Yinchuan

Kunlun Mountains

Qaidam Basin

Golmud

Qinghai Lake

Xining

Taiyu

C H I N A

Huang He (Yellow)

Lanzhou

4

Plateau of Tibet

Mount Li (Terracotta A

Siling Lake

Baoji

Xian

30°

TIBET

Yushu

Shiyan

Nam Lake

Chang Jiang (Yangtze)

Xiangfa

Brahmaputra

Salween

Mekong

Chengdu

Yichang

5

Himalayas

Lhasa

Gongga Shan 7,556m (24,790ft)

NEPAL

■ **Kathmandu**

Mount Everest 8,850m (29,035ft)

Leshan

Chongqing

Darjeeling

Thimphu

Changde

Darbhanga

BHUTAN

Dibrugarh

Xichang

Luzhou

Patna

Biratnagar

Brahmaputra

Chang Jiang (Yangtze)

25°

Ganges

Rangpur

Guwahati

Zunyi

Huaihua

Bhagalpur

Shillong

Panzhihua

INDIA

Ranchi

Asansol

Rajshahi

Sylhet

Imphal

Dali

Guiyang

Hengy

Tropic of Cancer

BANGLADESH

Myitkyina

Irrawaddy

6

Dhaka ■

Aizawl

Kunming

Guilin

Kolkata (Calcutta)

Khulna

Liuzhou

Chittagong

Lashio

Gejiu

Wuzhou

Cuttack

20°

Mouths of the Ganges

Monywa

Mandalay

Simao

Nanning

Yulin

Mount Victoria 3,053m (10,016ft)

Lao Cai

Bay of Bengal

Sittwe

BURMA (MYANMAR)

Taunggyi

Phongsali

Son La

Thai Nguyen

Zhanjiar

Red

Hanoi ■

Haikou

7

INDIAN OCEAN

Pyinmana

Salween

Louangphrabang

Hai Phong

Gulf of Tonkin

Sandoway

Pye

Mekong

Thanh Hoa

Hainan

Chiang Mai

LAOS

VIETNAM

Henzada

THAILAND

Vinh

Irrawaddy

Pathein

Pegu

■ **Vientiane**

Sanya

15°

298

Rangoon ■

Udon Thani

C 90°E D *Mouths of the Irrawaddy* Moulmein F 100° 95° G 105° 110°

Map labels (geographic features, cities, and key):

RUSSIA

MANCHURIA

NORTH KOREA

SOUTH KOREA

JAPAN

TAIWAN

PHILIPPINES

Hailar, Hulun Lake, Qiqihar, Daqing, Ulanhot, Harbin, Yichun, Hegang, Jiamusi, Jixi, Mudanjiang, Amur

Xilinhot, Changchun, Jilin, Yanji, Liaoyuan, Tongliao, Vladivostok, Nakhodka, Lake Khanka, Sikhote Alin Range

Greater Khingan Range

La Perouse Strait, Kuril Islands (Russia)

Asahikawa, Kushiro, Hokkaido, Sapporo, Tomakomai, Hakodate, Aomori, Akita

Sea of Japan

INNER MONGOLIA

Chifeng, Fuxin, Fushun, Shenyang, Hyesan, Kanggye, Kimchaek, Chongjin

Zhangjiakou, Jinzhou, Anshan, Dandong, Sinuiju, Hamhung, Wonsan, Sendai, Fukushima, Niigata

Datong, Beijing, Qinhuangdao, Tangshan, Korea Bay, Pyongyang, Nampo, Honshu, Utsunomiya

Baoding, Tianjin, Gulf of Chihli, Dalian, Seoul, Inchon, Suwon, Toyama, Kanazawa, Mount Fuji 3,776m (12,388ft), Tokyo

Shijiazhuang, Yantai, Chongju, Taejon, Fukui, Shizuoka, Hamamatsu, Nagoya, Kyoto

Handan, Zibo, Weifang, Qingdao, Yellow Sea, SOUTH KOREA, Taegu, Pusan, Okayama, Osaka, Wakayama, Hiroshima

Taian, Jining, Kwangju, Matsuyama, Shikoku

Huang He (Yellow)

Zhengzhou, Xuzhou, Lianyungang, Korea Strait, Fukuoka, Kitakyushu, Kumamoto

Grand Canal, Yancheng, Cheju, Nagasaki, Kyushu, Kagoshima

Nanjing, Hefei, Wuxi, Shanghai, Chang Jiang (Yangtze), Tai Lake, Hangzhou

Wuhan, Anqing, Ningbo

Poyang Lake, Jinhua, East China Sea, Ryukyu Islands (Japan), Amami

Nanchang, Linchuan, Wenzhou, Okinawa

Nanping, Fuzhou, Chilung, Taipei

Ganzhou, Yongan, Quanzhou, Taichung, Changhua, TAIWAN, Sakishima Islands

Shaoguan, Xiamen, Meizhou, Yu Shan 3,997m (13,113ft), Tainan, Kaohsiung

Canton (Guangzhou), Shantou, Taiwan Strait

Hong Kong (Xianggang)

South China Sea

PACIFIC OCEAN

Batan Islands, Luzon Strait, Babuyan Islands, Aparri, Laoag, Tuguegarao, Luzon

Tropic of Cancer

China, Korea and Japan

- Boreal forest
- Temperate forest
- Tropical forest
- Temperate grassland
- Savanna
- Semi-desert and scrub
- Hot desert
- Wetland
- Mountain
- Tundra
- Ice
- Cultivation
- Urban
- ■ National capital
- ● Internal capital
- ◉ Major city or town
- ○ Other town
- International boundary
- Internal boundary
- 2,490m (7,988ft) Height above or below sea level

See also main key on page 259.

1:14,000,000

0   200   400km

0   100   200   300 miles

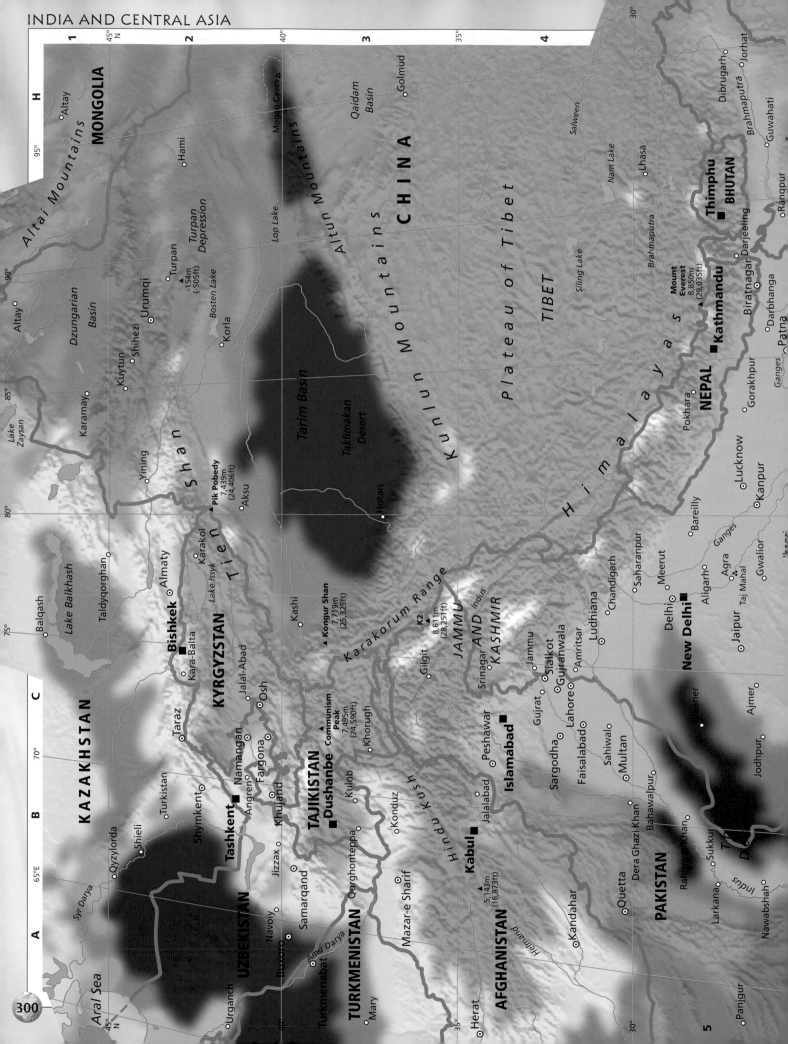

1   2   3   4

45° N

95°   90°   85°   80°   75°   70° 65°E   45° N

H

MONGOLIA

Altai Mountains

Altay

Altay

MONGOLIA

Hami

Dzungarian Basin

Qaidam Basin

Golmud

Mogao Caves

Urumqi

Shihezi

Turpan

Turpan Depression
▲ -154m (-505ft)

Bosten Lake

Korla

Lop Lake

Altun Mountains

CHINA

Salween

Lhasa

Nam Lake

Brahmaputra

Dibrugarh

Jorhat

Brahmaputra

Guwahati

Thimphu
BHUTAN

Rangpur

Siling Lake

Plateau of Tibet

TIBET

Kuytun

Karamay

Kuytun

Yining

Tarim Basin

Taklimakan Desert

Taklimakan Desert

Lake Zaysan

Lake Balkash

Balqash

Taldyqorghan

Shieli

Shieli

Tien

Shan

Aksu

▲ Pik Pobedy 7,439m (24,406ft)

Hotan

Kunlun Mountains

Karakol

Karakol

Almaty

Lake Issyk

Kashi

▲ Kongur Shan 7,719m (25,325ft)

Karakorum Range

Indus

Himalayas

Mount Everest 8,850m (29,035ft)

Kathmandu

NEPAL

Pokhara

Biratnagar

Darbhanga

Patna

Ganges

Gorakhpur

Lucknow

Kanpur

Bareilly

Ganges

Saharanpur

Meerut

Chandigarh

Aligarh

Agra
Taj Mahal

Gwalior

Delhi

New Delhi

Jaipur

Ajmer

Bikaner

Jodhpur

Bishkek
Kara-Balta

KYRGYZSTAN

Jalal-Abad

Osh

K2 8,611m (28,251ft)

JAMMU AND KASHMIR

Gilgit

Srinagar

Jammu

Sialkot
Gujranwala

Amritsar

Ludhiana

Jalal-Abad

Taraz

Namangan

Fargona

Khujand

Communism Peak 7,495m (24,590ft)

Khorugh

Kulob

Gujrat

Lahore

Faisalabad

Sahiwalo

KAZAKHSTAN

Qyzylorda

Turkistan

Shymkent

Tashkent

Angren

Jizzax

Samarqand

TAJIKISTAN

Dushanbe

Konduz

Hindu Kush

Peshawar

Islamabad

Kabul

Jalalabad

Sargodha

Multan

Dera Ghazi Khan

Bahawalpur

Rahimyar Khan

Sukkur

Larkana

Nawabshah

Indus

Navoiy

Buxoro

UZBEKISTAN

Qurghonteppa

Mazar-e Sharif

Hindu Kush

AFGHANISTAN

Kabul ▲ 5,143m (16,873ft)

Kandahar

Quetta

PAKISTAN

TURKMENISTAN

Turkmenabat

Mary

Amu Darya

Herat

Helmand

Syr Darya

Aral Sea

Urganch

A   B   C   H

30°

40°

35°

Shan

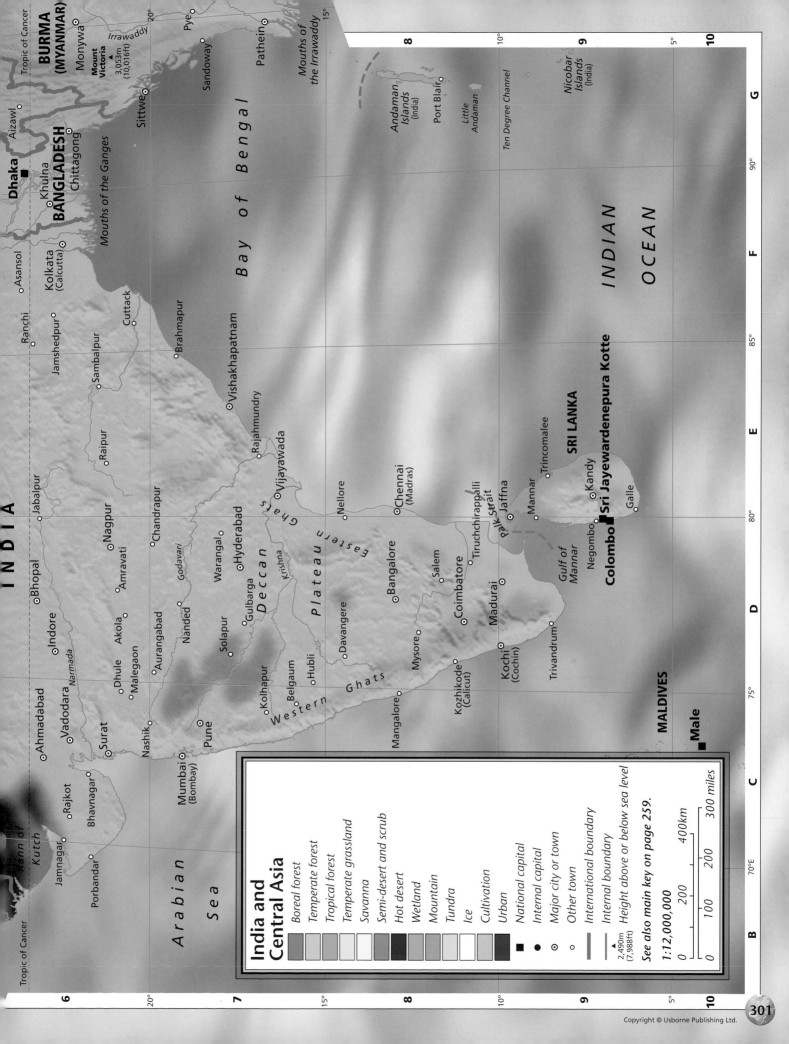

India and Central Asia

Boreal forest
Temperate forest
Tropical forest
Temperate grassland
Savanna
Semi-desert and scrub
Hot desert
Wetland
Mountain
Tundra
Ice
Cultivation
Urban

■ National capital
● Internal capital
⊙ Major city or town
○ Other town

International boundary
Internal boundary

▲ 2,490m (7,988ft) Height above or below sea level

See also main key on page 259.

1:12,000,000

0   100   200   300   400km
0   100   200   300 miles

BURMA (MYANMAR)

Aizawl
Monywa
Mount Victoria 3,053m (10,016ft) ▲
Pye
Sandoway
Pathein
Sittwe
Irrawaddy
Mouths of the Irrawaddy

BANGLADESH

Dhaka ■
Khulna
Chittagong

INDIA

Asansol
Ranchi
Jamshedpur
Kolkata (Calcutta)
Sambalpur
Raipur
Cuttack
Brahmapur
Vishakhapatnam
Rajahmundry
Vijayawada
Jabalpur
Nagpur
Chandrapur
Bhopal
Amravati
Narmada
Godavari
Warangal
Hyderabad
Krishna
Nellore
Chennai (Madras)
Indore
Akola
Nanded
Gulbarga
Solapur
Davangere
Bangalore
Salem
Tiruchchirappalli
Dhule
Malegaon
Aurangabad
Kolhapur
Belgaum
Hubli
Mysore
Coimbatore
Madurai
Nashik
Pune
Mangalore
Kozhikode (Calicut)
Kochi (Cochin)
Trivandrum
Surat
Vadodara
Bhavnagar
Ahmadabad
Rajkot
Jamnagar
Porbandar

Deccan Plateau
Eastern Ghats
Western Ghats

Rann of Kutch

Mouths of the Ganges

Tropic of Cancer

SRI LANKA

Jaffna
Mannar
Trincomalee
Kandy
Negombo
Colombo ■
Sri Jayewardenepura Kotte ●
Galle
Palk Strait
Gulf of Mannar

MALDIVES

Male ■

Andaman Islands (India)
Port Blair
Little Andaman
Ten Degree Channel

Nicobar Islands (India)

Bay of Bengal

Arabian Sea

INDIAN OCEAN

Tropic of Cancer

Copyright © Usborne Publishing Ltd.

301

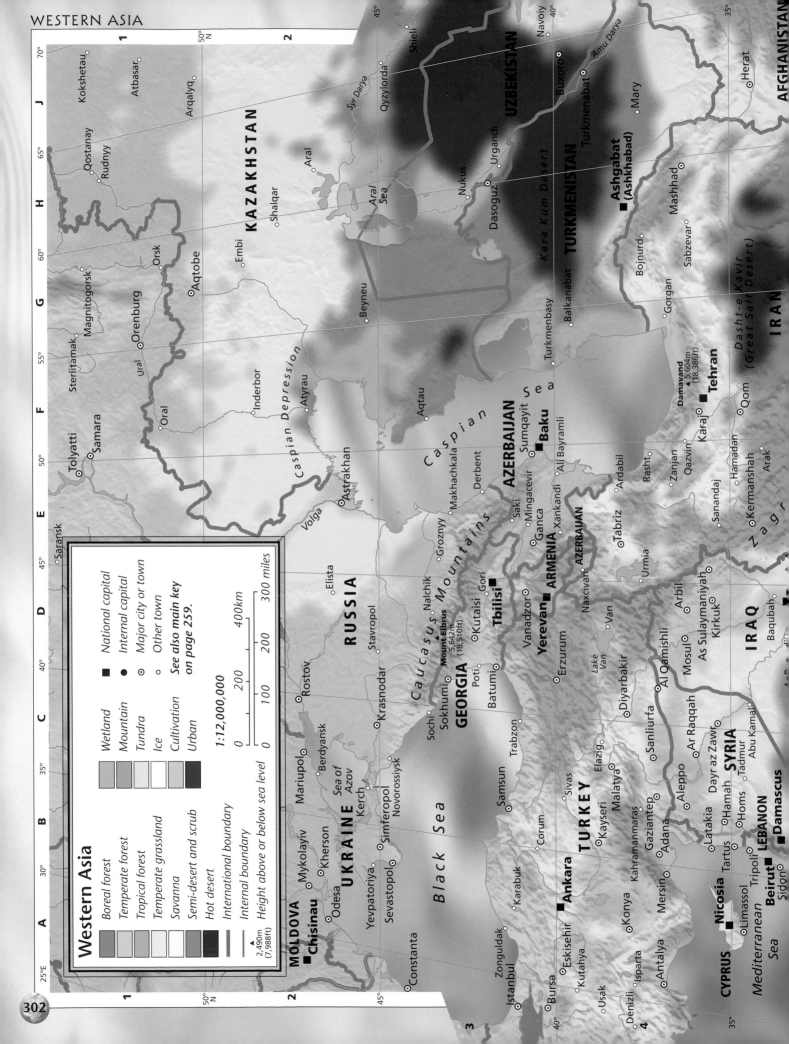

Western Asia

Boreal forest	■ National capital
Temperate forest	● Internal capital
Tropical forest	◉ Major city or town
Temperate grassland	○ Other town
Savanna	*See also main key*
Semi-desert and scrub	*on page 259.*
Hot desert	

1:12,000,000

0	100	200	400km
0	100	200	300 miles

Wetland
Mountain
Tundra
Ice
Cultivation
Urban

International boundary
Internal boundary
Height above or below sea level

▲ 2,490m
(7,988ft)

KAZAKHSTAN

Kokshetau
Qostanay
Atbasar
Rudnyy
Arqalyq
Shieli
Syr Darya
Qyzylorda
Shalqar
Aral
Aral Sea

UZBEKISTAN
Navoiy
Buxoro
Urganch
Amu Darya
Nukus
Dasoguz
Turkmenabat
Mary

TURKMENISTAN
■ **Ashgabat**
(Ashkhabad)
Kara Kum Desert
Balkanabat
Bojnurd
Gorgan
Sabzevar
Mashhad

AFGHANISTAN
Herat

IRAN
Dasht-e Kavir (Great Salt Desert)
▲ 5,604m
(18,386ft)
Damavand
■ **Tehran**
Karaj ◉
Qazvin
Qom
Hamadan
Qom
Arak
Zagros
Kermanshah
Sanandaj
Tabriz
Urmia
Ardabil
Rasht
Zanjan

Magnitogorsk
Orsk
Orenburg
Sterlitamak
Aqtobe
Embi
Inderbor
Ural
Oral
Atyrau
Caspian Depression

Tolyatti
Samara
Beyneu
Aqtau
Saransk
Astrakhan
Volga
Elista
Caspian Sea

RUSSIA
Stavropol
Rostov
Krasnodar
Novorossiysk
Sochi
Makhachkala
Derbent
Groznyy
Nalchik
Mount Elbrus ▲ 5,642m (18,510ft)
Caucasus Mountains

AZERBAIJAN
Sumqayit
■ **Baku**
Ali Bayramli
Saki
Mingacevir
Ganca
Xankandi
Naxcivan
AZERBAIJAN

GEORGIA
Poti
Batumi
Sokhumi
Kutaisi
Gori
● **Tbilisi**

ARMENIA
Vanadzor
■ **Yerevan**

IRAQ
Mosul
Arbil
Kirkuk
As Sulaymaniyah
Al Qamishli
Ar Raqqah
Dayr az Zawr
Baqubah

SYRIA
Aleppo
Hamah
Homs
Tadmur
Abu Kamal
Latakia
Tartus

LEBANON
Tripoli
■ **Beirut**
Sidon

CYPRUS
■ **Nicosia**
Limassol
Mediterranean Sea

TURKEY
■ **Ankara**
Istanbul
Bursa
Eskisehir
Kutahya
Usak
Denizli
Antalya
Isparta
Konya
Mersin
Adana
Gaziantep
Kahramanmaras
Sanliurfa
Diyarbakir
Lake Van
Van
Erzurum
Trabzon
Samsun
Sivas
Kayseri
Malatya
Elazig
Karabuk
Zonguldak
Corum

Black Sea
Constanta
Sea of Azov
Kerch
Simferopol
Sevastopol
Yevpatoriya

UKRAINE
Mykolayiv
Kherson
Odesa
Mariupol
Berdyansk

MOLDOVA
■ **Chisinau**

A 25°E 30° **B** 35° **C** 40° **D** 45° **E** 50° **F** 55° **G** 60° **H** 65° **J** 70°

50°N
45°N
40°
35°

PAKISTAN

Helmand

Zabol
Zahedan
Kerman
Iranshahr
Panjgur
Turbat

30°
25°

Suez Canal
Port Said
Gaza
Beer Sheva
Jerusalem
ISRAEL
Amman
JORDAN
Maan
Petra
Al Aqabah
Elat
Sinai
Mount Sinai
2,285m
(7,497ft)
Tabuk
Sharm el Sheikh
Hurghada

El Mansura
Ismailia
Cairo
Suez
Pyramids of Giza
Beni Suef
El Minya
Asyut
Sohag
Qena
Luxor
Valley of the Kings
Arabian Desert
EGYPT
Aswan
Aswan High Dam
Tropic of Cancer
Lake Nasser

Delta
Nile

30°
25°

Zabol
Iranshahr
Kerman
Sirjan
Shiraz
Persepolis
Bandar-e Abbas
Strait of Hormuz
Gulf of Oman
Sur
Masirah Island

Bushehr
Ahvaz
Abadan
Basra
Al Amarah
An Nasiriyah
Euphrates
Tigris
Syrian Desert

OMAN
Dubai
Sharjah
Al Ayn
UNITED ARAB
EMIRATES
Abu Dhabi
QATAR
Doha
Manama
BAHRAIN
Persian Gulf
(The Gulf)
Kuwait City
KUWAIT

Ad Dammam
Al Mubarrez
Haradh

Buraydah

Riyadh

SAUDI ARABIA

Arabian Peninsula

Rub al Khali
(Empty Quarter)

OMAN

Muscat
Suhar

Salalah

Socotra
(Yemen)

Cape Guardafui

INDIAN
OCEAN

Arabian Sea

Hadhramaut
Al Mukalla

YEMEN

Marib

Aden
Gulf of Aden

Najran
Sadah
Sana
3,760m
(12,336ft)
Dhamar
Ibb
Taizz

Abha
3,133m
(10,279ft)
Asir
At Taif
Mecca
Jedda
Medina

Hail

Hejaz
Red Sea

Farasan Islands

Al Hudaydah
Bab al Mandab

SOMALIA

Berbera
Hargeysa

DJIBOUTI
Djibouti
Dikhil
Assab

Karora
Massawa
Dahlak Archipelago

Keren
Asmara
ERITREA
Teseney
Kassala
Gedaref
Wad Medani

Atbarah
Port Sudan
SUDAN
Nubian Desert

Nile

-116m
(-381ft)
Kobar Sink
Mekele
Ras Dashen
4,620m
(15,157ft)
Gonder
Bahir Dar
Lake Tana
Blue Nile
ETHIOPIA
Dese
Dire Dawa

Ethiopian Highlands

60°
55°
50°
45°
40°
35°E

30°
25°

7
20°
8
15°
9

H
G
F

7
20°
8
15°
9

6

Tropic of Cancer

Copyright © Usborne Publishing Ltd.

303

60°   2   80°   A   1

ARCTI

UNITED
KINGDOM
London

B

Paris

Svalbard
(Norway)

20°

North
Sea

Norwegian
Sea

Arctic Circle

40°   Franz Josef
Land

C

BELGIUM
NETHERLANDS
LUXEMBOURG
FRANCE

NORWAY
Oslo

SWEDEN

North Cape

60°

GERMANY

Berlin

DENMARK

Stockholm

FINLAND

Murmansk

Barents
Sea

Novaya
Zemlya

80°

D

Baltic
Sea

Helsinki

Kola
Peninsula

Kara
Sea

3

CZECH
REPUBLIC

POLAND

LITHUANIA

ESTONIA

Lake
Ladoga

St. Petersburg

Arkhangelsk

Vorkuta

Noril

AUSTRIA

Warsaw

LATVIA

Vilnius

Lake
Onega

Cherepovets

Ukhta

SLOVAKIA

Budapest

HUNGARY

Minsk

BELARUS

Moscow

Novyy Urengoy

Lviv

West Siberian

Ural Mountains

Ob

ROMANIA

Kiev

Ryazan

Nizhniy Novgorod

Plain

MOLDOVA

UKRAINE

Voronezh

Volga

Kazan

Perm

Surgut

Ob

Yenisey

Chisinau

Kharkiv

Yekaterinburg

Odesa

Dnipropetrovsk

Samara

40°
N

Simferopol

Rostov

Chelyabinsk

R   U

Black
Sea

Volgograd

Oral

Orenburg

Tomsk

Krasnoya

Ankara

Krasnodar

Volga

Omsk

Novosibirsk

Aba

TURKEY

Mount Elbrus
5,642m
(18,510ft)

Astrakhan

Aqtobe

Barnaul

Adana

Atyrau

KAZAKHSTAN

GEORGIA

Tbilisi

Caspian Sea

Aqtau

Astana

Pavlodar

ARMENIA

Yerevan

AZERBAIJAN

Baku

Qaraghandy

Uskemen

Kyz

Aleppo

SYRIA

Mosul

Tabriz

Aral
Sea

Nukus

Qyzylorda

Balqash

Lake
Balkhash

Altay

Baghdad

IRAQ

Dasoguz

UZBEKISTAN

TURKMENISTAN

Shymkent

Tien Shan

Urumqi

4

Damavand
5,604m
(18,386ft)

Tehran

Ashgabat
(Ashkhabad)

Tashkent

Bishkek

Almaty

Ahvaz

Esfahan

Mashhad

Turkmenabat

Samarqand

KYRGYZSTAN

Osh

Aksu

Kuwait City

KUWAIT

IRAN

Shiraz

Dushanbe

TAJIKISTAN

Tarim Basin

Taklimakan Desert

SAUDI
ARABIA

Persian
(The Gulf)

Herat

Mazar-e Sharif

Riyadh

Manama

Bandar-e
Abbas

Zahedan

AFGHANISTAN

Kabul

K2
8,611m
(28,251ft)

Hotan

QATAR

Doha

Gulf

Kandahar

Islamabad

Srinagar

Abu Dhabi

PAKISTAN

Indus

Lahore

INDIA

Plateau of Tibet

C   60°E   D   80°   E

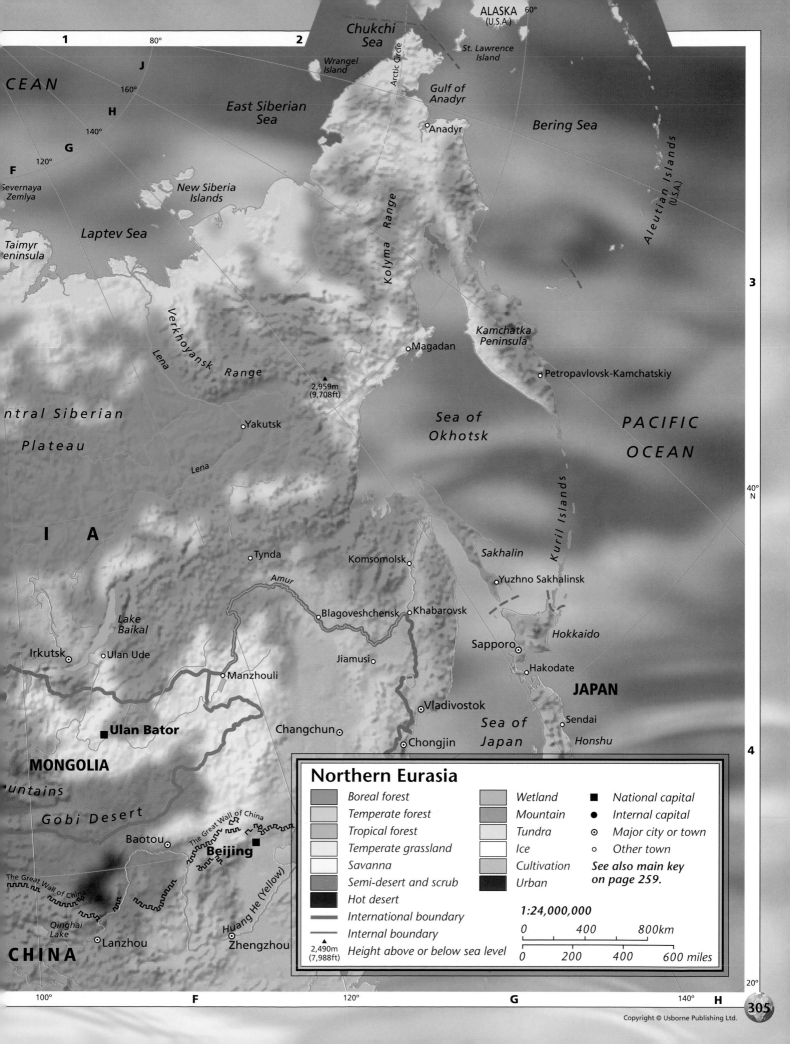

Northern Eurasia

CEAN

ALASKA
(U.S.A.)
60°

*Chukchi
Sea*

J

160°

H

140°

*East Siberian
Sea*

*Wrangel
Island*

Arctic Circle

*St. Lawrence
Island*

*Gulf of
Anadyr*

Bering Sea

G

120°

F

*Severnaya
Zemlya*

*New Siberia
Islands*

Anadyr

Aleutian Islands
(U.S.A.)

*Taimyr
Peninsula*

Laptev Sea

Kolyma Range

3

ntral Siberian

Plateau

Verkhoyansk Range

Lena

2,959m
(9,708ft)

Magadan

*Kamchatka
Peninsula*

Petropavlovsk-Kamchatskiy

**PACIFIC
OCEAN**

40°
N

Yakutsk

*Sea of
Okhotsk*

Lena

Kuril Islands

I   A

Tynda

Komsomolsk

Sakhalin

Yuzhno Sakhalinsk

Amur

Blagoveshchensk

Khabarovsk

Hokkaido

*Lake
Baikal*

Jiamusi

Sapporo

Irkutsk

Ulan Ude

Manzhouli

Hakodate

JAPAN

4

MONGOLIA

Changchun

Vladivostok

*Sea of
Japan*

Sendai

Honshu

Ulan Bator

Chongjin

untains

Gobi Desert

The Great Wall of China

Baotou

Beijing

The Great Wall of China

Huang He (Yellow)

*Qinghai
Lake*

Lanzhou

Zhengzhou

CHINA

Northern Eurasia

Boreal forest	Wetland	■	National capital
Temperate forest	Mountain	●	Internal capital
Tropical forest	Tundra	⊙	Major city or town
Temperate grassland	Ice	○	Other town
Savanna	Cultivation		
Semi-desert and scrub	Urban		
Hot desert			

*See also main key
on page 259.*

International boundary

Internal boundary

▲ 2,490m
(7,988ft)   Height above or below sea level

1:24,000,000

0   400   800km

0   200   400   600 miles

MAPS OF EUROPE

This is a satellite image of
Europe. You can see how
the continent joins on
to Asia to the east.

This is a red squirrel, a species which is widespread throughout Europe but declining in numbers in Britain.

Europe is a small continent, packed with over 40 countries and more than 700 million people. It has no deserts, but its geography ranges from high mountain ranges to icy tundra, rocky islands and lush farmland. With dozens of islands and peninsulas, many of Europe's countries are largely surrounded by sea.

The shading on this map is there to help you see clearly the different countries that make up the continent.

Arctic Circle

ARCTIC OCEAN

Reykjavik
ICELAND

Norwegian
Sea

Faroe Islands
(Denmark)

SWEDEN

Shetland
Islands

NORWAY

Oslo

Orkney
Islands

Stockholm

North

Sea

DENMARK
Copenhagen

Ba
Se

IRELAND
Dublin

UNITED

KINGDOM

Amsterdam

The
Hague   NETHERLANDS

Berlin

London

Brussels   GERMANY

POLA

BELGIUM   Bonn

Paris

LUXEMBOURG

Luxembourg

Prague
CZECH
REPUBLIC

Rhine

Vienna
Bratislava

Bay
of
Biscay

FRANCE   SWITZERLAND

LIECHTENSTEIN

Bern   Vaduz   AUSTRIA   Budape

HUNG

ATLANTIC

SLOVENIA
Ljubljana

Zagre

CROAT

OCEAN

MONACO

SAN MARINO

BOSNIA AN
HERZEGOVI

ANDORRA

PORTUGAL

Andorra
la Vella

ITALY

Sarajevo

Corsica

VATICAN CITY

Lisbon

Madrid

Rome

ALBA
Tir

SPAIN

Balearic
Islands

Sardinia

Mediterranean Sea

Sicily

MALTA
Valletta

Barents Sea

Murmansk

Arctic Circle

Arkhangelsk

FINLAND

R U S S I A

sinki

St. Petersburg

Tallinn
ESTONIA

Nizhniy Novgorod

Kazan

Riga   LATVIA

Moscow

THUANIA
Vilnius

A

Minsk

Volga

BELARUS

arsaw

Kiev

Volgograd

Dnieper

UKRAINE

VAKIA

MOLDOVA

Chisinau

ROMANIA

rade

Bucharest

Danube

Black Sea

&

GRO BULGARIA

Sofia

kopje
CEDONIA

TURKEY

EECE

Athens

Crete

Facts

Total land area 10,205,720 sq km (3,940,428 sq miles) (including European Russia)

Total population 727 million (including all of Russia)

Biggest city Paris, France

Biggest country Russia *Total area: 17,075,200 sq km (6,592,735 sq miles) Area of European Russia: 4,294,400 sq km (1,658,068 sq miles)*

Smallest country Vatican City *0.44 sq km (0.17 sq miles)*

Highest mountain Elbrus, Russia *5,642m (18,510ft)*

Longest river Volga *3,700km (2,298 miles)*

Biggest lake Lake Ladoga, Russia *17,700 sq km (6,834 sq miles)*

Highest waterfall Utigard, on the Jostedal Glacier, Norway *800m (2,625ft)*

Biggest desert No deserts in Europe

Biggest island Great Britain *229,870 sq km (88,753 sq miles)*

Main mineral deposits Bauxite, zinc, iron, potash, fluorspar

Main fuel deposits Oil, coal, natural gas, peat, uranium

A dairy cow in Devon, in the south of England

West Siberian Plain

Kotlas

Syktyvkar

Ivdel

Uray

Irtysh

Serov

Solikamsk

Berezniki

Tobolsk

Kirov

Kama Reservoir

Nizhniy Tagil

Tyumen

Glazov

Perm

R U S S I A

U r a l   M o u n t a i n s

Yekaterinburg

Votkinsk

Izhevsk

Tobol

Yoshkar-Ola

Sarapul

55° N

Kurgan

Cheboksary

Belaya

Chelyabinsk

Kazan

Zlatoust

Ershovka

Naberezhnyye Chelny

UY

Buinsk

Kuybyshev Reservoir

Ufa

Yamantau
▲
1,640m
(5,381ft)

Komsomolets

Qostanay

Almetyevsk

Oktyabrskiy

Beloretsk

Rudnyy

Ulyanovsk

Sterlitamak

Magnitogorsk

Tobyl

Semiozernoe

Volga

Tolyatti

Belaya

3

Syzran

Saratov Reservoir

Samara

Buzuluk

Zhetiqara

lands

Zhaylma

Balakovo

Orenburg

Ural

Orsk

Tolybay

aratov

50°

Engels

Oral

Aqsay

Torghay

olgograd
servoir

Aqtobe

K A Z A K H S T A N

Chapaev

Ural

4

Kaztalovka

Zhanibek

Inderbor

Eastern Europe

Boreal forest
Temperate forest
Tropical forest
Temperate grassland
Savanna
Semi-desert and scrub
Hot desert
International boundary
Internal boundary
2,490m
(7,988ft) Height above or below sea level

Wetland
Mountain
Tundra
Ice
Cultivation
Urban

■ National capital
● Internal capital
⊙ Major city or town
○ Other town

See also main key on page 259.

Topoli

1:7,000,000

0   100   200   300km

Balkuduk

0   100   200 miles

Volga

C a s p i a n   D e p r e s s i o n

Atyrau

45°

Astrakhan

Caspian Sea

M
1 68° N 2 64° 3 60° 4

Barents Sea

North Cape

Kola
Peninsula

White
Sea

Arctic Circle

Severomorsk

Murmansk

Monchegorsk
▲1,191m
3,907ft)
Apatity

Kandalaksha

Belomorsk

Lake Vyg

Lake
Onega

RUSSIA

Tikhvin

Volkhov

Kirishi

Borovichi

Petrozavodsk

St. Petersburg

Pushkin

Gatchina

Novgorod

Lake
Ilmen

L 36°

Soroya

Hammerfest

Alta

Vadso

Kirkenes

Utsjoki
Sevettijarvi
Kaamanen

Lake
Inari

Lokan
Reservoir

Sodankyla

Lake Top

Lake Pya

Lake
Kuyto

Kostomuksha

Lake
Seg

Lieksa
Medvezhyegorsk

Lake
Ladoga

Zelenogorsk

Vyborg

Volkhov

Kingisepp

Narva

Lake
Peipus

K 32°

J 28°

Tromso

Lapland

Rovaniemi

Kuusamo

Kuhmo

Kajaani

Kiuruvesi

Kuopio

Varkaus

Hauki Lake

Pihlaja
Lake

Saimaa
Lake

Lappeenranta

Kouvola

Kotka

ESTONIA

Haapsalu

H 24°

Narvik

Kebnekaise
▲
2,114m
(6,935ft)

Kiruna

Stora
Lule Lake

Boden

Pielis Lake

FINLAND

Oulu

Raahe

Kokkola

Jyvaskyla

Mikkeli
Paijanne
Lake

Tampere

Lahti

Hameenlinna

Helsinki

Espoo

Turku

Tallinn

Hiiumaa

G 20°

Svolvaer

Narvik

Horn Lake

Storavan
Lake

Skelleftea

Umea

Vaasa

Kurikka

Pori

Rauma

Aland
Islands

Gulf of Finland

F 16°

Mo-i
Rana

Bodo

Storuman
Lake

Ume

Sundsvall

Hudiksvall

Gavle

Stockholm

Sodertalje

E 12°

Namsos

Steinkjer

Ostersund

Indals

Stor
Lake

SWEDEN

Borlange

Uppsala

Eskilstuna

Lake Malar

D

Trondheim

Oppdal

Klar

Karlstad

Orebro

Lake
Vaner

C 8°

Galdhopiggen
▲
2,469m
(8,100ft)

Froya
Hitra

Smola

Kristiansund

Alesund

NORWAY

Lillehammer

Glama

Honefoss

Oslo

Drammen

Fredrikstad

Larvik

B

Bergen

Odda

Stavanger

Sotra

Sula

Karmoy

Varhaug

Arendal

Norwegian
Sea

Vikna

Namsos

A 4°W

1 68° N 2 64° 3 60° 4

312

N 0° **P** 4°E **Q** 8°

2 20°W **2** 16° **3**

64°
N

Langanes

Seydhisfjordhur

ICELAND

Vatnajokull

Hvannadalshnukur
▲
2,119m
(6,952ft)

Same scale as main map

Siglufjordhur

Isafjordhur

Faxafloi

Reykjavik

Keflavik

ATLANTIC OCEAN

Arctic Circle

64°
N

20°

24°W

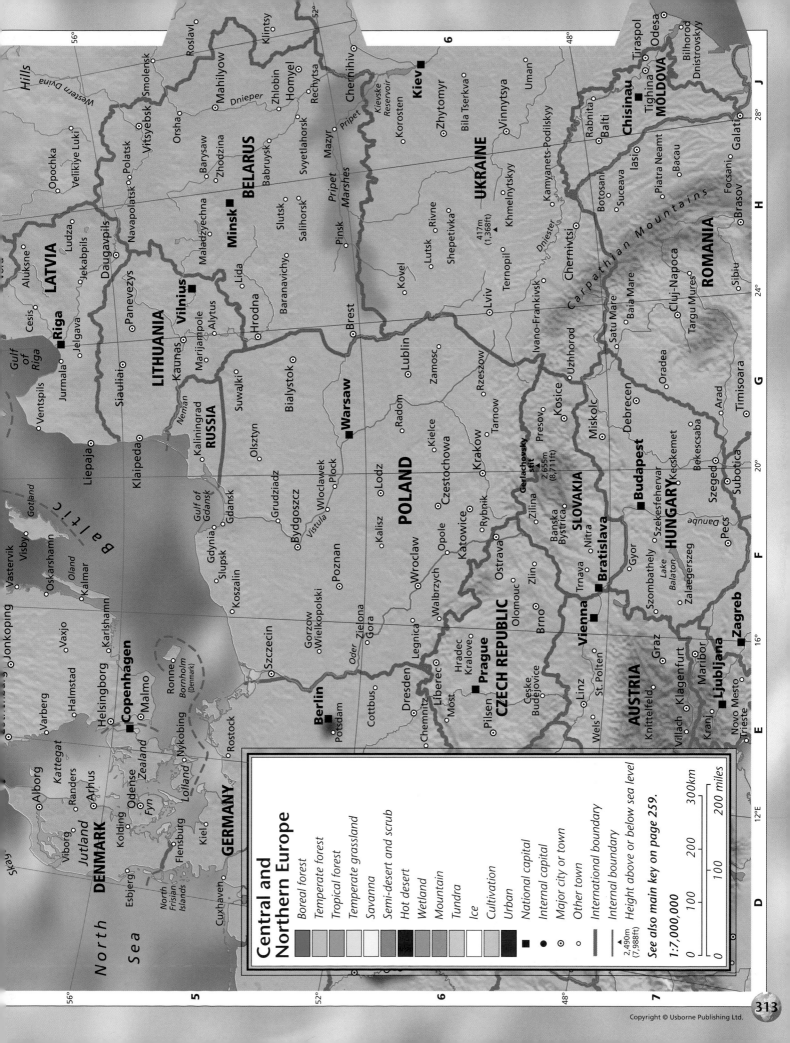

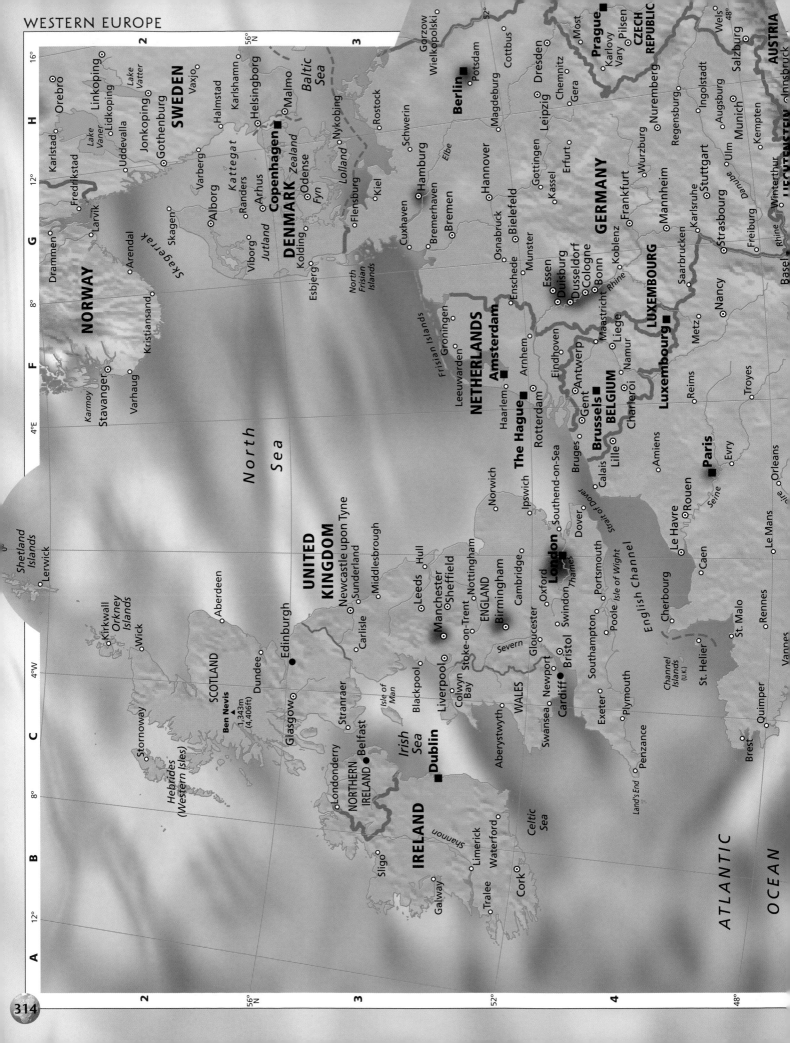

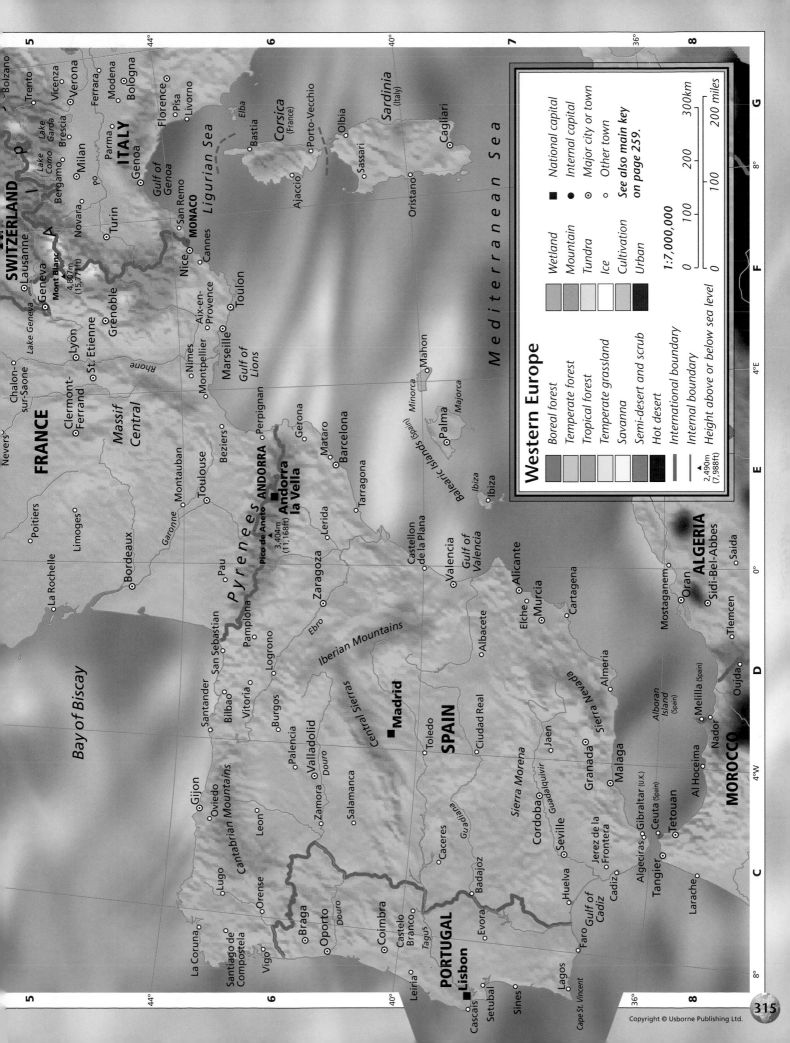

A 0° B 4°E C 8° D 12° E 16°

Cherbourg
Le Havre
Rouen
Caen
Amiens
Charleroi
Namur
BELGIUM
Koblenz
Erfurt
Gera
Chemnitz
Dresden
Wroclaw
Walbrzych
Opo

Paris
Reims
LUXEMBOURG
■ **Luxembourg**
Frankfurt
Wurzburg
Most
Liberec
Hradec Kralove
Karlovy Vary
Pilsen
■ **Prague**
CZECH REPUBLIC
Olomouc

Evry
Le Mans
Orleans
Troyes
Metz
Nancy
Saarbrucken
Mannheim
GERMANY
Nuremberg
Karlsruhe
Regensburg
Stuttgart
Ingolstadt
Ceske Budejovice
Brno
Zlin

48°N
Angers
Tours
Poitiers
Strasbourg
Rhine
Freiburg
Ulm
Danube
Augsburg
Munich
Linz
Wels
St. Polten
Vienna ■
Trna

FRANCE
Dijon
Besancon
Basel
Winterthur
Kempten
Salzburg
AUSTRIA
Knittelfeld
Szombathely
Bratislav ■
Gyor
La Balate

Limoges
Chalon-sur-Saone
Bern ■
Zurich
Lucerne
Vaduz ■
LIECHTENSTEIN
Innsbruck
Grossglockner
3,798m (12,461ft)
S
Graz ●
Villach
Klagenfurt
Maribor
Zalaegersz

Clermont-Ferrand
Geneva
Lausanne
SWITZERLAND
Lake Geneva
Bielo
A
l
p
Bolzano
Kranj
SLOVENIA
Novo Mesto
■ **Ljubljana**
■ **Zagreb**
CROATIA

St. Etienne
Lyon
Mont Blanc
4,807m (15,771ft)
Trento
Bergamo
Lake Como
Lake Garda
Vicenza
Trieste
Rijeka
Karlovac
Slavons
Br

44°N
Massif Central
Grenoble
Novara
Milan
Brescia
Verona
Venice
Pula
Banja Luka
BOSNIA

Garonne
Montauban
Turin
Po
Parma
Modena
Bologna
Ravenna
ITALY
Rimini
Zadar
Ancona
AND HERZEGOVIN
Zeni

Toulouse
Nimes
MONACO
Gulf of Genoa
Genoa
Pisa
Livorno
Florence
SAN MARINO
Split
Most

Montpellier
Aix-en-Provence
Nice
San Remo
Cannes
Perugia
A p e n n i n e s
Pescara
A d r i a t i c   S e a

Beziers
Marseille
Toulon
Gulf of Lions
Ligurian Sea
Bastia
Elba
Terni

Andorra la Vella ■

3

Corsica (France)
Ajaccio
Porto-Vecchio
VATICAN CITY
■ **Rome**
Foggia
Bari

Olbia
Sassari
Sardinia (Italy)
Naples
Pompeii
Salerno
Taranto

40°N
Oristano
Tyrrhenian
Cagliari
Sea
Cosenza
Catanzaro

4

M e d i t e r r a n e a n   S e a
Lipari Islands

Trapani
Palermo
Messina

Sicily
Mount Etna
3,323m (10,902ft)
Catania

Annaba
Bizerte
Menzel Bourguiba
Carthage
Agrigento
Syracuse
Ragusa

36°N
Guelma
■ **Tunis**
Pantelleria (Italy)
Nabeul

Souk Ahras
Pelagian Islands (Italy)

5
Tebessa
TUNISIA
Sousse
Kairouan
Monastir
MALTA
■ **Valletta**

Kasserine
El Jem

● Biskra

316

B 4°E C 8° D 12° E 16°

African elephants in Amboseli National Park, Kenya

This satellite image of Africa shows how the continent is dominated by deserts, particularly the Sahara in the north, which are represented here in yellow.

MAPS OF AFRICA

Africa

Africa is the second-biggest continent and has 53 countries altogether. More than a quarter of them are landlocked, with no access to the sea except through other countries. Africa is home to the world's longest river, the Nile, and its largest desert, the Sahara. It also has vast amounts of natural resources, such as gold, copper and diamonds. Many of them have not yet begun to be used.

A group of Masai people from East Africa silhouetted against a sunset over the flat grasslands

Algiers
Tunis
Rabat
Madeira (Portugal)
MOROCCO
TUNISIA
Tripoli
Canary Islands (Spain)
Laayoune
ALGERIA
LIBYA
Tropic of Cancer
WESTERN SAHARA (Morocco)
MAURITANIA
Nouakchott
MALI
Niger
NIGER
CHAD
CAPE VERDE
Praia
Dakar
SENEGAL
Bamako
Niamey
Ndjamen
THE GAMBIA
Banjul
Ouagadougou
Bissau
BURKINA FASO
GUINEA-BISSAU
GUINEA
BENIN
NIGERIA
Conakry
Abuja
Freetown
IVORY COAST
TOGO
SIERRA LEONE
GHANA
Porto-Novo
CENTRAL AFRIC REPUB
Monrovia
Yamoussoukro
Lome
CAMEROON
Bangui
LIBERIA
Accra
Malabo
Yaounde
EQUATORIAL GUINEA
Con
Equator
Libreville
CONGO
SAO TOME AND PRINCIPE
GABON
Brazzaville
Kinshas
ATLANTIC
Luanda
OCEAN
ANGOLA
NAMIBIA
Tropic of Capricorn
Windhoek
Oran
Cape Town

The shading on this map is there to help you see clearly the different countries that make up the continent.

Cairo

EGYPT

Tropic of Cancer

Nile

Khartoum

ERITREA
Asmara

SUDAN

DJIBOUTI • Djibouti

Addis Ababa   SOMALIA

ETHIOPIA

ONGO

UGANDA
Kampala   KENYA   Mogadishu

DEM.   Kigali • Nairobi
Equator
EP.)   RWANDA
BURUNDI
Bujumbura

Dodoma   Victoria
SEYCHELLES

TANZANIA • Dar es Salaam

INDIAN

MALAWI   Moroni
COMOROS

AMBIA   Lilongwe
Lusaka   OCEAN

Zambezi

Harare   MOZAMBIQUE
ZIMBABWE   Antananarivo

TSWANA   MAURITIUS
MADAGASCAR   Port Louis

orone   Reunion
(France)   Tropic of Capricorn
Pretoria • Maputo
Mbabane • SWAZILAND
Lobamba
mfontein • Maseru
LESOTHO

UTH
RICA

Facts

Total land area 30,311,690 sq km (11,703,343 sq miles)

Total population 794 million

Biggest city Cairo, Egypt

Biggest country Sudan 2,505,810 sq km (967,493 sq miles)

Smallest country Seychelles 455 sq km (176 sq miles)

Highest mountain Kilimanjaro, Tanzania 5,895m (19,340ft)

Longest river Nile, running from to Burundi to Egypt 6,671km (4,145 miles)

Biggest lake Lake Victoria, between Tanzania, Kenya and Uganda 69,215 sq km (26,724 sq miles)

Highest waterfall Tugela Falls, on the Tugela River, South Africa 610m (2,000ft)

Biggest desert Sahara, North Africa 9,100,000 sq km (3,500,000 sq miles)

Biggest island Madagascar 587,040 sq km (226,656 sq miles)

Main mineral deposits Gold, copper, diamonds, iron ore, manganese, bauxite

Main fuel deposits Coal, uranium, natural gas

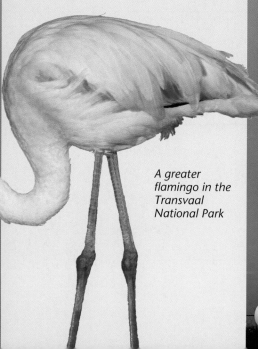

A greater flamingo in the Transvaal National Park

A   0°   B   5°E

Saida
Djelfa
Batna
Biskra
Tebessa
Atlas Mountains
Ghardaia
El Oued
Touggourt
Ouargla

Annaba
Menzel Bourguiba
Bizerte
Carthage
Tunis

Sicily (Italy)
Catania
Syracuse

GREECE
Athe

20°

Kairouan
Sousse
Monastir
El Jem
Sfax

Pantelleria (Italy)

MALTA
Valletta

M e d i t e r r a n e a

Gafsa
Tozeur
Chott el Jerid

Kerkennah Islands

Gulf of Gabes
Gabes
Jerba

Pelagian Islands (Italy)

2

Tataouine

TUNISIA

Tripoli
Al Khums

Misratah

Leptis Magna

Cyrene
Darnah
Al Bayda

Gharyan

Benghazi

Tubruq

30°N

Tademait Plateau

Ghadamis

Surt

Gulf of Sidra

Ajdabiya

Great Eastern Erg

3

ALGERIA

Illizi

Sabha

LIBYA

Liby

25°

Murzuq

Ahaggar Mountains
Ghat

Tropic of Cancer
Mount Tahat
2,918m
(9,573ft)▲

Al Ja

4

Tamanrasset

Djado Plateau

Tibesti Mountains

20°

Emi Koussi
3,415m
(11,204ft)▲

MALI
S   A   H   A   R   A

5

Agadez

NIGER

Faya-Largeau

Bodele Depression

Ennedi Plateau

15°

Tahoua

CHAD

Dosso
Maradi
Zinder
Mao

Sokoto
S   A   H   E   L
Abeche

6

Birnin-Kebbi
Katsina

Lake Chad

Mount

Kandi
Gusau
Kano
Mongo

Zaria
Maiduguri
Ndjamena

Potiskum

10°

Kaduna
NIGERIA
Kainji Reservoir

Am Timan

Saki
Minna
Jos
Kumo
Maroua

7
Bida
Niger

Abuja
CAMEROON
Bongor
Birao

B   5°E   C   10°   D   15°   E   20°   F

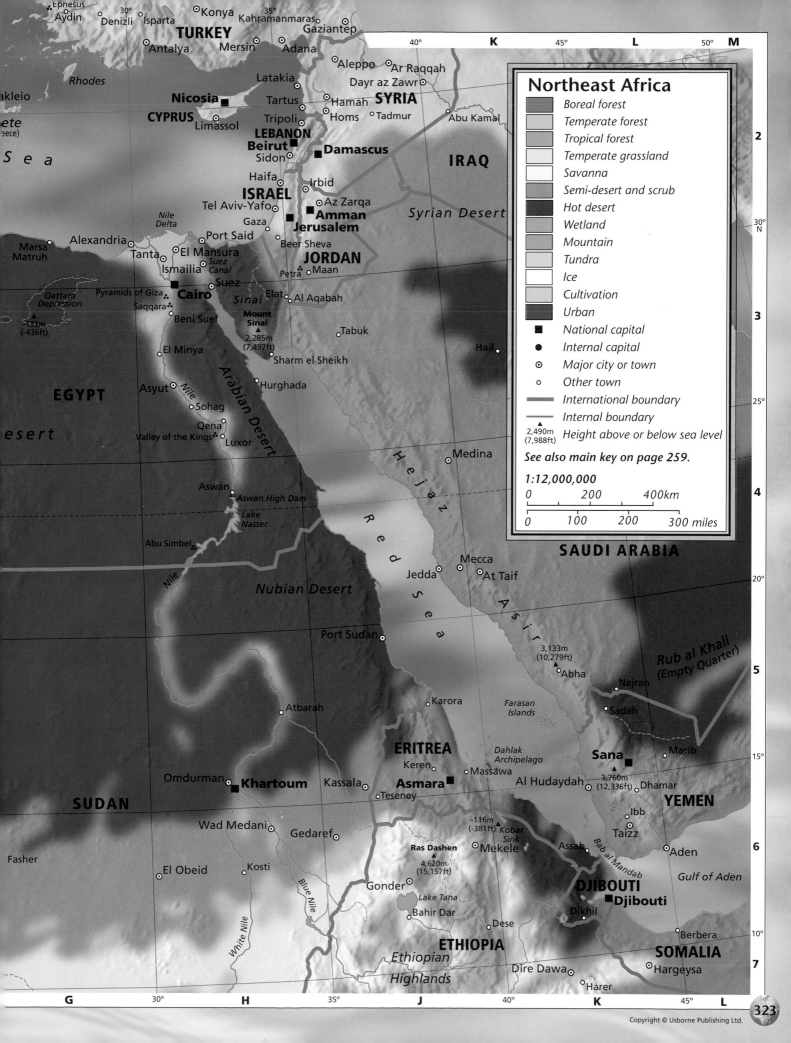

Epnesus
Aydin · Denizli Isparta · 30° · Konya · 35° · Kahramanmaras · Gaziantep
*akleio · Antalya · Mersin · Adana · TURKEY

Rhodes · Latakia · Aleppo · Ar Raqqah · K · 40° · 45° · L · 50° · M
Nicosia · Tartus · Hamah · Dayr az Zawr · SYRIA
CYPRUS · Tripoli · Homs · Tadmur · Abu Kamal · IRAQ · 2
Limassol
LEBANON · Beirut · Damascus
Sidon
Haifa · Irbid · Az Zarqa
ISRAEL · Amman · 30°N
Tel Aviv-Yafo · Jerusalem · Syrian Desert
Gaza · Beer Sheva · JORDAN
Nile Delta · Port Said · Petra · Maan
Alexandria · El Mansura · Suez Canal
Marsa Matruh · Tanta · Ismailia · Suez · Elat · Al Aqabah
Qattara Depression · Pyramids of Giza · Cairo · Sinai · Tabuk · Hail · 3
-133m (-436ft) · Saqqara · Beni Suef · Mount Sinai 2,285m (7,497ft)
EGYPT · El Minya · Sharm el Sheikh
Asyut · Nile · Hurghada · 25°
Sohag · Arabian Desert
esert · Qena · Valley of the Kings · Luxor
Aswan · Medina
Aswan High Dam · Hejaz · 4
Lake Nasser
Abu Simbel · Red Sea
Nile · Nubian Desert · Asir · Rub al Khali (Empty Quarter) · 20°
Mecca · SAUDI ARABIA
Jedda · At Taif · 3,133m (10,279ft) · Abha
Port Sudan · Najran · 5
Atbarah · Karora · Sadah · Marib
Farasan Islands
Omdurman · Khartoum · ERITREA · Dahlak Archipelago · Sana · 15°
SUDAN · Kassala · Keren · Massawa · Al Hudaydah · 3,760m (12,336ft) · Dhamar · YEMEN
Asmara · Teseney · Ibb
Wad Medani · Gedaref · -116m (-381ft) · Kobar Sink · Taizz · Aden · 6
Fasher · Ras Dashen · Mekele · Assab · Bab al Mandab · Gulf of Aden
El Obeid · Kosti · 4,620m (15,157ft) · DJIBOUTI · Djibouti
Gonder · Dikhil · Berbera · 10°
Blue Nile · Lake Tana · SOMALIA
White Nile · Bahir Dar · Dese
ETHIOPIA · Dire Dawa · Hargeysa · 7
Ethiopian · Harer
Highlands
G · 30° · H · 35° · J · 40° · K · 45° · L

Northeast Africa

■	Boreal forest
	Temperate forest
	Tropical forest
	Temperate grassland
	Savanna
	Semi-desert and scrub
	Hot desert
	Wetland
	Mountain
	Tundra
	Ice
	Cultivation
	Urban

■ National capital
● Internal capital
⊙ Major city or town
○ Other town
━━━ International boundary
━━━ Internal boundary
▲ 2,490m (7,988ft) Height above or below sea level

See also main key on page 259.

1:12,000,000

0 · 200 · 400km
0 · 100 · 200 · 300 miles

323

A B C D E F G H

J K

1 2 3 4

30°W 20° 30°W 25° 20°

ATLANTIC OCEAN

K

10

Flores

Azores
(Portugal)

Terceira
Angra do
Heroísmo

São Miguel
Pico Ponta Delgada

Same scale as main map

K

40°
N

40°
N

25°

35°

PORTUGAL

Lisbon

Sines

Lagos

SPAIN

Seville

Cordoba

Cadiz

Granada
Malaga

Alicante
Murcia

Ibiza

Majorca

Balearic Islands
(Spain)

Gibraltar (U.K.)
Ceuta (Spain)
Tetouan
Al Hoceima

Tangiers

Larache

Kenitra

Rabat

Casablanca

El Jadida

Safi

Essaouira

Agadir

Fes

Meknes

Khouribga

Beni Mellal

Marrakech

Toubkal ▲
4,165m
(13,665ft)

Ouarzazate

MOROCCO

Atlas Mountains

Taza

Oujda

Tlemcen

Mediterranean Sea

Almeria

Melilla
(Spain)

Oran

Mostaganem

Sidi-Bel-Abbes

Saida

Algiers

Blida

Bordj Bou
Arreridj

Bejaia

Skikda

Djemila

Setif

Batna

Constantine

Annaba

Tebessa

Biskra

El Oued

Touggourt

Djelfa

Ghardaia

Ouargla

Sardinia
(Italy)

Cagliari

Menzel
Bourguiba
Bizerte
Carthage
Tunis

Sousse
Monastir
El Jem

Kairouan

Sfax

Gabes

Tataouine

Ghadamis

Kerkenah
Islands

Jerba

Gafsa

Tozeur

Chott
el Jerid

TUNISIA

LIBYA

Tropic of Cancer

Illizi

Mount Tahat
2,918m
(9,573ft) ▲

Tamanrasset

Ahaggar
Mountains

Great
Eastern Erg

ALGERIA

Tademait
Plateau

Great
Western Erg

Bechar

Adrar

Er Rachidia

Erfoud

Chech Erg

AHAGGAR

Kidal

SAHARA

MALI

Tindouf

Es Semara

Tan-Tan

WESTERN
SAHARA
(Morocco)

Laayoune

Boujdour

Ad Dakhla

Zouerat

Atar

Akjoujt

Tidjikja

MAURITANIA

Nouadhibou

Cape Blanc

Tropic of Cancer

ATLANTIC OCEAN

Canary Islands
(Spain)

Lanzarote

Fuerteventura

Gran
Canaria

Tenerife

La Gomera

La Palma

El Hierro

Madeira
(Portugal)

Funchal

35°

5°W

0°

5°E

10°

30°

25°

20°

10°

15°

10°

5°W

0°

Northwest Africa

Map Key

■	National capital	
●	Internal capital	
⊙	Major city or town	
○	Other town	

See also main key on page 259.

1:12,000,000

| 0 | 100 | 200 | 300 miles |
| 0 | 200 | 400km | |

Boreal forest
Temperate forest
Tropical forest
Temperate grassland
Savanna
Semi-desert and scrub
Hot desert

Wetland
Mountain
Tundra
Ice
Cultivation
Urban

International boundary
Internal boundary

▲ 2,490m (7,988ft) Height above or below sea level

Labels

NIGER

Agadez
Maradi
Katsina
Gusau
Tahoua
Sokoto
Birnin-Kebbi
Zaria
Kaduna
Minna
Bida
Abuja
NIGERIA
Ilorin
Ogbomoso
Enugu
Onitsha
Warri
Owo
Ibadan
Abeokuta
Benin City
Port Harcourt
Lagos
Saki
Kainji Reservoir
Niger
Niger Delta

Niamey
Dosso
BURKINA FASO
Kandio
BENIN
Natitingou
Djougou
Parakou
Abomey
Cotonou
Porto-Novo
Lome
TOGO
Sokode
Fada-Ngourma
Bawku
Tenkodogo
Tillaberi
Ouagadougou
White Volta
Dori
Ouahigouya
Koudougou
Bobo-Dioulasso
Banfora
Wa
Tamale
Damongo
Wenchi
GHANA
Lake Volta
Koforidua
Accra
Cape Coast
Sekondi-Takoradi
Tarkwa
Kumasi

Gao
Tombouctou (Timbuktu)
Goundam
Mopti
Niono
San
Tougan
Segou
Bamako
Koutiala
Sikasso
Bougouni
Black Volta
Korhogo
Bouna
Bondoukou
Bouake
Katiola
Yamoussoukro
IVORY COAST
Adzope
Abidjan
Divo
Gagnoa
Daloa
Man
Odienne
Niger
Kita
Kankan
Siguiri
Nzerekore
1,752m (5,748ft)
Gueckedou
Zorzor
Tubmanburg
Monrovia
LIBERIA
San Pedro
Harper
Cape Palmas

Nema
Ayoun el Atrous
Nioro du Sahel
Kayes
Selibabi
Kaedi
Tambacounda
Kolda
SENEGAL
Kaolack
Thies
St. Louis
Louga
Dara
Dakar
Banjul
THE GAMBIA
Bignona
Ziguinchor
GUINEA-BISSAU
Bissau
Bissagos Archipelago
Boke
Kindia
Conakry
Labe
GUINEA
Kedougou
Kindia
Makeni
Sefadu
Bo
Kenema
SIERRA LEONE
Freetown

ATLANTIC OCEAN

Gulf of Guinea

Bight of Benin

Cape Three Points

S A H A R A
S A H E L

Inset — Cape Verde / Sao Tome and Principe

SAO TOME AND PRINCIPE
Principe
Sao Tome
Equator

L | M
ATLANTIC OCEAN
Santo Antao
Mindelo
Sao Nicolau
Sal
Boa Vista
CAPE VERDE
Sao Tiago
Maio
Fogo
Praia
Same scale as main map

325

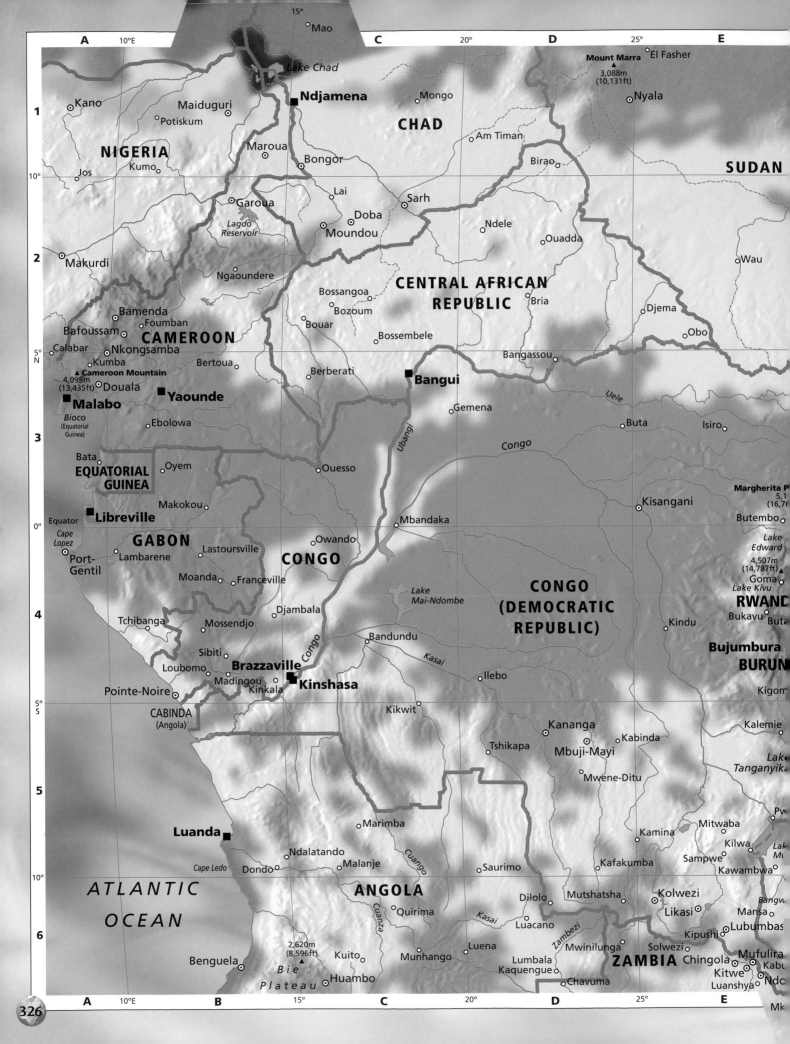

Obeid
Kosti
Ras Dashen ▲ 4,620m (15,157ft)
Mekele
Assab
Taizz
YEMEN
Aden
Gulf of Aden
Cape Guardafui

Gonder
Lake Tana
DJIBOUTI
Dikhil ■ **Djibouti**
Berbera
Boosaaso

Malakal
Bahir Dar
Dese
Ethiopian Highlands
Dire Dawa
Hargeysa
SOMALIA

Gambela
Nekemte
Addis Ababa
Harer
Eyl

White Nile
Debre Zeyit ⊙ Nazret
ETHIOPIA
Jima

Awasa
Lake Abaya
Gode

White Nile
Juba
Beledweyne

Gulu
Soroti ⊙ **Mount Elgon** ▲4,321m (14,176ft)
Moyale
Mandera
Baydhabo

UGANDA
Lake Albert
Lake Kyoga
Mbale
Kitale
Baardheere
Mogadishu

Kampala ■ ⊙ Jinja
Eldoret
Juba
Marka

Entebbe
Kisumu
KENYA
Meru

Masaka
Nakuru
Garissa

Mbarara
Kisii
Nyeri
▲ **Kirinyaga (Mount Kenya)** 5,199m (17,057ft)
Kismaayo

igali
Lake Victoria
Nairobi ■ ⊙ Thika
⊙ Machakos

Mwanza
Kilimanjaro 5,895m (19,340ft) ▲
Moshi
Malindi

Great Rift Valley
Arusha
Mombasa

Tabora
Tanga
Pemba Island
INDIAN OCEAN

Dodoma ■
Zanzibar ⊙
Zanzibar Island

TANZANIA
Morogoro
Dar es Salaam ■

Lake Rukwa
Iringa
Mafia Island

Mbeya
Makumbako
Ilonga
Njinjo

Rift Valley
Liwale

Kasama
Karonga
Songea
Lindi
Mtwara

Isoka
Lupilichi
Tunduru
Masasi
Palma
Cape Delgado
COMOROS
Grand Comoro (Njazidja)

AMBIA
Mzuzu
Nungo
Mecula
Mueda
Moroni ■
Anjouan Island (Nzwani)

Mpika
Lundazi
Lake Nyasa (Lake Malawi)
Lichinga
Tunduma
Mutsamudu
Fomboni
Mamoudzou

Chipata
MALAWI
MOZAMBIQUE
Mohilla Island (Mwali)
Mayotte (France)

Petauke
Lilongwe ■
Kasungu
Cuamba
Pemba

Luangwa
Ruvuma

Central Africa

	Boreal forest
	Temperate forest
	Tropical forest
	Temperate grassland
	Savanna
	Semi-desert and scrub
	Hot desert
	Wetland
	Mountain
	Tundra
	Ice
	Cultivation
	Urban
■	National capital
●	Internal capital
⊙	Major city or town
○	Other town
——	International boundary
——	Internal boundary
▲ 2,490m (7,988ft)	Height above or below sea level

See also main key on page 259.

1:12,000,000

0   200   400km

0   100   200   300 miles

327

Mbeya
Makumbako
ft Valley
duma
Ilonga
Njinjo
Karonga
Liwale
TANZANIA
Lindi
Mtwara
Masasi
Palma
Songea
Tunduru
Cape Delgado
Mzuzu
Ruvuma
Lupilichi
Mueda
Mecula
Lake Nyasa
(Lake Malawi)
Lichinga
Nungo
Pemba
Lundazi
Kasungu
ata
Lilongwe
Cuamba
MALAWI
Cape Melamo
Zomba
Lake
Chilwa
Nacala
Nampula
Mozambique
ongo
Blantyre
Milange
Mocuba
te
Zambezi
Angoche
angani
592m
504ft)
Quelimane
tare
MOZAMBIQUE
imanimani
Beira
spungabera
Nova
Mambone
Massangena
Chigubo
Barra Falsa Point
Massinga
Barra Point
Inhambane
Xai-Xai
aputo

SEYCHELLES
Aldabra Group
Providence
St. Pierre
Bancs
Cosmoledo Group
Providence
Assumption
Astove
Farquhar
Group

Grand
Comoro
(Njazidja)
COMOROS
Moroni
Anjouan Island
(Nzwani)
Mutsamudu
Fomboni
Mohilla Island
(Mwali)
Mamoudzou
Mayotte
(France)
Glorioso Islands
(Reunion)
Cape Amber
Antsiranana
Nosy Be
Ambilobe
Ambanja
Bealanana
Analalava
Antalaha
Mahajanga
Maroantsetra
Cape St. Andrew
Mandritsara
Besalampy
Maevatanana
Ikopa
Nosy
Boraha
Juan de Nova
(Reunion)
Antsalova
Tsiroanomandidy
Toamasina
Belo-
Tsiribihina
Antananarivo
Mania
Antsirabe
Malaimbandy
Ambositra
Bassas da India
(Reunion)
MADAGASCAR
Morombe
Manja
Beroroha
Fianarantsoa
Europa
Island
(Reunion)
Ihosy
2,658m
(8,720ft)
Manakara
St. Denis
Reunion
(France)
Toliara
Betroka
Tropic of Capricorn
Bekily
Androka
Tolanaro
Cape St. Mary

INDIAN

OCEAN

St. Lucia

Southern Africa

▢ Boreal forest	▢ Wetland	■ National capital
▢ Temperate forest	▢ Mountain	● Internal capital
▢ Tropical forest	▢ Tundra	⊙ Major city or town
▢ Temperate grassland	▢ Ice	○ Other town
▢ Savanna	▢ Cultivation	
▢ Semi-desert and scrub	▢ Urban	**See also main key**
▢ Hot desert		**on page 259.**

—— International boundary

—— Internal boundary

▲ 2,490m
(7,988ft)   Height above or below sea level

1:12,000,000

0   200   400km

0   100   200   300 miles

Inset map (Mauritius)

K   55°E   L
INDIAN OCEAN
3   3
MAURITIUS
Port Louis
20°S   20°S
St. Denis
4   4
Reunion
(France)
Same scale as main map
K   55°E   L

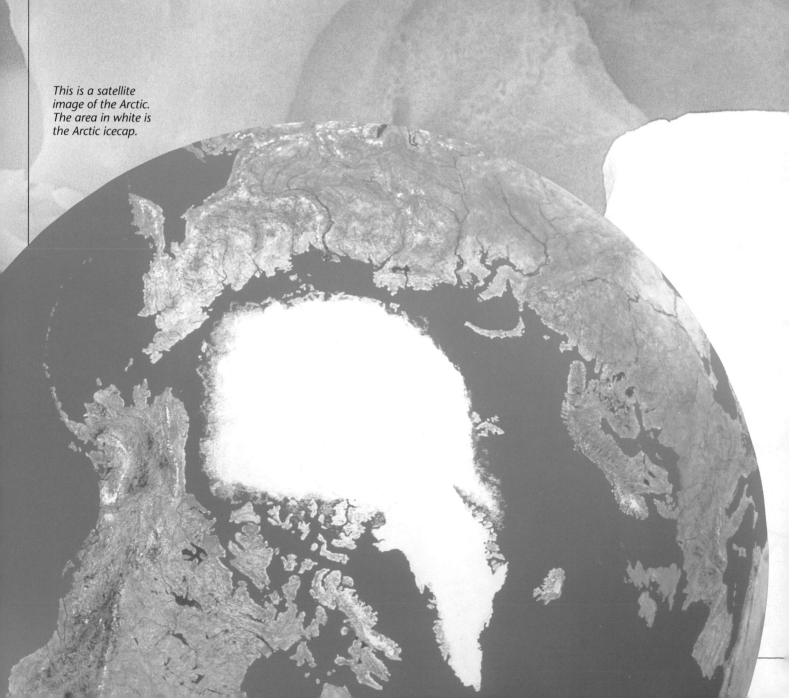

MAPS OF THE ARCTIC AND ANTARCTICA

This is a satellite image of the Arctic. The area in white is the Arctic icecap.

This is a satellite image of Antarctica with its permanent white icecap.

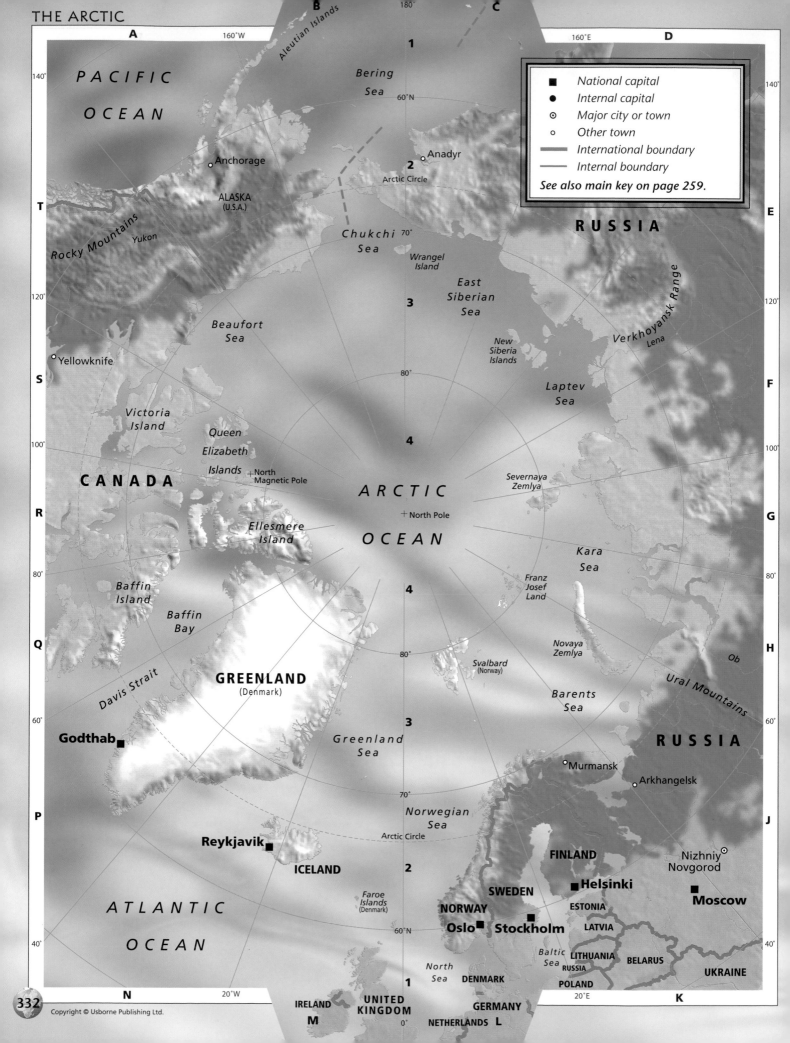

PACIFIC
OCEAN

A   160°W   B   180   C   160°E   D

140°

Aleutian Islands

1

Bering
Sea

60°N

T

Anchorage

2   Anadyr

Arctic Circle

ALASKA
(U.S.A.)

RUSSIA

Rocky Mountains

Yukon

Chukchi   70°
Sea

120°

Wrangel
Island

East
Siberian
Sea

3

Verkhoyansk Range

Lena

S

Yellowknife

Beaufort
Sea

New
Siberia
Islands

80°

Laptev
Sea

F

120°

Victoria
Island

4

100°

Queen
Elizabeth
Islands

North
Magnetic Pole

Severnaya
Zemlya

CANADA

ARCTIC

R

North Pole

G

Ellesmere
Island

OCEAN

80°

Kara
Sea

Baffin
Island

Franz
Josef
Land

Q

Baffin
Bay

Novaya
Zemlya

H

Ob

Davis Strait

GREENLAND
(Denmark)

Svalbard
(Norway)

Barents
Sea

Ural Mountains

60°

Godthab

Greenland
Sea

3

RUSSIA

Murmansk

Arkhangelsk

70°

Norwegian
Sea

P

Arctic Circle

J

Reykjavik

2

Nizhniy
Novgorod

ICELAND

FINLAND

40°

Faroe
Islands
(Denmark)

SWEDEN

Helsinki

Moscow

ATLANTIC

NORWAY

ESTONIA

OCEAN

Oslo   Stockholm

LATVIA

60°N

Baltic   LITHUANIA   BELARUS
Sea   RUSSIA

1

North
Sea   DENMARK

POLAND   UKRAINE

N   20°W   0°   20°E   K

IRELAND   GERMANY

M   UNITED   L
KINGDOM   NETHERLANDS

Key

■ National capital
● Internal capital
⊙ Major city or town
○ Other town
━ International boundary
─ Internal boundary
See also main key on page 259.

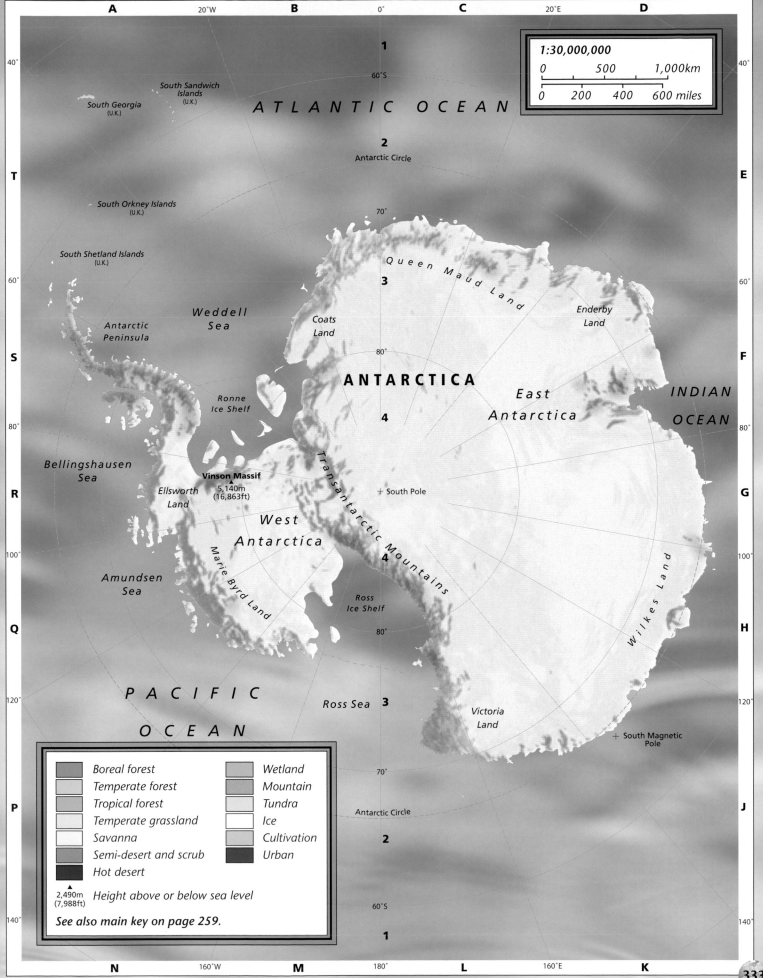

ATLANTIC OCEAN

South Georgia
(U.K.)

South Sandwich
Islands
(U.K.)

1:30,000,000

| 0 | 500 | 1,000km |

| 0 | 200 | 400 | 600 miles |

Antarctic Circle

South Orkney Islands
(U.K.)

South Shetland Islands
(U.K.)

Queen Maud Land

Weddell
Sea

Coats
Land

Enderby
Land

Antarctic
Peninsula

ANTARCTICA

East
Antarctica

INDIAN
OCEAN

Ronne
Ice Shelf

Bellingshausen
Sea

Vinson Massif
▲
5,140m
(16,863ft)

Ellsworth
Land

+ South Pole

West
Antarctica

Transantarctic Mountains

Amundsen
Sea

Marie Byrd Land

Ross
Ice Shelf

Wilkes Land

PACIFIC

Ross Sea

Victoria
Land

+ South Magnetic
Pole

OCEAN

Antarctic Circle

	Boreal forest		Wetland
	Temperate forest		Mountain
	Tropical forest		Tundra
	Temperate grassland		Ice
	Savanna		Cultivation
	Semi-desert and scrub		Urban
	Hot desert		

▲
2,490m
(7,988ft)   Height above or below sea level

See also main key on page 259.

Stalactites and stalagmites in the Cave of the Winds,
Colorado Springs, U.S.A.

FACT FILE

GEOGRAPHERS AND SCIENTISTS

Geography is the scientific study of the Earth. *Geo* is Greek for "Earth", and "graphy" comes from the Greek "graphein", which means "to write". Sciences that relate to the Earth are known as Earth sciences or geosciences.

Many geographers and scientists are involved in studying different aspects of the Earth. The table below lists some of these areas of study, the scientists and geographers who study them and the area each one deals with.

Name of study	Name of scientist/geographer	What is it?
Biogeography	Biogeographer	The study of the distribution of plants and animals
Geography	Geographer	The study of the Earth's features and processes, climates, resources and the way people relate to the Earth
Historical geography	Historical geographer	The geographic study of a place or region at a specific time in the past, or the study of geographic change over a period of time
Regional geography	Regional geographer	The study of the interrelationship between human and physical geography in a particular region
Urban geography	Urban geographer	The geographical study of cities
Geology	Geologist	The study of planet Earth, what it is made of, how it formed and how it is changing
Mineralogy	Mineralogist	The study of minerals
Geomorphology	Geomorphologist	The study of landforms (the shapes and features on the Earth's surface) and the processes which cause them
Volcanology	Volcanologist	The study of volcanoes
Seismology	Seismologist	The study of earthquakes and earth tremors
Oceanography	Oceanographer	The study of seas and oceans and the seabed
Meteorology	Meteorologist	The study of the weather and weather forecasting
Climatology	Climatologist	The study of climates past and present
Ecology	Ecologist	The study of the relationship between living things (including humans) and their surroundings on Earth
Pedology	Pedologist	The study of soil, which is also often known as soil science
Cartography	Cartographer	The science of designing and making maps, and collecting the information needed to make them

These are some of the famous scientists and geographers who have contributed to our understanding of how the Earth and its processes work, and explored other aspects of geography.

al-Idrisi (c.1100–c.1165)
Arabic geographer and author who explored the Mediterranean region, created an early map of the world, and wrote a book, *The Book of Roger*, describing his travels.

Aristotle (384BC–322BC)
Greek scientist and philosopher who wrote on many subjects. He realized that the Earth was a sphere, although it took a long time for everyone to accept this. (Until about AD1500, many people still thought the world was flat.)

Darwin, Charles (1809–1882)
English scientist who developed the theory of natural selection, which argues that plant and animal species change, or evolve, over long periods of time. This theory was controversial, partly because it suggested that the Earth was much older than many people believed.

Davis, William Morris (1850–1934) American geologist and meteorologist who founded the science of geomorphology. He developed a theory of how the process of erosion forms a cycle and was famous for his detailed diagrams showing how features of the Earth's crust are formed.

Democritus (c.460BC–c.370BC)
Greek philosopher who was the first to claim that all matter was made up of tiny particles, or atoms. He also studied earthquakes, volcanoes, the water cycle and erosion.

Eratosthenes (c.276BC–c.196BC)
Greek scientist and geographer who made the first measurement of the distance around the Earth, using the stars as a guide. He was the first person to use the word *geography*.

Gould, Stephen Jay (born 1941)
American geologist and paleontologist (person who studies fossils) who built on the theories of Charles Darwin. He has written many popular books, such as *Wonderful Life* (1989).

Hartshorne, Richard (1899–1992)
A leading American philosopher of geography. His major work was *Perspective on the Nature of Geography*, published in 1939, in which he argued for the study of specific places and regions.

Henry the Navigator (1394–1460)
A prince of Portugal who planned and paid for many journeys of exploration to Africa. He opened a school which taught explorers how to navigate (find their way) and record their discoveries.

Herodotus (c.484BC–c.425BC)
Greek historian known as the "father of history", but also regarded as the founder of geography because he was the first person to put historical events in a geographical setting.

Humboldt, Alexander von (1769–1859)
German explorer who contributed to geography, geology, meteorology and oceanography. He explored South America and wrote *Kosmos* (The Cosmos), in 1844, describing the geography and geology of the world.

Hutton, James (1726–1797)
Scottish scientist who studied rocks and minerals, and is sometimes called "the father of geology". He said that the Earth's crust changed gradually through erosion, volcanic eruptions and other processes.

Kant, Immanual (1724–1804)
Famous German philosopher who taught physical geography.

Lyell, Sir Charles (1797–1875)
Scottish geologist who developed the theories of James Hutton. He was also a friend of Charles Darwin and his ideas helped Darwin with his theory of natural selection.

Mackinder, Sir Halford J. (1861–1947)
Leading British geographer in the early 20th century. He was head of the first university geography department in the United Kingdom.

Ptolemy (c.AD100–c.AD170)
Egyptian geographer and astronomer. He devised an early system of latitude and longitude and used it to create many maps.

Ritter, Carl (1779–1859)
German geographer who was the first professor of geography at Berlin University. He wrote his major work, the 19-volume *Erdkunde* (Earth Science), in 1817 and is seen as the founder of modern regional geography.

Strabo (c.64BC–c.AD20)
Greek historian and geographer. He wrote *Geography*, a 17-volume book which provides geographical information on the Roman Empire.

Varenius, Bernhardus (1622–1650)
Dutch geographer. He wrote a major book, *Geographia Generalis* (General Geography) in 1650, in which he was one of the first people to distinguish between physical and human geography.

Wegener, Alfred (1880–1930)
German meteorologist who claimed that the Earth's continents were once joined together in one big continent, which he named Pangaea. His theories were not widely accepted until the 1960s when they were used to develop the theory of plate tectonics.

WORLD RECORDS

Here are some of the Earth's longest rivers, highest mountains and other amazing world records. But the world is always changing; mountains wear down, rivers change shape, and new buildings are constructed. Ways of measuring things can also change. That's why you may find slightly different figures in different books.

Highest mountains	
Everest, Nepal/China	8,850m (29,035ft)
K2, Pakistan/China	8,611m (28,251ft)
Kanchenjunga, India/Nepal	8,597m (28,208ft)
Lhotse I, Nepal/China	8,511m (27,923ft)
Makalu I, Nepal/China	8,481m (27,824ft)
Lhotse II, Nepal/China	8,400m (27,560ft)
Dhaulagiri, Nepal	8,172m (26,810ft)
Manaslu I, Nepal	8,156m (26,760ft)
Cho Oyu, Nepal/China	8,153m (26,750ft)
Nanga Parbat, Pakistan	8,126m (26,660ft)

Longest rivers	
Nile, Africa	6,671km (4,145 miles)
Amazon, South America	6,440km (4,000 miles)
Chang Jiang (Yangtze), China	6,380km (3,964 miles)
Mississippi/Missouri, U.S.A.	6,019km (3,741 miles)
Yenisey/Angara, Russia	5,540km (3,442 miles)
Huang He (Yellow), China	5,464km (3,395 miles)
Ob/Irtysh/Black Irtysh, Asia	5,411km (3,362 miles)
Amur/Shilka/Onon, Asia	4,416km (2,744 miles)
Lena, Russia	4,400km (2,734 miles)
Congo, Africa	4,374km (2,718 miles)

Biggest natural lakes	
Caspian Sea	370,999 sq km (143,243 sq miles)
Lake Superior	82,414 sq km (31,820 sq miles)
Lake Victoria	69,215 sq km (26,724 sq miles)
Lake Huron	59,596 sq km (23,010 sq miles)
Lake Michigan	58,016 sq km (22,400 sq miles)
Lake Tanganyika	32,764 sq km (12,650 sq miles)
Lake Baikal	31,500 sq km (12,162 sq miles)
Great Bear Lake	31,328 sq km (12,096 sq miles)
Lake Nyasa	29,928 sq km (11,555 sq miles)
Aral Sea	28,600 sq km (11,042 sq miles)

Deepest ocean
The Mariana Trench, part of the Pacific Ocean, is the deepest part of the sea at 11,022m (36,740ft) deep.

Deepest lake
Lake Baikal in Russia is the deepest lake in the world. At its deepest point it is 1,637m (5,370ft) deep.

Biggest islands	
Greenland	2,175,600 sq km (840,000 sq miles)
New Guinea	800,000 sq km (309,000 sq miles)
Borneo	751,100 sq km (290,000 sq miles)
Madagascar	587,040 sq km (226,656 sq miles)
Baffin Island	507,451 sq km (195,928 sq miles)
Sumatra	437,607 sq km (184,706 sq miles)
Great Britain	234,410 sq km (90,506 sq miles)
Honshu	227,920 sq km (88,000 sq miles)
Victoria Island	217,290 sq km (83,896 sq miles)
Ellesmere Island	196,236 sq km (75,767 sq miles)

Tallest inhabited buildings	
Petronas Towers, Malaysia	452m (1,483ft)
Sears Tower, U.S.A.	443m (1,454ft)
Jin Mao Building, China	420m (1,378ft)
CITIC Plaza, China	391m (1,283ft)
Shun Hing Square, China	384m (1,260ft)
Plaza Rakyat, Malaysia	382m (1,254ft)
Empire State Building, U.S.A.	381m (1,250ft)
Central Plaza, China	373m (1,227ft)
Bank of China, China	368m (1,209ft)
Emirates Tower, U.A.E.	350m (1,148ft)

Biggest cities/urban areas	
Tokyo, Japan	26.4 million
Mexico City, Mexico	18.1 million
Bombay, India	18.1 million
Sao Paulo, Brazil	17.8 million
New York, U.S.A	16.6 million
Lagos, Nigeria	13.4 million
Los Angeles, U.S.A.	13.1 million
Calcutta, India	12.9 million
Shanghai, China	12.9 million
Buenos Aires, Argentina	12.6 million

Famous waterfalls	Height
Angel Falls, Venezuela	979m (3,212ft)
Sutherland Falls, New Zealand	580m (1,904ft)
Mardalfossen, Norway	517m (1,696ft)
Jog Falls, India	253m (830ft)
Victoria Falls, Zimbabwe/Zambia	108m (355ft)
Iguacu Falls, Brazil/Argentina	82m (269ft)
Niagara Falls, Canada/U.S.A.	57m (187ft)

Natural disasters

Natural disasters can be measured in different ways. For example, some earthquakes score highly on the Richter scale, while others cause more destruction. The earthquakes, volcanic eruptions, floods, hurricanes and tornadoes listed here are among the most famous and destructive disasters in history.

Earthquakes	Richter scale	Deaths and other effects
San Francisco, U.S.A., 1906	7.9	3,000; deadliest in U.S.; Great Fire
Messina, Italy, 1908	7.5	70-100,000; tsunami killed many
Tokyo-Kanto, Japan, 1923	8.3	142,807; caused Great Tokyo Fire
Quetta, Pakistan, 1935	7.5	30-60,000; Quetta city destroyed
Concepcion, Chile, 1960	8.7	2,000; strongest quake ever
Alaska, U.S.A., 1964	8.6	125; strongest quake ever in U.S.A.
Tangshan, China, 1976	7.9	655,237; deadliest quake of 1900s
Manjil-Rudbar, Iran, 1990	7.7	50,000; landslides; cities destroyed
Kobe, Japan, 1995	6.8	5,500; over $147bn damage
Gujarat, India, 2001	8.0	20,085; strongest quake in India ever

Volcanic eruptions	Disastrous effects
Mount Vesuvius, Italy, AD79	Pompeii flattened; up to 20,000 died
Tambora, Indonesia, 1815	92,000 people starved to death
Krakatau, Indonesia, 1883	36,500 drowned in resulting tsunami
Mount Pelee, Martinique, 1902	Nearly 30,000 people buried in ash flows
Kelut, Indonesia, 1919	Over 5,000 people drowned in mud
Agung, Indonesia, 1963	1,200 people suffocated in hot ash
Mount St. Helens, U.S.A., 1980	Only 61 died but a large area was destroyed
Ruiz, Colombia, 1985	25,000 people died in giant mud flows
Mt. Pinatubo, Philippines, 1991	800 killed by collapsing roofs and disease
Island of Montserrat, 1995	Volcano left most of the island uninhabitable

Floods	Disastrous effects
Holland, 1228	100,000 drowned by a sea flood
Kaifeng, China, 1642	300,000 died after rebels destroyed a dyke
Johnstown, U.S.A., 1889	2,200 killed in a flood caused by rain
Italy, 1963	Vaoint Dam overflowed; 2–3,000 killed
East Pakistan, 1970	Giant wave caused by cyclone killed 250,000
Bangladesh, 1988	1,300 died, 30m homeless in monsoon flood
Southern U.S.A., 1993	$12bn of damage after Mississippi flooded
China, 1998	Chang Jiang overflow left 14m homeless
Venezuela, 1999	Floods and mudslides killed 5,000-20,000
Southeast Asia, 2004	Tsunamis killed over 222,000 people

Storms	Disastrous effects
Caribbean "Great Hurricane", 1780	Biggest ever hurricane killed over 20,000
Hong Kong typhoon, China, 1906	10,000 people died in this giant hurricane
Killer tornado, U.S.A., 1925	Up to 700 people died in Ellington, Missouri
Tropical Storm Agnes, U.S.A., 1972	$3.5bn damage, 129 dead
Hurricane Fifi, Honduras, 1974	8,000 people died and 100,000 left homeless
Hurricane Georges, U.S.A., 1998	Caribbean and U.S.A. hit; $5bn of damage
Hurricane Mitch, C. America, 1998	Over 9,000 killed across Central America

Amazing Earth facts

The Earth is 12,103km (7,520 miles) across. Its circumference (the distance around the Equator) is 38,022km (23,627 miles) and it is 149,503,000 km (92,897,000 miles) away from the Sun.

To make one complete orbit around the Sun, the Earth has to travel 938,900,000km (583,400,000 miles). To do this in just a year, it has to travel very fast. Because of the atmosphere surrounding the Earth, you can't feel it moving. But in fact you are zooming through space faster than any rocket.

• **Orbit speed** The Earth travels around the Sun at a speed of about 106,000kph (65,868mph).

• **Spinning speed** The Earth also spins around an axis, but the speed you are spinning at depends on where you live. Places on the Equator move at 1,600kph (995mph). New York moves at around 1,100kph (684mph). Near the poles, the spinning is not very fast at all. (You can see how this works by looking at a spinning globe.)

• **Solar System speed** The whole Solar System, including the Sun, the Earth and its moon, and the other planets and their moons, is moving at 72,400kph (45,000 mph) through the galaxy.

• **Galaxy speed** Our galaxy, the Milky Way, whizzes through the universe at a speed of 2,172,150kph (1,350,000mph).

CYCLES OF PLANET EARTH

The Earth is constantly going through repeated processes, or cycles, such as the orbit of the Earth around the Sun, the way it spins and tilts as it moves through space, the orbit of the Moon around the Earth, and the sequence of the tides.

Days and years

Days and years are created by the movement of the Earth in relation to the Sun. Here are some facts and figures about the Earth's orbit.

• One **day** is the amount of time it takes the Earth to spin around on its axis. We divide each day into 24 hours of 60 minutes each.

• The exact amount of time it takes the Earth to make one complete orbit around the Sun is 365.26 days. This is known as a **solar year**.

• Instead of having 365.26 days, a normal **year** on Earth has exactly 365 days (because this is easier for us). Every four years another day is added to make up the difference. A year with an extra day in it is called a **leap year**. The extra day is added to February, so in leap years February has 29 days instead of 28.

• Making every fourth year a leap year does not even things out exactly, so some leap years are missed. Usually, every fourth year is a leap year, such as 1988, 1992 and 1996. But century years, such as 1700, 1800 and 1900, are not leap years. However, millennium years, such as the year 2000, *are* leap years.

Calendars

A **calendar** is a system of measuring years, months, weeks and days. People don't all agree when the world began, so years cannot be measured from then. Several different calendars, mostly based on religious beliefs, are used today.

Years ago	Christian calendar	Muslim calendar	Chinese calendar	Hebrew calendar
5,800				
5,600				*This is when Jews believe the world began.*
5,400				
5,200				
5,000				
4,800				
4,600			*Emperor Huang Di is said to have invented the Chinese calendar 4,600 years ago.*	
4,400				
4,200				
4,000				
3,800				
3,600				
3,400				
3,200				
3,000				
2,800				
2,600				
2,400				
2,200				
2,000				
1,800	*The Christian calendar begins with the birth of Jesus Christ.*			
1,600				
1,400				
1,200		*This is when the Muslim prophet Mohammed fled from Mecca to Medina.*		
1,000				
800				
600				
400				
200				
0				

This chart shows how many years ago the different calendars began. When the Christian calendar is on the year 2000, the Muslim calendar is on the year 1378, and so on.

The Moon

A **moon** is a ball of rock orbiting (moving around) a planet. The Earth only has one moon, but some planets have more. Saturn, for example, has at least 30 moons.

Our Moon orbits the Earth once every 27 days, 7 hours and 43 minutes. The Moon "shines" because it is reflecting light from the Sun. Whether we see a full moon, a thin crescent moon, or something in between, depends on what position the Moon is in and how much sunlight it can reflect onto the Earth. These different shapes are called the phases of the Moon.

This diagram shows the phases of the Moon as it orbits the Earth.

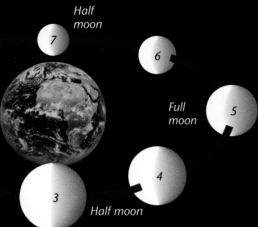

Light rays from the Sun

1. New moon 3. Half moon 5. Full moon 7. Half moon

2. Waxing crescent 4. Waxing gibbous 6. Waning gibbous 8. Waning crescent

Phases of the Moon

• A **new moon** does not shine at all. The Moon's cycle begins when the Moon is between the Earth and the Sun, so none of the light it reflects can reach the Earth.

• A **half moon** appears when the Moon has moved around and is alongside the Earth. We see half of it reflecting the Sun.

• A **full moon** is what you see when the Moon is on the opposite side of the Earth from the Sun. When the Moon is in this position, you can see sunlight reflecting off the whole of the surface facing Earth.

More Moon facts

• When the Moon is moving away from the Sun and growing fuller, it is **waxing**. When it moves around toward the Sun again and seems to be getting smaller, it is **waning**.

• A **crescent moon** is between a new moon and a half moon, and looks like a crescent or C-shape.

• A **gibbous moon** is between a half moon and a full moon, and is a fat oval shape.

• A **lunar month** is the amount of time it takes the Moon to complete its cycle: 29 days, 12 hours and 44 minutes. This is longer than the orbit time, because while the Moon is making its orbit around the Earth, the Earth is moving around the Sun and so changing its own position.

• Like the Earth, the Moon spins around on its axis. It does this every 27 days, 7 hours and 43 minutes. This is exactly the same amount of time as the time it takes to travel around the Earth, which means we always see the same side of the Moon from Earth. However, we can see the other side of the Moon in pictures taken by spacecraft.

• The Moon is 3,476km (2,160 miles) across, about a quarter of the width of the Earth. Its circumference is 10,927km (6,790 miles) and its distance away from the Earth varies between 356,399 and 384,403km (221,456 and 238,857 miles). It orbits the Earth at about 3,700kph (2,300mph).

• A **month** on Earth is a period of time based on the Moon's cycle. But to make 12 months fit into a year, an average month is about 30 days long, slightly longer than a lunar month.

• A **blue moon** happens when there are two full moons within one Earth month. The second full moon of the two is called the blue moon.

Tides

The water in the Earth's seas and oceans rises and falls twice a day. These movements are called tides, and they are caused by the gravity of the Moon.

As the Earth spins, different parts of its surface move past the Moon. The part nearest the Moon has a high tide, when the water rises as the Moon pulls it.

At the same time, a high tide also happens on the opposite side of the Earth, because of a reaction called centrifugal force, created by the way the Earth and the Moon move around each other.

While this is happening, there is a low tide on the parts of the Earth's surface that are not facing or opposite the Moon. Each part of the world has two high tides and two low tides every day.

TIME ZONES

When it's midday in Rio de Janeiro, it's midnight in Tokyo. This is because we divide the Earth into different time zones. Within each zone, people usually set their clocks to the same time. If you fly between two zones, you change your watch to the time in the new zone.

Dividing up time

There are 25 different time zones. They are separated by one-hour intervals and there is a new time zone roughly every 15 degrees of longitude*. The zones are measured in hours ahead of or behind Greenwich Mean Time, or GMT, which is the time at the Prime Meridian Line*.

Governments can change their countries' time zones. So, for convenience, whole countries usually keep the same local time instead of sticking to the zones exactly. For example, China could be divided into several time zones, but instead the whole country keeps the same time. A few areas, such as India, Iran and parts of Australia, use non-standard half hour deviations.

Summer time

Some countries adjust their clocks in summer. For example, in the U.K. everybody's clocks go forward one hour. This is known as Daylight Saving Time or Summer Time. It is a way of getting more out of the days by giving people an extra hour of daylight in the evening. It reduces energy use because people don't use as much electricity for lights.

Changing dates

On the opposite side of the world from the Prime Meridian Line is the International Date Line, which runs mostly through the Pacific Ocean and bends to avoid the land. Places to the west of it are 24 hours ahead of places to the east. This means that if you travel east across it you lose a day and if you travel west across it you gain a day.

This map shows the different time zones. The times at the top of the map tell you the time it is in the different zones when it is noon at the Prime Meridian Line. The numbers in circles tell you how many hours ahead of or behind Greenwich Mean Time an area is.

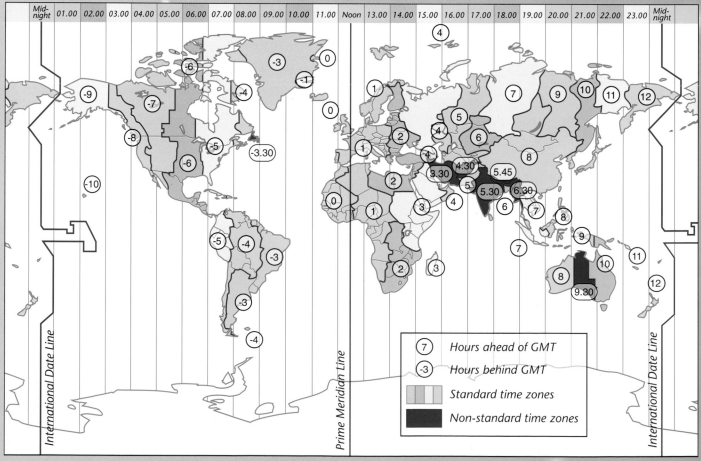

*Longitude, 250; Prime Meridian Line, 250

LOOKING AT THE STARS

On a clear night you can see a huge number of stars from Earth. If you look carefully, you will soon be able to recognize individual stars and groups of stars, known as constellations. The star maps on the following pages will show you which stars to look for.

Internet links

Website 1 Read the stories behind the names of some of the stars and constellations.

Website 2 Find out about the life cycle of stars, read star facts and see amazing NASA photographs of stars.

For links to these websites, go to **www.usborne-quicklinks.com**

Pegasus

Andromeda

Perseus

In these pictures, the red dots show the stars that make up a constellation and the white outlines show the figures they are supposed to represent.

Constellations

To make it easier to find and identify different stars, people divided them into constellations and gave them names, often based on characters in stories. The constellations on the star maps in this book appear in capital letters and some have been joined together with lines to make them easier to recognize.

Star maps

On the next eight pages there are star maps for each season. This is because as the Earth orbits the Sun, the part of the sky that we can see changes. In addition, many of the stars you can see from the northern hemisphere are different from the ones you can see from the southern hemisphere, so there are different maps for each of these.

You can observe the stars with your naked eye, but binoculars or a telescope like this one will make them look much bigger and brighter.

Using the maps

To use the star maps, choose the right hemisphere and season and look in the direction indicated at the bottom of the map. You will find it easiest to see stars on a clear, dark night, away from city lights. You can look at them with just your naked eye or you can use binoculars or a telescope to see the fainter ones more clearly. On each pair of star maps there is a note of the dates and times when the star maps will match up exactly with the night sky.

THE NIGHT SKY IN SPRING

Star maps for the northern hemisphere

The only star in the sky that doesn't seem to change its position is Polaris, in the middle of the top map. Polaris is flanked by Capella and Aldebaran on its left, and Deneb and Vega on its right.

Look out for Ursa Major (the Great Bear) overhead and Taurus (the Bull) in the west. The bright streak in the sky is the starry trail of the Milky Way.

March 15th 11:00pm
April 15th 10:00pm
May 15th 9:00pm

West   Looking north   East

Regulus is the bright star in the middle of the sky. It is part of the constellation of Leo (the Lion).

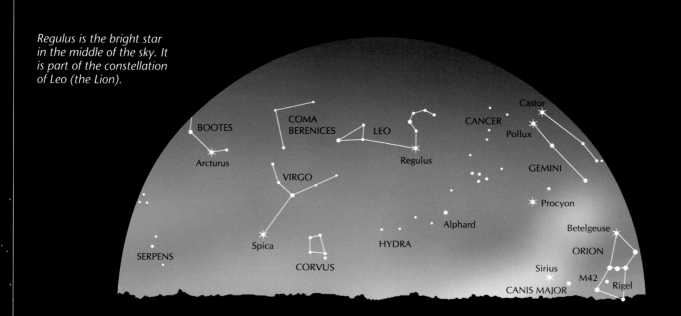

East   Looking south   West

Star maps for the southern hemisphere

The most famous constellation is Crux, or the Southern Cross. It can never be seen from the northern hemisphere. Facing north, the constellations of Pegasus and Andromeda dominate the sky.

Internet links

Website 1 Find tips on how to observe the night sky.

Website 2 Follow simple instructions on how to see different constellations in each season.

For links to these websites, go to
www.usborne-quicklinks.com

M31, just above the horizon, is a spiral-shaped galaxy.

September 15th 11:00pm
October 15th 10:00pm
November 15th 9:00pm

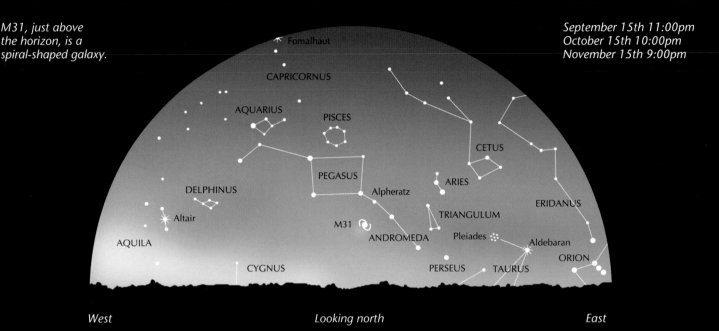

West — Looking north — East

Sirius is the brightest star in the sky. Canopus is the second brightest.

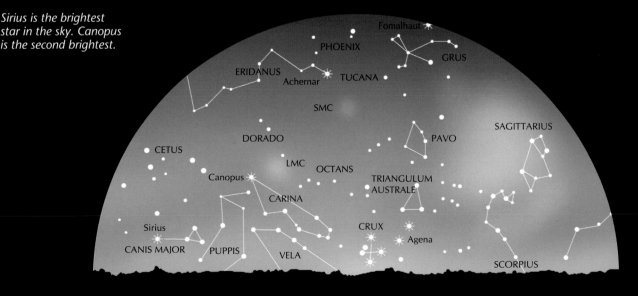

East — Looking south — West

THE NIGHT SKY IN SUMMER

Maps for the northern hemisphere

The sky never really gets dark in summer, so only the brightest stars show up clearly. If the sky is clear on August 12th, stay up to watch shooting stars coming from the constellation of Perseus.

Capella, Regulus and Deneb are the brightest stars in the northern sky at this time of year.

June 15th 11:00pm
July 15th 10:00pm
August 15th 9:00pm

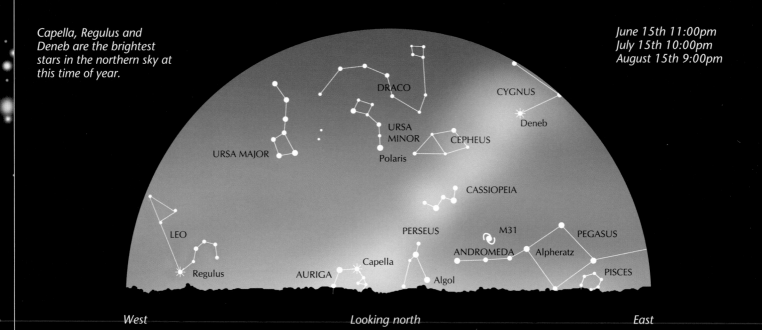

West   *Looking north*   East

Look out for Antares shining brightly above the southern horizon.

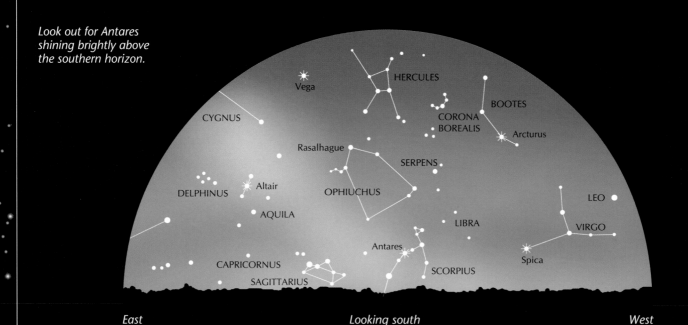

East   *Looking south*   West

Maps for the southern hemisphere

Facing north, the easiest constellations to spot are Orion and Canis Major (the Great Dog) and over to the east you can see Leo (the Lion). Sirius (the Dog Star), one of the stars in Canis Major, is the brightest star in the sky.

Internet links

Website 1 See a different NASA picture of the universe each day, accompanied by a brief explanation from a professional astronomer.

Website 2 See star maps for the northern and southern hemispheres.

For links to these websites, go to **www.usborne-quicklinks.com**

Look out for the cluster of stars known as Pleiades, or Seven Sisters, in the constellation of Taurus.

December 15th 11:00pm
January 15th 10:00pm
February 15th 9:00pm

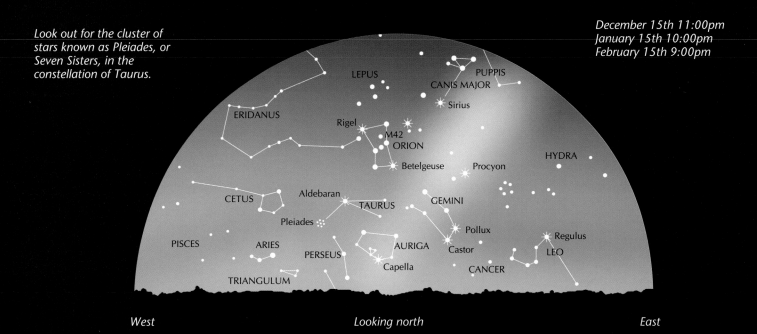

West   Looking north   East

LMC and SMC stand for Large and Small Magellanic Cloud. These are small galaxies.

East   Looking south   West

THE NIGHT SKY IN AUTUMN

Maps for the northern hemisphere

Facing north, look for Ursa Major, which is below
Polaris and parallel with the horizon. Looking south,
you should be able to see Pegasus (the Winged
Horse), which has a square of stars in the middle.

*In the east, the winter
stars are beginning to
rise, including the red
star Aldebaran.*

September 15th 11:00pm
October 15th 10:00pm
November 15th 9:00pm

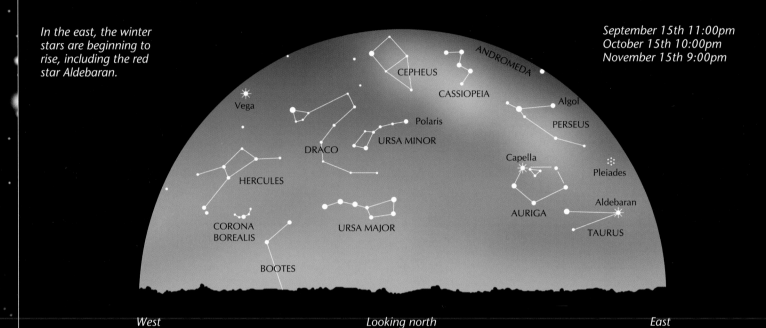

West   Looking north   East

*This is the best time to see
M31, a huge distant galaxy.
It is just visible with the
naked eye, but binoculars
will show it as a misty oval.*

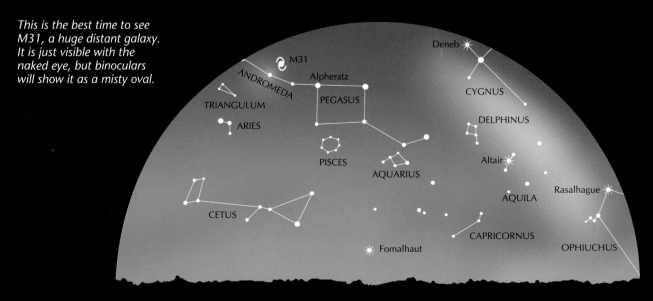

East   Looking south   West

Maps for the southern hemisphere

Facing north, a triangle of three bright stars dominates the sky: Regulus, which is blue, yellow Arcturus and blue-white Spica. Facing south, the Milky Way crosses the sky in a wide band.

Internet links

Website 1 Find out what to look out for on each night of the year.

Website 2 Discover fascinating facts about stars and read the latest space science news.

For links to these websites, go to **www.usborne-quicklinks.com**

Look out for the constellations of Virgo (the Virgin) and Leo (the Lion).

March 15th 11:00pm
April 15th 10:00pm
May 15th 9:00pm

West — Looking north — East

Above Crux (the Southern Cross) is Centaurus (the Centaur). A centaur was a mythical creature that was half man and half horse.

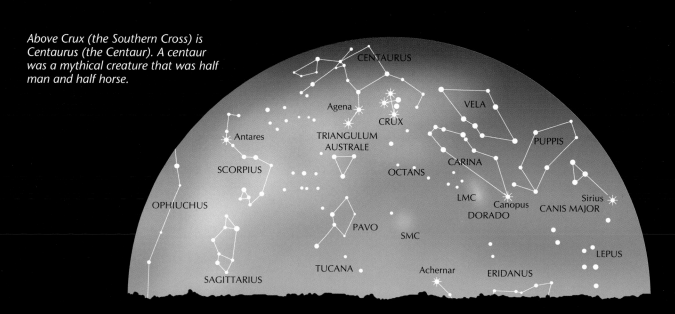

East — Looking south — West

THE NIGHT SKY IN WINTER

Maps for the northern hemisphere

Winter is a good time to look for shooting stars. Set your alarm for just before dawn on December 14th to see shooting stars coming from Gemini. Looking south, you can see Orion, one of the brightest constellations.

Facing north, look for Ursa Major balancing on its tail, and Cygnus (the Swan).

December 15th 11:00pm
January 15th 10:00pm
February 15th 9:00pm

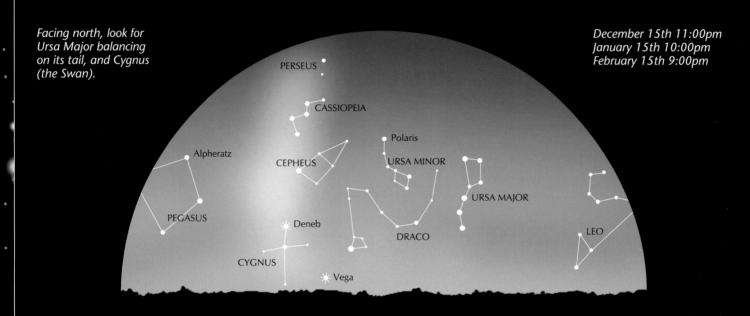

West   Looking north   East

If you find the bright constellation of Orion, it will help you to locate the other constellations.

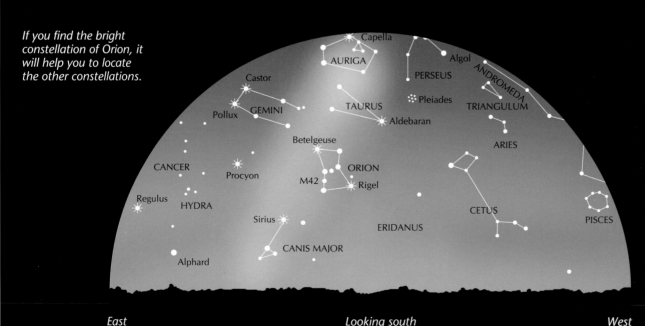

East   Looking south   West

Maps for the southern hemisphere

There are plenty of bright stars to look for at this time of the year. Try to spot Deneb, Spica, Altair, Vega and Fomalhaut. The Milky Way is seen at its best, cutting the sky in half.

Internet links

Website 1 See night-time constellations without leaving your computer.

Website 2 Go on an amazing virtual journey through the stars.

For links to these websites, go to
www.usborne-quicklinks.com

Look out for Ophiuchus (the Serpent Bearer), a very large group of stars, and Hercules, named after a Greek hero.

June 15th 11:00pm
July 15th 10:00pm
August 15th 9:00pm

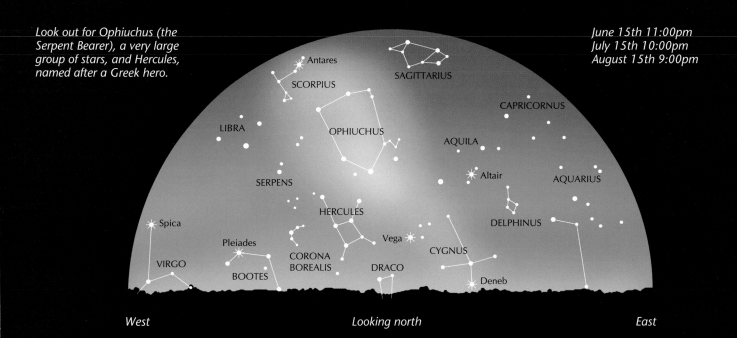

West   Looking north   East

The Milky Way runs through Crux (the Southern Cross) and Centaurus (the Centaur).

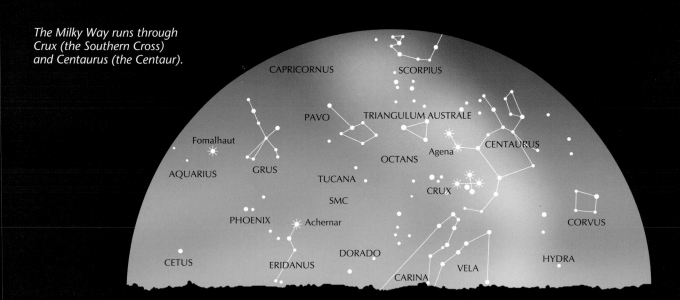

East   Looking south   West

MEASUREMENTS

Measuring things – distance, area, weight, volume, time and temperature – is one of the most important parts of science. There are two main systems of measurement: metric and imperial. This page shows how each measuring system works, and also how to convert from one into the other.

Imperial

This system of measurement is very old, dating from the 12th century or even earlier. It can be hard to use because it is not based on the decimal (base 10) system which we use for numbers. Some of the units have symbols or abbreviations. For example, the symbol for an inch is ".

Length and distance

12 inches (") = 1 foot (')
3 feet = 1 yard (yd)
1,760 yards = 1 mile
3 miles = 1 league

Area

144 square inches = 1 square foot
9 square feet = 1 square yard
4,840 square yards = 1 acre
640 acres = 1 square mile

Weight

16 drams (dr) = 1 ounce (oz)
16 ounces = 1 pound (lb)
14 pounds = 1 stone
2,240 pounds (160 stone) = 1 ton
2,000 pounds = 1 short ton

Volume and capacity

1,728 cubic inches = 1 cubic foot (ft^3)
27 cubic feet = 1 cubic yard (yd^3)
5 fluid ounces (fl oz) = 1 gill (gi)

20 fluid ounces = 1 pint (pt) (U.K.)
16 fluid ounces = 1 pint (U.S.)
2 pints = 1 quart (qt)
8 pints (4 quarts) = 1 gallon (gal)

Temperature

The imperial unit of temperature is one degree (°) Fahrenheit (F). The freezing point of water is 32° F and the boiling point of water is 212° F.

Metric

The metric or decimal system is based on the metre or meter, a unit of measurement which was first used in France in the 1790s. Metric units are multiples of each other by 10, 100 or 1,000. Countries around the world are gradually switching from imperial to metric. Many of the metric units have both U.S. spellings (-er) and European spellings (-re).

Length and distance

10 millimeters/millimetres (mm) =
      1 centimeter/centimetre (cm)
100 cm = 1 meter/metre (m)
1,000 m = 1 kilometer/kilometre (km)

Area

100 square mm (mm^2) =
      1 square cm (cm^2)
10,000 square cm =
      1 square m (m^2)
10,000 square m = 1 hectare
1,000,000 square m = 1 square
      kilometer/kilometre (km^2)

Weight

1,000 grams (g) = 1 kilogram (kg)
1,000 kilograms = 1 tonne (t)

Volume and capacity

1 cubic cm (cc or cm^3) = 1
      milliliter/millilitre (ml)
1,000 ml = 1 liter/litre (l)
1,000 l = 1 cubic m (m^3)

Temperature

The metric temperature unit is one degree (°) Celsius (C). Water freezes at 0°C and boils at 100° C.

Conversion tables

You can convert between metric and imperial with this table. Use a calculator to do the multiplications.

To convert	into	multiply by
cm	inches	0.394
m	yards	1.094
km	miles	0.621
grams	ounces	0.35
kilograms	pounds	2.205
tonnes	tons	0.984
square cm	square inches	0.155
square m	square yards	1.196
square km	square miles	0.386
hectares	acres	2.471
liters/litres	pints	1.76
inches	cm	2.54
yards	m	0.914
miles	km	1.609
ounces	grams	28.35
pounds	kilograms	0.454
tons	tonnes	1.016
square inches	square cm	6.452
square yards	square m	0.836
square miles	square km	2.59
acres	hectares	0.405
pints	liters/litres	0.5683

TYPES OF GOVERNMENTS

Most states have one main leader along with a parliament or assembly of politicians. The main types of governments are listed and explained below. A state can have a combination of more than one of these types of governments. For example, the United States of America is a federal republic.

Anarchy
Anarchy means a situation where there is no government. This can happen after a civil war, when a government has been destroyed and rival groups are battling to take its place.

Capitalist state
In a Capitalist or free-market state, people can own their own businesses and property, and buy services such as healthcare privately. However, most Capitalist governments also provide national health, education and welfare services.

Commonwealth
This word is sometimes used to mean a democratic republic, in which all the state's citizens are seen as having an equal interest in the functioning of the state.

Communist state
Under Communism, the state owns things like factories, farms and businesses, and provides healthcare, welfare and education for its people.

Democracy
In a democracy, the government is elected by the people, using a voting system.

Dictatorship
This is a state run by a single, unelected leader, who may use force to keep control. In a military dictatorship, the army is in power.

Federal government
In a federal system, such as that of the U.S.A., a central government shares power with a number of smaller regional governments.

Monarchy
A monarchy is a state with a king or queen. In some traditional monarchies, the monarch has complete power. A constitutional monarchy, however, also has a separate, usually democratic, government and the monarch's powers are limited.

Regional or local government
A government that controls a smaller area within a state. Some regional governments have very limited powers, and are largely directed by the central government. Others, such as the regional governments in the U.S.A., have much more power and can make their own laws.

Republic
A republic is a state with no monarch. The head of state is usually an elected president.

Revolutionary government
After a revolution, when a government is overthrown by force, the new regime is sometimes called a revolutionary government.

Totalitarian state
This is a state with only one political party, in which individuals are forced to obey the government and may also be prevented from leaving the country.

Transitional government
A government that is changing from one system to another is known as a transitional government. For example, a dictatorship may become a democracy after the dictator dies, but the transition between the systems can take several years.

GAZETTEER OF STATES

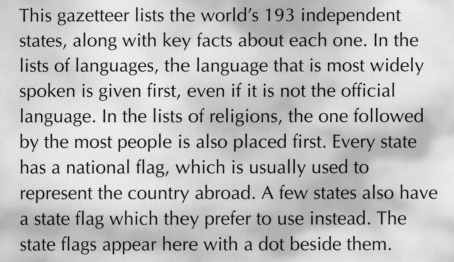

This gazetteer lists the world's 193 independent states, along with key facts about each one. In the lists of languages, the language that is most widely spoken is given first, even if it is not the official language. In the lists of religions, the one followed by the most people is also placed first. Every state has a national flag, which is usually used to represent the country abroad. A few states also have a state flag which they prefer to use instead. The state flags appear here with a dot beside them.

Afghanistan

Albania

Algeria

Andorra

Angola

Antigua and Barbuda

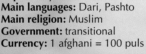

• **Argentina**

Armenia

Australia

Austria

Azerbaijan

Bahamas, The

Bahrain

Bangladesh

AFGHANISTAN (Asia)
Area: 647,500 sq km (249,935 sq miles)
Population: 25,838,797
Capital city: Kabul
Main languages: Dari, Pashto
Main religion: Muslim
Government: transitional
Currency: 1 afghani = 100 puls

ALBANIA (Europe)
Area: 28,750 sq km (11,100 sq miles)
Population: 3,510,484
Capital city: Tirana
Main language: Albanian
Main religions: Muslim, Albanian Orthodox
Government: emerging democracy
Currency: 1 lek = 100 qintars

ALGERIA (Africa)
Area: 2,381,740 sq km (919,589 sq miles)
Population: 31,193,917
Capital city: Algiers
Main languages: Arabic, French, Berber dialects
Main religion: Sunni Muslim
Government: republic
Currency: 1 Algerian dinar = 100 centimes

ANDORRA (Europe)
Area: 468 sq km (181 sq miles)
Population: 67,627
Capital city: Andorra la Vella
Main languages: Catalan, Spanish
Main religion: Roman Catholic
Government: parliamentary democracy
Currency: 1 euro = 100 cents

ANGOLA (Africa)
Area: 1,246,700 sq km (481,351 sq miles)
Population: 10,366,031
Capital city: Luanda
Main languages: Kilongo, Kimbundu, other Bantu languages, Portuguese
Main religions: indigenous, Roman Catholic, Protestant
Government: transitional
Currency: 1 kwanza = 100 lwei

ANTIGUA AND BARBUDA (North America)
Area: 442 sq km (171 sq miles)
Population: 66,970
Capital city: Saint John's
Main languages: Caribbean Creole, English
Main religion: Protestant
Government: constitutional monarchy
Currency: 1 East Caribbean dollar = 100 cents

ARGENTINA (South America)
Area: 2,780,400 sq km (1,073,512 sq miles)
Population: 36,955,182
Capital city: Buenos Aires
Main language: Spanish
Main religion: Roman Catholic
Government: republic
Currency: 1 peso = 100 centavos

ARMENIA (Asia)
Area: 29,800 sq km (11,506 sq miles)
Population: 3,336,100
Capital city: Yerevan
Main language: Armenian
Main religion: Armenian Orthodox
Government: republic
Currency: 1 dram = 100 luma

AUSTRALIA (Australasia/Oceania)
Area: 7,686,850 sq km (2,967,124 sq miles)
Population: 19,357,594
Capital city: Canberra
Main language: English
Main religion: Christian
Government: federal democratic monarchy
Currency: 1 Australian dollar = 100 cents

AUSTRIA (Europe)
Area: 83,858 sq km (32,378 sq miles)
Population: 8,150,835
Capital city: Vienna
Main language: German
Main religion: Roman Catholic
Government: federal republic
Currency: 1 euro = 100 cents

Barbados

Belarus

Belgium

Belize

Benin

Bhutan

• **Bolivia**

AZERBAIJAN (Asia)
Area: 86,600 sq km (33,436 sq miles)
Population: 7,771,092
Capital city: Baku
Main language: Azeri
Main religion: Muslim
Government: republic
Currency: 1 manat = 100 gopiks

BAHAMAS, THE (North America)
Area: 13,940 sq km (5,382 sq miles)
Population: 297,852
Capital city: Nassau
Main languages: Bahamian Creole, English
Main religion: Christian
Government: parliamentary democracy
Currency: 1 Bahamian dollar = 100 cents

BAHRAIN (Asia)
Area: 678 sq km (261 sq miles)
Population: 645,361
Capital city: Manama
Main languages: Arabic, English
Main religion: Muslim
Government: traditional monarchy
Currency: 1 Bahraini dinar = 1,000 fils

BANGLADESH (Asia)
Area: 144,000 sq km (55,598 sq miles)
Population: 131,269,860
Capital city: Dhaka
Main languages: Bengali, English
Main religions: Muslim, Hindu
Government: republic
Currency: 1 taka = 100 poisha

BARBADOS (North America)
Area: 430 sq km (166 sq miles)
Population: 275,330
Capital city: Bridgetown
Main languages: Bajan, English
Main religion: Christian
Government: parliamentary democracy
Currency: 1 Barbadian dollar = 100 cents

BELARUS (Europe)
Area: 207,600 sq km (80,154 sq miles)
Population: 10,350,194
Capital city: Minsk
Main language: Belarusian
Main religion: Eastern Orthodox
Government: republic
Currency: 1 Belarusian ruble = 100 kopecks

BELGIUM (Europe)
Area: 30,510 sq km (11,780 sq miles)
Population: 10,258,762
Capital city: Brussels
Main languages: Dutch, French
Main religions: Roman Catholic, Protestant
Government: constitutional monarchy
Currency: 1 euro = 100 cents

BELIZE (North America)
Area: 22,960 sq km (8,865 sq miles)
Population: 256,062
Capital city: Belmopan
Main languages: Spanish, Belize Creole, English, Garifuna, Maya

Main religions: Roman Catholic, Protestant
Government: parliamentary democracy
Currency: 1 Belizean dollar = 100 cents

BENIN (Africa)
Area: 112,620 sq km (43,483 sq miles)
Population: 6,590,782
Capital city: Porto-Novo
Main languages: Fon, French, Yoruba
Main religions: indigenous, Christian, Muslim
Government: republic
Currency: 1 CFA* franc = 100 centimes

BHUTAN (Asia)
Area: 47,000 sq km (18,146 sq miles)
Population: 2,049,412
Capital city: Thimphu
Main languages: Dzongkha, Nepali
Main religions: Muslim, Hindu
Government: monarchy
Currency: 1 ngultrum = 100 chetrum

BOLIVIA (South America)
Area: 1,098,580 sq km (424,162 sq miles)
Population: 8,300,463
Capital cities: La Paz, Sucre
Main languages: Spanish, Quechua, Aymara
Main religion: Roman Catholic
Government: republic
Currency: 1 boliviano = 100 centavos

BOSNIA AND HERZEGOVINA (Europe)
Area: 51,129 sq km (19,741 sq miles)
Population: 3,922,205
Capital city: Sarajevo
Main languages: Bosnian, Serbian, Croatian
Main religions: Muslim, Orthodox, Roman Catholic
Government: emerging federal democracy
Currency: 1 marka = 100 pfenninga

BOTSWANA (Africa)
Area: 600,372 sq km (231,743 sq miles)
Population: 1,586,119
Capital city: Gaborone
Main languages: Setswana, Kalanga, English
Main religions: indigenous, Christian
Government: parliamentary republic
Currency: 1 pula = 100 thebe

BRAZIL (South America)
Area: 8,547,400 sq km (3,300,151 sq miles)
Population: 174,468,575
Capital city: Brasilia
Main language: Portuguese
Main religion: Roman Catholic
Government: federal republic
Currency: 1 real = 100 centavos

BRUNEI (Asia)
Area: 5,770 sq km (2,228 sq miles)
Population: 343,653
Capital city: Bandar Seri Begawan
Main languages: Malay, English, Chinese
Main religions: Muslim, Buddhist
Government: constitutional sultanate (a type of monarchy)
Currency: 1 Bruneian dollar = 100 cents

Bosnia and Herzegovina

Botswana

Brazil

Brunei

Bulgaria

Burkina Faso

Burma (Myanmar)

*CFA = Communaute Financiere Africaine

GAZETTEER OF STATES CONTINUED:

Burundi

Cambodia

Cameroon

Canada

Cape Verde

Central African Republic

Chad

BULGARIA (Europe)
Area: 110,910 sq km (42,822 sq miles)
Population: 7,707,495
Capital city: Sofia
Main language: Bulgarian
Main religions: Bulgarian Orthodox, Muslim
Government: republic
Currency: 1 lev = 100 stotinki

BURKINA FASO (Africa)
Area: 274,200 sq km (105,869 sq miles)
Population: 12,272,289
Capital city: Ouagadougou
Main languages: Moore, Jula, French
Main religions: Muslim, indigenous
Government: republic
Currency: 1 CFA* franc = 100 centimes

BURMA (MYANMAR) (Asia)
Area: 678,500 sq km (261,969 sq miles)
Population: 50,438,300
Capital city: Rangoon
Main language: Burmese
Main religion: Buddhist
Government: military dictatorship
Currency: 1 kyat = 100 pyas

BURUNDI (Africa)
Area: 27,830 sq km (10,745 sq miles)
Population: 6,223,897
Capital city: Bujumbura
Main languages: Kirundi, French, Swahili
Main religions: Christian, indigenous
Government: republic
Currency: 1 Burundi franc = 100 centimes

CAMBODIA (Asia)
Area: 181,040 sq km (69,900 sq miles)
Population: 12,491 501
Capital city: Phnom Penh
Main language: Khmer
Main religion: Buddhist
Government: constitutional monarchy
Currency: 1 new riel = 100 sen

CAMEROON (Africa)
Area: 475,440 sq km (183,567 sq miles)
Population: 15,803,220
Capital city: Yaounde
Main languages: Cameroon Pidgin English, Ewondo, Fula, French, English
Main religions: indigenous, Christian, Muslim
Government: republic
Currency: 1 CFA* franc = 100 centimes

CANADA (North America)
Area: 9,970,610 sq km (3,849,653 sq miles)
Population: 31,592,805
Capital city: Ottawa
Main languages: English, French
Main religions: Roman Catholic, Protestant
Government: federal democracy
Currency: 1 Canadian dollar = 100 cents

CAPE VERDE (Africa)
Area: 4,033 sq km (1,557 sq miles)
Population: 405,163
Capital city: Praia
Main languages: Crioulo*, Portuguese

Main religions: Roman Catholic, Protestant
Government: republic
Currency: 1 Cape Verdean escudo = 100 centavos

CENTRAL AFRICAN REPUBLIC (Africa)
Area: 622,436 sq km (240,322 sq miles)
Population: 3,576,884
Capital city: Bangui
Main languages: Sangho, French
Main religions: indigenous, Christian, Muslim
Government: republic
Currency: 1 CFA* franc = 100 centimes

CHAD (Africa)
Area: 1,284,000 sq km (495,752 sq miles)
Population: 8,707,078
Capital city: Ndjamena
Main languages: Arabic, Sara, French
Main religions: Muslim, Christian, indigenous
Government: republic
Currency: 1 CFA* franc = 100 centimes

CHILE (South America)
Area: 756,626 sq km (292,133 sq miles)
Population: 15,328,467
Capital city: Santiago
Main language: Spanish
Main religions: Roman Catholic, Protestant
Government: republic
Currency: 1 Chilean peso = 100 centavos

CHINA (Asia)
Area: 9,596,960 sq km (3,705,386 sq miles)
Population: 1,273,111,290
Capital city: Beijing
Main languages: Mandarin Chinese, Yue, Wu
Main religions: Taoist, Buddhist
Government: Communist state
Currency: 1 yuan = 10 jiao

COLOMBIA (South America)
Area: 1,138,910 sq km (439,733 sq miles)
Population: 40,349,388
Capital city: Bogota
Main language: Spanish
Main religion: Roman Catholic
Government: republic
Currency: 1 Colombian peso = 100 centavos

COMOROS (Africa)
Area: 1,862 sq km (719 sq miles)
Population: 596,202
Capital city: Moroni
Main languages: Comorian*, French, Arabic
Main religion: Sunni Muslim
Government: republic
Currency: 1 Comoran franc = 100 centimes

CONGO (Africa)
Area: 342,000 sq km (132,046 sq miles)
Population: 2,894,336
Capital city: Brazzaville
Main languages: Munukutuba, Lingala, French
Main religions: Christian, animist
Government: republic
Currency: 1 CFA* franc = 100 centimes

Chile

China

Colombia

Comoros

Congo

Congo (Democratic Republic)

Costa Rica

*CFA = Communaute Financiere Africaine; Comorian = a blend of Swahili and Arabic; Crioulo = a blend of Portuguese and West African

Croatia

Cuba

Cyprus

Czech Republic

Denmark

Djibouti

Dominica

CONGO (DEMOCRATIC REPUBLIC) (Africa)
Area: 2,345,410 sq km (905,563 sq miles)
Population: 53,624,718
Capital city: Kinshasa
Main languages: Lingala, Swahili, Kikongo, Tshiluba, French
Main religions: Roman Catholic, Protestant, Kimbanguist, Muslim
Government: transitional
Currency: 1 Congolese franc = 100 centimes

COSTA RICA (North America)
Area: 51,100 sq km (19,730 sq miles)
Population: 3,773,057
Capital city: San Jose
Main language: Spanish
Main religions: Roman Catholic, Evangelical
Government: democratic republic
Currency: 1 Costa Rican colon = 100 centimos

CROATIA (Europe)
Area: 56,538 sq km (21,829 sq miles)
Population: 4,334,142
Capital city: Zagreb
Main language: Croatian
Main religions: Roman Catholic, Orthodox
Government: parliamentary democracy
Currency: 1 kuna = 100 lipas

CUBA (North America)
Area: 110,860 sq km (42,803 sq miles)
Population: 11,184,023
Capital city: Havana
Main language: Spanish
Main religion: Roman Catholic
Government: Communist state
Currency: 1 Cuban peso = 100 centavos

CYPRUS (Europe)
Area: 9,250 sq km (3,571 sq miles)
Population: 762,887
Capital city: Nicosia
Main languages: Greek, Turkish
Main religions: Greek Orthodox, Muslim
Government: republic with a self-proclaimed independent Turkish area
Currency: Greek Cypriot area: 1 Cypriot pound = 100 cents; Turkish Cypriot area: 1 Turkish lira = 100 kurus

CZECH REPUBLIC (Europe)
Area: 78,866 sq km (30,450 sq miles)
Population: 10,264,212
Capital city: Prague
Main language: Czech
Main religion: Roman Catholic
Government: parliamentary democracy
Currency: 1 koruna = 100 haleru

DENMARK (Europe)
Area: 43,094 sq km (16,639 sq miles)
Population: 5,352,815
Capital city: Copenhagen
Main language: Danish
Main religion: Evangelical Lutheran
Government: constitutional monarchy
Currency: 1 Danish krone = 100 oere

DJIBOUTI (Africa)
Area: 23,200 sq km (8,957 sq miles)
Population: 460,700
Capital city: Djibouti
Main languages: Afar, Somali, Arabic, French
Main religion: Muslim
Government: republic
Currency: 1 Djiboutian franc = 100 centimes

DOMINICA (North America)
Area: 751 sq km (290 sq miles)
Population: 70,786
Capital city: Roseau
Main languages: English, French patois
Main religions: Roman Catholic, Protestant
Government: democratic republic
Currency: 1 East Caribbean dollar = 100 cents

DOMINICAN REPUBLIC (North America)
Area: 48,511 sq km (18,731 sq miles)
Population: 8,581,477
Capital city: Santo Domingo
Main language: Spanish
Main religion: Roman Catholic
Government: democratic republic
Currency: 1 Dominican peso = 100 centavos

EAST TIMOR (Asia)
Area: 24,000 sq km (9,266 sq miles)
Population: 737,811
Capital city: Dili
Main languages: Tetun (Tetum), Bahasa Indonesia, Portuguese
Main religions: Roman Catholic, animist
Government: republic
Currency: 1 U.S. dollar = 100 cents

ECUADOR (South America)
Area: 283,560 sq km (109,483 sq miles)
Population: 13,183,978
Capital city: Quito
Main languages: Spanish, Quechua
Main religion: Roman Catholic
Government: republic
Currency: 1 sucre = 100 centavos

EGYPT (Africa)
Area: 1,001,450 sq km (386,660 sq miles)
Population: 69,536,644
Capital city: Cairo
Main language: Arabic
Main religion: Sunni Muslim
Government: republic
Currency: 1 Egyptian pound = 100 piasters

EL SALVADOR (North America)
Area: 21,040 sq km (8,124 sq miles)
Population: 6,237,662
Capital city: San Salvador
Main language: Spanish
Main religion: Roman Catholic
Government: republic
Currency: 1 Salvadoran colon = 100 centavos

EQUATORIAL GUINEA (Africa)
Area: 28,050 sq km (10,830 sq miles)
Population: 486,060
Capital city: Malabo
Main languages: Fang, Bubi, other Bantu

• **Dominican Republic**

East Timor

• **Ecuador**

Egypt

• **El Salvador**

Equatorial Guinea

Eritrea

*CFA = Communaute Financiere Africaine

GAZETTEER OF STATES CONTINUED:

Estonia

Ethiopia

Federated States of Micronesia

Fiji

Finland

France

Gabon

languages, Spanish, French, Pidgin English
Main religion: Christian
Government: republic
Currency: 1 CFA* franc = 100 centimes

ERITREA (Africa)
Area: 117,600 sq km (45,405 sq miles)
Population: 4,298,269
Capital city: Asmara
Main languages: Tigrinya, Afar, Arabic
Main religions: Muslim, Coptic Christian, Roman Catholic, Protestant
Government: transitional
Currency: 1 nafka = 100 cents

ESTONIA (Europe)
Area: 45,226 sq km (17,462 sq miles)
Population: 1,423,316
Capital city: Tallinn
Main languages: Estonian, Russian
Main religions: Evangelical Lutheran, Russian and Estonian Orthodox, other Christian
Government: parliamentary democracy
Currency: 1 Estonian kroon = 100 senti

ETHIOPIA (Africa)
Area: 1,127,127 sq km (435,184 sq miles)
Population: 65,891,874
Capital city: Addis Ababa
Main languages: Amharic, Tigrinya, Arabic
Main religions: Muslim, Ethiopian Orthodox, animist
Government: federal republic
Currency: 1 birr = 100 cents

FEDERATED STATES OF MICRONESIA (Australasia/Oceania)
Area: 702 sq km (271 sq miles)
Population: 134,597
Capital city: Palikir
Main languages: Chuuk, Ponapean, English
Main religions: Roman Catholic, Protestant
Government: democracy
Currency: 1 U.S. dollar = 100 cents

FIJI (Australasia/Oceania)
Area: 18,270 sq km (7,054 sq miles)
Population: 844,330
Capital city: Suva
Main languages: Fijian, Hindustani, English
Main religions: Christian, Hindu
Government: republic
Currency: 1 Fijian dollar = 100 cents

FINLAND (Europe)
Area: 337,030 sq km (130,127 sq miles)
Population: 5,175,783
Capital city: Helsinki
Main language: Finnish
Main religion: Evangelical Lutheran
Government: republic
Currency: 1 euro = 100 cents

FRANCE (Europe)
Area: 547,030 sq km (211,208 sq miles)
Population: 59,551,227
Capital city: Paris
Main language: French

Main religion: Roman Catholic
Government: republic
Currency: 1 euro = 100 cents

GABON (Africa)
Area: 267,670 sq km (103,347 sq miles)
Population: 1,221,175
Capital city: Libreville
Main languages: Fang, Myene, French
Main religions: Christian, animist
Government: republic
Currency: 1 CFA* franc = 100 centimes

GAMBIA, THE (Africa)
Area: 11,300 sq km (4,363 sq miles)
Population: 1,411,205
Capital city: Banjul
Main languages: Mandinka, Fula, Wolof, English
Main religion: Muslim
Government: democratic republic
Currency: 1 dalasi = 100 butut

GEORGIA (Asia)
Area: 69,700 sq km (26,911 sq miles)
Population: 4,989,285
Capital city: Tbilisi
Main languages: Georgian, Russian
Main religions: Georgian Orthodox, Muslim, Russian Orthodox
Government: republic
Currency: 1 lari = 100 tetri

GERMANY (Europe)
Area: 357,021 sq km (137,846 sq miles)
Population: 83,029,536
Capital city: Berlin
Main language: German
Main religions: Protestant, Roman Catholic
Government: federal republic
Currency: 1 euro = 100 cents

GHANA (Africa)
Area: 238,540 sq km (92,100 sq miles)
Population: 19,894,014
Capital city: Accra
Main languages: Twi, Fante, Ga, Hausa, Dagbani, Ewe, Nzemi, English
Main religions: indigenous, Muslim, Christian
Government: democratic republic
Currency: 1 new cedi = 100 pesewas

GREECE (Europe)
Area: 131,940 sq km (50,942 sq miles)
Population: 10,623,835
Capital city: Athens
Main language: Greek
Main religion: Greek Orthodox
Government: parliamentary republic
Currency: 1 euro = 100 cents

GRENADA (North America)
Area: 340 sq km (131 sq miles)
Population: 89,227
Capital city: Saint George's
Main languages: English, French patois
Main religions: Roman Catholic, Protestant
Government: constitutional monarchy
Currency: 1 East Caribbean dollar = 100 cents

Gambia, The

Georgia

Germany

Ghana

Greece

Grenada

Guatemala

*CFA = Communaute Financiere Africaine

Guinea

Guinea-Bissau

Guyana

• **Haiti**

Honduras

Hungary

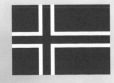

Iceland

GUATEMALA (North America)
Area: 108,890 sq km (42,042 sq miles)
Population: 12,974,361
Capital city: Guatemala City
Main languages: Spanish, Amerindian languages including Quiche, Kekchi, Cakchiquel, Mam
Main religions: Roman Catholic, Protestant, indigenous Mayan beliefs
Government: democratic republic
Currency: 1 quetzal = 100 centavos

GUINEA (Africa)
Area: 245,860 sq km (94,927 sq miles)
Population: 7,613,870
Capital city: Conakry
Main languages: Fuuta Jalon, Mallinke, Susu, French
Main religion: Muslim
Government: republic
Currency: 1 Guinean franc = 100 centimes

GUINEA-BISSAU (Africa)
Area: 36,120 sq km (13,946 sq miles)
Population: 1,315,822
Capital city: Bissau
Main languages: Crioulo*, Balante, Pulaar, Mandjak, Mandinka, Portuguese
Main religions: indigenous, Muslim
Government: republic
Currency: 1 CFA* franc = 100 centimes

GUYANA (South America)
Area: 214,970 sq km (83,000 sq miles)
Population: 697,181
Capital city: Georgetown
Main languages: Guyanese Creole,English, Amerindian languages, Caribbean Hindi
Main religions: Christian, Hindu
Government: republic
Currency: 1 Guyanese dollar = 100 cents

HAITI (North America)
Area: 27,750 sq km (10,714 sq miles)
Population: 6,964,549
Capital city: Port-au-Prince
Main languages: Haitian Creole, French
Main religions: Roman Catholic, Protestant, Voodoo
Government: republic
Currency: 1 gourde = 100 centimes

HONDURAS (North America)
Area: 112,090 sq km (43,278 sq miles)
Population: 6,406,052
Capital city: Tegucigalpa
Main language: Spanish
Main religion: Roman Catholic
Government: republic
Currency: 1 lempira = 100 centavos

HUNGARY (Europe)
Area: 93,030 sq km (35,919 sq miles)
Population: 10,106,017
Capital city: Budapest
Main language: Hungarian
Main religions: Roman Catholic, Calvinist
Government: parliamentary democracy
Currency: 1 forint = 100 filler

ICELAND (Europe)
Area: 103,000 sq km (39,768 sq miles)
Population: 277,906
Capital city: Reykjavik
Main language: Icelandic
Main religion: Evangelical Lutheran
Government: republic
Currency: 1 Icelandic krona = 100 aurar

INDIA (Asia)
Area: 3,287,590 sq km (1,269,339 sq miles)
Population: 1,029,991,145
Capital city: New Delhi
Main languages: Hindi, English, Bengali, Urdu, over 1,600 other languages and dialects
Main religions: Hindu, Muslim
Government: federal republic
Currency: 1 Indian rupee = 100 paise

INDONESIA (Asia)
Area: 1,919,440 sq km (741,096 sq miles)
Population: 228,437,870
Capital city: Jakarta
Main languages: Bahasa Indonesia, English, Dutch, Javanese
Main religion: Muslim
Government: republic
Currency: 1 Indonesian rupiah = 100 sen

IRAN (Asia)
Area: 1,648,000 sq km (636,293 sq miles)
Population: 66,128,965
Capital city: Tehran
Main languages: Farsi and other Persian dialects, Azeri
Main religions: Shi'a Muslim, Sunni Muslim
Government: Islamic republic
Currency: 10 Iranian rials = 1 toman

IRAQ (Asia)
Area: 437,072 sq km (168,754 sq miles)
Population: 23,331,985
Capital city: Baghdad
Main languages: Arabic, Kurdish
Main religion: Muslim
Government: republic under a military regime
Currency: 1 Iraqi dinar = 1,000 fils

IRELAND (Europe)
Area: 70,280 sq km (27,135 sq miles)
Population: 3,840,838
Capital city: Dublin
Main languages: English, Irish (Gaelic)
Main religion: Roman Catholic
Government: republic
Currency: 1 euro = 100 cents

ISRAEL (Asia)
Area: 20,770 sq km (8,019 sq miles)
Population: 5,938,093
Capital city: Jerusalem
Main languages: Hebrew, Arabic
Main religions: Jewish, Muslim
Government: parliamentary democracy
Currency: 1 Israeli shekel = 100 agorot

ITALY (Europe)
Area: 301,230 sq km (116,305 sq miles)

India

Indonesia

Iran

Iraq

Ireland

Israel

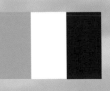

Italy

*CFA = Communaute Financiere Africaine;
Crioulo = a blend of Portuguese and West African

GAZETTEER OF STATES CONTINUED:

Ivory Coast

Population: 57,679,825
Capital city: Rome
Main language: Italian
Main religion: Roman Catholic
Government: republic
Currency: 1 euro = 100 cents

IVORY COAST (Africa)
Area: 322,460 sq km (124,502 sq miles)
Population: 16,393,221
Capital city: Yamoussoukro
Main languages: Baoule, Dioula, French
Main religions: Christian, Muslim, animist
Government: republic
Currency: 1 CFA* = 100 centimes

Jamaica

JAMAICA (North America)
Area: 10,990 sq km (4,243 sq miles)
Population: 2,665,636
Capital city: Kingston
Main languages: Southwestern Caribbean Creole, English
Main religion: Protestant
Government: parliamentary democracy
Currency: 1 Jamaican dollar = 100 cents

Japan

JAPAN (Asia)
Area: 377,835 sq km (145,882 sq miles)
Population: 126,771,662
Capital city: Tokyo
Main language: Japanese
Main religions: Shinto, Buddhist
Government: constitutional monarchy
Currency: 1 yen = 100 sen

Jordan

JORDAN (Asia)
Area: 92,190 sq km (35,585 sq miles)
Population: 5,153,378
Capital city: Amman
Main languages: Arabic, English
Main religion: Sunni Muslim
Government: constitutional monarchy
Currency: 1 Jordanian dinar = 1,000 fils

Kazakhstan

KAZAKHSTAN (Asia)
Area: 2,717,300 sq km (1,049,150 sq miles)
Population: 16,731,303
Capital city: Astana
Main languages: Kazakh, Russian
Main religions: Muslim, Russian Orthodox
Government: republic
Currency: 1 Kazakhstani tenge = 100 tiyn

Kenya

KENYA (Africa)
Area: 582,650 sq km (224,961 sq miles)
Population: 30,765,916
Capital city: Nairobi
Main languages: Swahili, English, Bantu languages
Main religions: Christian, indigenous
Government: republic
Currency: 1 Kenyan shilling = 100 cents

Kiribati

KIRIBATI (Australasia/Oceania)
Area: 717 sq km (277 sq miles)
Population: 94,149
Capital city: Bairiki (on Tarawa island)
Main languages: Gilbertese, English
Main religions: Roman Catholic,

Protestant
Government: republic
Currency: 1 Australian dollar = 100 cents

KUWAIT (Asia)
Area: 17,820 sq km (6,880 sq miles)
Population: 2,041,961
Capital city: Kuwait City
Main languages: Arabic, English
Main religion: Muslim
Government: monarchy
Currency: 1 Kuwaiti dinar = 1,000 fils

Kuwait

KYRGYZSTAN (Asia)
Area: 198,500 sq km (76,641 sq miles)
Population: 4,753,003
Capital city: Bishkek
Main languages: Kyrgyz, Russian
Main religions: Muslim, Russian Orthodox
Government: republic
Currency: 1 Kyrgyzstani som = 100 tyiyn

Kyrgyzstan

LAOS (Asia)
Area: 236,800 sq km (91,428 sq miles)
Population: 5,638,967
Capital city: Vientiane
Main languages: Lao, French, English
Main religions: Buddhist, animist
Government: Communist state
Currency: 1 new kip = 100 at

Laos

LATVIA (Europe)
Area: 64,589 sq km (24,938 sq miles)
Population: 2,385,231
Capital city: Riga
Main languages: Latvian, Russian
Main religions: Lutheran, Roman Catholic, Russian Orthodox
Government: parliamentary democracy
Currency: 1 Latvian lat = 100 santims

Latvia

LEBANON (Asia)
Area: 10,400 sq km (4,015 sq miles)
Population: 3,627,774
Capital city: Beirut
Main languages: Arabic, French, English
Main religions: Muslim, Christian
Government: republic
Currency: 1 Lebanese pound = 100 piasters

Lebanon

LESOTHO (Africa)
Area: 30,350 sq km (11,718 sq miles)
Population: 2,177,062
Capital cities: Maseru, Lobamba
Main languages: Sesotho, English, Zulu, Xhosa
Main religions: Christian, indigenous
Government: constitutional monarchy
Currency: 1 loti = 100 lisente

Lesotho

LIBERIA (Africa)
Area: 111,370 sq km (43,000 sq miles)
Population: 3,225,837
Capital city: Monrovia
Main languages: Kpelle, English, Bassa
Main religions: indigenous, Christian, Muslim
Government: republic
Currency: 1 Liberian dollar = 100 cents

Liberia

*CFA = Communaute Financiere Africaine

LIBYA (Africa)
Area: 1,759,540 sq km (679,358 sq miles)
Population: 5,240,599
Capital city: Tripoli
Main languages: Arabic, Italian, English
Main religion: Sunni Muslim
Government: military rule
Currency: 1 Libyan dinar = 1,000 dirhams

Libya

LIECHTENSTEIN (Europe)
Area: 160 sq km (62 sq miles)
Population: 32,528
Capital city: Vaduz
Main languages: German, Alemannic
Main religion: Roman Catholic
Government: constitutional monarchy
Currency: 1 Swiss franc = 100 centimes

Liechtenstein

LITHUANIA (Europe)
Area: 65,200 sq km (25,174 sq miles)
Population: 3,610,535
Capital city: Vilnius
Main languages: Lithuanian, Polish, Russian
Main religions: Roman Catholic, Lutheran, Russian Orthodox
Government: democracy
Currency: 1 Lithuanian litas = 100 centas

Lithuania

LUXEMBOURG (Europe)
Area: 2,586 sq km (998 sq miles)
Population: 442,972
Capital city: Luxembourg
Main languages: Luxemburgish, German, French
Main religion: Roman Catholic
Government: constitutional monarchy
Currency: 1 euro = 100 cents

Luxembourg

MACEDONIA (Europe)
Area: 25,333 sq km (9,781 sq miles)
Population: 2,046,209
Capital city: Skopje
Main languages: Macedonian, Albanian
Main religions: Macedonian Orthodox, Muslim
Government: emerging democracy
Currency: 1 Macedonian denar = 100 deni

Macedonia

MADAGASCAR (Africa)
Area: 587,040 sq km (226,656 sq miles)
Population: 15,982,563
Capital city: Antananarivo
Main languages: Malagasy, French
Main religions: indigenous beliefs, Christian
Government: republic
Currency: 1 Malagasy franc = 100 centimes

Madagascar

MALAWI (Africa)
Area: 118,480 sq km (45,745 sq miles)
Population: 10,548,250
Capital city: Lilongwe
Main languages: Chichewa, English
Main religions: Protestant, Roman Catholic, Muslim
Government: parliamentary democracy
Currency: 1 Malawian kwacha = 100 tambala

MALAYSIA (Asia)
Area: 329,750 sq km (127,316 sq miles)
Population: 22,229,040

Malawi

Capital city: Kuala Lumpur
Main languages: Bahasa Melayu, English, Chinese dialects, Tamil
Main religions: Muslim, Buddhist, Daoist
Government: constitutional monarchy
Currency: 1 ringgit = 100 sen

Malaysia

MALDIVES (Asia)
Area: 300 sq km (116 sq miles)
Population: 310,764
Capital city: Male
Main languages: Maldivian, English
Main religion: Sunni Muslim
Government: republic
Currency: 1 rufiyaa = 100 laari

Maldives

MALI (Africa)
Area: 1,240,000 sq km (478,764 sq miles)
Population: 11,008,518
Capital city: Bamako
Main languages: Bambara, Fulani, Songhai, French
Main religion: Muslim
Government: republic
Currency: 1 CFA* franc = 100 centimes

Mali

MALTA (Europe)
Area: 316 sq km (122 sq miles)
Population: 394,583
Capital city: Valletta
Main languages: Maltese, English
Main religion: Roman Catholic
Government: democratic republic
Currency: 1 Maltese lira = 100 cents

Malta

MARSHALL ISLANDS (Australasia/Oceania)
Area: 181 sq km (70 sq miles)
Population: 70,822
Capital city: Majuro
Main languages: Marshallese, English
Main religion: Protestant
Government: republic
Currency: 1 U.S. dollar = 100 cents

Marshall Islands

MAURITANIA (Africa)
Area: 1,030,700 sq km (397,953 sq miles)
Population: 2,747,312
Capital city: Nouakchott
Main languages: Arabic, Wolof, French
Main religion: Muslim
Government: republic
Currency: 1 ouguiya = 5 khoums

Mauritania

MAURITIUS (Africa)
Area: 1,860 sq km (718 sq miles)
Population: 1,189,825
Capital city: Port Louis
Main languages: Mauritius Creole French, French, Hindi, Bhojpuri, Urdu, Tamil, English
Main religions: Hindu, Christian, English
Government: parliamentary democracy
Currency: 1 Mauritian rupee = 100 cents

MEXICO (North America)
Nationality: Mexican
Area: 1,972,550 sq km (761,602 sq miles)
Population: 101,879,171
Capital city: Mexico City

Mauritius

*CFA = Communaute Financiere Africaine

GAZETTEER OF STATES CONTINUED:

Mexico

Main languages: Spanish, Mayan, Nahuatl
Main religion: Roman Catholic
Government: federal republic
Currency: 1 New Mexican peso = 100 centavos

MOLDOVA (Europe)
Area: 33,843 sq km (13,067 sq miles)
Population: 4,431,570
Capital city: Chisinau
Main languages: Moldovan, Russian, Gagauz
Main religion: Eastern Orthodox
Government: republic
Currency: 1 Moldovan leu = 100 bani

Moldova

MONACO (Europe)
Area: 1.95 sq km (0.75 sq miles)
Population: 31,842
Capital city: Monaco
Main languages: French, Monegasque, Italian
Main religion: Roman Catholic
Government: constitutional monarchy
Currency: 1 euro = 100 cents

Monaco

MONGOLIA (Asia)
Area: 1,565,000 sq km (604,247 sq miles)
Population: 2,654,999
Capital city: Ulan Bator
Main language: Khalkha Mongol
Main religion: Tibetan Buddist Lamaist
Government: republic
Currency: 1 tugrik = 100 mongos

Mongolia

MOROCCO (Africa)
Area: 446,550 sq km (172,413 sq miles)
Population: 30,645,305
Capital city: Rabat
Main languages: Arabic, Berber, French
Main religion: Muslim
Government: constitutional monarchy
Currency: 1 Moroccan dirham = 100 centimes

Morocco

MOZAMBIQUE (Africa)
Area: 801,590 sq km (309,494 sq miles)
Population: 19,371,057
Capital city: Maputo
Main languages: Makua, Tsonga, Portuguese
Main religions: indigenous, Christian, Muslim
Government: republic
Currency: 1 metical = 100 centavos

Mozambique

NAMIBIA (Africa)
Area: 825,418 sq km (318,694 sq miles)
Population: 1,797,677
Capital city: Windhoek
Main languages: Afrikaans, German, English
Main religions: Christian, indigenous
Government: republic
Currency: 1 Namibian dollar = 100 cents

NAURU (Australasia/Oceania)
Area: 21 sq km (8 sq miles)
Population: 12,088
Capital city: Yaren
Main languages: Nauruan, English
Main religion: Christian
Government: republic
Currency: 1 Australian dollar = 100 cents

Namibia

NEPAL (Asia)
Area: 147,181 sq km (56,827 sq miles)
Population: 25,284,463
Capital city: Kathmandu
Main languages: Nepali, Maithili
Main religions: Hindu, Buddhist
Government: constitutional monarchy
Currency: 1 Nepalese rupee = 100 paisa

NETHERLANDS (Europe)
Area: 41,532 sq km (16,036 sq miles)
Population: 15,981,472
Capital cities: Amsterdam, The Hague
Main language: Dutch
Main religion: Christian
Government: constitutional monarchy
Currency: 1 euro = 100 cents

NEW ZEALAND (Australasia/Oceania)
Area: 268,680 sq km (103,737 sq miles)
Population: 3,864,129
Capital city: Wellington
Main languages: English, Maori
Main religion: Christian
Government: parliamentary democracy
Currency: 1 New Zealand dollar = 100 cents

NICARAGUA (North America)
Area: 129,494 sq km (49,998 sq miles)
Population: 4,918,393
Capital city: Managua
Main language: Spanish
Main religion: Roman Catholic
Government: republic
Currency: 1 gold cordoba = 100 centavos

NIGER (Africa)
Area: 1,267,000 sq km (489,189 sq miles)
Population: 10,355,156
Capital city: Niamey
Main languages: Hausa, Djerma, French
Main religion: Muslim
Government: republic
Currency: 1 CFA* franc = 100 centimes

NIGERIA (Africa)
Area: 923,768 sq km (356,667 sq miles)
Population: 126,635,626
Capital city: Abuja
Main languages: Hausa, Yoruba, Igbo, English
Main religions: Muslim, Christian, indigenous
Government: republic
Currency: 1 naira = 100 kobo

NORTH KOREA (Asia)
Area: 120,540 sq km (46,540 sq miles)
Population: 21,968,228
Capital city: Pyongyang
Main language: Korean
Main religions: Buddhist, Confucianist
Government: authoritarian socialist
Currency: 1 North Korean won = 100 chon

NORWAY (Europe)
Area: 324,220 sq km (125,181 sq miles)
Population: 4,503,440
Capital city: Oslo

Nauru

Nepal

Netherlands

New Zealand

Nicaragua

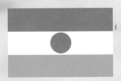

Niger

Nigeria

*CFA = Communaute Financiere Africaine

North Korea

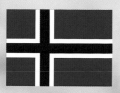

Norway

Oman

Pakistan

Palau

Panama

Papua New Guinea

Main language: Norwegian
Main religion: Evangelical Lutheran
Government: constitutional monarchy
Currency: 1 Norwegian krone = 100 oere

OMAN (Asia)
Area: 212,460 sq km (82,031 sq miles)
Population: 2,622,198
Capital city: Muscat
Main languages: Arabic, English, Baluchi
Main religion: Muslim
Government: monarchy
Currency: 1 Omani rial = 1,000 baiza

PAKISTAN (Asia)
Area: 803,940 sq km (310,401 sq miles)
Population: 144,616,639
Capital city: Islamabad
Main languages: Punjabi, Sindhi, Urdu, English
Main religion: Muslim
Government: federal republic
Currency: 1 Pakistani rupee = 100 paisa

PALAU (Australasia/Oceania)
Area: 459 sq km (177 sq miles)
Population: 19,092
Capital city: Koror
Main languages: Palauan, English
Main religions: Christian, Modekngei
Government: democratic republic
Currency: 1 U.S. dollar = 100 cents

PANAMA (North America)
Area: 78,200 sq km (30,193 sq miles)
Population: 2,845,647
Capital city: Panama City
Main languages: Spanish, English
Main religions: Roman Catholic, Protestant
Government: democracy
Currency: 1 balboa = 100 centesimos

PAPUA NEW GUINEA
(Australasia/Oceania)
Area: 462,840 sq km (178,703 sq miles)
Population: 5,049,055
Capital city: Port Moresby
Main languages: Tok Pisin, Hiri Motu, English
Main religions: Christian, indigenous
Government: parliamentary democracy
Currency: 1 kina = 100 toea

PARAGUAY (South America)
Area: 406,750 sq km (157,046 sq miles)
Population: 5,734,139
Capital city: Asuncion
Main languages: Guarani, Spanish
Main religion: Roman Catholic
Government: republic
Currency: 1 guarani = 100 centimos

PERU (South America)
Area: 1,285,220 sq km (496,223 sq miles)
Population: 27,483,864
Capital city: Lima
Main languages: Spanish, Quechua, Aymara
Main religion: Roman Catholic
Government: republic
Currency: 1 nuevo sol = 100 centimos

PHILIPPINES (Asia)
Area: 300,000 sq km (115,830 sq miles)
Population: 82,841,518
Capital city: Manila
Main languages: Tagalog, English, Ilocano
Main religion: Roman Catholic
Government: republic
Currency: 1 Philippine peso = 100 centavos

POLAND (Europe)
Area: 312,685 sq km (120,727 sq miles)
Population: 38,633,912
Capital city: Warsaw
Main language: Polish
Main religion: Roman Catholic
Government: democratic republic
Currency: 1 zloty = 100 groszy

PORTUGAL (Europe)
Area: 92,391 sq km (35,672 sq miles)
Population: 10,066,253
Capital city: Lisbon
Main language: Portuguese
Main religion: Roman Catholic
Government: democratic republic
Currency: 1 euro = 100 cents

QATAR (Asia)
Area: 11,437 sq km (4,416 sq miles)
Population: 769,152
Capital city: Doha
Main languages: Arabic, English
Main religion: Muslim
Government: monarchy
Currency: 1 Qatari riyal = 100 dirhams

ROMANIA (Europe)
Area: 237,500 sq km (91,699 sq miles)
Population: 22,364,022
Capital city: Bucharest
Main languages: Romanian, Hungarian, German
Main religion: Romanian Orthodox
Government: republic
Currency: 1 leu = 100 bani

RUSSIA (Europe and Asia)
Area: 17,075,200 sq km (6,592,735 sq miles)
Population: 145,470,197
Capital city: Moscow
Main language: Russian
Main religions: Russian Orthodox, Muslim
Government: federal government
Currency: 1 ruble = 100 kopeks

RWANDA (Africa)
Area: 26,338 sq km (10,169 sq miles)
Population: 7,312,756
Capital city: Kigali
Main languages: Kinyarwanda, French, English, Swahili
Main religions: Roman Catholic, Protestant,
Government: transitional
Currency: 1 Rwandan franc = 100 centimes

SAINT KITTS AND NEVIS
(North America)
Area: 269 sq km (104 sq miles)
Population: 38,756
Capital city: Basseterre

Paraguay

• Peru

Philippines

Poland

Portugal

Qatar

Romania

GAZETTEER OF STATES CONTINUED:

Russia

Main language: English
Main religions: Protestant, Roman Catholic
Government: constitutional monarchy
Currency: 1 East Caribbean dollar = 100 cents

SAINT LUCIA (North America)
Area: 620 sq km (239 sq miles)
Population: 158,178
Capital city: Castries
Main languages: French patois, English
Main religion: Roman Catholic
Government: parliamentary democracy
Currency: 1 East Caribbean dollar = 100 cents

Rwanda

SAINT VINCENT AND THE GRENADINES (North America)
Area: 389 sq km (150 sq miles)
Population: 115,942
Capital city: Kingstown
Main languages: English, French patois
Main religions: Protestant, Roman Catholic
Government: parliamentary democracy
Currency: 1 East Caribbean dollar = 100 cents

Saint Kitts and Nevis

SAMOA (Australasia/Oceania)
Area: 2,860 sq km (1,104 sq miles)
Population: 179,058
Capital city: Apia
Main languages: Samoan, English
Main religion: Christian
Government: constitutional monarchy
Currency: 1 tala = 100 sene

SAN MARINO (Europe)
Area: 61 sq km (24 sq miles)
Population: 27,336
Capital city: San Marino
Main language: Italian
Main religion: Roman Catholic
Government: republic
Currency: 1 euro = 100 cents

Saint Lucia

SAO TOME AND PRINCIPE (Africa)
Area: 1,001 sq km (386 sq miles)
Population: 165,034
Capital city: Sao Tome
Main languages: Crioulo* dialects, Portuguese
Main religion: Christian
Government: republic
Currency: 1 dobra = 100 centimos

Saint Vincent and the Grenadines

SAUDI ARABIA (Asia)
Area: 2,149,690 sq km (829,995 sq miles)
Population: 22,757,092
Capital city: Riyadh
Main language: Arabic
Main religion: Muslim
Government: monarchy
Currency: 1 Saudi riyal = 100 halalah

Samoa

SENEGAL (Africa)
Area: 196,190 sq km (75,749 sq miles)
Population: 10,284,929
Capital city: Dakar
Main languages: Wolof, French, Pulaar
Main religion: Muslim
Government: democratic republic
Currency: 1 CFA* franc = 100 centimes

• San Marino

SERBIA AND MONTENEGRO (Europe)
Area: 102,350 sq km (39,517 sq miles)
Population: 10,677,290
Capital city: Belgrade
Main languages: Serbian, Montenegrin
Main religions: Orthodox, Muslim
Government: republic
Currency: 1 dinar = 100 paras (Serbia),
1 1 euro = 100 cents (Montenegro)

SEYCHELLES (Africa)
Area: 455 sq km (176 sq miles)
Population: 79,715
Capital city: Victoria
Main language: Seselwa
Main religion: Roman Catholic
Government: republic
Currency: 1 Seychelles rupee = 100 cents

SIERRA LEONE (Africa)
Area: 71,740 sq km (27,699 sq miles)
Population: 5,426,618
Capital city: Freetown
Main languages: Mende, Temne, Krio, English
Main religions: Muslim, indigenous, Christian
Government: republic
Currency: 1 leone = 100 cents

SINGAPORE (Asia)
Area: 648 sq km (250 sq miles)
Population: 4,300,419
Capital city: Singapore
Main languages: Chinese, Malay, English, Tamil
Main religions: Buddhist, Muslim
Government: parliamentary republic
Currency: 1 Singapore dollar = 100 cents

SLOVAKIA (Europe)
Area: 48,845 sq km (18,859 sq miles)
Population: 5,414,937
Capital city: Bratislava
Main languages: Slovak, Hungarian
Main religion: Roman Catholic
Government: parliamentary democracy
Currency: 1 koruna = 100 halierov

SLOVENIA (Europe)
Area: 20,253 sq km (7,820 sq miles)
Population: 1,930,132
Capital city: Ljubljana
Main language: Slovenian
Main religion: Roman Catholic
Government: democratic republic
Currency: 1 tolar = 100 stotins

SOLOMON ISLANDS (Australasia/Oceania)
Area: 28,450 sq km (10,985 sq miles)
Population: 480,442
Capital city: Honiara
Main languages: Solomon pidgin, Kwara'ae, To'abaita, English
Main religion: Christian
Government: parliamentary democracy
Currency: 1 dollar = 100 cents

SOMALIA (Africa)
Area: 637,657 sq km (246,199 sq miles)
Population: 7,488,773
Capital city: Mogadishu

Sao Tome and Principe

Saudi Arabia

Senegal

Serbia and Montenegro

Seychelles

Sierra Leone

Singapore

*CFA = Communaute Financiere Africaine; Crioulo = a blend of Portuguese and West African

Slovakia

• **Slovenia**

Solomon Islands

Somalia

South Africa

South Korea

• **Spain**

Main languages: Somali, Arabic, Oromo
Main religion: Sunni Muslim
Government: currently has no government
Currency: 1 Somali shilling = 100 cents

SOUTH AFRICA (Africa)
Area: 1,219,912 sq km (471,008 sq miles)
Population: 43,586,097
Capital cities: Pretoria, Cape Town, Bloemfontein
Main languages: Zulu, Xhosa, Afrikaans, Pedi, English, Tswana, Sotho, Tsonga, Swati, Venda, Ndebele
Main religions: Christian, indigenous
Government: republic
Currency: 1 rand = 100 cents

SOUTH KOREA (Asia)
Area: 98,480 sq km (38,023 sq miles)
Population: 47,904,370
Capital city: Seoul
Main language: Korean
Main religions: Christian, Buddhist
Government: republic
Currency: 1 South Korean won = 100 chun

SPAIN (Europe)
Area: 504,750 sq km (194,884 sq miles)
Population: 40,037,995
Capital city: Madrid
Main languages: Castilian Spanish, Catalan
Main religion: Roman Catholic
Government: constitutional monarchy
Currency: 1 euro = 100 cents

SRI LANKA (Asia)
Area: 65,610 sq km (25,332 sq miles)
Population: 19,408,635
Capital cities: Colombo, Sri Jayewardenepura Kotte
Main languages: Sinhala, Tamil, English
Main religions: Buddhist, Hindu
Government: republic
Currency: 1 Sri Lankan rupee = 100 cents

SUDAN (Africa)
Area: 2,505,810 sq km (967,493 sq miles)
Population: 36,080,373
Capital city: Khartoum
Main languages: Arabic, English
Main religions: Sunni Muslim, indigenous
Government: Islamic republic
Currency: 1 Sudanese dinar = 100 piastres

SURINAM (South America)
Area: 163,270 sq km (63,039 sq miles)
Population: 433,998
Capital city: Paramaribo
Main languages: Sranang Tongo, Dutch, English
Main religions: Christian, Hindu, Muslim
Government: republic
Currency: 1 Surinamese guilder, gulden or florin = 100 cents

SWAZILAND (Africa)
Area: 17,363 sq km (6,704 sq miles)
Population: 1,104,343
Capital cities: Mbabane, Lobamba

Main languages: Swati, English
Main religions: Protestant, indigenous, Muslim
Government: monarchy
Currency: 1 lilangeni = 100 cents

SWEDEN (Europe)
Area: 449,964 sq km (173,731 sq miles)
Population: 8,875,053
Capital city: Stockholm
Main language: Swedish
Main religion: Lutheran
Government: constitutional monarchy
Currency: 1 Swedish krona = 100 oere

SWITZERLAND (Europe)
Area: 41,290 sq km (15,942 sq miles)
Population: 7,283,274
Capital city: Bern
Main languages: German, French, Italian
Main religions: Roman Catholic, Protestant
Government: federal republic
Currency: 1 Swiss franc, franken or frano = 100 centimes, rappen or centesimi

SYRIA (Asia)
Area: 185,180 sq km (71,498 sq miles)
Population: 16,728,808
Capital city: Damascus
Main languages: Arabic, Kurdish
Main religions: Muslim, Christian
Government: republic under military regime
Currency: 1 Syrian pound = 100 piastres

TAIWAN (Asia)
Area: 35,980 sq km (13,892 sq miles)
Population: 22,370,461
Capital city: Taipei
Main languages: Taiwanese, Mandarin Chinese, Hakka Chinese
Main religions: Buddhist, Confucian, Daoist
Government: democracy
Currency: 1 New Taiwan dollar = 100 cents

TAJIKISTAN (Asia)
Area: 143,100 sq km (55,251 sq miles)
Population: 6,578,681
Capital city: Dushanbe
Main languages: Tajik, Russian
Main religion: Sunni Muslim
Government: republic
Currency: 1 somoni = 100 dirams

TANZANIA (Africa)
Area: 945,087 sq km (364,898 sq miles)
Population: 36,232,074
Capital cities: Dar es Salaam, Dodoma
Main languages: Swahili, English, Sukuma
Main religions: Christian, Muslim, indigenous
Government: republic
Currency: 1 Tanzanian shilling = 100 cents

THAILAND (Asia)
Area: 514,000 sq km (198,455 sq miles)
Population: 61,797,751
Capital city: Bangkok
Main languages: Thai, English, Chaochow
Main religion: Buddhist
Government: constitutional monarchy
Currency: 1 baht = 100 satang

Sri Lanka

Sudan

Surinam

Swaziland

Sweden

Switzerland

Syria

CFA = Communaute Financiere Africaine

GAZETTEER OF STATES CONTINUED:

Taiwan

TOGO (Africa)
Area: 56,785 sq km (21,925 sq miles)
Population: 5,153,088
Capital city: Lome
Main languages: Mina, Ewe, Kabye, French
Main religions: indigenous, Christian, Muslim
Government: republic
Currency: 1 CFA* franc = 100 centimes

TONGA (Australasia/Oceania)
Area: 748 sq km (289 sq miles)
Population: 104,227
Capital city: Nukualofa
Main languages: Tongan, English
Main religion: Christian
Government: constitutional monarchy
Currency: 1 pa'anga = 100 seniti

Tajikistan

TRINIDAD AND TOBAGO (North America)
Area: 5,128 sq km (1,980 sq miles)
Population: 1,169,682
Capital city: Port-of-Spain
Main languages: English, French, Spanish, Hindi
Main religions: Christian, Hindu
Government: republic
Currency: 1 Trinidad and Tobago dollar = 100 cents

TUNISIA (Africa)
Area: 163,610 sq km (63,170 sq miles)
Population: 9,705,102
Capital city: Tunis
Main languages: Arabic, French
Main religion: Muslim
Government: republic
Currency: 1 Tunisian dinar = 1,000 millimes

Tanzania

TURKEY (Europe and Asia)
Area: 780,580 sq km (301,382 sq miles)
Population: 66,493,970
Capital city: Ankara
Main language: Turkish
Main religion: Muslim
Government: democratic republic
Currency: 1 Turkish lira = 100 kurus

Thailand

TURKMENISTAN (Asia)
Area: 488,100 sq km (188,455 sq miles)
Population: 4,603,244
Capital city: Ashgabat (Ashkhabad)
Main languages: Turkmen, Russian
Main religion: Muslim
Government: republic
Currency: 1 Turkmen manat = 100 tenesi

TUVALU (Australasia/Oceania)
Area: 26 sq km (10 sq miles)
Population: 10,991
Capital city: Funafuti
Main languages: Tuvaluan, English
Main religion: Congregationalist
Government: constitutional monarchy
Currency: 1 Tuvaluan dollar or 1 Australian dollar = 100 cents

Togo

UGANDA (Africa)
Area: 236,040 sq km (91,135 sq miles)
Population: 23,985,712
Capital city: Kampala

Tonga

Main languages: Luganda, English, Swahili
Main religion: Christian, Muslim, indigenous
Government: republic
Currency: 1 Ugandan shilling = 100 cents

UKRAINE (Europe)
Area: 603,700 sq km (233,089 sq miles)
Population: 49,153,027
Capital city: Kiev
Main languages: Ukrainian, Russian
Main religion: Ukrainain Orthodox
Government: republic
Currency: 1 hryvnia = 100 kopiykas

UNITED ARAB EMIRATES (Asia)
Area: 82,880 sq km (32,000 sq miles)
Population: 2,407,460
Capital city: Abu Dhabi
Main languages: Arabic, English
Main religion: Muslim
Government: federation
Currency: 1 Emirati dirham = 100 fils

UNITED KINGDOM (Europe)
Area: 244,820 sq km (94,525 sq miles)
Population: 59,647,790
Capital city: London
Main language: English
Main religions: Anglican, Roman Catholic
Government: constitutional monarchy
Currency: 1 British pound = 100 pence

UNITED STATES OF AMERICA (North America)
Area: 9,629,091 sq km (3,717,792 sq miles)
Population: 278,058,881
Capital city: Washington D.C.
Main language: English
Main religions: Protestant, Roman Catholic
Government: federal republic
Currency: 1 U.S. dollar = 100 cents

URUGUAY (South America)
Area: 176,220 sq km (68,039 sq miles)
Population: 3,360,105
Capital city: Montevideo
Main language: Spanish
Main religion: Roman Catholic
Government: republic
Currency: 1 Uruguayan peso = 100 centesimos

UZBEKISTAN (Asia)
Area: 447,400 sq km (172,741 sq miles)
Population: 25,155,064
Capital city: Tashkent
Main languages: Uzbek, Russian
Main religions: Muslim, Eastern Orthodox
Government: republic
Currency: 1 Uzbekistani sum = 100 tyyn

VANUATU (Australasia/Oceania)
Area: 12,189 sq km (4,706 sq miles)
Population: 192,910
Capital city: Port-Vila
Main languages: Bislama, French, English
Main religion: Christian
Government: republic
Currency: 1 vatu = 100 centimes

Trinidad and Tobago

Tunisia

Turkey

Turkmenistan

Tuvalu

Uganda

Ukraine

United Arab Emirates

United Kingdom

United States of America

Uruguay

Uzbekistan

Vanuatu

VATICAN CITY (Europe)
Area: 0.44 sq km (0.17 sq miles)
Population: 880
Capital city: Vatican City
Main languages: Italian, Latin
Main religion: Roman Catholic
Government: led by the Pope
Currency: 1 euro = 100 cents

VENEZUELA (South America)
Area: 912,050 sq km (352,143 sq miles)
Population: 23,916,810
Capital city: Caracas
Main language: Spanish
Main religion: Roman Catholic
Government: federal republic
Currency: 1 bolivar = 100 centimos

VIETNAM (Asia)
Area: 329,560 sq km (127,243 sq miles)
Population: 79,939,014
Capital city: Hanoi
Main languages: Vietnamese, French, English, Khmer, Chinese
Main religion: Buddhist
Government: Communist state
Currency: 1 new dong = 100 xu

YEMEN (Asia)
Area: 527,970 sq km (203,849 sq miles)
Population: 18,078,035
Capital city: Sana
Main language: Arabic
Main religion: Muslim
Government: republic
Currency: 1 Yemeni rial = 100 fils

ZAMBIA (Africa)
Area: 752,614 sq km (290,584 sq miles)
Population: 9,770,199
Capital city: Lusaka
Main languages: Bemba, Tonga, Nyanja, English
Main religions: Christian, Muslim, Hindu
Government: republic
Currency: 1 Zambian kwacha = 100 ngwee

ZIMBABWE (Africa)
Area: 390,580 sq km (150,803 sq miles)
Population: 11,365,366
Capital city: Harare
Main languages: Shona, Ndebele, English
Main religions: Christian, indigenous
Government: republic
Currency: 1 Zimbabwean dollar = 100 cents

Vatican City

Venezuela

Vietnam

Yemen

Zambia

Zimbabwe

The United Nations

The United Nations (U.N.) is an organization which aims to bring different countries together to work for peace and development. Of the world's 193 states, 191 are members of the U.N. Those that don't belong are Taiwan and the Vatican City.

Kofi Annan, the Secretary-General of the U.N., with U.N. ambassador Pele

Internet links
Play a game where you have to match countries and their flags.

For a link to this website, go to
www.usborne-quicklinks.com

GLOSSARY

This glossary explains some of the words you may come across when reading about the Earth and its peoples. Words in *italic type* have their own entry elsewhere in the glossary.

ablation zone The lower end of a *glacier*, where the ice melts and flows into streams and rivers, or into the sea.

abyssal plain A huge, flat expanse of seabed that forms most of the ocean floor.

accumulation zone The top of a *glacier*, where snow falls and is gradually compacted into ice.

acid rain Rain containing dissolved chemicals from polluted air. The chemicals make the water acidic, which means it can eat away at rock and damage plant life.

active volcano An active volcano is one which might *erupt* at any time.

adaptation The way a plant or animal *species* develops over time to suit its *habitat*.

aid Any kind of help, especially that given by one country to another. The help can be money, food, equipment or expert help from teachers and engineers.

animism The belief that plants, stones and other natural objects have living souls or spirits.

anticyclone An area of high *atmospheric pressure*, which pushes winds outward. It is the opposite of a *cyclone*.

apartheid A system, such as the one used in South Africa until 1994, which separates people according to their race.

aquifer A layer of *porous* rock which can hold water and carry it along under the ground.

arable Arable land is suitable for growing crops (plants). Arable farming means crop farming.

archipelago A group of islands.

asteroid A small rock that *orbits* the Sun. There are thousands of asteroids in the part of the *Solar System* known as the Asteroid Belt.

atmosphere A layer of gases that surrounds the Earth and some other planets and stars.

atmospheric pressure The force the *atmosphere* exerts on Earth. It can change according to how warm the air is and how high you are above sea level.

atom A tiny particle. All *elements* are made up of atoms.

aurora Flickering lights, caused by *magnetic* particles from the Sun, that sometimes appear in the sky near the poles. The lights in the north are named the aurora borealis and those in the south are the aurora australis.

axis An imaginary line running through the middle of the Earth, from the *North Pole* to the *South Pole*, around which the Earth spins.

bacterium (plural: **bacteria**) A tiny *organism* found in the soil, in the air, and in plants and animals.

bedrock The solid layer of rock that lies underneath the soil, covering the Earth's surface.

biome An area with a *climate* that supports a particular range of plants and animals. For example, deserts, mountains and seas are all biomes.

black smoker A kind of *hydrothermal vent* which churns out black water containing many dissolved minerals. The minerals gradually build up around the vent, forming a chimney.

border A line separating political or geographical areas, especially countries. Borders are drawn up by governments and can change over time.

camouflage Patterns or features, that help plants and animals to look like their backgrounds and avoid being seen. For example, a tiger's stripes blend in with long grass.

canopy The thick upper layer of leaves and branches in a rainforest.

carnivore An animal or plant that feeds on animals.

caste An inherited class, also known as *Jati*, in traditional Indian *culture*.

census An official count of the number of people in a country. Other information, such as age, sex and occupation, may also be noted in a census.

central business district (CBD) The main business area of a city, where most of the stores, banks and offices are found.

chlorofluorocarbon (CFC) Any of various chemicals that are thought to damage the layer of *ozone* in the Earth's *atmosphere*.

chlorophyll A green chemical in plants which enables them to convert sunlight into food.

civilization The process of human development from small prehistoric groups to complex human societies with cities, governments, laws and communication systems.

civil war A war between people of the same country.

climate The typical or average weather conditions in a particular region.

colonization The process of establishing a settlement or settlements in another country. It may involve imposing a new *culture*, language or religion.

comet A chunk of dirty ice mixed with dust and grit which travels around the *Sun*.

compass A device containing a *magnetic* needle that points to the *North Pole*. A compass is used to find your direction.

conservation Protecting and preserving *environments,* including the plants, animals and buildings that form a part of them, and trying to reduce the damage caused to them by *pollution*.

constellation A group of *stars* that form a recognizable pattern.

continent One of the Earth's major land masses.

continental crust Part of the Earth's *crust* that forms land masses. Continental crust is made mostly of a rock called granite and similar light rocks.

continental shelf A wide shelf of seabed that surrounds most land masses, making the sea much shallower near the land than it is in the middle of the oceans.

continental slope The steep slope leading from the edge of the *continental shelf* down to the deeper seabed.

coral reef A structure made up of the skeletons of small sea animals called coral polyps. A reef builds up gradually as old polyps die and new ones grow on top.

core The central part of the inside of the Earth, which scientists think is made of the metals iron and nickel.

Coriolis effect The effect of the spinning of the Earth, which forces winds and *currents* into a spiral.

creole A language formed from a European language and another language. The word creole can also be used to describe a person who is descended from Europeans and another ethnic group.

crevasse A crack in a *glacier*.

crop rotation Changing the crop grown on a particular piece of land each year, to give the soil the opportunity to recover.

crust The Earth's solid outer layer. It consists of *continental crust* which forms the land, and *oceanic crust* which forms the seabed.

culture The way of life of a group of people. It includes their customs, hobbies, food, fashions and beliefs.

current A body of water or air which moves in a definite direction, often through a stiller surrounding body. For example, the Gulf Stream is a current that carries warm water across the Atlantic Ocean from the Caribbean to northern Europe.

cyclone An area of low *atmospheric pressure* where winds rotate inward.

debris Any kind of loose rock, mud or other matter – such as the rocks carried along by a *glacier*, or the material carried and deposited by a flowing river.

deforestation Reducing or removing forests by cutting down or burning trees. Soil is washed away more easily in deforested areas.

degree One 360th of a circle. Degrees are used with *latitude* and *longitude* to measure distance on the Earth's surface. One degree is one 360th of the distance around the Earth.

delta A fan-shaped system of streams, created when a river splits up into many smaller branches and deposits *debris* as it nears the sea.

deposition Dropping or leaving behind rocks or other *debris*.

desertification The process of non-desert land becoming desert.

development The improvement of a country's industry, wealth and standard of living.

DNA Material, like a set of "coded instructions", in living *organisms* that contains the information they need to function and develop.

dormant volcano A volcano that is temporarily inactive, but could *erupt* in the future. The word dormant means "sleeping".

drumlin A small hill formed from *debris* deposited by a moving *glacier*, lengthened in the direction of the movement of the glacier to form an oval shape.

dyke A barrier built at the coast to stop the sea from flooding the land at high *tide*.

ecosystem A living system that includes a group of plants and animals and the *habitat* they live in.

ecotourism A type of tourism that aims to protect the environment, for example by charging tourists to visit nature reserves to spot wildlife.

element A substance, such as iron, oxygen or silicon, made of one type of *atom*. There are over a hundred elements on Earth.

El Niño A weather phenomenon that sometimes makes part of the Pacific Ocean get much warmer than normal, causing severe storms.

emergent A tree that rises above the main *canopy* in a rainforest.

emigration Movement from one country to settle in another.

environment Surroundings, including the landscape, living things and the *atmosphere*.

Equator An imaginary line around the middle of the Earth, exactly halfway between the *North Pole* and the *South Pole*.

erratic A large boulder that has been deposited by a *glacier* and is left standing away from its source.

eruption The ejection of *lava*, rocks, hot ash and gases from a volcano.

estuary A wide channel that forms where a river joins the sea.

ethnic group A group of people who share things like language, *culture* and religion, and who often live together in the same area.

Eurasia The continent of Europe and Asia.

evolution The gradual development of plants and animals, over many generations, to fit in better with their *habitats*.

exfoliation A process which involves shedding layers. When a rock exfoliates, its outer layers peel off like the layers of an onion. This is caused by changes in temperature, which make rock shrink and expand.

export A product sent abroad to be sold.

extinction The death of a *species* of plant or animal.

fallow Fallow land is farmland that is being left to rest and recover between crops.

famine A widespread shortage of food, which can lead to starvation and the spread of diseases.

Far East The most easterly countries of Asia, especially China and Japan.

fault A crack in the Earth's *crust*.

fault creep The gradual movement of two pieces of the Earth's *crust* along a *fault*.

fertile Fertile land is land that is good for growing plants. Fertile also means able to reproduce.

fertilizer A substance, such as manure, that contains *nitrates* and other chemicals and is put on land to make it more *fertile*.

fold mountains A mountain range formed by the Earth's *crust* buckling up into folds when the *plates* of the crust push together.

food chain A sequence showing which *species* eat which.

food web A network of *food chains* showing which *species* eat each other in an *ecosystem*.

footloose industry An industry that does not have to locate near its raw materials, either because it hardly uses any, or because the raw materials it does use are light and easy to transport. Also known as light industry.

fossil The shape or remains of a plant or animal that died long ago, hardened and preserved in rock.

fossil fuel A fuel, such as coal, oil or gas, made from the compressed bodies of plants and animals that died many years ago.

freeze-thaw action The action of water that seeps into cracks in rocks and then freezes, which makes it expand. This expansion forces the cracks apart, so they gradually get bigger.

fungus (plural: **fungi**) A type of *organism*, including mushrooms, that is similar to a plant but has no leaves or flowers.

galaxy A huge group of stars and planets. There are millions of galaxies in the universe.

genetically modified food Food crops which have been genetically changed. This may be to make them grow faster or resist frost or pests.

genetic engineering Changing the *DNA* of plants and animals to benefit medicine, farming and industry. In farming, for example, scientists can create new plant species which work better as crops.

geostationary Moving in such a way as to remain above the same point on the Earth's surface. For example, geostationary *satellites* orbit the Earth at the same speed as the Earth spins, so they always stay above the same part of the Earth.

geyser A spring that discharges water and steam, heated up inside the Earth, in bursts.

glacial valley A deep U-shaped valley carved by a flowing *glacier*, left behind after the glacier melts.

glacier A mass of ice that flows very slowly downhill.

globalization The organization of industry on a worldwide scale.

global warming The gradual warming-up of the Earth's atmosphere, possibly due to the *greenhouse effect*.

gorge A deep, narrow valley, shaped by a river gradually cutting down into the land it flows across.

gravity The pulling force that holds the *atmosphere* and objects in place on the Earth and stops them from floating out into space.

greenhouse effect The effect of certain gases in the *atmosphere* which trap heat from the Sun, causing the Earth to heat up.

greenhouse gas A gas, such as carbon dioxide, which contributes to the *greenhouse effect*.

gross national product (GNP) The total value of the goods and *services* produced by a nation over a year.

groundwater Water that has soaked into the ground and is stored inside *porous* rock.

habitat The place where an animal or plant *species* lives.

hanging valley A valley found high up the side of a *glacial valley*. Hanging valleys once contained mini-glaciers that flowed into a large glacier. When glaciers melt, hanging valleys are left behind, high up the mountainside.

heat expansion The increase in size of many substances, such as wood or rock, as they get warmer.

heavy industry An industry, such as ship-building, that uses heavy raw materials and needs large machines.

hemisphere Half of the Earth.

herbivore An animal that eats plants.

horizon A layer in soil. It is also the line where you can see the land meeting the sky when you look into the distance.

hot spot An area of the Earth's *crust* where *magma* breaks through and forms a volcano.

hot spring See **thermal spring.**

Human Development Index A system developed by the United Nations for measuring the standard of living in different countries.

humidity The amount of water contained in the air.

humus The part of soil that makes it *fertile*. Humus is made from rotted plant and animal matter.

hunter-gatherer Someone who survives by hunting animals and collecting wild plants, instead of by farming.

hydroelectric power (HEP) Power created from the energy of flowing water.

hydrothermal vent A hole in the seabed, through which a *thermal spring* emerges. See also **black smoker**.

Ice age A period when the Earth was much colder than average. There have been several major Ice ages since the Earth began.

iceberg A huge chunk of a *glacier* that has broken off into the sea.

ice sheet A sheet of ice covering a large area, such as the ice that covers Antarctica. An ice sheet is a type of large *glacier* which flows outward from the middle.

igneous rock Rock formed when *magma* escapes from inside the Earth, and then cools and hardens.

immigration Movement of people into a new country, usually to settle there permanently.

impermeable Not allowing water to pass through.

import A product or service brought into a country from another country.

indigenous Originating naturally in an area. Indigenous people are the people who first lived in a particular place.

infrared A type of energy that *radiates* from hot things. It is invisible to the human eye, but can be detected by infrared cameras.

intensive farming A type of farming that involves using chemicals and technology to increase *yield*.

interglacial A period of time within an *Ice age* when the climate gets slightly warmer for a while.

International Date Line An imaginary line on the Earth's surface, to the east of which the date is one day earlier than to the west. It runs on the opposite side of the world to the *Prime Meridian Line* at 180° of *longitude*, except where it bends to avoid time change in populated areas.

irrigation The artificial watering of land to help grow crops.

isobar A line that links points with the same *atmospheric pressure*. The isobars on a weather map show patterns of atmospheric pressure.

isthmus A narrow strip of land connecting two larger land areas. For example, Central America is an isthmus connecting North and South America.

landslide A sudden slippage of rocks and soil down a hillside, usually caused by heavy rain or earthquakes.

latitude A measurement of how many *degrees* a place is north or south of the *Equator*. Lines of latitude are imaginary lines around the Earth, parallel to the *Equator*.

lava Hot molten rock which bursts or flows out of volcanoes. Lava also sometimes seeps out of holes in the ground, called vents.

leap year A year every four years that has 366 days instead of 365. The extra day is added in February, to make February 29th.

less developed country (LDC) A poor country which has not yet been industrialized and has low standards of living.

lithosphere The outer layers of Earth, made up of the *crust* and upper *mantle*.

longitude A measurement of how many *degrees* a place is east or west of the *Prime Meridian Line*. Lines of longitude are imaginary lines that run around the Earth from north to south.

magma Hot, molten rock inside the Earth.

magnet An object that has magnetic force, an invisible force that attracts iron and steel. The ends of a magnet are known as its poles.

magnetic poles The Earth is like a giant *magnet*, and the ends of this magnet are called the magnetic poles. They move gradually over time, and are not in exactly the same place as the geographic *North Pole* and *South Pole*.

malaria A disease, affecting millions of people, which is spread by insects called mosquitoes.

mantle The thick layer of rock under the Earth's *crust*. Some of it is solid and some is *magma*.

manufacturing industry Industry, such as ship-building or clothes-making, that involves making new products.

matriarchy A system in which women are the most powerful members of families and of society.

meander A bend or long loop in a river. Meanders form when rivers flow across gently sloping land.

Mediterranean A type of *climate* that has warm winters and hot summers, and is good for growing many types of crops. It is named after the region around the Mediterranean Sea, but is also found in other parts of the world.

megacity A name for a city that has more than ten million people.

mestizo A Spaniard or Portuguese person of mixed origin, especially with Native American ancestors.

metamorphic rock Rock that has been changed by heat or pressure. For example, when a rock called shale is squashed, it hardens into a type of metamorphic rock called slate.

meteoroid Dust or a small chunk of rock which *orbits* the *Sun*.

Middle East An area of Asia between the Red Sea and Persian Gulf, as well as Israel, Jordan, Syria, Lebanon, Iraq and Iran.

migration Moving from one place to another. Many animals migrate each season to find food.

Milky Way The *galaxy* of which the *Sun* and *Solar System* are a part. It can often be seen as a broad band of light in the night sky.

mineral A non-living substance found in the Earth, such as salt, iron, diamond or quartz.

missionary A member of a group sent by a religious body to do religious or social work in another country.

molecule Two or more *atoms* bonded together.

monsoon A strong seasonal change in the weather that affects certain parts of Asia. Monsoon regions have three seasons – a long, cool, dry season, a hot, humid season and a rainy season.

moon A natural *satellite* which *orbits* a *planet*. The Earth has one moon which orbits it once a month.

moraine Boulders, clay and other *debris* left behind by a *glacier*.

more developed country (MDC) A wealthy country with well-developed industry and a high standard of living.

national park An area of natural beauty protected by law from building and development.

native Belonging to a particular place.

natural selection The theory that those animals and plants that are best suited to their *environment* are the most likely to survive.

newly industrialized country (NIC) A country that has recently increased its wealth and standard of living through the development of modern industry.

New World A phrase used to mean North, Central and South America. The term was first applied by European explorers.

niche A particular plant or animal *species'* place in an *ecosystem*.

nitrate Any of a group of chemicals found in soil that helps plants grow.

nomad Someone who has no permanent home and travels around to make a living. Many nomads herd animals.

northern hemisphere The half of the Earth that lies north of the *Equator*.

North Pole The most northern point on the Earth, and one end of the *axis* the Earth spins around.

nuclear power Energy produced by splitting *atoms* of a *radioactive element* called uranium.

oasis A *fertile* area in a desert, supplied by water from an *aquifer*.

oceanic crust Part of the Earth's *crust* that forms the seabed. Oceanic crust is made mostly of a rock called basalt.

oceanic ridge A raised ridge on the seabed, caused by the *plates* of the Earth's *crust* pulling apart and *magma* pushing up in between.

oceanic trench A deep trench in the seabed that forms where one *plate* pushes underneath another.

official language The language of a country that is spoken at work, at school and in government. The official language may be different from the language spoken in homes or with friends, and is not always the language spoken by the majority of the population.

omnivore An animal that eats both meat and plants. Omnivore means "everything-eater".

orbit The path of an object as it travels around, or orbits, another.

ore Rock containing metal that can be extracted.

organic farming A type of farming that doesn't use artificial chemicals and methods.

organic food Food produced by organic farming that contains no artificial chemicals.

organism A living thing, such as a plant, animal or *bacterium*.

outback The remote bush country of Australia.

outcrop An area of land where part of a rock formation reaches the surface.

oxbow lake A curved lake left behind when a river *meander* gets cut off from the rest of the river.

ozone A type of oxygen in which each *molecule* contains three oxygen *atoms* instead of two.

ozone layer A layer of *ozone* in the Earth's *atmosphere*, from 20 to 50km (12 to 30 miles) above the Earth's surface, which protects the Earth from the *Sun's* rays. The ozone layer may be being damaged by *chlorofluorocarbons*, or *CFCs*.

Pangaea The name scientists give to a huge continent that they think once existed on Earth. It gradually broke up to form the *continents* we have today.

passport An official document issued by the government of a country to a person who belongs to that country. A passport can allow travel to foreign countries, act as an identity card and give its owner the right to re-enter his or her *native* country.

pastoral farming A type of farming that involves raising and breeding animals.

patriarchy A system in which men are the most powerful members of families and of society.

peninsula A long piece of land that sticks out into the sea.

permafrost A layer of the ground that is permanently frozen.

photosynthesis A chemical process in plants, which converts sunlight into food.

pidgin A language made up of elements of two or more languages to help groups who speak different languages communicate.

pilgrimage A journey to a sacred place.

planet A celestial body that *orbits* a *star*. For example, Earth and Mars are planets which orbit the *Sun*.

plate One of the large pieces of *lithosphere* that make up the Earth's surface layer.

plate tectonics The theory that *plates* gradually move around and rub against each other.

poles The *North Pole* and the *South Pole*, the coldest points of the Earth and those that are farthest away from the *Equator*.

pollution Waste or dirt, such as exhaust from cars, that builds up faster than it can be broken down.

population The number of people living in a particular place.

porous Able to soak up water. Porous rock can soak up water like a sponge and store it underground.

port A town or city where ships can load and unload.

precipitation Rain, snow, hail or any other water falling from the sky.

precision farming A type of farming that uses the latest science and technology to grow crops more efficiently.

primary industry An industry that takes raw materials from the Earth. Mining and fishing are primary industries.

Prime Meridian Line An imaginary line that runs from north to south through Greenwich, England, at zero *degrees* of *longitude*. The time along the Prime Meridian Line is called Greenwich Mean Time.

projection A representation of the Earth's surface on a flat map.

quaternary industry An industry, such as accountancy, in which information is bought and sold.

radar A system that detects objects such as clouds by sending out radio waves and collecting the signals that bounce back. Radar stands for **RA**dio **D**etecting **A**nd **R**anging.

radiation Energy, such as light, heat or *radioactive* particles, that radiates (flows outward) from an energy source. For example, the *Sun* radiates light and heat.

radioactive A substance that gives out *radiation*. Radioactive substances, such as uranium, give off particles which can be harmful.

refugee A person who has fled from their country to escape some danger or problem.

remote sensing Recording information from a long distance away; for example, measuring sea temperatures from a *satellite*.

reservation An area of public land set aside for a special purpose. For example, in North America European settlers forced Native Americans to live on reservations.

rift valley A valley formed on land where two *plates* of the Earth's *crust* pull away from each other.

Ring of Fire A group of volcanoes and *faults* that forms a huge ring in the Pacific Ocean.

satellite An object that *orbits* a *planet*. Many satellites are built to do particular jobs, such as monitoring the weather.

scale The size of a map in relation to the area it represents. If a map's scale is 1:100, 1cm on the map represents 100cm of the area shown.

secondary industry An industry, such as building or making cloth in a factory, that makes things out of raw materials.

sedimentary rock Rock made up of particles of sand, mud and other *debris* that have settled on the seabed and been squashed down to form hard rock.

selective breeding Developing plants and animals by choosing those with good qualities for farming.

service industry An industry, such as banking or waitressing, that involves people doing or supplying something for other people. See also **tertiary industry**.

settlement A collection of homes forming a community.

sewage Waste and dirty water from sinks and bathrooms.

shaman A religious leader who is believed to have magical powers.

shanty town A makeshift town on the outskirts of a city where people build their own homes out of waste materials.

shifting agriculture A system of farming in which people clear a small area of forest to use as farmland. After a few years, they move on to another area.

site The place where a *settlement* has been built.

situation A *settlement's* position in the surrounding area, such as in a gap in a range of hills.

smog A mixture of smoke and fog. Also a general word for *pollution*.

Solar System The *Sun* and the *planets, satellites* and other objects that *orbit* it.

solar year The amount of time it takes the Earth to *orbit* the *Sun* once. A solar year is 365.26 days.

sonar A method of bouncing sounds off objects and measuring the results in order to make maps. Sonar is used to map the seabed.

southern hemisphere The half of the Earth that lies south of the *Equator*.

South Pole The most southern point on the Earth, and one end of the *axis* the Earth spins around.

species (plural: **species**) A type of plant, animal or other living thing.

stalactite A column of stone hanging down inside a cave, made by water dripping from the roof and depositing dissolved minerals.

stalagmite A tower of stone rising from the ground in a cave, made by water dripping onto the floor and depositing dissolved minerals.

star A huge ball of burning gas in space. The *Sun*, in the middle of our *Solar System*, is a star.

state An area of land that has its own government, laws and money. It can also mean one of a number of regional governments forming a federation under a central government, as in the U.S.A.

stoma (plural: **stomata**) One of the tiny holes in the leaves of plants. A stoma allows gases and water in and out. See also **transpiration**.

stratum (plural: **strata**) A layer of rock.

subduction zone An area of the seabed where one *plate* of the Earth's *lithosphere* plunges beneath another, forming a deep trench.

submersible A small submarine used by scientists to explore the oceans and the seabed.

Sun The medium-sized *star* that lies in the middle of our *Solar System*.

temperate A type of *climate* that is mild and damp.

terrace One of a series of large steps dug into hillsides to hold soil and water in place for farming.

tertiary industry An industry, such as teaching or banking, that provides services for others.

thermal spring A flow of water heated by underground rocks that emerges on the Earth's surface. Also known as a hot spring.

tidal wave A type of very large wave. *Tsunamis* are not tidal waves, as they are caused by underwater volcanoes or earthquakes and have nothing to do with tides.

tide The daily rise and fall of the sea, caused by the Moon's *gravity*.

time zone A region where the same standard time is used.

topsoil The rich, uppermost layer of soil. It contains *humus* and *organisms* that make it *fertile*.

transpiration A process where water that has been sucked in through a plant's roots travels up to the leaves, and transpires, or evaporates, through the *stomata*.

treeline The height up a mountain above which there are no more trees (because it is too cold and windy for them to survive).

tributary A river that flows into a bigger river, instead of into the sea.

tropics The warm, wet areas on either side of the *Equator*, between the Tropic of Cancer and the Tropic of Capricorn.

tsunami A giant wave made by an earthquake, landslide or volcanic activity on the seabed causing the water to make waves.

tundra A type of land, found in the Arctic, where a layer of the ground is permanently frozen.

turbine A machine that converts turning power (such as the spinning of a waterwheel) into electricity.

ultraviolet (UV) A type of invisible *radiation* from the Sun which can cause skin damage.

understorey The level of a rainforest where small trees and plants grow, between the *canopy* and the forest floor.

urbanization An increase in the number of people living in towns and cities rather than in the countryside.

visa A stamp on a *passport* from the government of a country which shows that the owner is allowed to travel through that country for a fixed period of time.

water table The top level of *groundwater* that is stored in underground rock.

yield The amount of food or other produce that is grown on a particular piece of land.

MAP INDEX

This is an index of the places and features named on the maps. Each entry consists of the following parts: the name (given in bold type), the country or region within which it is located (given in italics), the page on which the name can be found (given in bold type), and the grid reference (also given in bold type). For some names, there is also a description explaining what kind of place it is – for example a country, internal administrative area (state or province), national capital or internal capital. To find a place on a map, first find the map indicated by the page reference. Then use the grid reference to find the square containing the name or town symbol. See page 251 for help with using the grid.

a

Abaco, *The Bahamas*, **271 L5**
Abadan, *Iran*, **303 E5**
Abakan, *Russia*, **304 E3**
Abaya, Lake, *Ethiopia*, **327 G2**
Abeche, *Chad*, **322 F6**
Abeokuta, *Nigeria*, **325 F7**
Aberdeen, *United Kingdom*, **314 D2**
Aberystwyth, *United Kingdom*, **314 C3**
Abha, *Saudi Arabia*, **303 D8**
Abidjan, *Ivory Coast*, **325 E7**
Abilene, *U.S.A.*, **270 G4**
Abomey, *Benin*, **325 F7**
Abu Dhabi, *United Arab Emirates, national capital*, **303 F7**
Abuja, *Nigeria, national capital*, **325 G7**
Abu Kamal, *Syria*, **302 D5**
Abu Simbel, *Egypt*, **323 H4**
Acapulco, *Mexico*, **272 E4**
Accra, *Ghana, national capital*, **325 E7**
Acklins Island, *The Bahamas*, **271 L6**
Aconcagua, *Argentina*, **280 E6**
Adana, *Turkey*, **302 C4**
Adapazari, *Turkey*, **317 J3**
Ad Dakhla, *Western Sahara*, **324 B4**
Ad Dammam, *Saudi Arabia*, **303 F6**
Addis Ababa, *Ethiopia, national capital*, **327 G2**
Adelaide, *Australia, internal capital*, **288 G6**
Aden, *Yemen*, **303 E9**
Aden, Gulf of, *Africa/Asia*, **303 E9**
Admiralty Islands, *Papua New Guinea*, **295 L4**
Adrar, *Algeria*, **324 E3**
Adriatic Sea, *Europe*, **316 E3**
Adzope, *Ivory Coast*, **325 E7**
Aegean Sea, *Europe*, **317 H4**
Afghanistan, *Asia, country*, **300 A4**
Africa, **263**
Agadez, *Niger*, **322 C5**
Agadir, *Morocco*, **324 D2**
Agra, *India*, **300 D5**
Agrigento, *Italy*, **316 E4**
Agua Prieta, *Mexico*, **272 C1**
Aguascalientes, *Mexico*, **272 D3**
Agulhas, Cape, *South Africa*, **328 C6**
Agulhas Negras, Mount, *Brazil*, **280 K4**
Ahaggar Mountains, *Algeria*, **324 G4**
Ahmadabad, *India*, **301 C6**
Ahvaz, *Iran*, **303 E5**
Aix-en-Provence, *France*, **315 F6**
Aizawl, *India*, **301 G6**
Ajaccio, *France*, **315 G6**
Ajdabiya, *Libya*, **322 F2**
Ajmer, *India*, **300 C5**
Akhisar, *Turkey*, **317 H4**
Akita, *Japan*, **299 P3**
Akjoujt, *Mauritania*, **324 C5**
Akola, *India*, **301 D6**
Aksaray, *Turkey*, **317 K4**
Aksu, *China*, **300 E2**
Alabama, *U.S.A., internal admin. area*, **271 J4**
Al Amarah, *Iraq*, **303 E5**
Aland Islands, *Finland*, **312 F3**
Alanya, *Turkey*, **317 J4**
Al Aqabah, *Jordan*, **303 C6**
Alaska, *U.S.A., internal admin. area*, **268 D2**

Alaska, Gulf of, *North America*, **268 E3**
Alaska Peninsula, *U.S.A.*, **268 D3**
Alaska Range, *U.S.A.*, **268 D2**
Alavus, *Finland*, **312 G3**
Al Ayn, *United Arab Emirates*, **303 G7**
Albacete, *Spain*, **315 D7**
Albania, *Europe, country*, **317 F3**
Albany, *Australia*, **288 C7**
Albany, *Georgia, U.S.A.*, **271 K4**
Albany, *New York, U.S.A., internal capital*, **271 M2**
Al Bayda, *Libya*, **322 F2**
Alberta, *Canada, internal admin. area*, **268 H3**
Albert, Lake, *Africa*, **327 F3**
Albino Point, *Angola*, **328 B3**
Alboran Island, *Spain*, **315 D7**
Alborg, *Denmark*, **313 D4**
Albuquerque, *U.S.A.*, **270 E3**
Aldabra Group, *Seychelles*, **329 J1**
Aleppo, *Syria*, **302 C4**
Alesund, *Norway*, **312 C3**
Aleutian Islands, *U.S.A.*, **269 A3**
Alexander Archipelago, *Canada*, **268 F3**
Alexander Bay, *South Africa*, **328 C5**
Alexandria, *Egypt*, **323 G2**
Algeciras, *Spain*, **315 C7**
Algeria, *Africa, country*, **324 F3**
Algiers, *Algeria, national capital*, **324 F1**
Al Hillah, *Iraq*, **302 D5**
Al Hoceima, *Morocco*, **324 E1**
Al Hudaydah, *Yemen*, **303 D9**
Ali Bayramli, *Azerbaijan*, **302 E4**
Alicante, *Spain*, **315 D7**
Alice Springs, *Australia*, **288 F4**
Aligarh, *India*, **300 D5**
Al Jawf, *Libya*, **322 F4**
Al Khums, *Libya*, **322 D2**
Al Kut, *Iraq*, **303 E5**
Allahabad, *India*, **300 E5**
Almaty, *Kazakhstan*, **300 D2**
Almeria, *Spain*, **315 D7**
Almetyevsk, *Russia*, **311 G3**
Almirante, *Panama*, **273 H6**
Al Mubarrez, *Saudi Arabia*, **303 E6**
Al Mukalla, *Yemen*, **303 E9**
Alor Setar, *Malaysia*, **294 B2**
Alps, *Europe*, **316 D2**
Al Qamishli, *Syria*, **302 D4**
Alta, *Norway*, **312 G1**
Altai Mountains, *Asia*, **298 D1**
Altamira, *Brazil*, **279 H4**
Altay, *China*, **300 F1**
Altay, *Mongolia*, **298 E1**
Altun Mountains, *China*, **300 G3**
Aluksne, *Latvia*, **313 H4**
Alytus, *Lithuania*, **313 H5**
Amadjuak Lake, *Canada*, **269 M2**
Amami, *Japan*, **299 L5**
Amarillo, *U.S.A.*, **270 F3**
Amazon, *South America*, **278 H4**
Amazon Delta, *Brazil*, **279 J3**
Ambanja, *Madagascar*, **329 J2**
Ambato, *Ecuador*, **278 C4**
Amber, Cape, *Madagascar*, **329 J2**
Ambilobe, *Madagascar*, **329 J2**
Ambon, *Indonesia*, **295 G4**
Ambositra, *Madagascar*, **329 J4**

American Samoa, *Oceania, dependency*, **286 F6**
America, United States of, *North America, country*, **270 F3**
Amiens, *France*, **314 E4**
Amman, *Jordan, national capital*, **303 C5**
Amravati, *India*, **301 D6**
Amritsar, *India*, **300 C4**
Amsterdam, *Netherlands, national capital*, **314 F3**
Am Timan, *Chad*, **322 F6**
Amu Darya, *Asia*, **302 H4**
Amundsen Gulf, *Canada*, **268 G1**
Amundsen Sea, *Antarctica*, **333 Q3**
Amur, *Asia*, **305 G3**
Anadyr, *Russia*, **305 J2**
Anadyr, Gulf of, *Asia*, **305 K2**
Analalava, *Madagascar*, **329 J2**
Anambas Islands, *Indonesia*, **294 C3**
Anchorage, *U.S.A.*, **268 E2**
Ancona, *Italy*, **316 E3**
Andaman Islands, *India*, **301 G8**
Andaman Sea, *Asia*, **296 C5**
Andara, *Namibia*, **328 D3**
Andes, *South America*, **280 E5**
Andorra, *Europe, country*, **315 E6**
Andorra la Vella, *Andorra, national capital*, **315 E6**
Andreanof Islands, *U.S.A.*, **269 B3**
Androka, *Madagascar*, **329 H5**
Andros, *The Bahamas*, **271 L6**
Aneto, Pico de, *Spain*, **315 E6**
Angel Falls, *Venezuela*, **278 F2**
Angers, *France*, **314 D5**
Angkor, *Cambodia*, **296 D5**
Angoche, *Mozambique*, **329 G3**
Angola, *Africa, country*, **328 C2**
Angra do Heroismo, *Azores*, **324 K10**
Angren, *Uzbekistan*, **300 C2**
Anguilla, *North America*, **272 M4**
Anjouan Island, *Comoros*, **329 H2**
Ankara, *Turkey, national capital*, **317 K3**
Annaba, *Algeria*, **324 G1**
An Najaf, *Iraq*, **303 D5**
Annapolis, *U.S.A., internal capital*, **271 L3**
An Nasiriyah, *Iraq*, **303 E5**
Anqing, *China*, **299 J4**
Anshan, *China*, **299 K2**
Antalaha, *Madagascar*, **329 K2**
Antalya, *Turkey*, **317 J4**
Antalya, Gulf of, *Turkey*, **317 J4**
Antananarivo, *Madagascar, national capital*, **329 J3**
Antarctica, **333 B4**
Antarctic Peninsula, *Antarctica*, **333 T2**
Anticosti Island, *Canada*, **269 N4**
Antigua and Barbuda, *North America, country*, **272 M4**
Antofagasta, *Chile*, **280 D4**
Antsalova, *Madagascar*, **329 H3**
Antsirabe, *Madagascar*, **329 J3**
Antsiranana, *Madagascar*, **329 J2**
Antwerp, *Belgium*, **314 F4**
Aomori, *Japan*, **299 P2**
Aoraki, *New Zealand*, **289 P8**
Apalachee Bay, *U.S.A.*, **271 K5**
Aparri, *Philippines*, **297 H4**
Apatity, *Russia*, **312 K2**

Apennines, *Italy*, **316 E3**
Apia, *Samoa, national capital*, **286 F6**
Appalachian Mountains, *U.S.A.*, **271 K3**
Aqsay, *Kazakhstan*, **311 G3**
Aqtau, *Kazakhstan*, **302 F3**
Aqtobe, *Kazakhstan*, **311 H3**
Arabian Desert, *Africa*, **323 H3**
Arabian Peninsula, *Asia*, **303 E7**
Arabian Sea, *Asia*, **303 G8**
Aracaju, *Brazil*, **279 L6**
Arad, *Romania*, **317 G2**
Arafura Sea, *Asia/Australasia*, **295 H5**
Araguaia, *Brazil*, **279 H6**
Araguaina, *Brazil*, **279 J5**
Arak, *Iran*, **302 E5**
Aral, *Kazakhstan*, **302 H2**
Aral Sea, *Asia*, **302 G2**
Arapiraca, *Brazil*, **279 L5**
Araraquara, *Brazil*, **280 J4**
Araure, *Venezuela*, **278 E2**
Arbil, *Iraq*, **302 D4**
Arctic Ocean, **332 A4**
Ardabil, *Iran*, **302 E4**
Arendal, *Norway*, **312 D4**
Arequipa, *Peru*, **278 D7**
Argentina, *South America, country*, **281 E7**
Argentino, Lake, *Argentina*, **281 D10**
Arhus, *Denmark*, **313 D4**
Arica, *Chile*, **280 D7**
Arica, Gulf of, *South America*, **278 D7**
Arizona, *U.S.A., internal admin. area*, **270 D4**
Arkansas, *U.S.A.*, **271 G3**
Arkansas, *U.S.A., internal admin. area*, **271 H4**
Arkhangelsk, *Russia*, **304 C2**
Armenia, *Asia, country*, **302 D3**
Armidale, *Australia*, **289 K6**
Arnhem, *Netherlands*, **314 F4**
Arnhem Land, *Australia*, **288 F2**
Arqalyq, *Kazakhstan*, **302 J1**
Ar Ramadi, *Iraq*, **302 D5**
Ar Raqqah, *Syria*, **302 C4**
Aruba, *North America*, **273 K5**
Aru Islands, *Indonesia*, **295 J5**
Arusha, *Tanzania*, **327 G4**
Arzamas, *Russia*, **310 E2**
Asahikawa, *Japan*, **299 P2**
Asansol, *India*, **301 F6**
Ashgabat, *Turkmenistan, national capital*, **302 G4**
Ashkhabad, *Turkmenistan, national capital*, **302 G4**
Asia, **263**
Asir, *Saudi Arabia*, **303 D7**
Asmara, *Eritrea, national capital*, **323 J5**
Assab, *Eritrea*, **323 K6**
As Sulaymaniyah, *Iraq*, **302 E4**
Assumption, *Seychelles*, **329 J1**
Astana, *Kazakhstan, national capital*, **304 D3**
Astove, *Seychelles*, **329 J2**
Astrakhan, *Russia*, **311 F4**
Asuncion, *Paraguay, national capital*, **280 G5**
Aswan, *Egypt*, **323 H4**
Aswan High Dam, *Egypt*, **323 H4**
Asyut, *Egypt*, **323 H3**
Atacama Desert, *Chile*, **280 E3**

Atalaia do Norte, *Brazil*, 278 D4
Atar, *Mauritania*, 324 C4
Atbarah, *Sudan*, 323 H5
Atbasar, *Kazakhstan*, 302 J1
Athabasca, *Canada*, 268 H3
Athabasca, Lake, *Canada*, 268 J3
Athens, *Greece, national capital*, 317 G4
Atka Island, *U.S.A.*, 269 B3
Atlanta, *U.S.A., internal capital*, 271 K4
Atlantic City, *U.S.A.*, 271 M3
Atlantic Ocean, 262
Atlas Mountains, *Africa*, 324 D2
At Taif, *Saudi Arabia*, 303 D7
Attapu, *Laos*, 296 E5
Attu Island, *U.S.A.*, 269 A3
Atyrau, *Kazakhstan*, 311 G4
Auckland, *New Zealand*, 289 P7
Augsburg, *Germany*, 314 G4
Augusta, *U.S.A., internal capital*, 271 N2
Aurangabad, *India*, 301 D7
Austin, *U.S.A., internal capital*, 270 G4
Australasia and Oceania, 263
Australia, *Australasia, country*, 288 E4
Australian Capital Territory, *Australia, internal admin. area*, 289 J6
Austria, *Europe, country*, 316 E2
Awasa, *Ethiopia*, 327 G2
Ayacucho, *Peru*, 278 D6
Aydin, *Turkey*, 317 H4
Ayers Rock, *Australia*, 288 F5
Ayoun el Atrous, *Mauritania*, 325 D5
Azerbaijan, *Asia, country*, 302 E3
Azores, *Atlantic Ocean*, 324 K10
Azov, Sea of, *Europe*, 317 K2
Az Zarqa, *Jordan*, 303 C5

b

Baardheere, *Somalia*, 327 H3
Babahoyo, *Ecuador*, 278 C4
Bab al Mandab, *Africa/Asia*, 323 K6
Babruysk, *Belarus*, 313 J5
Babuyan Islands, *Philippines*, 297 H4
Babylon, *Iraq*, 302 D5
Bacabal, *Brazil*, 279 K4
Bacau, *Romania*, 317 H2
Bac Lieu, *Vietnam*, 296 E6
Bacolod, *Philippines*, 297 H5
Badajoz, *Spain*, 315 C7
Baffin Bay, *Canada*, 269 N1
Baffin Island, *Canada*, 269 M2
Bafoussam, *Cameroon*, 326 B2
Bage, *Brazil*, 280 H6
Baghdad, *Iraq, national capital*, 302 D5
Bahamas, The, *North America, country*, 271 L5
Bahawalpur, *Pakistan*, 300 C5
Bahia, *Brazil*, 279 L6
Bahia Blanca, *Argentina*, 281 F7
Bahir Dar, *Ethiopia*, 327 G1
Bahrain, *Asia, country*, 303 F6
Baia Mare, *Romania*, 317 G2
Baie-Comeau, *Canada*, 269 N4
Baikal, Lake, *Russia*, 305 F3
Bairiki, *Kiribati, national capital*, 286 E4
Bakersfield, *U.S.A.*, 270 C3
Baku, *Azerbaijan, national capital*, 302 E3
Balakovo, *Russia*, 311 F3
Balaton, Lake, *Hungary*, 313 F7
Balbina Reservoir, *Brazil*, 279 G4
Baldy Peak, *U.S.A.*, 270 E4
Balearic Islands, *Spain*, 315 E7
Bali, *Indonesia*, 294 E5
Balikesir, *Turkey*, 317 H4
Balikpapan, *Indonesia*, 294 E4
Balkanabat, *Turkmenistan*, 302 F4
Balkan Mountains, *Europe*, 317 G3
Balkhash, Lake, *Kazakhstan*, 300 D1
Balkuduk, *Kazakhstan*, 311 F4
Balqash, *Kazakhstan*, 300 D1
Balti, *Moldova*, 317 H2
Baltic Sea, *Europe*, 313 F4
Baltimore, *U.S.A.*, 271 L3
Bamako, *Mali, national capital*, 325 D6
Bamenda, *Cameroon*, 326 B2
Bancs Providence, *Seychelles*, 329 K1
Banda Aceh, *Indonesia*, 294 A2

Bandar-e Abbas, *Iran*, 303 G6
Bandar Seri Begawan, *Brunei, national capital*, 294 D2
Banda Sea, *Indonesia*, 295 G5
Bandundu, *Democratic Republic of Congo*, 326 C4
Bandung, *Indonesia*, 294 C5
Banfora, *Burkina Faso*, 325 E6
Bangalore, *India*, 301 D8
Bangassou, *Central African Republic*, 326 D3
Bangka, *Indonesia*, 294 C4
Bangkok, *Thailand, national capital*, 296 D5
Bangladesh, *Asia, country*, 301 F6
Bangor, *U.S.A.*, 271 N2
Bangui, *Central African Republic, national capital*, 326 C3
Bangweulu, Lake, *Zambia*, 328 E2
Banja Luka, *Bosnia and Herzegovina*, 316 F2
Banjarmasin, *Indonesia*, 294 D4
Banjul, *The Gambia, national capital*, 325 B6
Banks Island, *Canada*, 268 G1
Banks Islands, *Vanuatu*, 289 N2
Banska Bystrica, *Slovakia*, 313 F6
Baoding, *China*, 299 J3
Baoji, *China*, 298 G4
Baotou, *China*, 298 G2
Baqubah, *Iraq*, 302 D5
Baranavichy, *Belarus*, 313 H5
Barbacena, *Brazil*, 280 K4
Barbados, *North America, country*, 272 N5
Barcelona, *Spain*, 315 E6
Barcelona, *Venezuela*, 278 F1
Bareilly, *India*, 300 D5
Barents Sea, *Europe*, 304 B2
Bari, *Italy*, 316 F3
Barinas, *Venezuela*, 278 D2
Barkly Tableland, *Australia*, 288 G3
Barnaul, *Russia*, 304 E3
Barquisimeto, *Venezuela*, 278 E1
Barra Falsa Point, *Mozambique*, 329 G4
Barranquilla, *Colombia*, 278 D1
Barra Point, *Mozambique*, 329 G4
Barreiras, *Brazil*, 280 J2
Barrow, Point, *U.S.A.*, 268 D1
Barysaw, *Belarus*, 313 J5
Basel, *Switzerland*, 316 C2
Basra, *Iraq*, 303 E5
Bassas da India, *Africa*, 329 G4
Basse-Terre, *Guadeloupe*, 272 M4
Basseterre, *St. Kitts and Nevis, national capital*, 272 M4
Bass Strait, *Australia*, 288 J7
Bastia, *France*, 315 G6
Bata, *Equatorial Guinea*, 326 A3
Batan Islands, *Philippines*, 297 H3
Batdambang, *Cambodia*, 296 D5
Bathurst, *Canada*, 269 N4
Bathurst, *U.S.A.*, 271 N1
Bathurst Island, *Canada*, 269 K1
Batna, *Algeria*, 324 G1
Baton Rouge, *U.S.A., internal capital*, 271 H4
Batumi, *Georgia*, 302 D3
Baturaja, *Indonesia*, 294 B4
Bawku, *Ghana*, 325 E6
Bayamo, *Cuba*, 273 J3
Baydhabo, *Somalia*, 327 H3
Bealanana, *Madagascar*, 329 J2
Beaufort Sea, *North America*, 268 F1
Beaufort West, *South Africa*, 328 D6
Beaumont, *U.S.A.*, 271 H4
Bechar, *Algeria*, 324 E2
Beer Sheva, *Israel*, 303 B5
Beijing, *China, national capital*, 299 J3
Beira, *Mozambique*, 329 G3
Beirut, *Lebanon, national capital*, 302 C5
Bejaia, *Algeria*, 324 F1
Bekescsaba, *Hungary*, 313 G7
Bekily, *Madagascar*, 329 J4
Belarus, *Europe, country*, 313 J5
Belaya, *Russia*, 311 G2
Belcher Islands, *Canada*, 269 L3
Beledweyne, *Somalia*, 327 J3

Belem, *Brazil*, 279 J4
Belfast, *United Kingdom, internal capital*, 314 C3
Belgaum, *India*, 301 C7
Belgium, *Europe, country*, 314 E4
Belgrade, *Serbia & Montenegro, national capital*, 317 G2
Belitung, *Indonesia*, 294 C4
Belize, *North America, country*, 272 G4
Bellingham, *U.S.A.*, 270 B1
Bellingshausen Sea, *Antarctica*, 333 R2
Belmopan, *Belize, national capital*, 272 G4
Belo Horizonte, *Brazil*, 280 K3
Belomorsk, *Russia*, 312 K2
Beloretsk, *Russia*, 311 H3
Belo-Tsiribihina, *Madagascar*, 329 H3
Bendigo, *Australia*, 288 H7
Bengal, Bay of, *Asia*, 301 F7
Benghazi, *Libya*, 322 F2
Bengkulu, *Indonesia*, 294 B4
Benguela, *Angola*, 328 B2
Beni Mellal, *Morocco*, 324 D2
Benin, *Africa, country*, 325 F6
Benin, Bight of, *Africa*, 325 F7
Benin City, *Nigeria*, 325 G7
Beni Suef, *Egypt*, 323 H3
Ben Nevis, *United Kingdom*, 314 C2
Benoni, *South Africa*, 328 E5
Berbera, *Somalia*, 327 J1
Berberati, *Central African Republic*, 326 C3
Berdyansk, *Ukraine*, 310 D4
Bereznici, *Russia*, 311 H2
Bergamo, *Italy*, 316 D2
Bergen, *Norway*, 312 C3
Bering Sea, *North America*, 268 C2
Bering Strait, *U.S.A.*, 268 B2
Berlin, *Germany, national capital*, 314 H3
Bern, *Switzerland, national capital*, 316 C2
Beroroha, *Madagascar*, 329 J4
Bertoua, *Cameroon*, 326 B3
Besalampy, *Madagascar*, 329 H3
Besancon, *France*, 315 F5
Bethel, *U.S.A.*, 268 C2
Bethlehem, *South Africa*, 328 E5
Betroka, *Madagascar*, 329 J4
Beyneu, *Kazakhstan*, 302 G2
Beysehir Lake, *Turkey*, 317 J4
Beziers, *France*, 315 E6
Bhagalpur, *India*, 300 F5
Bhavnagar *India*, 301 C6
Bhopal, *India*, 301 D6
Bhutan, *Asia, country*, 300 G5
Biak, *Indonesia*, 295 J4
Bialystok, *Poland*, 313 G5
Bida, *Nigeria*, 325 G7
Bielefeld, *Germany*, 314 G3
Biel, *Switzerland*, 316 C2
Bien Hoa, *Vietnam*, 296 E5
Bie Plateau, *Angola*, 328 B2
Bignona, *Senegal*, 325 B6
Bikaner, *India*, 300 C5
Bila Tserkva, *Ukraine*, 313 J6
Bilbao, *Spain*, 315 D6
Bilhorod Dnistrovskyy, *Ukraine*, 310 C4
Billings, *U.S.A.*, 270 E1
Bindura, *Zimbabwe*, 328 F3
Binga, *Zimbabwe*, 328 E3
Bintulu, *Malaysia*, 294 D3
Bioco, *Equatorial Guinea*, 326 A3
Birao, *Central African Republic*, 326 D1
Biratnagar, *Nepal*, 300 F5
Birjand, *Iran*, 302 G5
Birmingham, *United Kingdom*, 314 D3
Birmingham, *U.S.A.*, 271 J4
Birnin-Kebbi, *Nigeria*, 325 F6
Biscay, Bay of, *Europe*, 315 C5
Bishkek, *Kyrgyzstan, national capital*, 300 C2
Bisho, *South Africa*, 328 E6
Biskra, *Algeria*, 324 G2
Bismarck, *U.S.A., internal capital*, 270 F1
Bismarck Sea, *Papua New Guinea*, 295 L4
Bissagos Archipelago, *Guinea-Bissau*, 325 B6
Bissau, *Guinea-Bissau, national capital*, 325 B6

Bitola, *Macedonia*, 317 G3
Bitterfontein, *South Africa*, 328 C6
Bizerte, *Tunisia*, 322 C1
Blackpool, *United Kingdom*, 314 D3
Black Sea, *Asia/Europe*, 304 B3
Black Volta, *Africa*, 325 E6
Blagoevgrad, *Bulgaria*, 317 G3
Blagoveshchensk, *Russia*, 305 G3
Blanca Bay, *Argentina*, 281 F7
Blanc, Cape, *Africa*, 324 B4
Blanc, Mont, *Europe*, 315 F5
Blantyre, *Malawi*, 329 F3
Blida, *Algeria*, 324 F1
Bloemfontein, *South Africa, national capital*, 328 E5
Blue Nile, *Africa*, 323 H6
Bo, *Sierra Leone*, 325 C7
Boa Vista, *Brazil*, 278 F3
Boa Vista, *Cape Verde*, 325 M11
Bobo Dioulasso, *Burkina Faso*, 325 E6
Bodele Depression, *Africa*, 322 E5
Boden, *Sweden*, 312 G2
Bodo, *Norway*, 312 E2
Bogor, *Indonesia*, 294 C5
Bogota, *Colombia, national capital*, 278 D3
Bohol, *Philippines*, 297 H6
Boise, *U.S.A., internal capital*, 270 C2
Bojnurd, *Iran*, 302 G4
Boke, *Guinea*, 325 C6
Bolivar Peak, *Venezuela*, 278 D2
Bolivia, *South America, country*, 280 E3
Bologna, *Italy*, 316 D2
Bolzano, *Italy*, 316 D2
Bombay, *India*, 301 C7
Bondoukou, *Ivory Coast*, 325 E7
Bongor, *Chad*, 326 C1
Bonin Islands, *Japan*, 286 B2
Bonn, *Germany*, 314 F4
Boosaaso, *Somalia*, 327 J1
Boothia, Gulf of, *Canada*, 269 K1
Boothia Peninsula, *Canada*, 269 K1
Bordeaux, *France*, 315 D5
Bordj Bou Arreridj, *Algeria*, 324 F1
Borlange, *Sweden*, 312 E3
Borneo, *Asia*, 294 D4
Bornholm, *Denmark*, 313 E5
Borovichi, *Russia*, 312 K4
Bosnia and Herzegovina, *Europe, country*, 316 F2
Bosporus, *Turkey*, 317 J3
Bossangoa, *Central African Republic*, 326 C2
Bossembele, *Central African Republic*, 326 C2
Boston, *U.S.A., internal capital*, 271 M2
Bothnia, Gulf of, *Europe*, 312 F3
Botosani, *Romania*, 317 H2
Botswana, *Africa, country*, 328 D4
Bouake, *Ivory Coast*, 325 E7
Bouar, *Central African Republic*, 326 C2
Boujdour, *Western Sahara*, 324 C3
Bouna, *Ivory Coast*, 325 E7
Bozoum, *Central African Republic*, 326 C2
Braga, *Portugal*, 315 B6
Braganca, *Brazil*, 279 J4
Brahmapur, *India*, 301 E7
Brahmaputra, *Asia*, 300 G5
Braila, *Romania*, 317 H2
Brandon, *Canada*, 269 K4
Brandon, *U.S.A.*, 270 G1
Brasilia, *Brazil, national capital*, 280 J3
Brasov, *Romania*, 317 H2
Bratislava, *Slovakia, national capital*, 313 F6
Brazil, *South America, country*, 279 H5
Brazilian Highlands, *Brazil*, 280 K2
Brazzaville, *Congo, national capital*, 326 C4
Bremen, *Germany*, 314 G3
Bremerhaven, *Germany*, 314 G3
Brescia, *Italy*, 316 D2
Brest, *Belarus*, 313 G5
Brest, *France*, 314 C4
Bria, *Central African Republic*, 326 D2
Bridgetown, *Barbados, national capital*, 272 N5

Brisbane, *Australia, internal capital*, 289 K5
Bristol, *United Kingdom*, 314 D4
Bristol Bay, *U.S.A.*, 268 C3
British Columbia, *Canada, internal admin. area*, 268 G3
Brno, *Czech Republic*, 316 F1
Broken Hill, *Australia*, 288 H6
Brokopondo, *Surinam*, 279 G2
Brooks Range, *U.S.A.*, 268 D2
Brownsville, *U.S.A.*, 270 G5
Bruges, *Belgium*, 314 E4
Brunei, *Asia, country*, 294 D3
Brussels, *Belgium, national capital*, 314 F4
Bryansk, *Russia*, 310 C3
Bucaramanga, *Colombia*, 278 D2
Bucharest, *Romania, national capital*, 317 H2
Budapest, *Hungary, national capital*, 313 F7
Buenaventura, *Colombia*, 278 C3
Buenos Aires, *Argentina, national capital*, 280 G6
Buenos Aires, Lake, *South America*, 281 D9
Buffalo, *U.S.A.*, 271 L2
Buga, *Colombia*, 278 C3
Buinsk, *Russia*, 311 F3
Bujumbura, *Burundi, national capital*, 326 E4
Bukavu, *Democratic Republic of Congo*, 326 E4
Bulawayo, *Zimbabwe*, 328 E4
Bulgan, *Mongolia*, 298 F1
Bulgaria, *Europe, country*, 317 H3
Bunbury, *Australia*, 288 C6
Bundaberg, *Australia*, 289 K4
Buon Me Thuot, *Vietnam*, 296 E5
Buraydah, *Saudi Arabia*, 303 D6
Burgas, *Bulgaria*, 317 H3
Burgos, *Spain*, 315 D6
Burkina Faso, *Africa, country*, 325 E6
Burma, *Asia, country*, 296 C3
Bursa, *Turkey*, 317 J3
Buru, *Indonesia*, 295 G4
Burundi, *Africa, country*, 326 E4
Bushehr, *Iran*, 303 F6
Buta, *Democratic Republic of Congo*, 326 D3
Butare, *Rwanda*, 326 E4
Butembo, *Democratic Republic of Congo*, 326 E3
Buton, *Indonesia*, 295 F4
Butuan, *Philippines*, 297 J6
Buxoro, *Uzbekistan*, 300 A3
Buzau, *Romania*, 317 H2
Buzuluk, *Russia*, 311 G3
Bydgoszcz, *Poland*, 313 F5

C
Cabanatuan, *Philippines*, 297 H4
Cabinda, *Angola, enclave*, 326 B5
Cabonga Reservoir, *Canada*, 271 L1
Cabora Bassa Reservoir, *Mozambique*, 328 F3
Caceres, *Brazil*, 280 G3
Caceres, *Colombia*, 278 C2
Caceres, *Spain*, 315 C7
Cachoeiro de Itapemirim, *Brazil*, 280 K4
Cadiz, *Spain*, 315 C7
Cadiz, Gulf of, *Europe*, 315 C7
Caen, *France*, 314 D4
Cagayan de Oro, *Philippines*, 297 H6
Cagliari, *Italy*, 316 D4
Caicara, *Venezuela*, 278 E2
Cairns, *Australia*, 288 J3
Cairo, *Egypt, national capital*, 323 H3
Caiundo, *Angola*, 328 C3
Cajamarca, *Peru*, 278 C5
Calabar, *Nigeria*, 326 A2
Calais, *France*, 314 E4
Calama, *Chile*, 280 D4
Calamian Group, *Philippines*, 297 G5
Calapan, *Philippines*, 297 H5
Calbayog, *Philippines*, 297 H5
Calcutta, *India*, 301 F6
Calgary, *Canada*, 268 H3

Cali, *Colombia*, 278 C3
Calicut, *India*, 301 D8
California, *U.S.A., internal admin. area*, 270 C3
California, Gulf of, *Mexico*, 272 B2
Camaguey, *Cuba*, 273 J3
Cambodia, *Asia, country*, 296 E5
Cambridge, *United Kingdom*, 314 E3
Cameroon, *Africa, country*, 326 B2
Cameroon Mountain, *Cameroon*, 326 A3
Cameta, *Brazil*, 279 J4
Camiri, *Bolivia*, 280 F4
Campeche, *Mexico*, 272 F4
Campeche, Bay of, *Mexico*, 272 F3
Campina Grande, *Brazil*, 279 L5
Campinas, *Brazil*, 280 J4
Campo Grande, *Brazil*, 280 H4
Campos, *Brazil*, 280 K4
Canada, *North America, country*, 268 J3
Canadian, *U.S.A.*, 270 F3
Canakkale, *Turkey*, 317 H3
Canary Islands, *Atlantic Ocean*, 324 B3
Canaveral, Cape, *U.S.A.*, 271 K5
Canberra, *Australia, national capital*, 289 J7
Cancun, *Mexico*, 273 G3
Cangombe, *Angola*, 328 D2
Cannes, *France*, 315 F6
Cantabrian Mountains, *Spain*, 315 C6
Can Tho, *Vietnam*, 296 E6
Canton, *U.S.A.*, 271 H6
Cape Coast, *Ghana*, 325 E7
Cape Town, *South Africa, national capital*, 328 C6
Cape Verde, *Atlantic Ocean, country*, 325 L11
Cape York Peninsula, *Australia*, 288 H2
Cap-Haitien, *Haiti*, 273 K4
Caprivi Strip, *Namibia*, 328 D3
Caracas, *Venezuela, national capital*, 278 E1
Cardiff, *United Kingdom, internal capital*, 314 D4
Caribbean Sea, *North/South America*, 273 J4
Carlisle, *United Kingdom*, 314 D3
Carnarvon, *Australia*, 288 B4
Carnarvon, *South Africa*, 328 D6
Carnot, Cape, *Australia*, 288 G7
Caroline Islands, *Federated States of Micronesia*, 286 B4
Carpathian Mountains, *Europe*, 313 H7
Carpentaria, Gulf of, *Australia*, 288 G2
Carson City, *U.S.A., internal capital*, 270 C3
Cartagena, *Colombia*, 278 C1
Cartagena, *Spain*, 315 D7
Carthage, *Tunisia*, 322 D1
Cartwright, *Canada*, 269 P3
Caruaru, *Brazil*, 279 L5
Casablanca, *Morocco*, 324 D2
Cascade Range, *U.S.A.*, 270 B2
Cascais, *Portugal*, 315 B7
Cascavel, *Brazil*, 280 H4
Casper, *U.S.A.*, 270 E2
Caspian Depression, *Asia*, 302 F2
Caspian Sea, *Asia*, 311 G4
Castellon de la Plana, *Spain*, 315 D7
Castelo Branco, *Portugal*, 315 C7
Castries, *St. Lucia, national capital*, 272 M5
Catamarca, *Argentina*, 280 E5
Catania, *Italy*, 316 E4
Catanzaro, *Italy*, 316 F4
Cat Island, *The Bahamas*, 271 L6
Caucasus Mountains, *Asia/Europe*, 302 D3
Caxias do Sul, *Brazil*, 280 H5
Cayenne, *French Guiana, national capital*, 279 H3
Cayman Islands, *North America*, 273 H4
Cebu, *Philippines*, 297 H5
Cedar Lake *Canada*, 268 J3
Cedar Rapids, *U.S.A.*, 271 H2
Cedros Island, *Mexico*, 272 A2
Ceduna, *Australia*, 288 F6
Celaya, *Mexico*, 272 D3
Celebes, *Indonesia*, 295 F4

Celebes Sea, *Asia*, 297 H7
Celtic Sea, *Europe*, 314 C4
Central African Republic, *Africa, country*, 326 C2
Central Cordillera, *Peru*, 278 C5
Central Russian Uplands, *Russia*, 310 D3
Central Siberian Plateau, *Russia*, 305 F2
Central Sierras, *Spain*, 315 D6
Ceram, *Indonesia*, 295 G4
Ceram Sea, *Indonesia*, 295 G4
Cerro de Pasco, *Peru*, 278 C6
Cesis, *Latvia*, 313 H4
Ceske Budejovice, *Czech Republic*, 316 E1
Ceuta, *Africa*, 315 C8
Chacabuco, *Argentina*, 280 F6
Chad, *Africa, country*, 322 E5
Chad, Lake, *Africa*, 322 D6
Chala, *Peru*, 278 D7
Chalan Kanoa, *Northern Marianas*, 286 B3
Chalkida, *Greece*, 317 G4
Challapata, *Bolivia*, 280 E3
Chalon-sur-Saone, *France*, 315 F5
Chanaral, *Chile*, 280 D5
Chandigarh, *India*, 300 D4
Chandrapur, *India*, 301 D7
Changchun, *China*, 299 L2
Changde, *China*, 298 H5
Changhua, *Taiwan*, 299 K6
Chang Jiang, *China*, 299 J4
Changsha, *China*, 299 H5
Changzhi, *China*, 299 H3
Chania, *Greece*, 317 G5
Channel Islands, *Europe*, 314 D4
Channel Islands, *U.S.A.*, 270 C4
Chapaev, *Kazakhstan*, 311 G3
Charagua, *Bolivia*, 280 F3
Charleroi, *Belgium*, 314 F4
Charleston, *South Carolina, U.S.A.*, 271 L4
Charleston, *West Virginia, U.S.A., internal capital*, 271 K3
Charlotte, *U.S.A.*, 271 K3
Charlottesville, *U.S.A.*, 271 L3
Charlottetown, *Canada, internal capital*, 269 N4
Chatham Islands, *New Zealand*, 289 R8
Chattanooga, *U.S.A.*, 271 J3
Chavuma, *Zambia*, 328 D2
Chech Erg, *Africa*, 324 E3
Cheboksary, *Russia*, 311 F2
Cheju, *South Korea*, 299 L4
Chelyabinsk, *Russia*, 311 J2
Chemnitz, *Germany*, 314 H4
Chengdu, *China*, 298 F4
Chennai, *India*, 301 E8
Chenzhou, *China*, 299 H5
Cherbourg, *France*, 314 D4
Cherepovets, *Russia*, 310 D2
Cherkasy, *Ukraine*, 310 C4
Chernihiv, *Ukraine*, 310 C3
Chernivtsi, *Ukraine*, 313 H6
Chesterfield Islands, *New Caledonia*, 289 M3
Cheyenne, *U.S.A., internal capital*, 270 F2
Chiang Mai, *Thailand*, 296 C4
Chicago, *U.S.A.*, 271 J2
Chiclayo, *Peru*, 278 C5
Chico, *U.S.A.*, 270 B3
Chicoutimi, *Canada*, 269 M4
Chidley, Cape, *Canada*, 269 N2
Chifeng, *China*, 299 J2
Chigubo, *Mozambique*, 329 F4
Chihli, Gulf of, *China*, 299 J3
Chihuahua, *Mexico*, 272 C2
Chile, *South America, country*, 280 D6
Chillan, *Chile*, 281 D7
Chiloe Island, *Chile*, 281 C8
Chilung, *Taiwan*, 299 K5
Chilwa, Lake, *Africa*, 329 G3
Chimanimani, *Zimbabwe*, 329 F3
Chimbote, *Peru*, 278 C5
Chincha Alta, *Peru*, 278 C6
Chingola, *Zambia*, 328 E2
Chinhoyi, *Zimbabwe*, 328 F3
Chios, *Greece*, 317 H4
Chipata, *Zambia*, 329 F2

Chiredzi, *Zimbabwe*, 328 F4
Chisinau, *Moldova, national capital*, 313 J2
Chittagong, *Bangladesh*, 301 G6
Chongjin, *North Korea*, 299 L2
Chongju, *South Korea*, 299 L3
Chongqing, *China*, 298 G5
Chonos Archipelago, *Chile*, 281 C8
Chott el Jerid, *Tunisia*, 322 C2
Christchurch, *New Zealand*, 289 P8
Christmas Island, *Asia*, 294 C6
Chukchi Sea, *Arctic Ocean*, 332 B2
Chulucanas, *Peru*, 278 B5
Chumphon, *Thailand*, 296 C5
Churchill, *Canada*, 269 K3
Churchill Falls, *Canada*, 269 N3
Cienfuegos, *Cuba*, 273 H3
Cilacap, *Indonesia*, 294 C5
Cincinnati, *U.S.A.*, 271 K3
Ciudad Bolivar, *Venezuela*, 278 F2
Ciudad del Carmen, *Mexico*, 272 F4
Ciudad del Este, *Paraguay*, 280 H5
Ciudad Guayana, *Venezuela*, 278 F2
Ciudad Juarez, *Mexico*, 272 C1
Ciudad Obregon, *Mexico*, 272 C2
Ciudad Real, *Spain*, 315 D7
Ciudad Victoria, *Mexico*, 272 E3
Clark Hill Lake, *U.S.A.*, 271 K4
Clermont-Ferrand, *France*, 315 E5
Cleveland, *U.S.A.*, 271 K2
Cluj-Napoca, *Romania*, 317 G2
Coast Mountains, *Canada*, 268 F3
Coast Ranges, *U.S.A.*, 270 B2
Coats Land, *Antarctica*, 333 A3
Coatzacoalcos, *Mexico*, 272 F4
Cobija, *Bolivia*, 280 E2
Cochabamba, *Bolivia*, 280 E3
Cochin, *India*, 301 D9
Cocos Island, *Costa Rica*, 273 G6
Cod, Cape, *U.S.A.*, 271 N2
Coeur d'Alene, *U.S.A.*, 270 C1
Coiba Island, *Panama*, 273 H6
Coihaique, *Chile*, 281 D9
Coimbatore, *India*, 301 D8
Coimbra, *Portugal*, 315 B6
Colima, *Mexico*, 272 D4
Cologne, *Germany*, 314 F4
Colombia, *South America, country*, 278 D3
Colombo, *Sri Lanka, national capital*, 301 D9
Colon, *Panama*, 273 J6
Colorado, *Argentina*, 281 F7
Colorado, *U.S.A.*, 270 D4
Colorado, *U.S.A., internal admin. area*, 270 E3
Colorado Plateau, *U.S.A.*, 270 D3
Colorado Springs, *U.S.A.*, 270 F3
Columbia, *U.S.A.*, 270 C1
Columbia, *U.S.A., internal capital*, 271 K4
Columbine, Cape, *South Africa*, 328 C6
Columbus, *U.S.A., internal capital*, 271 K3
Colwyn Bay, *United Kingdom*, 314 D3
Communism Peak, *Tajikistan*, 300 C3
Como, Lake, *Italy*, 316 D2
Comodoro Rivadavia, *Argentina*, 281 E9
Comoros, *Africa, country*, 329 H2
Conakry, *Guinea, national capital*, 325 C7
Concepcion, *Bolivia*, 280 F3
Concepcion, *Chile*, 281 D7
Concepcion, *Paraguay*, 280 G4
Concord, *U.S.A., internal capital*, 271 M2
Concordia, *Argentina*, 280 G6
Congo, *Africa*, 326 C4
Congo, *Africa, country*, 326 C4
Congo, Democratic Republic of, *Africa, country*, 326 D4
Connecticut, *U.S.A., internal admin. area*, 271 M2
Con Son, *Vietnam*, 296 E6
Constanta, *Romania*, 317 J2
Constantine, *Algeria*, 324 G1
Cook Islands, *Oceania*, 286 G7
Cook, Mount, *New Zealand*, 289 P8
Cook Strait, *New Zealand*, 289 P8
Copenhagen, *Denmark, national capital*, 313 E5
Copiapo, *Chile*, 280 D5

Coquimbo, *Chile*, 280 D5
Coral Sea, *Oceania*, 289 K2
Coral Sea Islands Territory, *Oceania, dependency*, 289 K3
Cordoba, *Argentina*, 280 F6
Cordoba, *Spain*, 315 C7
Corfu, *Greece*, 317 F4
Cork, *Ireland*, 314 B4
Corner Brook, *Canada*, 269 P4
Coro, *Venezuela*, 278 E1
Coropuna, Mount, *Peru*, 278 D6
Corpus Christi, *U.S.A.*, 270 G5
Corrientes, *Argentina*, 280 G5
Corsica, *France*, 315 C4
Corum, *Turkey*, 317 K3
Corumba, *Brazil*, 280 G3
Cosenza, *Italy*, 316 F4
Cosmoledo Group, *Seychelles*, 329 J1
Costa Rica, *North America, country*, 273 G6
Cotonou, *Benin*, 325 F7
Cottbus, *Germany*, 314 H4
Cradock, *South Africa*, 328 E6
Craiova, *Romania*, 317 G2
Cravo Norte, *Colombia*, 278 D2
Crete, *Greece*, 317 H5
Criciuma, *Brazil*, 280 J5
Crimea, *Ukraine*, 317 K2
Cristobal Colon, *Colombia*, 278 D1
Croatia, *Europe, country*, 316 F2
Cruzeiro do Sul, *Brazil*, 278 D5
Cuamba, *Mozambique*, 329 G2
Cuangar, *Angola*, 328 C3
Cuango, *Africa*, 328 C1
Cuanza, *Angola*, 328 C2
Cuba, *North America, country*, 273 J3
Cucuta, *Colombia*, 278 D2
Cuenca, *Ecuador*, 278 C4
Cuiaba, *Brazil*, 280 G3
Culiacan, *Mexico*, 272 C3
Cumana, *Venezuela*, 278 F1
Cumberland Peninsula, *Canada*, 269 N2
Cunene, *Africa*, 328 C3
Curitiba, *Brazil*, 280 J5
Cusco, *Peru*, 278 D6
Cuttack, *India*, 301 F6
Cuxhaven, *Germany*, 314 G3
Cyclades, *Greece*, 317 H4
Cyprus, *Asia, country*, 317 J5
Cyrene, *Libya*, 322 F2
Czech Republic, *Europe, country*, 316 E1
Czestochowa, *Poland*, 313 F6

d

Dabeiba, *Colombia*, 278 C2
Dagupan, *Philippines*, 297 H4
Dahlak Archipelago, *Eritrea*, 323 K5
Dakar, *Senegal, national capital*, 325 B6
Dal, *Sweden*, 312 F3
Da Lat, *Vietnam*, 296 E5
Dali, *China*, 298 F5
Dalian, *China*, 299 K3
Dallas, *U.S.A.*, 271 G4
Daloa, *Ivory Coast*, 325 D7
Damascus, *Syria, national capital*, 302 C5
Damavand, *Iran*, 302 F4
Damongo, *Ghana*, 325 E7
Da Nang, *Vietnam*, 296 E4
Dandong, *China*, 299 K2
Danube, *Europe*, 313 F7
Danube, Mouths of the, *Europe*, 317 J2
Daqing, *China*, 299 L1
Darbhanga, *India*, 300 F5
Dar es Salaam, *Tanzania, national capital*, 327 G5
Darien, Gulf of, *Colombia*, 278 C2
Darjeeling, *India*, 300 F5
Darling, *Australia*, 288 H6
Darnah, *Libya*, 322 F2
Darwin, *Australia, internal capital*, 288 F2
Darwin, Mount, *Zimbabwe*, 328 F3
Dasht-e Kavir, *Iran*, 302 F5
Dasoguz, *Turkmenistan*, 302 G3
Datong, *China*, 299 H2
Daugavpils, *Latvia*, 313 H5
Davangere, *India*, 301 D8

Davao, *Philippines*, 297 J6
David, *Panama*, 273 H6
Davis Strait, *Canada*, 269 P2
Dawson, *Canada*, 268 F2
Dayr az Zawr, *Syria*, 302 D4
Daytona Beach, *U.S.A.*, 271 K5
De Aar, *South Africa*, 328 D6
Dease Lake, *Canada*, 268 G3
Death Valley, *U.S.A.*, 270 C3
Debrecen, *Hungary*, 313 G7
Debre Zeyit, *Ethiopia*, 327 G2
Deccan Plateau, *India*, 301 D7
Delgado, Cape, *Mozambique*, 329 H2
Delhi, *India*, 300 D5
Del Rio, *U.S.A.*, 270 F5
Delaware, *U.S.A., internal admin. area*, 271 L3
Democratic Republic of Congo, *Africa, country*, 326 D4
Denizli, *Turkey*, 317 J4
Denmark, *Europe, country*, 313 D5
Denpasar, *Indonesia*, 294 E5
D'Entrecasteaux Islands, *Papua New Guinea*, 295 M5
Denver, *U.S.A., internal capital*, 270 E3
Dera Ghazi Khan, *Pakistan*, 300 C4
Derbent, *Russia*, 302 E3
Des Moines, *U.S.A., internal capital*, 271 H2
Desna, *Europe*, 310 C3
Detroit, *U.S.A.*, 271 K2
Devon Island, *Canada*, 269 L1
Devonport, *Australia*, 288 J8
Dhaka, *Bangladesh, national capital*, 301 G6
Dhamar, *Yemen*, 303 D9
Dhule, *India*, 301 C6
Dibrugarh, *India*, 300 G5
Dijon, *France*, 315 F5
Dikhil, *Djibouti*, 323 K6
Dili, *East Timor, national capital*, 295 G5
Dilolo, *Democratic Republic of Congo*, 326 D6
Dinaric Alps, *Europe*, 316 E2
Dire Dawa, *Ethiopia*, 327 H2
Divo, *Ivory Coast*, 325 D7
Diyarbakir, *Turkey*, 302 D4
Djado Plateau, *Africa*, 322 D4
Djambala, *Congo*, 326 B4
Djelfa, *Algeria*, 324 F2
Djema, *Central African Republic*, 326 E2
Djemila, *Algeria*, 324 G1
Djibouti, *Africa, country*, 323 K6
Djibouti, *Djibouti, national capital*, 323 K6
Djougou, *Benin*, 325 F7
Dnieper, *Europe*, 310 C4
Dniester, *Europe*, 313 H6
Dniprodzerzhynsk, *Ukraine*, 310 C4
Dnipropetrovsk, *Ukraine*, 310 D4
Doba, *Chad*, 326 C2
Dobrich, *Bulgaria*, 317 H3
Dodecanese, *Greece*, 317 H4
Dodoma, *Tanzania, national capital*, 327 G5
Doha, *Qatar, national capital*, 303 F6
Dolak, *Indonesia*, 295 J5
Dolores, *Argentina*, 281 G7
Dominica, *North America, country*, 272 M4
Dominican Republic, *North America, country*, 273 L3
Don, *Russia*, 310 E4
Dondo, *Angola*, 328 B1
Dondo, *Mozambique*, 329 F4
Donets, *Europe*, 310 D4
Donetsk, *Ukraine*, 310 D4
Dongting Lake, *China*, 299 H5
Dori, *Burkina Faso*, 325 E6
Dosso, *Niger*, 325 F6
Douala, *Cameroon*, 326 A3
Douglas, *South Africa*, 328 D5
Dourados, *Brazil*, 280 H4
Douro, *Europe*, 315 C6
Dover, *United Kingdom*, 314 E4
Dover, *U.S.A., internal capital*, 271 L3

Dover, Strait of, *Europe*, 314 E4
Drakensberg, *South Africa*, 328 E6
Drake Passage, *South America*, 281 E11
Drammen, *Norway*, 312 D4
Dresden, *Germany*, 314 H4
Drobeta-Turnu Severin, *Romania*, 317 G2
Dryden, *Canada*, 269 K4
Dubai, *United Arab Emirates*, 303 G6
Dubawnt Lake, *Canada*, 268 J2
Dubbo, *Australia*, 289 J6
Dublin, *Ireland, national capital*, 314 C3
Dubrovnik, *Croatia*, 317 F3
Duisburg, *Germany*, 314 F4
Duitama, *Colombia*, 278 D2
Duluth, *U.S.A.*, 271 H1
Dumaguete, *Philippines*, 297 H6
Dundee, *United Kingdom*, 314 D2
Dunedin, *New Zealand*, 289 P9
Durango, *Mexico*, 272 D3
Durazno, *Uruguay*, 280 G6
Durban, *South Africa*, 328 F5
Durres, *Albania*, 317 F3
Dushanbe, *Tajikistan, national capital*, 300 B3
Dusseldorf, *Germany*, 314 F4
Dzhankoy, *Ukraine*, 317 K2
Dzungarian Basin, *China*, 300 F1

e

East Antarctica, *Antarctica*, 333 E3
East Cape, *New Zealand*, 289 Q7
East China Sea, *Asia*, 299 K5
Easter Island, *Pacific Ocean*, 287 N7
Eastern Cordillera, *Colombia*, 278 D3
Eastern Cordillera, *Peru*, 278 D6
Eastern Ghats, *India*, 301 D8
Eastern Sierra Madre, *Mexico*, 272 D2
East Falkland, *Falkland Islands*, 281 G10
East London, *South Africa*, 328 E6
East Siberian Sea, *Russia*, 305 J2
East Timor, *Asia, country*, 295 G5
Ebolowa, *Cameroon*, 326 B3
Ebro, *Spain*, 315 D6
Ecuador, *South America, country*, 278 B4
Edinburgh, *United Kingdom, internal capital*, 314 D2
Edirne, *Turkey*, 317 H3
Edmonton, *Canada, internal capital*, 268 H3
Edmundston, *Canada*, 269 N4
Edward, Lake, *Africa*, 326 E4
Edwards Plateau, *U.S.A.*, 270 F4
Efate, *Vanuatu*, 289 N3
Egypt, *Africa, country*, 323 G3
Eindhoven, *Netherlands*, 314 F4
Elat, *Israel*, 303 B6
Elazig, *Turkey*, 302 C4
Elba, *Italy*, 316 D3
Elbasan, *Albania*, 317 G3
Elbe, *Europe*, 314 G3
Elbrus, Mount, *Russia*, 302 D3
Elche, *Spain*, 315 D7
Eldorado, *Argentina*, 280 H5
Eldoret, *Kenya*, 327 G3
Elephant Island, *Atlantic Ocean*, 281 H12
Eleuthera, *The Bahamas*, 271 L5
El Fasher, *Sudan*, 323 G6
Elgon, Mount, *Uganda*, 327 F3
El Hierro, *Canary Islands*, 324 B3
Elista, *Russia*, 302 D2
El Jadida, *Morocco*, 324 D2
El Jem, *Tunisia*, 322 D1
Ellesmere Island, *Canada*, 332 R3
Ellsworth Land, *Antarctica*, 333 R3
El Mansura, *Egypt*, 323 H2
El Minya, *Egypt*, 323 H3
El Obeid, *Sudan*, 323 H6
El Oued, *Algeria*, 324 G2
El Paso, *U.S.A.*, 270 E4
El Salvador, *North America, country*, 272 G5

Enderby Land, *Antarctica*, 333 E3
Engels, *Russia*, 311 F3
England, *United Kingdom, internal admin. area*, 314 D3
English Channel, *Europe*, 314 D4
Ennedi Plateau, *Africa*, 322 F5
Enschede, *Netherlands*, 314 F3
Entebbe, *Uganda*, 327 F3
Enugu, *Nigeria*, 325 G7
Ephesus, *Turkey*, 317 H4
Equatorial Guinea, *Africa, country*, 326 A3
Erenhot, *China*, 298 H2
Erfurt, *Germany*, 314 G4
Erie, *U.S.A.*, 271 K2
Erie, Lake, *U.S.A.*, 271 K2
Eritrea, *Africa, country*, 323 J5
Er Rachidia, *Morocco*, 324 E2
Ershovka, *Kazakhstan*, 311 K3
Erzurum, *Turkey*, 302 D4
Esbjerg, *Denmark*, 313 D5
Esfahan, *Iran*, 302 F5
Eskilstuna, *Sweden*, 312 F4
Eskisehir, *Turkey*, 317 J4
Esmeraldas, *Ecuador*, 278 C3
Esperance, *Australia*, 288 D6
Espinosa, *Brazil*, 280 K2
Espiritu Santo, *Vanuatu*, 289 N3
Espoo, *Finland*, 312 H3
Espungabera, *Mozambique*, 329 F4
Esquel, *Argentina*, 281 D8
Essaouira, *Morocco*, 324 D2
Es Semara, *Western Sahara*, 324 C3
Essen, *Germany*, 314 F4
Estevan, *Canada*, 268 J4
Estonia, *Europe, country*, 312 H4
Ethiopia, *Africa, country*, 327 G2
Ethiopian Highlands, *Ethiopia*, 327 G1
Etna, Mount, *Italy*, 316 E4
Etosha Pan, *Namibia*, 328 C3
Euboea, *Greece*, 317 G4
Eugene, *U.S.A.*, 270 B2
Eugenia, Point, *Mexico*, 272 A2
Euphrates, *Asia*, 303 E5
Europa Island, *Africa*, 329 H4
Europe, 263
Evansville, *U.S.A.*, 271 J3
Everest, Mount, *Asia*, 300 F5
Everglades, The, *U.S.A.*, 271 K5
Evora, *Portugal*, 315 C7
Evry, *France*, 314 E4
Exeter, *United Kingdom*, 314 D4
Eyl, *Somalia*, 327 J2
Eyre, Lake, *Australia*, 288 G5

f

Fada-Ngourma, *Burkina Faso*, 325 F6
Fairbanks, *U.S.A.*, 268 E2
Faisalabad, *Pakistan*, 300 C4
Fakfak, *Indonesia*, 295 H4
Falkland Islands, *Atlantic Ocean*, 281 F10
Farasan Islands, *Saudi Arabia*, 303 D8
Farewell, Cape, *New Zealand*, 289 P8
Fargo, *U.S.A.*, 271 G1
Fargona, *Uzbekistan*, 300 C2
Farmington, *U.S.A.*, 270 E3
Faro, *Portugal*, 315 C7
Farquhar Group, *Seychelles*, 329 K1
Faxafloi, *Iceland*, 312 N2
Faya-Largeau, *Chad*, 322 E5
Federated States of Micronesia, *Oceania, country*, 286 C4
Feira de Santana, *Brazil*, 280 L2
Feodosiya, *Ukraine*, 317 K2
Fernandina, *Ecuador*, 278 N10
Ferrara, *Italy*, 316 D2
Fes, *Morocco*, 324 E2
Fianarantsoa, *Madagascar*, 329 J4
Fiji, *Oceania, country*, 289 Q3
Finland, *Europe, country*, 312 H2
Finland, Gulf of, *Europe*, 312 H4
Flagstaff, *U.S.A.*, 270 D3
Flensburg, *Germany*, 314 G3
Flinders Island, *Australia*, 289 J7
Flin Flon, *Canada*, 268 J3
Florence, *Italy*, 316 D3

Himalayas, *Asia*, 300 E4
Hindu Kush, *Asia*, 300 B3
Hinton, *Canada*, 268 H3
Hiroshima, *Japan*, 299 M4
Hispaniola, *North America*, 273 K4
Hitra, *Norway*, 312 D3
Hobart, *Australia, internal capital*, 288 J8
Ho Chi Minh City, *Vietnam*, 296 E5
Hohhot, *China*, 298 H2
Hokkaido, *Japan*, 299 P2
Holguin, *Cuba*, 273 J3
Homs, *Syria*, 302 C5
Homyel, *Belarus*, 313 J5
Honduras, *North America, country*, 273 G4
Honduras, Gulf of, *North America*, 273 G4
Honefoss, *Norway*, 312 D3
Hong Kong, *China*, 299 H6
Honiara, *Solomon Islands, national capital*, 286 D5
Honolulu, *U.S.A., internal capital*, 271 P7
Honshu, *Japan*, 299 N3
Horlivka, *Ukraine*, 310 D4
Hormuz, Strait of, *Asia*, 303 G6
Horn, Cape, *Chile*, 281 D11
Horn Lake, *Sweden*, 312 F2
Hotan, *China*, 300 D3
Hotazel, *South Africa*, 328 D5
Houston, *U.S.A.*, 271 G5
Hradec Kralove, *Czech Republic*, 316 E1
Hrodna, *Belarus*, 313 G5
Huacrachuco, *Peru*, 278 C5
Huaihua, *China*, 298 H5
Huambo, *Angola*, 328 C2
Huancayo, *Peru*, 278 C6
Huang He, *China*, 299 H3
Huanuco, *Peru*, 278 C5
Huascaran, Mount, *Peru*, 278 C5
Hubli, *India*, 301 D7
Hudiksvall, *Sweden*, 312 F3
Hudson Bay, *Canada*, 269 L3
Hudson Strait, *Canada*, 269 M2
Hue, *Vietnam*, 296 E4
Huelva, *Spain*, 315 C7
Hull, *United Kingdom*, 314 D3
Hulun Lake, *China*, 299 J1
Hungary, *Europe, country*, 313 F7
Huntsville, *Canada*, 269 M4
Huntsville, *U.S.A.*, 271 J4
Hurghada, *Egypt*, 323 H3
Huron, Lake, *U.S.A.*, 271 K2
Hvannadalshnukur, *Iceland*, 312 P2
Hwange, *Zimbabwe*, 328 E3
Hyderabad, *India*, 301 D7
Hyderabad, *Pakistan*, 300 B5
Hyesan, *North Korea*, 299 L2

i
Iasi, *Romania*, 317 H2
Ibadan, *Nigeria*, 325 F7
Ibague, *Colombia*, 278 C3
Ibarra, *Ecuador*, 278 C3
Ibb, *Yemen*, 303 D9
Iberian Mountains, *Spain*, 315 D6
Ibiza, *Spain*, 315 E7
Ica, *Peru*, 278 C6
Iceland, *Europe, country*, 312 P2
Idaho, *U.S.A., internal admin. area*, 270 C2
Idaho Falls, *U.S.A.*, 270 D2
Ierapetra, *Greece*, 317 H5
Iguacu Falls, *South America*, 280 H5
Ihosy, *Madagascar*, 329 J4
Ikopa, *Madagascar*, 329 J3
Ilagan, *Philippines*, 297 H4
Ilebo, *Democratic Republic of Congo*, 326 D4
Ilheus, *Brazil*, 280 L2
Iliamna Lake, *U.S.A.*, 268 D2
Iligan, *Philippines*, 297 H6
Illapel, *Chile*, 280 D6
Illimani, Mount, *Bolivia*, 280 E3
Illinois, *U.S.A., internal admin. area*, 271 J2
Illizi, *Algeria*, 324 G3
Ilmen, Lake, *Russia*, 312 J4
Iloilo, *Philippines*, 297 H5
Ilonga, *Tanzania*, 327 G5
Ilorin, *Nigeria*, 325 F7

Imperatriz, *Brazil*, 279 J5
Imphal, *India*, 301 G6
Inari, Lake, *Finland*, 312 H1
Inchon, *South Korea*, 299 L3
Indals, *Sweden*, 312 E3
Inderbor, *Kazakhstan*, 311 G4
India, *Asia, country*, 301 D6
Indiana, *U.S.A., internal admin. area*, 271 J2
Indianapolis, *U.S.A., internal capital*, 271 J3
Indore, *India*, 301 D6
Indus, *Asia*, 300 B5
Ingolstadt, *Germany*, 314 G4
Inhambane, *Mozambique*, 329 G4
Inner Mongolia, *China*, 299 H2
Innsbruck, *Austria*, 316 D2
Inukjuak, *Canada*, 269 M3
Inuvik, *Canada*, 268 F2
Invercargill, *New Zealand*, 289 N9
Inyangani, *Zimbabwe*, 329 F3
Ioannina, *Greece*, 317 G4
Ionian Sea, *Europe*, 317 F4
Iowa, *U.S.A., internal admin. area*, 271 H2
Ipiales, *Colombia*, 278 C3
Ipoh, *Malaysia*, 294 B3
Ipswich, *United Kingdom*, 314 E3
Iqaluit, *Canada, internal capital*, 269 N2
Iquique, *Chile*, 280 D4
Iquitos, *Peru*, 278 D4
Iran, *Asia, country*, 302 F5
Iranshahr, *Iran*, 303 H6
Iraq, *Asia, country*, 302 D5
Irbid, *Jordan*, 302 C5
Ireland, *Europe, country*, 314 B3
Iringa, *Tanzania*, 327 G5
Irish Sea, *Europe*, 314 C3
Irkutsk, *Russia*, 305 F3
Irrawaddy, *Burma*, 296 C4
Irrawaddy, Mouths of the, *Burma*, 296 B4
Irtysh, *Asia*, 304 D3
Isabela, *Ecuador*, 278 N10
Isafjordhur, *Iceland*, 312 N2
Isiro, *Democratic Republic of Congo*, 326 E3
Islamabad, *Pakistan, national capital*, 300 C4
Isle of Man, *Europe*, 314 C3
Isle of Wight, *United Kingdom*, 314 D4
Ismailia, *Egypt*, 323 H2
Isoka, *Zambia*, 329 F2
Isparta, *Turkey*, 317 J4
Israel, *Asia, country*, 303 B5
Issyk, Lake, *Kyrgyzstan*, 300 D2
Istanbul, *Turkey*, 317 J3
Itaituba, *Brazil*, 279 G4
Itajai, *Brazil*, 280 J5
Italy, *Europe, country*, 316 D2
Itapetininga, *Brazil*, 280 J4
Ivano-Frankivsk, *Ukraine*, 313 H6
Ivanovo, *Russia*, 310 E2
Ivdel, *Russia*, 311 J1
Ivory Coast, *Africa, country*, 325 D7
Ivujivik, *Canada*, 269 M2
Izhevsk, *Russia*, 311 G2
Izmir, *Turkey*, 317 H4

j
Jabalpur, *India*, 301 D6
Jackson, Mississippi, *U.S.A., internal capital*, 271 H4
Jackson, Tennessee, *U.S.A.*, 271 J3
Jacksonville, *U.S.A.*, 271 K4
Jaen, *Spain*, 315 D7
Jaffna, *Sri Lanka*, 301 E9
Jaipur, *India*, 300 D5
Jakarta, *Indonesia, national capital*, 294 C5
Jalalabad, *Afghanistan*, 300 C4
Jalal-Abad, *Kyrgyzstan*, 300 C2
Jamaica, *North America, country*, 273 J4
Jambi, *Indonesia*, 294 B4
James Bay, *Canada*, 269 L3
Jamestown, *U.S.A.*, 271 L2

Jammu, *India*, 300 C4
Jammu and Kashmir, *Asia*, 300 D4
Jamnagar, *India*, 301 C6
Jamshedpur, *India*, 301 F6
Japan, *Asia, country*, 299 N3
Japan, Sea of, *Asia*, 299 M2
Japura, *Brazil*, 278 E4
Jatai, *Brazil*, 280 H3
Java, *Indonesia*, 294 C5
Java Sea, *Indonesia*, 294 C5
Jayapura, *Indonesia*, 295 K4
Jedda, *Saudi Arabia*, 303 C7
Jefferson City, *U.S.A., internal capital*, 271 H3
Jekabpils, *Latvia*, 313 H4
Jelgava, *Latvia*, 313 G4
Jember, *Indonesia*, 294 D5
Jerba, *Tunisia*, 322 D2
Jerez de la Frontera, *Spain*, 315 C7
Jerusalem, *Israel, national capital*, 303 C5
Jhansi, *India*, 300 D5
Jiamusi, *China*, 299 M1
Jilin, *China*, 299 L2
Jima, *Ethiopia*, 327 G2
Jinhua, *China*, 299 J5
Jining, *China*, 299 J3
Jinja, *Uganda*, 327 F3
Jinzhou, *China*, 299 K2
Jixi, *China*, 299 M1
Jizzax, *Uzbekistan*, 300 B2
Joao Pessoa, *Brazil*, 279 M5
Jodhpur, *India*, 300 C5
Johannesburg, *South Africa*, 328 E5
Johnston Atoll, *Oceania*, 286 G3
Johor Bahru, *Malaysia*, 294 B3
Jolo, *Philippines*, 297 H6
Jonesboro, *U.S.A.*, 271 H3
Jonkoping, *Sweden*, 313 E4
Jordan, *Asia, country*, 303 C5
Jorhat, *India*, 300 G5
Jos, *Nigeria*, 326 A2
Juan de Nova, *Africa*, 329 H3
Juazeiro, *Brazil*, 279 K5
Juazeiro do Norte, *Brazil*, 279 L5
Juba, *Africa*, 327 H3
Juba, *Sudan*, 327 F3
Juchitan, *Mexico*, 272 E4
Juiz de Fora, *Brazil*, 280 K4
Juliaca, *Peru*, 278 D7
Juneau, *U.S.A., internal capital*, 268 F3
Jurmala, *Latvia*, 313 G4
Jurua, *Brazil*, 278 E5
Jutland, *Europe*, 313 D4
Jyvaskyla, *Finland*, 312 H3

k
K2, *Asia*, 300 D3
Kaamanen, *Finland*, 312 H1
Kabinda, *Democratic Republic of Congo*, 326 D5
Kabul, *Afghanistan, national capital*, 300 B4
Kabunda, *Democratic Republic of Congo*, 326 E6
Kabwe, *Zambia*, 328 E2
Kadoma, *Zimbabwe*, 328 E3
Kaduna, *Nigeria*, 325 G6
Kaedi, *Mauritania*, 325 C5
Kafakumba, *Democratic Republic of Congo*, 326 D5
Kafue, *Zambia*, 328 E3
Kagoshima, *Japan*, 299 M4
Kahramanmaras, *Turkey*, 302 C4
Kahului, *U.S.A.*, 271 P7
Kainji Reservoir, *Nigeria*, 325 F6
Kairouan, *Tunisia*, 322 D1
Kajaani, *Finland*, 312 H2
Kakhovske Reservoir, *Ukraine*, 310 C4
Kalahari Desert, *Africa*, 328 D4
Kalamata, *Greece*, 317 G4
Kalemie, *Democratic Republic of Congo*, 326 E5
Kalgoorlie, *Australia*, 288 D6
Kaliningrad, *Russia*, 313 G5
Kalisz, *Poland*, 313 F6
Kalkrand, *Namibia*, 328 C4

Kalmar, *Sweden*, 313 F4
Kaluga, *Russia*, 310 D3
Kamanjab, *Namibia*, 328 B3
Kama Reservoir, *Russia*, 311 H2
Kamativi, *Zimbabwe*, 328 E3
Kamchatka Peninsula, *Russia*, 305 H3
Kamenka, *Russia*, 310 F3
Kamina, *Democratic Republic of Congo*, 326 E5
Kamloops, *Canada*, 268 G3
Kampala, *Uganda, national capital*, 327 F3
Kampong Cham, *Cambodia*, 296 E5
Kampong Chhnang, *Cambodia*, 296 D5
Kampong Saom, *Cambodia*, 296 D5
Kamyanets-Podilskyy, *Ukraine*, 313 H6
Kamyshin, *Russia*, 310 F3
Kananga, *Democratic Republic of Congo*, 326 D5
Kanazawa, *Japan*, 299 N3
Kandahar, *Afghanistan*, 300 B4
Kandalaksha, *Russia*, 312 K2
Kandi, *Benin*, 325 F6
Kandy, *Sri Lanka*, 301 E9
Kang, *Botswana*, 328 D4
Kangaroo Island, *Australia*, 288 G7
Kanggye, *North Korea*, 299 L2
Kankan, *Guinea*, 325 D6
Kano, *Nigeria*, 322 C6
Kanpur, *India*, 300 E5
Kansas, *U.S.A., internal admin. area*, 270 G3
Kansas City, *U.S.A.*, 271 H3
Kanye, *Botswana*, 328 E4
Kaohsiung, *Taiwan*, 299 K6
Kaolack, *Senegal*, 325 B6
Kara-Balta, *Kyrgyzstan*, 300 C2
Karabuk, *Turkey*, 317 K3
Karachi, *Pakistan*, 301 B6
Karaj, *Iran*, 302 F4
Karakol, *Kyrgyzstan*, 300 D2
Karakorum Range, *Asia*, 300 D3
Kara Kum Desert, *Turkmenistan*, 302 G3
Karaman, *Turkey*, 317 K4
Karamay, *China*, 300 E1
Kara Sea, *Russia*, 304 D2
Kariba, *Zimbabwe*, 328 E3
Kariba, Lake, *Africa*, 328 E3
Karibib, *Namibia*, 328 C4
Karimata Strait, *Indonesia*, 294 C4
Karlovac, *Croatia*, 316 E2
Karlovy Vary, *Czech Republic*, 316 E1
Karlshamn, *Sweden*, 313 E4
Karlsruhe, *Germany*, 314 G4
Karlstad, *Sweden*, 312 E4
Karmoy, *Norway*, 312 C4
Karonga, *Malawi*, 329 F1
Karora, *Eritrea*, 323 J5
Karpathos, *Greece*, 317 H5
Karratha, *Australia*, 288 C4
Kasai, *Africa*, 326 C4
Kasama, *Zambia*, 328 F2
Kashi, *China*, 300 D3
Kassala, *Sudan*, 323 J5
Kassel, *Germany*, 314 G4
Kasungu, *Malawi*, 329 F2
Kataba, *Zambia*, 328 E2
Kathmandu, *Nepal, national capital*, 300 F5
Katiola, *Ivory Coast*, 325 D7
Katowice, *Poland*, 313 F6
Katsina, *Nigeria*, 325 G6
Kattegat, *Europe*, 313 D4
Kauai, *U.S.A.*, 271 P7
Kaukau Veld, *Africa*, 328 C4
Kaunas, *Lithuania*, 313 G5
Kavala, *Greece*, 317 H3
Kawambwa, *Zambia*, 328 E1
Kayes, *Mali*, 325 C6
Kayseri, *Turkey*, 302 C4
Kazakhstan, *Asia, country*, 304 C3
Kazan, *Russia*, 311 F2
Kaztalovka, *Kazakhstan*, 311 F4
Kebnekaise, *Sweden*, 312 F2
Kecskemet, *Hungary*, 313 F7
Kedougou, *Senegal*, 325 C6
Keetmanshoop, *Namibia*, 328 C5

Kefallonia, *Greece,* 317 F4
Keflavik, *Iceland,* 312 N2
Kelowna, *Canada,* 268 H4
Kempten, *Germany,* 314 G5
Kendari, *Indonesia,* 295 F4
Kenema, *Sierra Leone,* 325 C7
Kenhardt, *South Africa,* 328 D5
Kenitra, *Morocco,* 324 D2
Kenora, *Canada,* 269 K4
Kentucky, *U.S.A., internal admin. area,* 271 J3
Kentucky Lake, *U.S.A.,* 271 J3
Kenya, *Africa, country,* 327 G3
Kenya, Mount, *Kenya,* 327 G4
Kerch, *Ukraine,* 317 L2
Kerema, *Papua New Guinea,* 295 L5
Keren, *Eritrea,* 323 J5
Kerkenah Islands, *Tunisia,* 322 D2
Kermadec Islands, *New Zealand,* 289 Q6
Kerman, *Iran,* 303 G5
Kermanshah, *Iran,* 302 E5
Key West, *U.S.A.,* 271 K6
Khabarovsk, *Russia,* 305 G3
Khanka, Lake, *Asia,* 299 M2
Kharkiv, *Ukraine,* 310 D3
Khartoum, *Sudan, national capital,* 323 H5
Kherson, *Ukraine,* 310 C4
Khmelnytskyy, *Ukraine,* 313 H6
Khon Kaen, *Thailand,* 296 D4
Khorugh, *Tajikistan,* 300 C3
Khouribga, *Morocco,* 324 D2
Khujand, *Tajikistan,* 300 B2
Khulna, *Bangladesh,* 301 F6
Kidal, *Mali,* 324 F5
Kiel, *Germany,* 314 G3
Kielce, *Poland,* 313 G6
Kiev, *Ukraine, national capital,* 313 J6
Kievske Reservoir, *Ukraine,* 310 C3
Kiffa, *Mauritania,* 325 C5
Kigali, *Rwanda, national capital,* 327 F4
Kigoma, *Tanzania,* 326 E4
Kikwit, *Democratic Republic of Congo,* 326 C5
Kilimanjaro, *Africa,* 327 G4
Kilwa, *Democratic Republic of Congo,* 326 E5
Kimberley, *South Africa,* 328 D5
Kimberley Plateau, *Australia,* 288 E3
Kimchaek, *North Korea,* 299 L2
Kindia, *Guinea,* 325 C6
Kindu, *Democratic Republic of Congo,* 326 E4
Kineshma, *Russia,* 310 E2
King George Island, *Atlantic Ocean,* 281 G12
Kingisepp, *Russia,* 312 J4
King Island, *Australia,* 288 H7
Kings Peak, *U.S.A.,* 270 D2
Kingston, *Canada,* 269 M4
Kingston, *Jamaica, national capital,* 273 J4
Kingstown, *St. Vincent and the Grenadines, national capital,* 272 M5
King William Island, *Canada,* 269 K2
Kinkala, *Congo,* 326 B4
Kinshasa, *Democratic Republic of Congo, national capital,* 326 C4
Kipushi, *Democratic Republic of Congo,* 326 E6
Kiribati, *Oceania, country,* 286 F5
Kirikkale, *Turkey,* 317 K4
Kirinyaga, *Kenya,* 327 G4
Kirishi, *Russia,* 312 K4
Kirkenes, *Norway,* 312 J1
Kirkland Lake, *Canada,* 269 L4
Kirkuk, *Iraq,* 302 D4
Kirkwall, *United Kingdom,* 314 D2
Kirov, *Russia,* 311 F2
Kirovohrad, *Ukraine,* 310 C4
Kiruna, *Sweden,* 312 G2
Kisangani, *Democratic Republic of Congo,* 326 E3
Kisii, *Kenya,* 327 F4
Kismaayo, *Somalia,* 327 H4
Kisumu, *Kenya,* 327 F4
Kita, *Mali,* 325 D6

Kitakyushu, *Japan,* 299 M4
Kitale, *Kenya,* 327 G3
Kitwe, *Zambia,* 328 E2
Kiuruvesi, *Finland,* 312 H3
Kivu, Lake, *Africa,* 326 E4
Klagenfurt, *Austria,* 316 E2
Klaipeda, *Lithuania,* 313 G5
Klar, *Europe,* 312 E3
Klintsy, *Russia,* 313 K5
Knittelfeld, *Austria,* 316 E2
Knoxville, *U.S.A.,* 271 K3
Kobar Sink, *Ethiopia,* 323 K6
Koblenz, *Germany,* 314 F4
Kochi, *India,* 301 D9
Kodiak Island, *U.S.A.,* 268 D3
Koforidua, *Ghana,* 325 E7
Kohtla-Jarve, *Estonia,* 312 H4
Kokkola, *Finland,* 312 G3
Kokshetau, *Kazakhstan,* 302 J1
Kola Peninsula, *Russia,* 312 L2
Kolda, *Senegal,* 325 C6
Kolding, *Denmark,* 313 D5
Kolhapur, *India,* 301 C7
Kolkata, *India,* 301 F6
Kolomna, *Russia,* 310 D2
Kolwezi, *Democratic Republic of Congo,* 326 E6
Kolyma Range, *Russia,* 305 H2
Komsomolets, *Kazakhstan,* 311 J3
Komsomolsk, *Russia,* 305 G3
Konduz, *Afghanistan,* 300 B3
Kongur Shan, *China,* 300 D3
Konosha, *Russia,* 310 E1
Konya, *Turkey,* 317 K4
Korce, *Albania,* 317 G3
Korea Bay, *Asia,* 299 K3
Korea Strait, *Asia,* 299 L4
Korhogo, *Ivory Coast,* 325 D7
Korla, *China,* 300 F2
Koror, *Palau, national capital,* 286 A4
Korosten, *Ukraine,* 313 J6
Kosciuszko, Mount, *Australia,* 289 J7
Kosice, *Slovakia,* 313 G6
Kosti, *Sudan,* 323 H6
Kostomuksha, *Russia,* 312 J2
Kostroma, *Russia,* 310 E2
Koszalin, *Poland,* 313 F5
Kota, *India,* 300 D5
Kota Bharu, *Malaysia,* 294 B2
Kota Kinabalu, *Malaysia,* 294 E2
Kotka, *Finland,* 312 H3
Kotlas, *Russia,* 311 F1
Koudougou, *Burkina Faso,* 325 E6
Koutiala, *Mali,* 325 D6
Kouvola, *Finland,* 312 H3
Kovel, *Ukraine,* 313 H6
Kozhikode, *India,* 301 D8
Kragujevac, *Yugoslavia,* 317 G2
Krakatoa, *Indonesia,* 294 C5
Krakow, *Poland,* 313 G6
Kraljevo, *Yugoslavia,* 317 G3
Kramatorsk, *Ukraine,* 310 D4
Kranj, *Slovenia,* 316 E2
Krasnodar, *Russia,* 302 C2
Krasnoyarsk, *Russia,* 304 E3
Kremenchuk, *Ukraine,* 310 C4
Kremenchukske Reservoir, *Ukraine,* 310 C4
Krishna, *India,* 301 D7
Kristiansand, *Norway,* 312 C4
Kristiansund, *Norway,* 312 C3
Krong Kaoh Kong, *Cambodia,* 296 D5
Kroonstad, *South Africa,* 328 E5
Krugersdorp, *South Africa,* 328 E5
Kryvyy Rih, *Ukraine,* 310 C4
Kuala Lumpur, *Malaysia, national capital,* 294 B3
Kuala Terengganu, *Malaysia,* 294 B2
Kuantan, *Malaysia,* 294 B3
Kuching, *Malaysia,* 294 D3
Kuhmo, *Finland,* 312 J2
Kuito, *Angola,* 328 C2
Kulob, *Tajikistan,* 300 B3
Kumamoto, *Japan,* 299 M4
Kumanovo, *Macedonia,* 317 G3
Kumasi, *Ghana,* 325 E7

Kumba, *Cameroon,* 326 A3
Kumo, *Nigeria,* 326 A1
Kunlun Mountains, *China,* 300 E3
Kunming, *China,* 298 F5
Kuopio, *Finland,* 312 H2
Kupang, *Indonesia,* 295 F6
Kurgan, *Russia,* 311 K2
Kurikka, *Finland,* 312 G3
Kuril Islands, *Russia,* 305 H3
Kursk, *Russia,* 310 D3
Kushiro, *Japan,* 299 P2
Kutahya, *Turkey,* 317 J4
Kutaisi, *Georgia,* 302 D3
Kutch, Rann of, *India,* 301 B6
Kuujjuaq, *Canada,* 269 N3
Kuusamo, *Finland,* 312 J2
Kuwait, *Asia, country,* 303 E6
Kuwait City, *Kuwait, national capital,* 303 E6
Kuybyshev Reservoir, *Russia,* 311 F3
Kuyto, Lake, *Russia,* 312 K2
Kuytun, *China,* 300 F2
Kwangju, *South Korea,* 299 L3
Kyoga, Lake, *Uganda,* 327 F3
Kyoto, *Japan,* 299 N3
Kyrenia, *Cyprus,* 317 K5
Kyrgyzstan, *Asia, country,* 300 C2
Kythira, *Greece,* 317 G4
Kyushu, *Japan,* 299 M4
Kyzyl, *Russia,* 304 E3

l

Laayoune, *Western Sahara, national capital,* 324 C3
Labe, *Guinea,* 325 C6
Labrador City, *Canada,* 269 N3
Labrador Sea, *North America,* 269 P2
La Chorrera, *Colombia,* 278 D4
La Coruna, *Spain,* 315 B6
Ladoga, Lake, *Russia,* 312 J3
Ladysmith, *South Africa,* 328 E5
Lae, *Papua New Guinea,* 295 L5
Lagdo Reservoir, *Cameroon,* 326 B2
La Gomera, *Canary Islands,* 324 B3
Lagos, *Nigeria,* 325 F7
Lagos, *Portugal,* 315 B7
La Grande Reservoir, *Canada,* 269 M3
Lagunillas, *Venezuela,* 278 D1
Lahat, *Indonesia,* 294 B4
Lahore, *Pakistan,* 300 C4
Lahti, *Finland,* 312 H3
Lai, *Chad,* 326 C2
La Libertad, *Ecuador,* 278 B4
Lambarene, *Gabon,* 326 B4
Lamia, *Greece,* 317 G4
Lancaster Sound, *Canada,* 269 L1
Land's End, *United Kingdom,* 314 C4
Langanes, *Iceland,* 312 Q2
Langsa, *Indonesia,* 294 A3
Lansing, *U.S.A., internal capital,* 271 K2
Lanzarote, *Canary Islands,* 324 C3
Lanzhou, *China,* 298 F3
Laoag, *Philippines,* 297 H4
Lao Cai, *Vietnam,* 296 D3
La Oroya, *Peru,* 278 C6
Laos, *Asia, country,* 296 D4
La Palma, *Canary Islands,* 324 B3
La Palma, *Panama,* 273 J6
La Paz, *Bolivia, national capital,* 280 E3
La Paz, *Mexico,* 272 B3
La Perouse Strait, *Asia,* 299 P1
Lapland, *Europe,* 312 H1
La Plata, *Argentina,* 280 G6
Lappeenranta, *Finland,* 312 J3
Laptev Sea, *Russia,* 305 G2
Larache, *Morocco,* 324 D1
Laredo, *U.S.A.,* 270 G5
La Rioja, *Argentina,* 280 E5
Larisa, *Greece,* 317 G4
Larkana, *Pakistan,* 300 B5
Larnaca, *Cyprus,* 317 K5
La Rochelle, *France,* 315 D5
La Romana, *Dominican Republic,* 273 L4
Larvik, *Norway,* 312 D4
Lashio, *Burma,* 296 C3

Lastoursville, *Gabon,* 326 B4
Las Vegas, *U.S.A.,* 270 C3
Latakia, *Syria,* 302 C4
Latvia, *Europe, country,* 313 H4
Launceston, *Australia,* 288 J8
Lausanne, *Switzerland,* 316 C2
Lautoka, *Fiji,* 289 Q3
Lebanon, *Asia, country,* 302 C5
Lecce, *Italy,* 317 F3
Ledo, Cape, *Angola,* 328 B1
Leeds, *United Kingdom,* 314 D3
Leeuwarden, *Netherlands,* 314 F3
Leeuwin, Cape, *Australia,* 288 B6
Leeward Islands, *North America,* 272 M4
Legaspi, *Philippines,* 297 H5
Legnica, *Poland,* 313 F6
Le Havre, *France,* 314 E4
Leipzig, *Germany,* 314 H4
Leiria, *Portugal,* 315 B7
Le Mans, *France,* 314 E4
Lena, *Russia,* 305 G2
Leon, *Mexico,* 272 D3
Leon, *Nicaragua,* 273 G5
Leon, *Spain,* 315 C6
Leonardville, *Namibia,* 328 C4
Lerida, *Spain,* 315 E6
Lerwick, *United Kingdom,* 314 D1
Les Cayes, *Haiti,* 273 K4
Leshan, *China,* 298 F5
Leskovac, *Yugoslavia,* 317 G3
Lesotho, *Africa, country,* 328 E5
Lesser Antilles, *North America,* 272 M5
Lesser Sunda Islands, *Indonesia,* 294 E5
Lesvos, *Greece,* 317 H4
Lethbridge, *Canada,* 268 H4
Leticia, *Brazil,* 278 E4
Lewiston, *U.S.A.,* 270 C1
Lexington, *U.S.A.,* 271 K3
Lhasa, *China,* 300 G5
Lhokseumawe, *Indonesia,* 294 A2
Lianyungang, *China,* 299 J4
Liaoyuan, *China,* 299 L2
Liberec, *Czech Republic,* 316 E1
Liberia, *Africa, country,* 325 D7
Liberia, *Costa Rica,* 273 G5
Libreville, *Gabon, national capital,* 326 A3
Libya, *Africa, country,* 322 E3
Libyan Desert, *Africa,* 322 F3
Lichinga, *Mozambique,* 329 G2
Lida, *Belarus,* 313 H5
Lidkoping, *Sweden,* 312 E4
Liechtenstein, *Europe, country,* 316 D2
Liege, *Belgium,* 314 F4
Lieksa, *Finland,* 312 J3
Liepaja, *Latvia,* 313 G4
Ligurian Sea, *Europe,* 316 C3
Likasi, *Democratic Republic of Congo,* 326 E6
Lille, *France,* 314 E4
Lillehammer, *Norway,* 312 D3
Lilongwe, *Malawi, national capital,* 329 F2
Lima, *Peru, national capital,* 278 C6
Limassol, *Cyprus,* 317 K5
Limerick, *Ireland,* 314 B3
Limnos, *Greece,* 310 C3
Limoges, *France,* 315 E5
Limon, *Costa Rica,* 273 H5
Limpopo, *Africa,* 328 F4
Linares, *Chile,* 281 D7
Linchuan, *China,* 299 J5
Lincoln, *U.S.A., internal capital,* 271 G2
Lindi, *Tanzania,* 327 G6
Line Islands, *Kiribati,* 287 H4
Linhares, *Brazil,* 280 K3
Linkoping, *Sweden,* 312 E4
Linz, *Austria,* 316 E1
Lions, Gulf of, *Europe,* 315 F6
Lipari Islands, *Italy,* 316 E4
Lipetsk, *Russia,* 310 D3
Lisbon, *Portugal, national capital,* 315 B7
Lithuania, *Europe, country,* 313 G5
Little Andaman, *India,* 301 G8
Little Rock, *U.S.A., internal capital,* 271 H4
Liuzhou, *China,* 298 G6

Liverpool, *United Kingdom,* 314 D3
Livingstone, *Zambia,* 328 E3
Livorno, *Italy,* 316 D3
Liwale, *Tanzania,* 327 G5
Ljubljana, *Slovenia, national capital,* 316 E2
Llanos, *South America,* 278 D2
Lloydminster, *Canada,* 268 J3
Lobamba, *Lesotho, national capital,* 328 F5
Lodz, *Poland,* 313 F6
Lofoten, *Norway,* 312 E1
Logan, Mount, *Canada,* 268 F2
Logrono, *Spain,* 315 D6
Loire, *France,* 314 E5
Loja, *Ecuador,* 278 C4
Lokan Reservoir, *Finland,* 312 H2
Lolland, *Denmark,* 313 D5
Lombok, *Indonesia,* 294 E5
Lome, *Togo, national capital,* 325 F7
London, *Canada,* 269 L4
London, *United Kingdom, national capital,* 314 D4
Londonderry, *United Kingdom,* 314 C3
Londrina, *Brazil,* 280 H4
Long Island, *The Bahamas,* 271 L6
Long Xuyen, *Vietnam,* 296 D6
Lopez, Cape, *Gabon,* 326 A4
Lop Lake, *China,* 300 G2
Lord Howe Island, *Australia,* 289 L6
Los Angeles, *Chile,* 281 D7
Los Angeles, *U.S.A.,* 270 C4
Los Mochis, *Mexico,* 272 C2
Louangphrabang, *Laos,* 296 D4
Loubomo, *Congo,* 326 B4
Louga, *Senegal,* 325 B5
Louisiana, *U.S.A., internal admin. area,* 271 H4
Lower California, *Mexico,* 272 B2
Loyalty Islands, *New Caledonia,* 289 N4
Luacano, *Angola,* 328 D2
Luanda, *Angola, national capital,* 328 B1
Luangwa, *Africa,* 328 F2
Luanshya, *Zambia,* 328 E2
Lubango, *Angola,* 328 B2
Lubbock, *U.S.A.,* 270 F4
Lublin, *Poland,* 313 G6
Lubny, *Ukraine,* 310 C3
Lubumbashi, *Democratic Republic of Congo,* 326 E6
Lucena, *Philippines,* 297 H5
Lucerne, *Switzerland,* 316 D2
Lucira, *Angola,* 328 B2
Lucknow, *India,* 300 E5
Luderitz, *Namibia,* 328 C5
Ludhiana, *India,* 300 D4
Ludza, *Latvia,* 313 H4
Luena, *Angola,* 328 C2
Luganville, *Vanuatu,* 289 N3
Lugo, *Spain,* 315 C6
Luhansk, *Ukraine,* 310 D4
Luiana, *Angola,* 328 D3
Lukulu, *Zambia,* 328 D2
Lumbala Kaquengue, *Angola,* 328 D2
Lumbala Nguimbo, *Angola,* 328 D2
Lundazi, *Zambia,* 329 F2
Lupilichi, *Mozambique,* 329 G2
Lusaka, *Zambia, national capital,* 328 E3
Lutsk, *Ukraine,* 313 H6
Luxembourg, *Europe, country,* 314 F4
Luxembourg, *Luxembourg, national capital,* 314 F4
Luxor, *Egypt,* 323 H3
Luzhou, *China,* 298 G5
Luzon, *Philippines,* 297 H4
Luzon Strait, *Philippines,* 297 H4
Lviv, *Ukraine,* 313 H6
Lyon, *France,* 315 F5
Lysychansk, *Ukraine,* 310 D4

m

Maan, *Jordan,* 303 C5
Maastricht, *Netherlands,* 314 F4
Macae, *Brazil,* 280 K4
Macapa, *Brazil,* 279 H3
Macau, *China,* 299 H6

Macedonia, *Europe, country,* 317 G3
Maceio, *Brazil,* 279 L5
Machakos, *Kenya,* 327 G4
Machala, *Ecuador,* 278 C4
Machu Picchu, *Peru,* 278 D6
Mackay, *Australia,* 289 J4
Mackenzie, *Canada,* 268 G2
Mackenzie Bay, *Canada,* 268 F2
Mackenzie Mountains, *Canada,* 268 F2
Macon, *U.S.A.,* 271 K4
Madagascar, *Africa, country,* 329 J4
Madang, *Papua New Guinea,* 295 L5
Madeira, *Atlantic Ocean,* 324 B2
Madeira, *Brazil,* 278 F5
Madingou, *Congo,* 326 B4
Madison, *U.S.A., internal capital,* 271 J2
Madras, *India,* 301 E8
Madrid, *Spain, national capital,* 315 D6
Madurai, *India,* 301 D9
Maevatanana, *Madagascar,* 329 J3
Mafeteng, *Lesotho,* 328 E5
Mafia Island, *Tanzania,* 327 H5
Magadan, *Russia,* 305 H3
Magangue, *Colombia,* 278 D2
Magdalena, *Bolivia,* 280 F2
Magdeburg, *Germany,* 314 G3
Magellan, Strait of, *South America,* 281 E10
Magnitogorsk, *Russia,* 311 H3
Mahajanga, *Madagascar,* 329 J3
Mahalapye, *Botswana,* 328 E4
Mahilyow, *Belarus,* 313 J5
Mahon, *Spain,* 315 F7
Maiduguri, *Nigeria,* 322 D6
Mai-Ndombe, Lake, *Democratic Republic of Congo,* 326 C4
Maine, *U.S.A., internal admin. area,* 271 N1
Maine, Gulf of, *U.S.A.,* 271 N2
Maio, *Cape Verde,* 325 M11
Majorca, *Spain,* 315 E7
Majuro, *Marshall Islands, national capital,* 286 E4
Makarikari, *Botswana,* 328 D4
Makassar Strait, *Indonesia,* 295 E4
Makeni, *Sierra Leone,* 325 B7
Makgadikgadi Pans, *Botswana,* 328 D4
Makhachkala, *Russia,* 302 E3
Makkovik, *Canada,* 269 P3
Makokou, *Gabon,* 326 B3
Makumbako, *Tanzania,* 327 F5
Makurdi, *Nigeria,* 326 A2
Mala, *Peru,* 278 C6
Malabo, *Equatorial Guinea, national capital,* 326 A3
Maladzyechna, *Belarus,* 313 H5
Malaga, *Spain,* 315 C7
Malaimbandy, *Madagascar,* 329 J4
Malakal, *Sudan,* 327 F2
Malakula, *Vanuatu,* 289 N3
Malang, *Indonesia,* 294 D5
Malanje, *Angola,* 328 C1
Malar, Lake, *Sweden,* 312 F4
Malatya, *Turkey,* 302 C4
Malawi, *Africa, country,* 329 F2
Malawi, Lake, *Africa,* 327 F6
Malaysia, *Asia, country,* 294 B2
Maldives, *Asia, country,* 301 C9
Male, *Maldives, national capital,* 301 C10
Malegaon, *India,* 301 C6
Mali, *Africa, country,* 324 E5
Malindi, *Kenya,* 327 H4
Malmo, *Sweden,* 313 E5
Malpelo Island, *Colombia,* 278 B3
Malta, *Europe, country,* 316 E4
Mamoudzou, *Mayotte,* 329 J2
Mamuno, *Botswana,* 328 D4
Man, *Ivory Coast,* 325 D7
Manado, *Indonesia,* 295 F3
Managua, *Nicaragua, national capital,* 273 G5
Manakara, *Madagascar,* 329 J4
Manama, *Bahrain, national capital,* 303 F6
Manaus, *Brazil,* 279 G4
Manchester, *United Kingdom,* 314 D3
Manchuria, *China,* 299 K2
Mandalay, *Burma,* 296 C3

Mandera, *Kenya,* 327 H3
Mandritsara, *Madagascar,* 329 J3
Mandurah, *Australia,* 288 C6
Mangalore, *India,* 301 C8
Mania, *Madagascar,* 329 J3
Manicouagan Reservoir, *Canada,* 269 N3
Manila, *Philippines, national capital,* 297 H5
Manisa, *Turkey,* 317 H4
Man, Isle of, *Europe,* 314 C3
Manitoba, *Canada, internal admin. area,* 269 K3
Manitoba, Lake, *Canada,* 269 K3
Manizales, *Colombia,* 278 C2
Manja, *Madagascar,* 329 H4
Mannar, *Sri Lanka,* 301 E9
Mannar, Gulf of, *Asia,* 301 D9
Mannheim, *Germany,* 314 G4
Mansa, *Zambia,* 328 E2
Manta, *Ecuador,* 278 B4
Manzhouli, *China,* 305 F3
Mao, *Chad,* 322 E6
Maoke Range, *Indonesia,* 295 J4
Maputo, *Mozambique, national capital,* 329 F5
Maraba, *Brazil,* 279 J5
Maracaibo, *Venezuela,* 278 D1
Maracaibo, Lake, *Venezuela,* 278 D2
Maracay, *Venezuela,* 278 E1
Maradi, *Niger,* 322 C6
Maranon, *Peru,* 278 C4
Mar del Plata, *Argentina,* 281 G7
Margarita Island, *Venezuela,* 278 F1
Margherita Peak, *Africa,* 326 E3
Marib, *Yemen,* 303 E8
Maribor, *Slovenia,* 316 E2
Marie Byrd Land, *Antarctica,* 333 Q3
Mariental, *Namibia,* 328 C4
Marijampole, *Lithuania,* 313 G5
Marilia, *Brazil,* 280 J4
Marimba, *Angola,* 328 C1
Mariupol, *Ukraine,* 310 D4
Marka, *Somalia,* 327 H3
Marmara, Sea of, *Turkey,* 317 J3
Maroantsetra, *Madagascar,* 329 J3
Maroua, *Cameroon,* 326 B1
Marquesas Islands, *French Polynesia,* 287 K5
Marrakech, *Morocco,* 324 D2
Marra, Mount, *Sudan,* 322 F6
Marsa Matruh, *Egypt,* 323 G2
Marseille, *France,* 315 F6
Marshall Islands, *Oceania, country,* 286 D3
Martapura, *Indonesia,* 294 D4
Martinique, *North America,* 272 M5
Mary, *Turkmenistan,* 302 H4
Maryland, *U.S.A., internal admin. area,* 271 L3
Masaka, *Uganda,* 327 F4
Masasi, *Tanzania,* 327 G6
Masbate, *Philippines,* 297 H5
Maseru, *Lesotho, national capital,* 328 E5
Mashhad, *Iran,* 302 G4
Masirah Island, *Oman,* 303 G7
Massachusetts, *U.S.A., internal admin. area,* 271 M2
Massangena, *Mozambique,* 329 F4
Massawa, *Eritrea,* 323 J5
Massif Central, *France,* 315 E5
Massina, *Mozambique,* 329 G4
Masvingo, *Zimbabwe,* 328 F4
Matagalpa, *Nicaragua,* 273 G5
Matala, *Angola,* 328 B2
Matamoros, *Mexico,* 272 E2
Mataram, *Indonesia,* 294 E5
Mataro, *Spain,* 315 E6
Matehuala, *Mexico,* 272 D3
Mato Grosso, Plateau of, *Brazil,* 279 G6
Matsuyama, *Japan,* 299 M4
Maturin, *Venezuela,* 278 F2
Maui, *U.S.A.,* 271 P7
Maun, *Botswana,* 328 D3
Mauritania, *Africa, country,* 324 C5
Mauritius, *Indian Ocean, country,* 329 L3

Mavinga, *Angola,* 328 D3
Mayotte, *Africa,* 329 J2
Mazar-e Sharif, *Afghanistan,* 300 B3
Mazatlan, *Mexico,* 272 C3
Mazyr, *Belarus,* 313 J5
Mbabane, *Swaziland, national capital,* 328 F5
Mbala, *Zambia,* 328 F1
Mbale, *Uganda,* 327 F3
Mbandaka, *Democratic Republic of Congo,* 326 C3
Mbarara, *Uganda,* 327 F4
Mbeya, *Tanzania,* 327 F5
Mbuji-Mayi, *Democratic Republic of Congo,* 326 D5
McClintock Channel, *Canada,* 268 J1
McClure Strait, *Canada,* 268 G1
McKinley, Mount, *U.S.A.,* 268 D2
Mead, Lake, *U.S.A.,* 270 D3
Mecca, *Saudi Arabia,* 303 C7
Mecula, *Mozambique,* 329 G2
Medan, *Indonesia,* 294 A3
Medellin, *Colombia,* 278 C2
Medford, *U.S.A.,* 270 B2
Medina, *Saudi Arabia,* 303 C7
Mediterranean Sea, *Africa/Europe,* 263
Medvezhyegorsk, *Russia,* 312 K3
Meerut, *India,* 300 D5
Meiktila, *Burma,* 296 C3
Meizhou, *China,* 299 J6
Mekele, *Ethiopia,* 327 G1
Meknes, *Morocco,* 324 D2
Mekong, *Asia,* 296 E5
Melaka, *Malaysia,* 294 B3
Melamo, Cape, *Mozambique,* 329 H2
Melanesia, *Oceania,* 286 D5
Melbourne, *Australia, internal capital,* 288 H7
Melilla, *Africa,* 315 D7
Melitopol, *Ukraine,* 310 D4
Melo, *Uruguay,* 280 H6
Melville Island, *Australia,* 288 F2
Melville Island, *Canada,* 268 H1
Melville Peninsula, *Canada,* 269 L2
Memphis, *U.S.A.,* 271 J3
Mendoza, *Argentina,* 280 E6
Menongue, *Angola,* 328 C2
Mentawai Islands, *Indonesia,* 294 A4
Menzel Bourguiba, *Tunisia,* 322 C1
Mergui, *Burma,* 296 C5
Mergui Archipelago, *Burma,* 296 C5
Merida, *Mexico,* 272 G3
Meridian, *U.S.A.,* 271 J4
Merlo, *Argentina,* 280 E6
Mersin, *Turkey,* 302 B4
Meru, *Kenya,* 327 G3
Messina, *Italy,* 316 E4
Messina, *South Africa,* 328 F4
Metz, *France,* 314 F4
Mexicali, *Mexico,* 272 A1
Mexico, *North America, country,* 272 D3
Mexico City, *Mexico, national capital,* 272 E4
Mexico, Gulf of, *North America,* 272 F3
Mexico, Plateau of, *Mexico,* 272 D2
Miami, *U.S.A.,* 271 K5
Michigan, *U.S.A., internal admin. area,* 271 J2
Michigan, Lake, *U.S.A.,* 271 J2
Michurinsk, *Russia,* 310 E3
Micronesia, *Oceania,* 286 C4
Micronesia, Federated States of, *Oceania, country,* 286 C4
Middlesbrough, *United Kingdom,* 314 D3
Midway Islands, *Pacific Ocean,* 286 F2
Mikkeli, *Finland,* 312 H3
Milan, *Italy,* 316 D2
Milange, *Mozambique,* 329 G3
Mildura, *Australia,* 288 H6
Milwaukee, *U.S.A.,* 271 J2
Minas, *Uruguay,* 280 G6
Mindanao, *Philippines,* 297 H6
Mindelo, *Cape Verde,* 325 M11
Mindoro, *Philippines,* 297 H5
Mingacevir, *Azerbaijan,* 302 E3
Minna, *Nigeria,* 325 G7

Prince George, *Canada*, 268 G3
Prince of Wales Island, *Canada*, 269 K1
Prince Rupert, *Canada*, 268 F3
Principe, *Sao Tome and Principe*, 325 G8
Pripet, *Europe*, 313 J6
Pripet Marshes, *Europe*, 313 H5
Pristina, *Yugoslavia*, 317 G3
Providence, *Seychelles*, 329 K1
Providence, *U.S.A., internal capital*, 271 M2
Providence, Cape, *New Zealand*, 289 N9
Provo, *U.S.A.*, 270 D2
Prudhoe Bay, *U.S.A.*, 268 E1
Pskov, *Russia*, 313 J4
Pskov, Lake, *Europe*, 312 J4
Pucallpa, *Peru*, 278 D5
Puebla, *Mexico*, 272 E4
Pueblo, *U.S.A.*, 270 F3
Puerto Ayora, *Ecuador*, 278 N10
Puerto Cabezas, *Nicaragua*, 273 H5
Puerto Deseado, *Argentina*, 281 E9
Puerto Inirida, *Colombia*, 278 E3
Puerto Leguizamo, *Colombia*, 278 D4
Puerto Maldonado, *Peru*, 278 E6
Puerto Montt, *Chile*, 281 D8
Puerto Natales, *Chile*, 281 D10
Puerto Paez, *Venezuela*, 278 E2
Puerto Princesa, *Philippines*, 297 G6
Puerto Rico, *North America*, 272 L4
Puerto Suarez, *Bolivia*, 280 G3
Puerto Vallarta, *Mexico*, 272 C3
Pula, *Croatia*, 316 E2
Pulog, Mount, *Philippines*, 297 H4
Puncak Jaya, *Indonesia*, 295 J4
Pune, *India*, 301 C7
Puno, *Peru*, 278 D7
Punta Arenas, *Chile*, 281 D10
Puntarenas, *Costa Rica*, 273 H5
Purus, *Brazil*, 278 E5
Pusan, *South Korea*, 299 L3
Pushkin, *Russia*, 312 J4
Puula Lake, *Finland*, 312 H3
Pweto, *Democratic Republic of Congo*, 326 E5
Pya, Lake, *Russia*, 312 J2
Pye, *Burma*, 296 C4
Pyinmana, *Burma*, 296 C4
Pyongyang, *North Korea, national capital*, 299 L3
Pyramids of Giza, *Egypt*, 323 H3
Pyrenees, *Europe*, 315 D6
Pyrgos, *Greece*, 317 G4

q

Qaidam Basin, *China*, 300 G3
Qaraghandy, *Kazakhstan*, 304 D3
Qatar, *Asia, country*, 303 F6
Qattara Depression, *Egypt*, 323 G3
Qazvin, *Iran*, 302 E4
Qena, *Egypt*, 323 H3
Qingdao, *China*, 299 K3
Qinghai Lake, *China*, 298 F3
Qinhuangdao, *China*, 299 J3
Qiqihar, *China*, 299 K1
Qom, *Iran*, 302 F5
Qostanay, *Kazakhstan*, 311 J3
Quanzhou, *China*, 299 J6
Quebec, *Canada, internal admin. area*, 269 M3
Quebec, *Canada, internal capital*, 269 M4
Queen Charlotte Islands, *Canada*, 268 F3
Queen Elizabeth Islands, *Canada*, 268 H1
Queen Maud Land, *Antarctica*, 333 C3
Queensland, *Australia, internal admin. area*, 288 H4
Quelimane, *Mozambique*, 329 G3
Quellon, *Chile*, 281 D8
Quetta, *Pakistan*, 300 B4
Quevedo, *Ecuador*, 278 C4
Quezaltenango, *Guatemala*, 272 F4
Quezon City, *Philippines*, 297 H5
Quibdo, *Colombia*, 278 C2
Quillabamba, *Peru*, 278 D6
Quimper, *France*, 314 C5
Quincy, *U.S.A.*, 271 H3
Qui Nhon, *Vietnam*, 296 E5
Quirima, *Angola*, 328 C2

Quito, *Ecuador, national capital*, 278 C4
Qurghonteppa, *Tajikistan*, 300 B3
Qyzylorda, *Kazakhstan*, 302 J3

r

Raahe, *Finland*, 312 H2
Rabat, *Morocco, national capital*, 324 D2
Rabaul, *Papua New Guinea*, 295 M4
Rabnita, *Moldova*, 317 J2
Radisson, *Canada*, 269 M3
Radom, *Poland*, 313 G6
Ragusa, *Italy*, 316 E4
Rahimyar Khan, *Pakistan*, 300 C5
Raipur, *India*, 301 E6
Rajahmundry, *India*, 301 E7
Rajkot, *India*, 301 C6
Rajshahi, *Bangladesh*, 301 F6
Rakops, *Botswana*, 328 D4
Raleigh, *U.S.A., internal capital*, 271 L3
Ralik Islands, *Marshall Islands*, 286 D3
Ramnicu Valcea, *Romania*, 317 H2
Rancagua, *Chile*, 280 D6
Ranchi, *India*, 301 F6
Randers, *Denmark*, 313 D4
Rangoon, *Burma, national capital*, 296 C4
Rangpur, *Bangladesh*, 300 F5
Rapid City, *U.S.A.*, 270 F2
Ras Dashen, *Ethiopia*, 327 G1
Rasht, *Iran*, 302 E4
Ratak Islands, *Marshall Islands*, 286 E3
Rat Islands, *U.S.A.*, 269 A3
Rauma, *Finland*, 312 G3
Ravenna, *Italy*, 316 E2
Rawalpindi, *Pakistan*, 300 C4 (not present)
Rawson, *Argentina*, 281 E8
Rechytsa, *Belarus*, 313 J5
Recife, *Brazil*, 279 M5
Reconquista, *Argentina*, 280 G5
Red, *Asia*, 298 F6
Red, *U.S.A.*, 271 G4
Red Deer, *Canada*, 268 H3
Redding, *U.S.A.*, 270 B2
Red Sea, *Africa/Asia*, 323 J4
Regensburg, *Germany*, 314 H4
Regina, *Canada, internal capital*, 268 J3
Regina, *French Guiana*, 279 H3
Rehoboth, *Namibia*, 328 C4
Reims, *France*, 314 F4
Reindeer Lake, *Canada*, 268 J3
Rennell Island, *Solomon Islands*, 289 M2
Rennes, *France*, 314 D4
Reno, *U.S.A.*, 270 C3
Reunion, *Indian Ocean*, 329 L4
Revelstoke, *Canada*, 268 H3
Revillagigedo Islands, *Mexico*, 272 B4
Reykjavik, *Iceland, national capital*, 312 N2
Rhine, *Europe*, 314 F4
Rhode Island, *U.S.A., internal admin. area*, 271 M2
Rhodes, *Greece*, 317 J4
Rhone, *Europe*, 315 F5
Riau Islands, *Indonesia*, 294 B3
Ribeirao Preto, *Brazil*, 280 J4
Riberalta, *Bolivia*, 280 E2
Richards Bay, *South Africa*, 328 F5
Richmond, *U.S.A., internal capital*, 271 L3
Riga, *Latvia, national capital*, 313 H4
Riga, Gulf of, *Europe*, 313 G4
Rijeka, *Croatia*, 316 E2
Rimini, *Italy*, 316 E2
Rio Branco, *Brazil*, 278 E5
Rio Cuarto, *Argentina*, 280 F6
Rio de Janeiro, *Brazil*, 280 K4
Rio Gallegos, *Argentina*, 281 E10
Rio Grande, *Argentina*, 281 E10
Rio Grande, *Brazil*, 280 H6
Rio Grande, *U.S.A.*, 270 F5
Riohacha, *Colombia*, 278 D1
Rivas, *Nicaragua*, 273 G5
Rivera, *Uruguay*, 280 G6
Riverside, *U.S.A.*, 270 C4
Rivne, *Ukraine*, 313 H6
Riyadh, *Saudi Arabia, national capital*, 303 E7
Roanoke, *U.S.A.*, 271 L3
Robson, Mount, *Canada*, 268 H3

Rochester, *U.S.A.*, 271 L2
Rockford, *U.S.A.*, 271 J2
Rockhampton, *Australia*, 289 K4
Rocky Mountains, *U.S.A.*, 270 D1
Romania, *Europe, country*, 317 G2
Rome, *Italy, national capital*, 316 E3
Rondonopolis, *Brazil*, 280 H3
Ronne, *Denmark*, 313 E5
Ronne Ice Shelf, *Antarctica*, 333 S3
Roraima, Mount, *South America*, 278 F2
Rosario, *Argentina*, 280 F6
Roseau, *Dominica, national capital*, 272 M4
Roslavl, *Russia*, 313 K5
Ross Ice Shelf, *Antarctica*, 333 M4
Rosso, *Mauritania*, 325 B5
Ross Sea, *Antarctica*, 333 M3
Rostock, *Germany*, 314 H3
Rostov, *Russia*, 310 D4
Roti, *Indonesia*, 295 F6
Rotorua, *Australia*, 289 Q7
Rotterdam, *Netherlands*, 314 F4
Rouen, *France*, 314 E4
Rovaniemi, *Finland*, 312 H2
Roxas, *Philippines*, 297 H5
Rub al Khali, *Asia*, 303 E8
Rudnyy, *Kazakhstan*, 311 J3
Rufino, *Argentina*, 280 F6
Rufunsa, *Zambia*, 328 E3
Rukwa, Lake, *Tanzania*, 327 F5
Rundu, *Namibia*, 328 C3
Rurrenabaque, *Bolivia*, 280 E2
Ruse, *Bulgaria*, 317 H3
Russia, *Asia/Europe, country*, 304 E3
Ruvuma, *Africa*, 327 G6
Rwanda, *Africa, country*, 326 E4
Ryazan, *Russia*, 310 D3
Rybinsk, *Russia*, 310 D2
Rybinsk Reservoir, *Russia*, 310 D2
Rybnik, *Poland*, 313 F6
Ryukyu Islands, *Japan*, 299 L5
Rzeszow, *Poland*, 313 G6
Rzhev, *Russia*, 310 C2

s

Saarbrucken, *Germany*, 314 F4
Saarijarvi, *Finland*, 312 H3
Sabha, *Libya*, 322 D3
Sabzevar, *Iran*, 302 G4
Sacramento, *U.S.A., internal capital*, 270 B3
Sadah, *Yemen*, 303 E8
Safi, *Morocco*, 324 D2
Sahara, *Africa*, 322 C5
Saharanpur, *India*, 300 D5
Sahel, *Africa*, 322 C6
Sahiwal, *Pakistan*, 300 C4
Saida, *Algeria*, 324 F2
Saigon, *Vietnam*, 296 E5
Saimaa Lake, *Finland*, 312 H3
St. Andrew, Cape, *Madagascar*, 329 H3
St. Denis, *Reunion*, 329 L4
St. Etienne, *France*, 315 F5
St. Francis, Cape, *South Africa*, 328 D6
St. George, *U.S.A.*, 270 D3
St. George's, *Grenada, national capital*, 272 M5
St. Helier, *Channel Islands*, 314 D4
Saint John, *Canada*, 269 N4
St. John's, *Antigua and Barbuda, national capital*, 272 M4
St. John's, *Canada, internal capital*, 269 P4
St. Kitts and Nevis, *North America, country*, 272 M4
St. Lawrence, *Canada*, 269 M4
St. Lawrence, Gulf of, *Canada*, 269 N4
St. Lawrence Island, *U.S.A.*, 268 B2
St. Louis, *Senegal*, 325 B5
St. Louis, *U.S.A.*, 271 H3
St. Lucia, *North America, country*, 272 M5
St. Lucia, Cape, *South Africa*, 329 F5
St. Malo, *France*, 314 D4
St. Martha, Cape, *Angola*, 328 B2
St. Martin, *North America*, 272 M4
St. Mary, Cape, *Madagascar*, 329 J5
St. Paul, *U.S.A., internal capital*, 271 H1

St. Petersburg, *Russia*, 312 J4
St. Petersburg, *U.S.A.*, 271 K5
St. Pierre, *Seychelles*, 329 J1
St. Pierre and Miquelon, *North America*, 269 P4
St. Polten, *Austria*, 316 E1
St. Vincent and the Grenadines, *North America, country*, 272 M5
St. Vincent, Cape, *Portugal*, 315 B7
Sakhalin, *Russia*, 305 H3
Saki, *Azerbaijan*, 302 E3
Saki, *Nigeria*, 325 F7
Sakishima Islands, *Japan*, 299 K6
Sal, *Cape Verde*, 325 M11
Salado, *Argentina*, 280 F5
Salalah, *Oman*, 303 F8
Salamanca, *Spain*, 315 C6
Salem, *India*, 301 D8
Salem, *U.S.A., internal capital*, 270 B1
Salerno, *Italy*, 316 E3
Salihorsk, *Belarus*, 313 H5
Salinas, *U.S.A.*, 270 B3
Salta, *Argentina*, 280 E4
Saltillo, *Mexico*, 272 D2
Salt Lake City, *U.S.A., internal capital*, 270 D2
Salto, *Uruguay*, 280 G6
Salton Sea, *U.S.A.*, 270 C4
Salvador, *Brazil*, 279 L6
Salween, *Asia*, 296 C4
Salzburg, *Austria*, 316 E2
Samar, *Philippines*, 297 J5
Samara, *Russia*, 311 G3
Samarinda, *Indonesia*, 294 E4
Samarqand, *Uzbekistan*, 300 B3
Sambalpur, *India*, 301 E6
Samoa, *Oceania, country*, 286 F6
Sampwe, *Democratic Republic of Congo*, 326 E5
Sam Rayburn Reservoir, *U.S.A.*, 271 H4
Samsun, *Turkey*, 302 C3
San, *Mali*, 325 E6
Sana, *Yemen, national capital*, 303 D8
Sanandaj, *Iran*, 302 E4
San Andres Island, *Colombia*, 273 H5
San Antonio, *U.S.A.*, 270 G5
San Antonio, Cape, *Argentina*, 281 G7
San Antonio Oeste, *Argentina*, 281 F8
San Cristobal, *Ecuador*, 278 P10
San Cristobal, *Venezuela*, 278 D2
Sandakan, *Malaysia*, 295 E2
San Diego, *U.S.A.*, 270 C4
Sandoway, *Burma*, 296 B4
San Fernando, *Chile*, 280 D6
San Fernando de Apure, *Venezuela*, 278 E2
San Francisco, *Argentina*, 280 F6
San Francisco, *U.S.A.*, 270 B3
San Francisco, Cape, *Ecuador*, 278 B3
Sangihe Islands, *Indonesia*, 295 G3
San Jorge, Gulf of, *Argentina*, 281 E9
San Jose, *Costa Rica, national capital*, 273 H6
San Jose, *U.S.A.*, 270 B3
San Jose de Chiquitos, *Bolivia*, 280 F3
San Jose del Guaviare, *Colombia*, 278 D3
San Juan, *Argentina*, 280 E6
San Juan, *Puerto Rico*, 272 L4
San Julian, *Argentina*, 281 E9
Sanliurfa, *Turkey*, 302 C4
San Lucas, Cape, *Mexico*, 272 B3
San Luis, *Argentina*, 280 E6
San Luis Obispo, *U.S.A.*, 270 B3
San Luis Potosi, *Mexico*, 272 D3
San Marino, *Europe, country*, 316 E3
San Matias, Gulf of, *Argentina*, 281 F8
San Miguel de Tucuman, *Argentina*, 280 E5
San Nicolas de los Arroyos, *Argentina*, 280 F6
San Pedro, *Ivory Coast*, 325 D8
San Pedro de Atacama, *Chile*, 280 E4
San Rafael, *Argentina*, 280 E6
San Remo, *Italy*, 316 C3
San Salvador, *Ecuador*, 278 N10
San Salvador, *El Salvador, national capital*, 272 G5
San Salvador de Jujuy, *Argentina*, 280 E4

GENERAL INDEX

In this index, words that have a lot of page numbers may have a number in **bold** to show where to find the main explanation. The maps are listed in a separate index on pages 376–389.

a

ablation zone 66, 368
abyssal plain 70, 368
abyssal zone 71
Accra (Ghana) 245
accumulation zone 66, 368
acid rain 32, 33, 60, 368
acids 32, 33, 60
active volcanoes **39**, 46, 193, 368
adaptation **109**, 110, 111, 117, 123, 128, 131, 368
Adelaide (Australia) 190
aerial photographs 248, 254
Afghanistan 354
Africa 20, 21, 58, 59, 118, 119, 123, 152, 155, 162, 168, 170, 171, 174, 175, 180, 181, 185, 228, 229, **230–245**, **318–329**, 337
– Central 238–239
– East 144, **240–241**, 320
– North **236–237**, 321
– Southern 143, **242–243**
– West 105, 232, **238–239**
African National Congress (ANC) 242
aftershocks 51
Agra (India) 210
agriculture – see farming
aid **156**, 240, 368
air 69, 98, 108
– and breathing 12, 94, 111
– currents in 79, 80, 83, **96**
– and erosion 60, 68
– gases in 28, 32, 78, 87, 98, 99, 108
– in mountain areas 101, 130, 131
– pollution in 114
– and weather **77**, 79, 80, 82, 83, 124, 126
airports 115, 150
Alaska (U.S.A.) 161, 164, 175, 265, 267
Albania 354
Albanians 222
Alberta (Canada) 164
Algeria 236, 244, 354
al–Idrisi 337
Alps 21
alternative energy sources 63, 103, 115, 225

Amazon rainforest 182, 276
America 161, 162, 353 (see also U.S.A.)
– Central 160, 161, 166, **168–169**, 266, 277
– Latin 175 (see also Central America and South America)
– North 12, 50, 55, 127, 152, 155, **158–171**, 232, **264–273**
– South 12, 16, 20, 55, 59, 97, 168, 170, **172–185**, 229, 232, 253, 256, 266, **274–281**, 337
Americans, Native **160**, 165, 166, 168, 174, 175, 176, 178, 180, 184
ammonia 98
ammonites 23
amphibians 110
Amsterdam (Netherlands) 60
anarchy 353
ANC (African National Congress) 242
ancestor worship 209, 213
ancient Chinese 208
ancient Egypt 237, 245
ancient Greece 228
ancient Greeks 218
Andes 21, 130, 174, **176–177**, 275
Andorra 354
Angola 234, 354
animals 12, 22, 26, 78, 84, 98, 99, 100, 103, 104, 108, 109, **110–111**, 127, 135, 139, 185, 191, 207, 243, 336, 337
– alpacas 176
– antelopes 240
– badgers 110
– bears 128, 129
– birds 58, 73, 105, 110, 112, 115, 119, 122, 128, 135, 137, 174, 179, 185, 197, 265, 267, 321, 331
– boar, wild 136
– bullocks 155
– bulls 221
– caimans 179
– camels 123, 132, 207, 276
– cats 115
– cattle 185, 190, 240, 241, 244
– cheetahs 112, 119
– colugos 117
– coral polyps 71
– cougars 130
– cows 211, 233, 309
– crabs 43, 69
– crocodiles 59

– deer 110, 143, 225
– desert 122, 123
– dogs 53, 115
– donkeys 143
– dormice 127
– and earthquakes 53
– earthworms 28
– and ecosystems 112, 113, 114, 115
– elephants 113, 213, 318
– endangered 115
– farm animals **134–137**, 148, 155, 176, 240
– fish 56–57, 70, 71, 72, 282, 285
– fossilized 23, 105
– foxes 129
– frogs 88, 89, 107, 277
– gazelles 112, 119
– gerenuks 113
– goats 130, 131
– golden lion tamarins 117
– grassland 119, 240
– guanacos 111, 276
– guinea pigs 180
– hares 129, 130
– hippopotamuses 58
– horses 185
– iguanas 180
– insects 28, 58, 77, 98, 110, 111, 117, 119, 121, 137 180
– kangaroos 188
– koalas 188
– lemmings 112
– leopards 115, 240
– lions 119, 240
– llamas 176
– mammals 110, 128
– marsupials 188
– moose 101
– mountain 130, 131, 176
– orang-utans 251
– oxen 128, 220
– pandas 110
– pigs 136, 137, 195, 197
– polar 128, 129
– polar bears 128, 129
– rainforest 117, 169, 178
– reptiles 110
– sacred 211
– seals 128, 185
– in seas 71
– seashore 69, 73
– sheep 130, 190, 192
– snakes 274
– snow leopards 115
– in soil 28, 30
– squirrels 307
– tarantulas 179

– tigers 291
– tubeworms 43
– turtles 71
– warthogs 113
– and weather 77, 83, 85, 87, 88, 89
– and weathering 32, 33
– wild boar 136
– wildebeest 119
– yaks 134
– zebras 110
animism 239, 368
Anlo-Ewe people 235
Antarctic (Antarctica) 67, 86, 95, **128–129**, 250, 331, 333
Antarctic Circle 17, 126, 250
Antarctic Ocean 128
anticyclones 368
Antigua and Barbuda 354
Aotearoa 193
apartheid 242, 368
apatite 25
aquifers 64, 368
Arabia 206, 213, 240
arable farming 134, 368
Arabs and Arabic peoples 206, 240, 243
archaeologists 241
arches 68
archipelagos 213, 368
architecture 183, 184, 204, 215, 218, 219, 223, 229
Arctic 14, **128–129**, 224, 250, 290, 330, 332
Arctic Circle 17, 126, 165, 205, 250
Arctic Ocean 128
Argentina 130, 152, 176, 180, 181, **184–185**, 277, 354
Aristotle 337
Arizona 161
Armenia 354
art 189, 195, 204, 208, 212, 218, 219, 238, **244–45**
ash, volcanic 38, 39, 41, 44, 45, 47, 105
Ashanti people 244
Asia 174, 175, 192, **198–215**, 243, **290–305**, 306
– Southeast 120, 189, 194, 196, **212–213**, 243
Asiatic Russia 293
asteroids 11, 104, 368
asthma 114
astronomy 337, **343–351**
Aswan High Dam 84, 237
Atlanta (U.S.A.) 146
Atlantic Ocean 20, 59, 70, 97, 124, 169
atlas maps 246–333

atmosphere 15, 76, 77, 87, 88, **94–95**, 99, 102, 103, 104, 117, 368
atmospheric pressure 90, 91, **96**, 368
atomic oxygen 95
atoms 27, 368
auroras 88, 94, 368
Australasia 186–197, 282–289
Australia 16, 32, 55, 115, 124, 188, **190–191**, 192, 194, 283, 284, 285, 342, 354
Austria 354
autumn **14**, 126, 348–349
axis **10**, 16, 339, 341, 368
Azerbaijan 355
azimuthal projections 254, **255**
Aztecs 166

b

bacteria 28, 29, 43, 98, 121, 368
Bahamas, the 171, 355
Bahrain 206, 355
Bali (Indonesia) 116, 212, 213
ball lightning 81
Baltimore (U.S.A.) 248
Bangladesh 77, 149, 210, 355
banking 150, 201, 214, 220
Bantu people 234
Barbados 355
barrios 184
basalt 19
basalt lava 45
Basque people 131
battery farming 137
bauxite 277, 285, 309, 321
bays 68
beaches 45, **68–69**, 73, 125, 170, 197
Bedouin people 207
bedrock 29, 368
Belarus 257, 355
Belgium 226, 232, 355
Belize 168, 355
Benin 355
Berber people 234
Berlin (Germany) 219, 256
Berlin Wall 219, 256
Bhutan 355
biogeography 336
biological pest control 137
biological weathering 33
biomes 100, 113, 368
birds 110, 115, 122, 128, 185, 267
– chickens 197
– condors 174
– eagles 110, 265, 267

392

ACKNOWLEDGEMENTS

Every effort has been made to trace the copyright holders of the material in this book. If any rights have been omitted, the publishers offer to rectify this in any subsequent edition, following notification. The publishers are grateful to the following organizations and individuals for their contributions and permission to reproduce material (t=top, m=middle, b=bottom, l=left, r=right):

Cover NASA; © Digital Vision; Stephen Moncrieff; **Endpapers** © Digital Vision; **p1** © Tony Arruza/CORBIS; **p2–3** © Don Hammond/CORBIS; **p4–5** © Digital Vision; **p6–7** © Digital Vision; **p6** (tr) Jeremy Gower; **p8–9** © Digital Vision; **p10** (bl) Courtesy of SOHO/Extreme Ultraviolet Imaging Telescope (EIT) consortium. SOHO is a project of international cooperation between ESA and NASA; (ml) Mariner 10, Astrogeology team, U.S. Geological Survey; (m + tr) JPL/NASA; (mr) © Digital Vision; **p11** (l + tr) © Digital Vision; (tl + mr) NASA/U.S. Geological Survey; (tm) NASA; (tr) Alan Stern (Southwest Research Institute), Marc Buie (Lowell Observatory), NASA and ESA; (br) WFI, European Southern Observatory; **p12** (bl) © Digital Vision; (tr) © Digital Vision; **p13** (tr) © Digital Vision; (r) Courtesy Canadian Space Agency © 2001; **p14** (l) © Dave G. Houser/CORBIS; (r) © Digital Vision; (b) Jeremy Gower; **p14–15** (t) © Digital Vision; **p15** (m, bm + b) © Digital Vision; **p16** (bl) Jeremy Gower; (mr + br) © Digital Vision; **p17** (t) Chris Lyon; (tr) Gary Bines; (b) Science Photo Library/© Simon Fraser; **p18–19** Gary Bines/© Digital Vision; **p19** (tl) Jeremy Gower; (bm) Chris Lyon; (mr) Andy Burton; (br) Howard Allman; **p20** (m) Guy Smith; (b) Jeremy Gower; **p20–21** (t) Jeremy Gower; **p21** (b) © Galen Rowell/CORBIS; (tr) Guy Smith; (mr) © Yann Arthus-Bertrand/CORBIS; **p22–23** (b) G.S.F Picture Library/© Dr. B. Booth; **p22** Mike Freeman; **p23** Mike Freeman; **p24** (bl) © Kevin Fleming/CORBIS; (tr) Jeremy Gower; **p25** (l) Mike Freeman and Science Photo Library/© Roberto de Gugliemo; (tr) Science Photo Library/Rosenfeld Images Ltd; (br) © Dorothy Burrows, Eye Ubiquitous/CORBIS; **p26** (bl) © Digital Vision; **p26–27** © Digital Vision; **p27** (tr) © Digital Vision; (br) Laura Fearn; **p28** (b) © Ken Wilson, Papilio/CORBIS; (t) © Robert Pickett/CORBIS; **p29** (tl) Andrew Beckett; (b) © Bob Rowan, Progressive Image/CORBIS; (tr) © Michael Boys/CORBIS; **p30** (t) © Richard Hamilton Smith/CORBIS; (b) © Eric Crichton/CORBIS; **p31** (b) Still Pictures/© Alan Watson; (tm) © Dean Conger/CORBIS; (tr) © Ancient Art and Architecture; **p32–33** John Farmer, Cordaiy Photo Library Ltd/CORBIS; **p33** (tr) Jeremy Gower; (br) © Robert Holmes/CORBIS; **p34–35** (b) Layne Kennedy/CORBIS; **p34** (t) Jeremy Gower; **p35** (tl) © Richard A. Cooke/CORBIS; (br) © Wolfgang Kaehler/CORBIS; **p36–37** Douglas Peebles/CORBIS; **p38** (bl + m) Jeremy Gower; (br) Chris Shields; **p38–39** (m) G.S.F Picture Library/© Dr. B. Booth; **p39** (br) Chris Shields; **p40** (main) © Digital Vision; (bl, tr + br) Jeremy Gower; **p41** (bl) © Digital Vision; (r) © Julian Cotton Photo Library/Powerstock Zefa; **p42–43** © Michael T. Sedam/CORBIS; **p42** (tr) Jeremy Gower; **p43** (tl) © Ralph White/CORBIS; (br) Still Pictures/© D. Drain; **p44** (bl) Jeremy Gower; **p44–45** © Amos Nachoum/CORBIS; **p45** (b) © Douglas Peebles/CORBIS; (tr) G.S.F. Picture Library/© Solarfilm A; **p46** (bl) © Philip James Corwin/CORBIS; **p46–47** G.S.F. Picture Library/© Univ. California; **p48–49** Oxford Scientific Films/© Vinay Parelkar Dinodia; **p48** (tr) © Grant Smith/CORBIS; **p49** (t) Photo courtesy of Kinemetrics Inc.; (r) Peter Bull; **p50** (main) © Kevin Shafer/CORBIS; (ml, bl + br) Jeremy Gower; **p51** Jeremy Gower; **p52** (t) Jeremy Gower; (b) © Roger Rossmeyer/CORBIS; **p53** (bl) Warren Photographic/Jane Burton; (r) © Richard Cummins/CORBIS; **p54** (b) Jeremy Gower; (tr) © Costas Syrolakis; **p55** (b) Still Pictures/© UNEP/Foto; (tr) Jeremy Gower; **p56–57** © Lawson Wood/CORBIS; **p58** (bl + tr) © Digital Vision; (br) Ian Jackson; **p59** (ml) Shuttle Views of the Earth: Geology from Space. Compiled by Pat Jones, courtesy of LPI; (b) © Digital Vision; (tr) Frans Lanting/Tony Stone Images; **p60** (bl) © David Muench/CORBIS; (tr) © NASA/CORBIS; **p60–61** (b) © John and Dallas Heaton/CORBIS; **p61** (tl + br) Jeremy Gower; **p62** (m) © Charles and Josette Lenars/CORBIS; (tr) Rex Features/Mansell Collection; **p63** (tl) © Michael T. Sedam/CORBIS; (b) © Philip James Corwin/CORBIS; (tr) © Charles and Josette Lenars/CORBIS; **p64** (b) Jeremy Gower; (m) Evian Natural Mineral Water; (tr) Photography courtesy of The Strathmore Mineral Water Company; **p65** (b) © Macduff Everton/CORBIS; (tr) © Richard Hamilton Smith/CORBIS; **p66–67** © Neil Rabinovitz/CORBIS; **p66** (bl) Chris Lyon; **p67** (tm) Jeremy Gower; (mr) Ralph A. Clevenger/CORBIS; **p68–69** (background) © Digital Vision; **p68** (ml) Laura Fearn; (bl) Chris Lyon; (mr) © Shaun Egan/Tony Stone Images; **p69** (b) © Digital Vision; (tr) © Anthony Bannister, ABPL/CORBIS; **p70** (tl) © Lawson Wood/CORBIS; (m) Science Photo Library/Dr. Ken McDonald; (b) © Amos Nachoum/CORBIS; **p71** (tl) © Digital Vision; (b) © Digital Vision; (tr) Peter Dennis; **p72–73** © Michael S. Yamashita/CORBIS; **p72** (ml + tr) © Michael S. Yamashita/CORBIS; **p73** (tl) © Charles O'Rear/CORBIS; (br) © Digital Vision; **p74–75** © Steve Kaufman/CORBIS; **p76–77** (background) © Craig Aurniss/CORBIS; **p76** (l) © Michael Yashmita/CORBIS; (tr) Ian Jackson; **p77** (m) Ian Jackson; (tm) © Digital Vision; (br) © Wolfgang Kaehler/CORBIS; **p78–79** (background) Shuttle Views of the Earth: Clouds from Space. Compiled by Pat Jones, courtesy of LPI; **p78** (bl) Peter Dennis; (tr) Science Photo Library/Scott Camazine; **p79** (tl + tr) Shuttle Views of the Earth: Clouds from Space. Compiled by Pat Jones, courtesy of LPI; (ml) © Wolfgang Kaehler/CORBIS; (bl) © Digital Vision; **p79** (tr margin) Science Photo Library/Scott Camazine; (br) Ian Jackson; **p80–81** Glen Alison/Tony Stone Images; **p80** (bl) Shuttle Views of the Earth: Clouds from Space. Compiled by Pat Jones, courtesy of LPI; **p81** (tr) Fortean Picture Library/Werner Burger; **p82–83** John Lund/Tony Stone Images; **p82** (b) Guy Smith; (tr) Shuttle Views of the Earth: Clouds from Space. Compiled by Pat Jones, courtesy of LPI; **p84–85** © Michael S. Yamashita/CORBIS; **p84** (tr) Shuttle Views of the Earth: Geology from Space. Compiled by Pat Jones, courtesy of LPI; **p85** (ml + tr) © Digital Vision; **p86** (b) Robert H. Pearson, Canada; (tr) Brian and Cherry Alexander; **p87** (l) Will and Deni McIntyre/Tony Stone Images; (tr) Seymour Snowman Sun Protection Campaign, NSW Cancer Council and NSW Health Department; (br) © Peter Turnley/CORBIS; **p88** (bl) © Digital Vision; (tr) Science Photo Library/Magrath/Folsom; **p88–89** Science Photo Library/Pekka Parviainen; **p89** (m) Fortean Picture Library/Llewellyn Publications; (tr) © Alamy and E. Vicens/CORBIS; **p90–91** © Digital Vision; **p90** (mb) European Space Agency; (t) © Digital Vision; **p91** (tr) International Weather Productions; **p92–93** © Scott T. Smith/CORBIS; **p94–95** © George Hall/CORBIS; **p94** (tl) © Digital Vision; (ml) © Jonathan Blair/CORBIS; (bl) NASA; (b) © Digital Vision; **p95** (tr) Science Photo Library/NASA; **p96–97** (background) Shuttle Views of the Earth: Oceans from Space. Compiled by Pat Jones and Gordon Wells, courtesy of LPI; **p96** (b) Science Photo Library/NASA; **p97** (t) Science Photo Library/Los Alamos National Laboratory; (bl) Shuttle Views of the Earth: Oceans from Space. Compiled by Pat Jones and Gordon Wells, courtesy of LPI; **p98** (bl) © Karl Switak, ABPL/CORBIS; (m) Peter Bull; (tr) Science Photo Library/Dr. Jeremy Burgess; **p99** (tl) Still Pictures/Nick Cobbing; (b) Peter Bull; (r) © Chinch Gryniewicz, Ecoscene/CORBIS; **p100** (m) Science Photo Library/PLI; **p100–101** (t) © Dewitt Jones/CORBIS; **p101** (bl) © Paul A. Souders/CORBIS; (br) © Digital Vision; **p102–103** © Vince Streano/CORBIS; **p102** (bl) © Digital Vision; (tr) © Ron Boardman, FLPA/CORBIS; **p103** (t) © Wolfgang Kaehler/CORBIS; **p104–105** © Digital Vision; **p104** (t) Science Photo Library/Arc Science Simulations; **p105** (bl) © Digital Vision; (tr) Still Pictures/© Kevin Schafer; **p106–107** © Michael and Patricia Fogden/CORBIS; **p108** (tl, mr + bm) © Digital Vision; (br) © Ron Boardman, FLPA/CORBIS; **p109** (t) © Digital Vision; (bl) Howard Allman; (r) © Galen Rowell/CORBIS; **p110** (ml) Ian Jackson; (b) Chris Shields; **p110–111** © Stuart Westmoreland/CORBIS; **p111** (tr + mr) Ian Jackson; (mr) Jeremy Gower; (b) Ian Jackson; **p112** (ml) © Tom Brakefield/CORBIS; (tr) Ian Jackson; (br) David Wright; **p113** © Digital Vision; **p114–115** © Digital Vision; **p114** (b) © Digital Vision; **p115** (ml) Still Pictures/Michael Viard; (tr) © Digital Vision; (br) Ian Jackson; **p116–117** © Reinhard Eisele/CORBIS; **p116** (b) Nicola Butler; **p117** (bl, m + mr) Ian Jackson; (tr) © Digital Vision; **p118–119** © Buddy Mays/CORBIS; **p118** (tr) Nicola Butler; **p119** (t) © Buddy Mays/CORBIS; (mr) Ian Jackson; (br) © Anthony Bannister, ABPL/CORBIS; **p120–121** © Kit Kittle/CORBIS; **p120** (bl) Jeremy Gower; **p121** (ml) Yann Layma/Tony Stone Images; (tr) Science Photo Library/David Scharf; **p122–123** © Christine Osborne/CORBIS; **p122** (m) © Jeremy Horner/CORBIS; (tr) Nicola Butler; **p123** (m) Ian Jackson; **p124** (b) © Gail Mooney/CORBIS; (tr) Nicola Butler; **p125** (tr) Still Pictures/Carlos Guarita; (ml) Richard Passmore/Tony Stone Images; (mb) Still Pictures/Carlos Guarita; **p126** (ml) Nicola Butler; (r) © Stuart Westmoreland/CORBIS; **p127** (tl) Ron Watts/CORBIS; (tr) © Stuart Westmoreland/CORBIS; (br) © George MacCarthy/CORBIS; **p128–129** (background) © Digital Vision; **p128** (m) NOAA; (b) © Digital Vision; **p129** (m) © Digital Vision; (b) Ian Jackson; **p130–131** © Galen Rowell/CORBIS; **p130** (tr) © David Muench/CORBIS; **p131** (tr) © William A. Bake/CORBIS; (br) © Catherine Karnow/CORBIS; **p132–133** © Yann Arthus Bertrand/CORBIS; **p134–135** © Keren Su/CORBIS; **p134** (m) Ian Jackson; (tr) Fiona Patchett and Laura Fearn; **p135** (tl) © W. Wayne Lockwood, M.D./CORBIS; (mr) Ian Jackson; **p136** (bl) Ian Jackson; (br) Rachel Lockwood; (mr) Ian Jackson; **p137** (t) © Richard Hamilton Smith/CORBIS; (bl) Ian Jackson; (br) © Digital Vision; **p138–139** (t) Science Photo Library/Volker Steger, PETER ARNOLD INC.;

(b) Still Pictures/Jans Peter Lahall; **p138** (m) Stephen Moncrieff; **p139** (tr) Science Photo Library/Ed Young/AGSTOCK; **p140–141** (b) © Hans **p140** (tr) Still Pictures/Ron Giling; **p141** (m) Craig Asquith; **p142–143** © Nathan Benn/CORBIS; **p143** (t) Still Pictures/Mark Edwards; (b) © Steve Raymer/CORBIS; **p144–145** © Marc Garanger/CORBIS; **p144** (tr) © Digital Vision; **p145** (bl) © Liba Taylor/CORBIS; (tr) © Morton Beebe, S.F./CORBIS; **p146–147** © Bob Krist/CORBIS; **p146** (tr) Stephen Moncrieff; **p147** (tr) Still Pictures/Ron Giling; **p148** (l) Still Pictures/Harmut Schwarzbach; **p149** (tl) Still Pictures/Shehzad Noorani; (br) © Bob Krist/CORBIS; **p150–151** © Digital Vision; **p150** (r) Still Pictures/Thomas Raupach; **p151** (bl) © Richard Cummins/CORBIS; **p152** (bl) © David and Peter Turnley/CORBIS; (tr) © Hartmut Schwarzbach/CORBIS; **p152–153** Bruce Coleman Collection/Jules Cowan; **p154** (l) Still Pictures/Harmut Scharzbach; (tr) Photo courtesy of Boeing Satellite Systems; **p155** (tl) © Macduff Everton/CORBIS; (br) Still Pictures/Jean Luc and F. Ziegler; **p156** Wateraid/Jim Holmes; **p157** (t) Greenpeace/Borstelman; (b) Greenpeace/Morgan; **p158–159** © Phil Schermeister/CORBIS; **p160–161** © Craig Aurness/CORBIS; **p160** (tr) © Gunter Marx/CORBIS; **p161** (tr) © Joseph Sohm; Chromo Sohm Inc./CORBIS; **p162** (background) © Ron Watts/CORBIS; (bl) © Flip Schulke/CORBIS; **p162–163** (t) © Kevin Fleming/CORBIS; **p163** (bl) © Douglas Peebles/CORBIS; (r) © Digital Vision; **p164** (m) © Marc Muench/CORBIS; (tr) © Gunter Marx/CORBIS; (br) © Lowell Georgia/CORBIS; **p165** (tr) © Michael Lewis/Bruce Coleman; (br) © Galen Rowell/CORBIS; **p166** (tr) © Gianni Dagli Orti/CORBIS; (b) Howard Allman; **p167** © Charles and Josette Lenars/CORBIS; **p168** (bl) © Robert Francis/Hutchison; (tr) © Bill Gentile/CORBIS; **p169** (tl) Howard Allman; (b) © Danny Lehman/CORBIS; **p170** (l + tr) Howard Allman; **p171** (r) © Philip Gould/CORBIS; **p172–173** © Jeremy Horner/CORBIS; **p174–175** Brian Vikander/CORBIS; **p170–171** © Bob Krist/CORBIS; **p174** (tr) Galen Rowell/CORBIS; **p175** (r) © Annie Griffiths Belt/CORBIS; **p176–177** (t) © Jeremy Horner/CORBIS; (b) © Jeremy Horner/Hutchison; **p176** (bl) © Pablo Corral V/CORBIS; **p177** (br) © Sarah Errinton/Hutchison; **p178–179** © The Purcell Team/CORBIS; **p178** (bl) © Wolfgang Kaehler/CORBIS; (tr) © Sesco Von Puttamer/ Hutchison; **p179** (tr) © Luiz Claudio Marigo/Bruce Coleman; **p180–181** © Edward Parker/Hutchison; **p180** (b) © S. Molins/Hutchison; (tr) © Jeremy Horner/Hutchison; **p181** (tr) © Inge Yspeert/CORBIS; **p182–183** (background) © Bruce Coleman/Nicholas Devore; **p182** (bl) © Will and Deni McIntyre/Tony Stone Images; **p183** (b) © Diego Lezama Orezzoli/CORBIS; (tr) © Edward Parker/Hutchison; **p184–185** © Travel Ink/CORBIS; **p184** (tr) © Bettman/CORBIS; **p185** (tr) © Dennis Degnan/CORBIS; **p186–187** © Earl and Nazima Kowall/CORBIS; **p188–189** © Jack Fields/CORBIS; **p188** (tl) Michael S. Yamashita/CORBIS; **p189** (tl) © Adam Woolfitt/CORBIS (br) © Charles and Josette Lenars/CORBIS; **p190–191** (background) © John Cancalosi/Bruce Coleman; **p190** (b) © Roger Ressmeyer/CORBIS; (tr) © Patrick Ward/CORBIS; **p191** (tl) © Australian Picture Library/CORBIS; (br) © Charles and Josette Lenars/CORBIS; **p192–193** © Gerald S. Cubitt/Bruce Coleman; **p192** (tr) © Robert Francis/Hutchison; **p193** (t) © Doug Armand/Tony Stone Images; (br) © Pacific Stock/Bruce Coleman; **p194** (b) © Isabella Tree/Hutchison; **p195** (tl) © Chris Rainier/CORBIS; (br) © Fritz Prenzel/Bruce Coleman; **p196–197** © Pacific Stock/Bruce Coleman; **p196** (bl) © Pacific Stock/Bruce Coleman; (tr) © Jan Butchofsky-Houser/CORBIS; **p197** (tr) © Jack Fields/CORBIS; **p198–199** © Steve Raymer/CORBIS; **p200–201** © Keren Su/CORBIS; **p200** (bl) © Neil Rabinowitz/CORBIS; **p201** (tm) © Bob Krist/CORBIS; (b) © Wolfgang Kaehler/CORBIS; **p202–203** © Alain Compost/Bruce Coleman; **p202** (bl) © Isabella Tree/Hutchison; **p203** (ml) © Kenneth Fischer/Bruce Coleman; (r) © Robin Constable/Hutchison; **p204–205** (background) © Digital Vision **p204** © Dave Saunders/Tony Stone Images; (tr) © Charles and Josette Lenars/CORBIS; **p205** (tl) © Staffan Widstrand/Bruce Coleman; (br) © Christina Dodwell/Hutchison; **p206–207** © B. Gerard/Hutchison; **p206** (bl) © Dave G. Houser/CORBIS; (tr) © Nik Wheeler/CORBIS; **p207** (bl) © Dean Conger/CORBIS; (r) © Kevin Schafer/CORBIS; **p208** (l) © Wally McNamee/CORBIS; (tr) © Peter Turnley/CORBIS; **p209** (tl) © Christine Osborne/CORBIS; (b) © Kevin R. Morris/CORBIS; **p210–211** (background) © Wolfgang Kaehler/CORBIS; **p210** (b) © Michael MacIntyre/Hutchison; (tr) © David Cliverd/Hutchison; **p211** (bl) © Jeremy Horner/Hutchison; (tr) © Catherine Karnow/CORBIS; **p212–213** © Gerald S. Cubitt/Bruce Coleman; **p212** (bl) © Pacific Stock/Bruce Coleman; (tr) © Paul Almasy/CORBIS; **p213** (br) © Alain Compost/Bruce Coleman; **p214** (bl) © Ric Ergenbright/CORBIS; **p214–215** (t) Powerstock Zefa/Charles Tyler; (b) © Eye Ubiquitous, John Dakers/CORBIS; **p215** (r) AFP Photos/Yoshikazu Tsuno; **p216–217** © Fulvio Roiter/CORBIS; **p218–219** (background) © Larry Lee Photography/CORBIS; **p218** (l) © Gianni Dagli Orti/CORBIS; **p219** (tl) Deutsche Presse-Agentur GmbH; (r) Graeme Peacock, courtesy of Gateshead Council; **p220** (tl) Howard Allman; **p220–221** © Bob Krist/CORBIS; **p221** (t) © Todd Gipstein/CORBIS; (r) © Elke Stolzenberg/CORBIS; **p222** (b) © Rethly Akos; (tr) © Greenpeace/Shirly; **p223** © Franz-Marc Frei/CORBIS; **p224–225** © Jan Jordan; **p224** (bl) © J.F.Causse/Tony Stone Images; (tr) © Les Gibbon; Cordaiy Photo Library Ltd./CORBIS; **p225** (r) © Brian and Cherry Alexander; **p226** (tr) Photo © European Parliament; (b) © Powerstock Zefa; **p227** (tl) © European Communities; (tr) © European Communities; (b) © Peter Turnley/CORBIS; **p228** © Bettman/CORBIS; **p229** (tl) © Catherine Karnow/CORBIS; (br) © Nik Wheeler/CORBIS; **p230–231** © Charles and Josette Lenars/CORBIS; **p232–233** Still Pictures/Glen Christian; **p233** (tr) © Karen Tweedy-Holmes/CORBIS; (br) © David Reed/CORBIS; **p234–235** © Adrian Arbib/CORBIS; **p234** (tr) © Margaret Courtney-Clarke/CORBIS; **p235** © Daniel Lainé/CORBIS; **p236–237** © Christine Osborne/CORBIS; **p236** (tr) © J.Wright/Hutchison; (br) © Ian Jackson; **p237** (b) © Roger Wood/CORBIS; **p238–239** (b) © Sarah Errington/Hutchison; **p238** (l) © Mary Jellife/ Hutchison; **p239** (tl) © Daniel Lainé/CORBIS; (tr) © Hutchison; **p240** (tr) © Digital Vision; (b) © Kevin Fleming/CORBIS; **p241** © Hutchison; **p242–243** © Nevada Wier/CORBIS; **p242** (bl) © Peter Turnley/CORBIS; (tr) Ian Jackson; **p243** (tr) © Chris Hellier/CORBIS; (b) © Peter Johnson/CORBIS; **p244–245** (background) © Sarah Errington/Hutchison; **p244** (l) © Bruce Coleman Inc.; **p245** (bl) © Crispin Hughes/Hutchison; (tl) © CORBIS; (r) © Contemporary African Art Collection Limited/CORBIS; **p246–247** © Digital Vision; **p248** (ml) Stephen Moncrieff; (bl) © Air Photographics, Inc., CNOVS-969-20; (tr) © Digital Vision; **p249** (t, bm + br) European Map Graphics Ltd; **p250** (b) Stephen Moncrieff; (tr) © Dan Guravich/CORBIS; **p251** (bl) European Map Graphics Ltd; (tr) © W. Perry Conway/CORBIS; **p252–253** (background) © Digital Vision; **p252** (mr) PHOTO ESA; **p253** (tl) © NERC Satellite Station, University of Dundee www.sat.dundee.ac.html; (br) Science Photo Library/European Space Agency; **p254** (b) © Christopher Cormack/CORBIS; **p255** Stephen Moncrieff/Craig Asquith; **p256–257** © Raymond Gehman/CORBIS; **p256** (tr) © Owen Franken/CORBIS; **p257** (tr) © Adam Woolfitt/CORBIS; **p258–259** European Map Graphics Ltd; **p264–265** © Still Pictures/Thomas D. Mangelsen; **p264** (b) © Science Photo Library/Julian Baum and David Angus; **p266–267** © Richard Cummins/CORBIS; **p267** (br) © W. Perry Conway/CORBIS; **p274–275** © Still Pictures/John Cancalosi; **p275** © Science Photo Library/Julian Baum and David Angus; **p276–277** © Galen Rowell/CORBIS; **p277** (tr) © Eye Ubiquitous/CORBIS; **p282–283** © Amos Nachoum/CORBIS; (t) © Science Photo Library/Worldsat International; **p284–285** © Still Pictures/Pascal Kobeh; **p285** (br) © Bates Littlehales/CORBIS; **p290** Science Photo Library/ © Tom Van Sant; **p290–291** © Chase Swift/CORBIS; **p292–293** © Michael S. Yamashita/CORBIS; **p293** (br) © Keren Su/CORBIS; **p306–307** © NHPA/Stephan Dalton; **p306** © Science Photo Library/Julian Baum and David Angus; **p308–309** © Digital Vision **p309** (r) Agripicture/© Peter Dean; **p318–319** © SteveBloom.com; **p319** Science Photo Library/Julian Baum and David Angus; **p320–321** © Tom Brakefield/CORBIS; **p321** (b) © Gallo Images/CORBIS; **p330–331** © Digital Vision; **p330** (b) Science Photo Library/Julian Baum and David Angus; **p331** (tr) Science Photo Library/ Julian Baum and David Angus; **p334–335** © David Muench/CORBIS; **p336–337** (background) © Digital Vision; **p338–339** (background) © Digital Vision; **p341** (m) Susannah Owen/© Digital Vision; **p342** (b) Craig Asquith; **p343** (ml) Peter Bull; (b) Howard Allman; **p344–351** Mike Olley; **p352–353** (background) © Digital Vision; **p354–367** © Flag Institute Enterprises Ltd; (background) © Digital Vision; **p367** (b) AFP Photos/Henry Ray Abrams; **p368–375** (background) © Digital Vision Maps based on data distributed by the EROS Data Center Distributed Active Archive Center (EDC DAAC), located at the U.S. Geological Survey's EROS Data Center in Sioux Falls, South Dakota.

With thanks also to: Matthew Preston, Lecturer in Politics, Wadham College, Oxford; Stuart Atkinson, astronomy consultant; Ruth Brocklehurst; Alice Pearcey; Katie Daynes